No Place Like *Home*

For Daddy

No Place Like *Home*

Jojo Barr of House Nine Design

FRANCES
LINCOLN

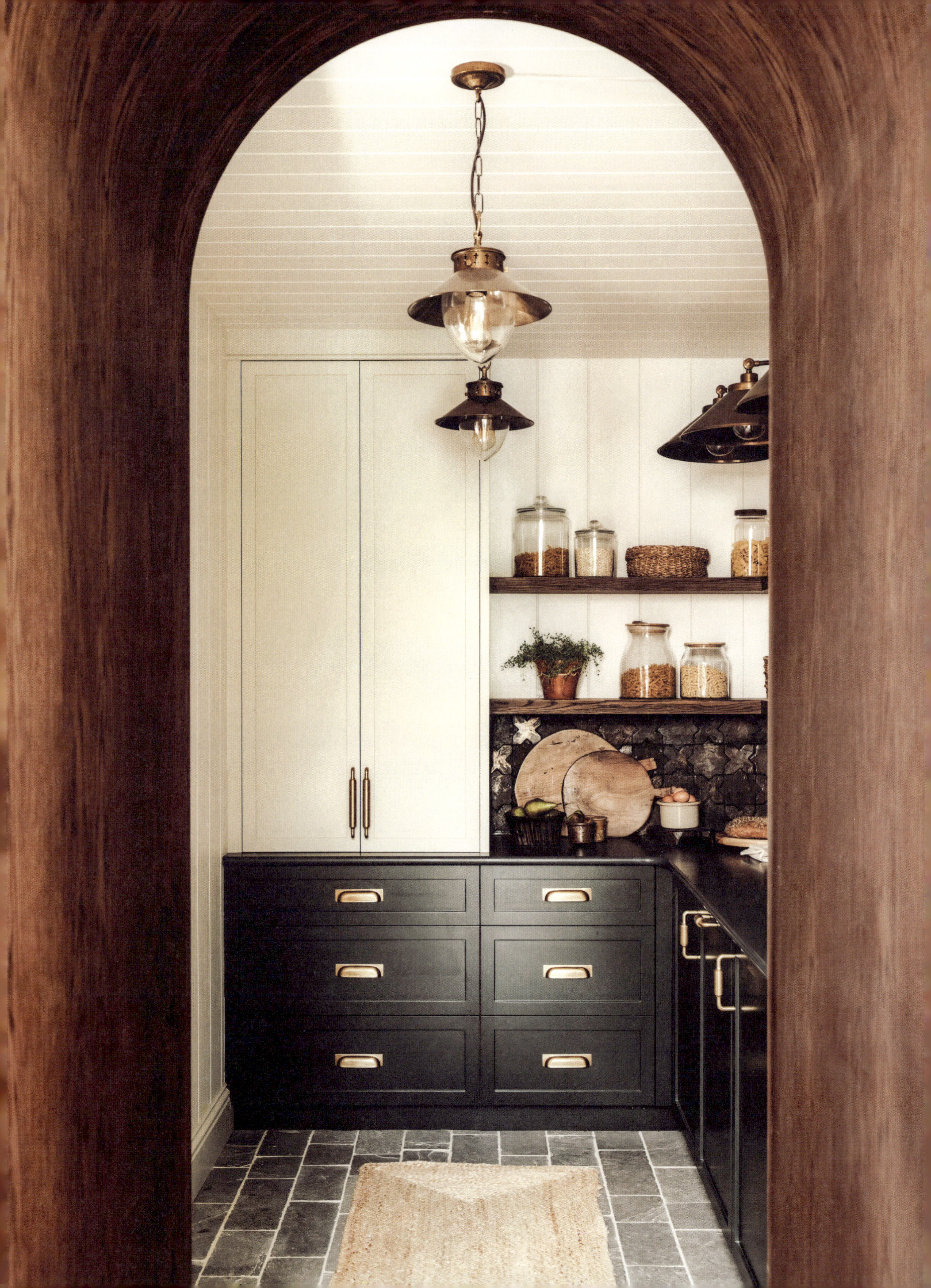

"There's no place like home.
There's no place like home.
There's no place like home."

DOROTHY – THE WIZARD OF OZ

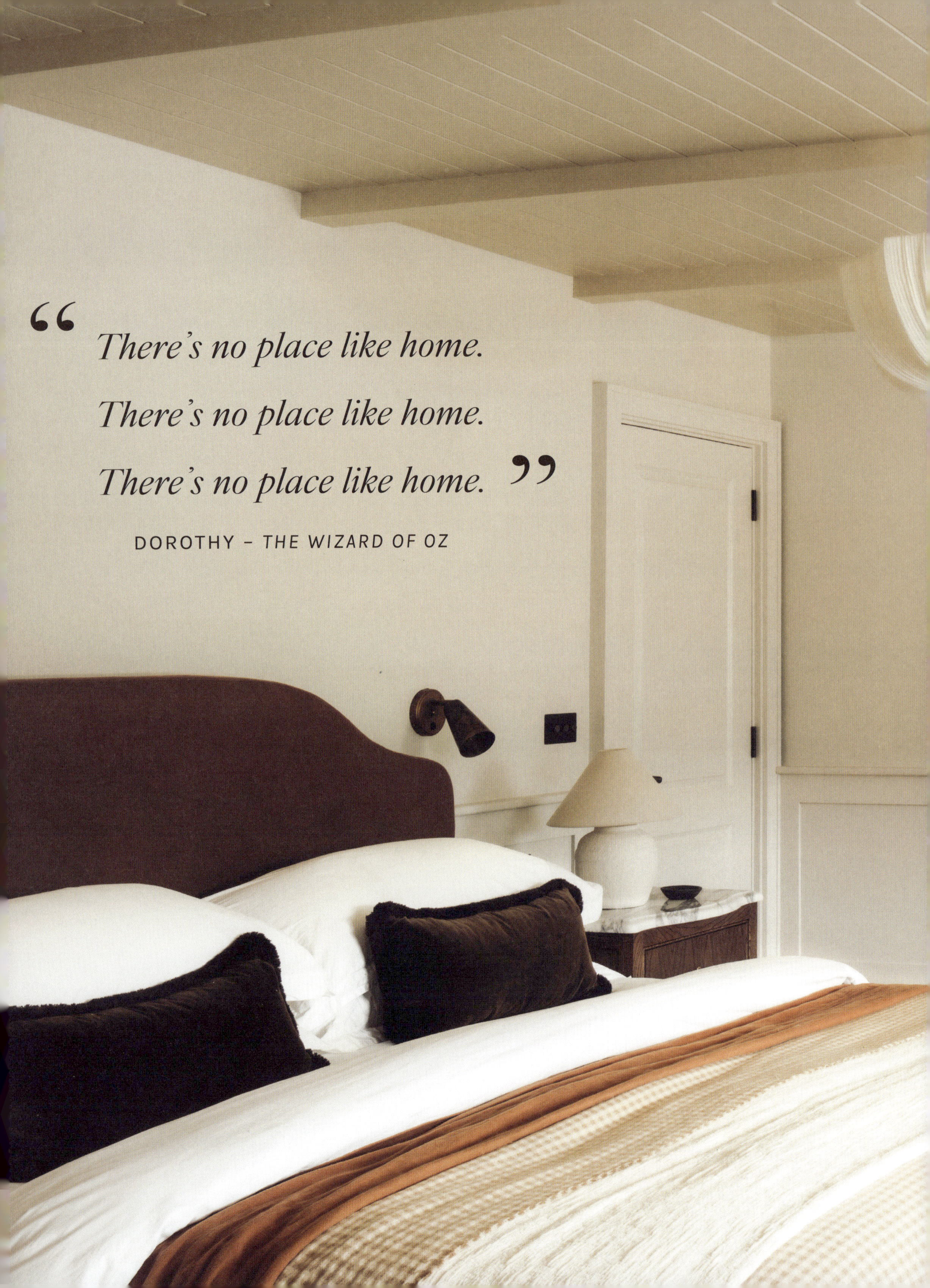

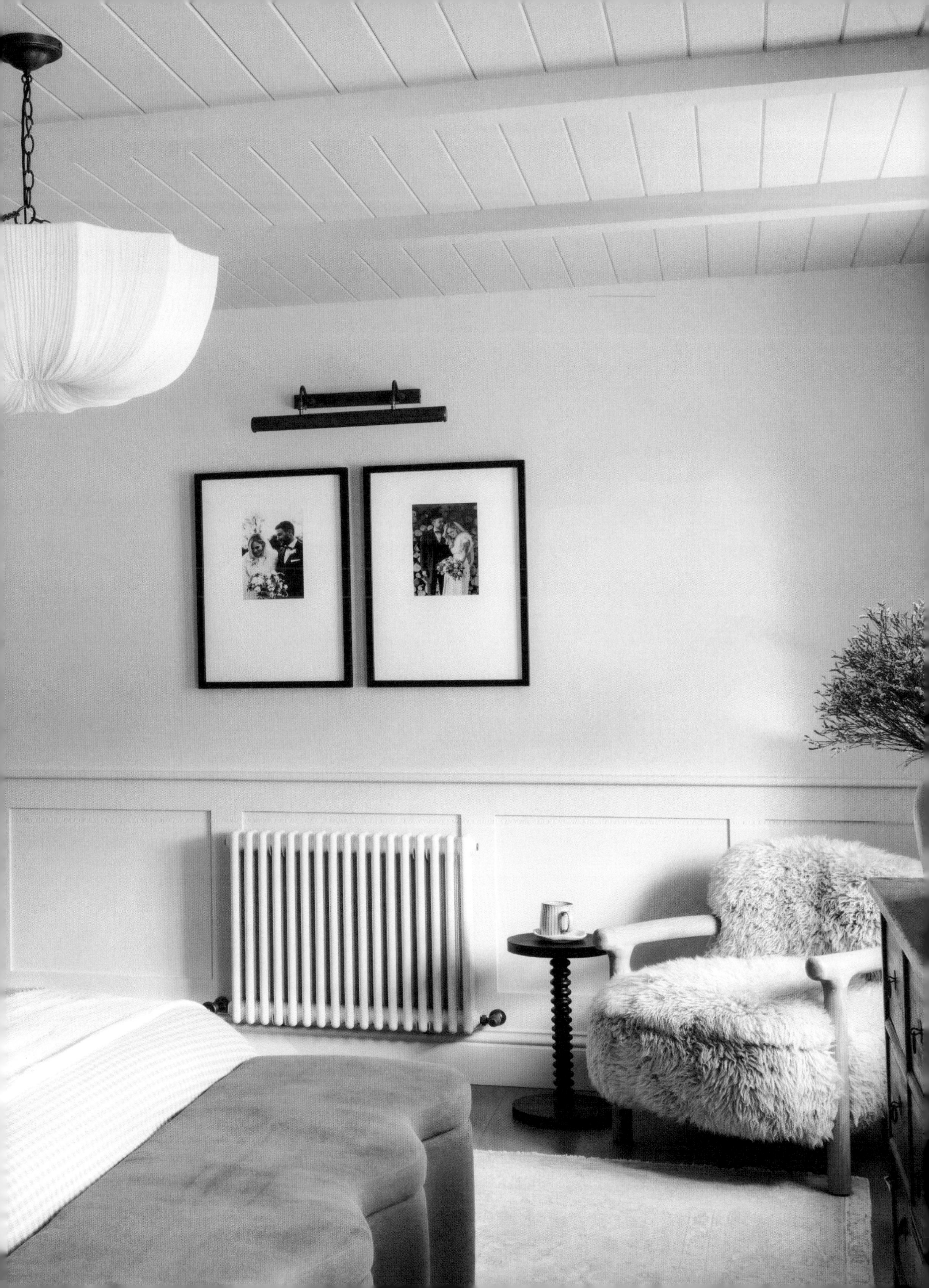

INTRODUCTION

When I think about the word home, the first images that come to my mind aren't interiors from glossy magazines or the perfectly curated rooms that fill our screens; they're memories. My memories. The familiar hum of a house alive with family, routines, and all the little objects that have somehow become part of our story.

For me, home has always been less about perfection and more about feeling. It's about how a space makes you exhale when you walk through the door, and how it seems to wrap itself around the rhythms of your daily life. Yes, I love beautiful things. Yes, I spend my days designing homes for clients. But what I've learned, both from my work and my own life, is that beauty without soul leaves you cold. A house only becomes a home when it reflects the people who live there.

My very first home was on Cicada Road in Wandsworth, south London. I was only about two or three at the time and my memories are hazy, but certain details have stayed vivid, such as the black and white tiled path up to the shiny black door and the cicada shoehorn on the mat. Tiny fragments, yet proof that even at a young age, our surroundings leave their mark.

We were only there for the first few years of my life, but the next house my family moved to left a much greater impression. My parents "upped sticks" and moved us out of London to Woldingham in Surrey, into a Georgian home surrounded by countryside. From the outside, it had beautiful proportions and a kind of quiet scruffy grandeur. On the inside, my father would later tell me, it was in fact a crumbling nightmare of repairs – "a money pit", as he called it. But to me, as a child, it was magical. It felt like a castle – a place of safety and adventure, full of corners to explore and mischief to be made.

We had the roof repaired not long after moving in, and I remember the scaffolding going up around the house, which was insanely exciting. Mine and my sisters' shared room was at the very top of the house, and our father would let us sit with him on the scaffolding, high above the garden, feeling like we were on top of a bean stalk. Once, in the hope it might return, we threw a boomerang out of the window – it all felt wonderfully anarchic. I was fortunate to have had a very happy childhood.

The house was divided into two homes, a man quietly occupying one half while we filled the other, but that hardly registered in my mind. To me, it was entirely ours – our fortress. The house was a perfect blend of shabby elegance and eccentricity. Every bathroom had carpet – a feature that definitely left its mark, as I now consider this a crime against interiors! One even boasted a peach bathroom suite. The conservatory had an original clay-tiled floor and bougainvillea climbing up the walls out of a large French urn. The rooms were filled with a jumble of mahogany furniture, antiques, and the odd bit of inherited chaos. All our sofas wore pale green slipcovers, and the whole house had that slightly worn, lived-in Laura Ashley look. It wasn't polished but it was layered and homely and somewhat eclectic.

My mother and her mother before her – my grandmother Mardi – were both fiercely house-proud. Beds always made; each item in its right place; organised drawers. And perhaps, a few too many of everything. Countless salad bowls, side plates, and endless pieces of china; trinkets and thimbles; silver cutlery polished for special occasions. Their homes felt layered and lived in, never minimal but expressive and tenderly personal.

My mother was always on the move – rearranging furniture, sewing new curtains, or finding yet another corner to improve. Almost every weekend, the dining table was being dressed for another dinner party. My mother was the ultimate host

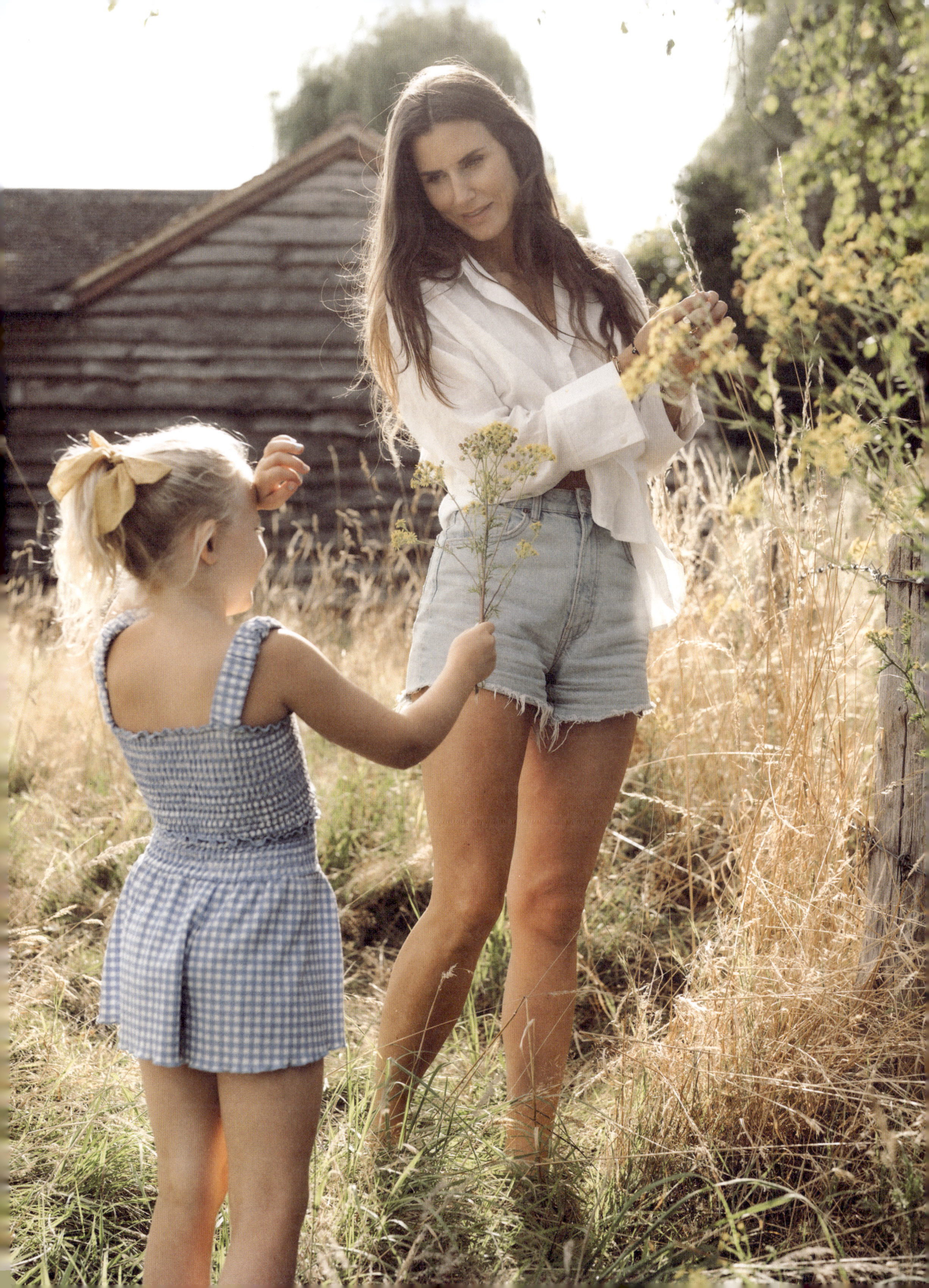

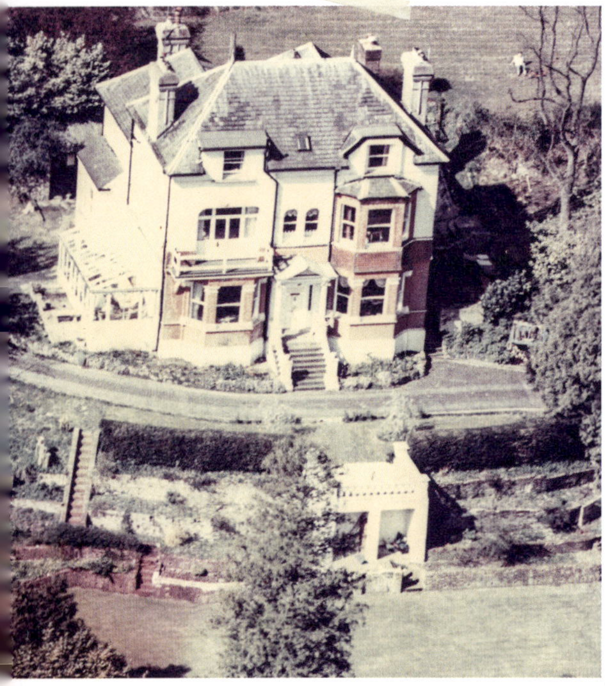
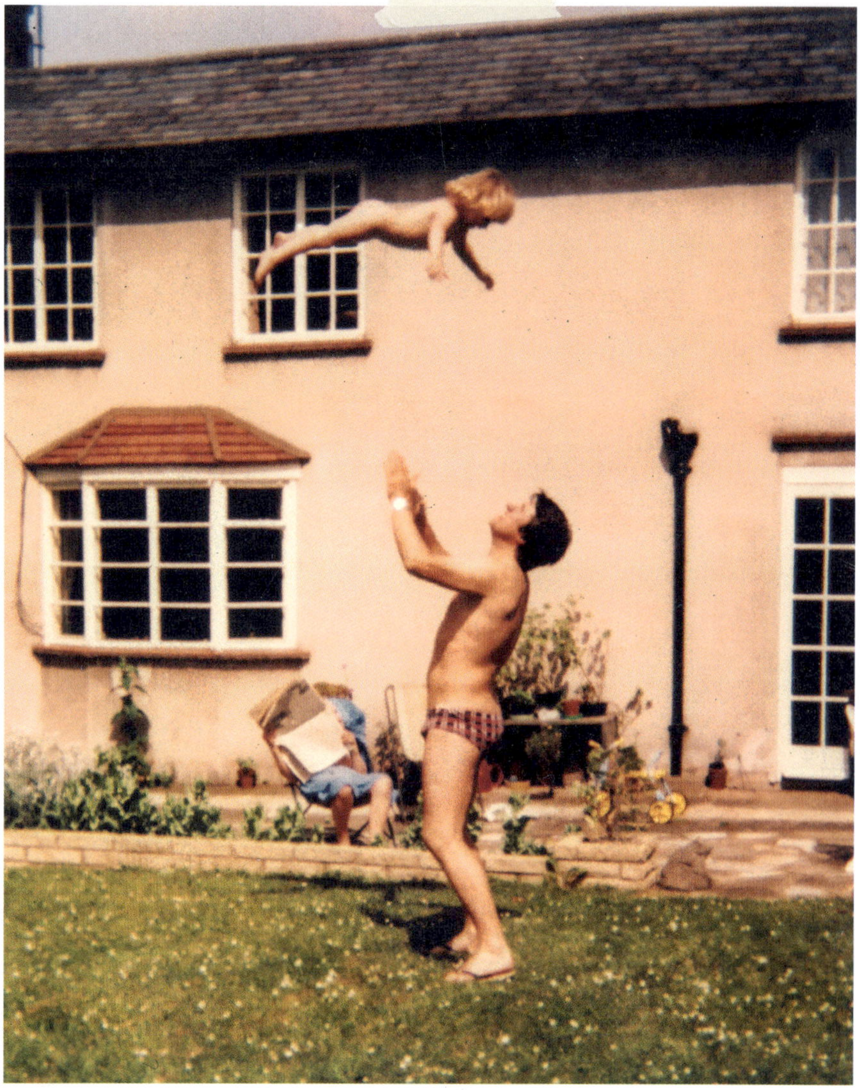
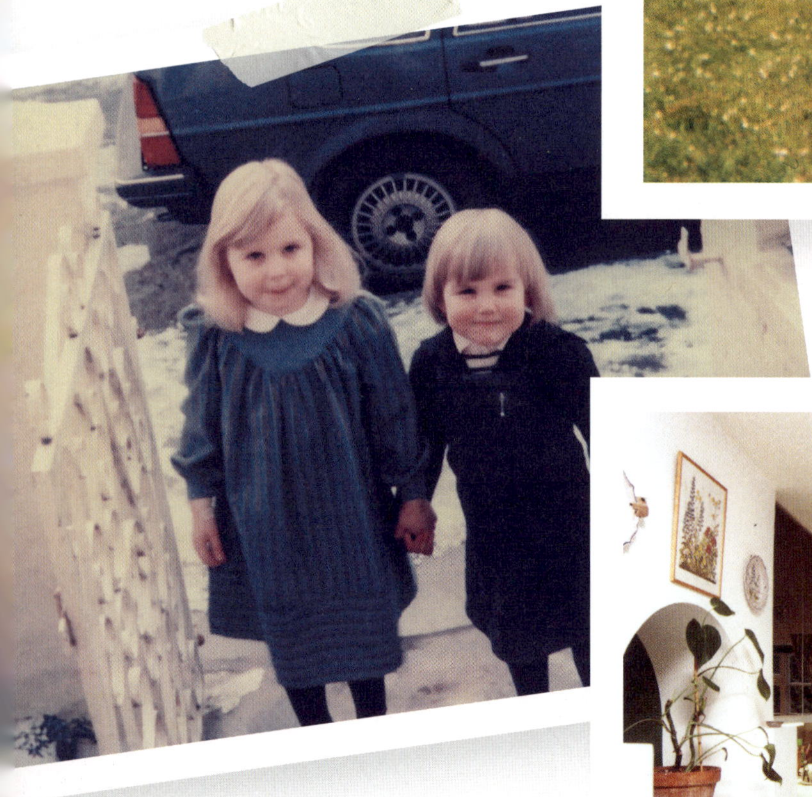
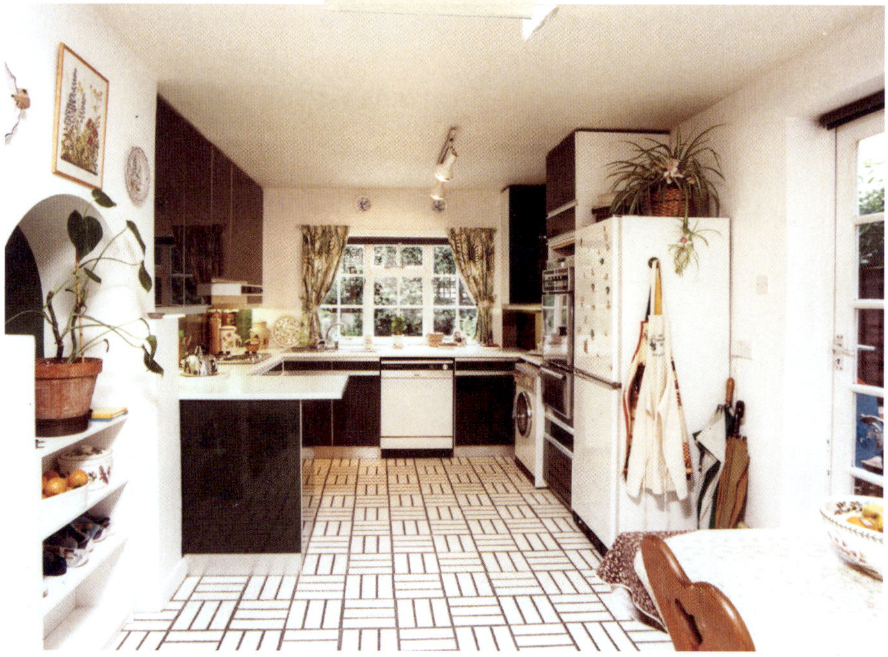

"For me, home has always been less about perfection and more about feeling."

– candles lit, napkins pressed, every plate and glass perfectly placed. My father, in the wine trade, worked the room – topping up glasses, cracking rude jokes, pairing the perfect bottle with each course (and a different shaped glass for every wine). The clean-up operation afterwards was always epic, but it never seemed to matter. The house pulsed with people, laughter, music, and the happy clatter of a life being thoroughly enjoyed.

That sense of things having their place and a use, nothing ever going to waste, and a gratitude for the things we have has stayed with me. It taught me that a home is always evolving, just as we are. The things we bring into it – souvenirs, heirlooms, mistakes, treasures – tell the story of where we've been and who we're becoming. Those early lessons now sit at the heart of my design practice, shaping the way I approach interiors as living, adaptable spaces and ones that honour what already exists while making room for what's still to come.

I often find myself turning to nature for inspiration, because nature, too, is imperfectly perfect. It's full of contrast – light and shade, stillness and movement, decay and renewal. It reminds me that nothing truly beautiful is flawless. Just as seasons change, our homes shift with us; weathering, softening, and settling into their own kind of harmony.

This book is my way of helping you uncover your story and translating it into a home that feels like you. Think of it as a companion, not a rulebook, offering both guidance and reassurance. Because if there's one thing I know, it's that home design isn't about achieving some impossible ideal; it's about balance and flow. It's about creating spaces that feel coherent but never contrived and finding joy in the process, rather than waiting for a "finished" result that never really comes.

Over the years, I've discovered that the rooms that stay with you are rarely the perfect ones. They're the ones with a little patina, a bit of chaos, and a piece of life showing through. They have soul. They tell stories. They welcome you in.

Of course, there are principles that can help – a scaffolding to build upon: flow, light, colour, proportion, layering. I'll walk you through the frameworks I return to again and again. But it's never about following the rule to the letter – it's about using it as a springboard. These are guidelines, not commandments. Because the truth is, a home is never finished. It grows with you, shifts with you, changes with the seasons of your life. I know mine has. It's an evolving tapestry of treasured antiques, things I've saved up for and, let's be honest, pieces bought in a rush because last-minute guests were arriving. Together, they tell my story of travel, family, work, and life.

So, if you're picking up this book feeling overwhelmed, lost in the endless swirl of inspiration online falling down a deep, dark Pinterest hole, let me reassure you – there is no right or wrong. There's only your story and your way of living. The best homes are the ones that tell those stories unapologetically.

This book will give you tools, yes. But more than that, it will give you permission. Permission to let your home evolve. Permission to hold onto the things that matter, even if they don't "match". Permission to find beauty in the imperfect. Because there really is no place like home.

> “*You can find inspiration in everything. If you can’t, then you’re not looking properly.*”

PAUL SMITH

Inspire

FIND YOUR VISION

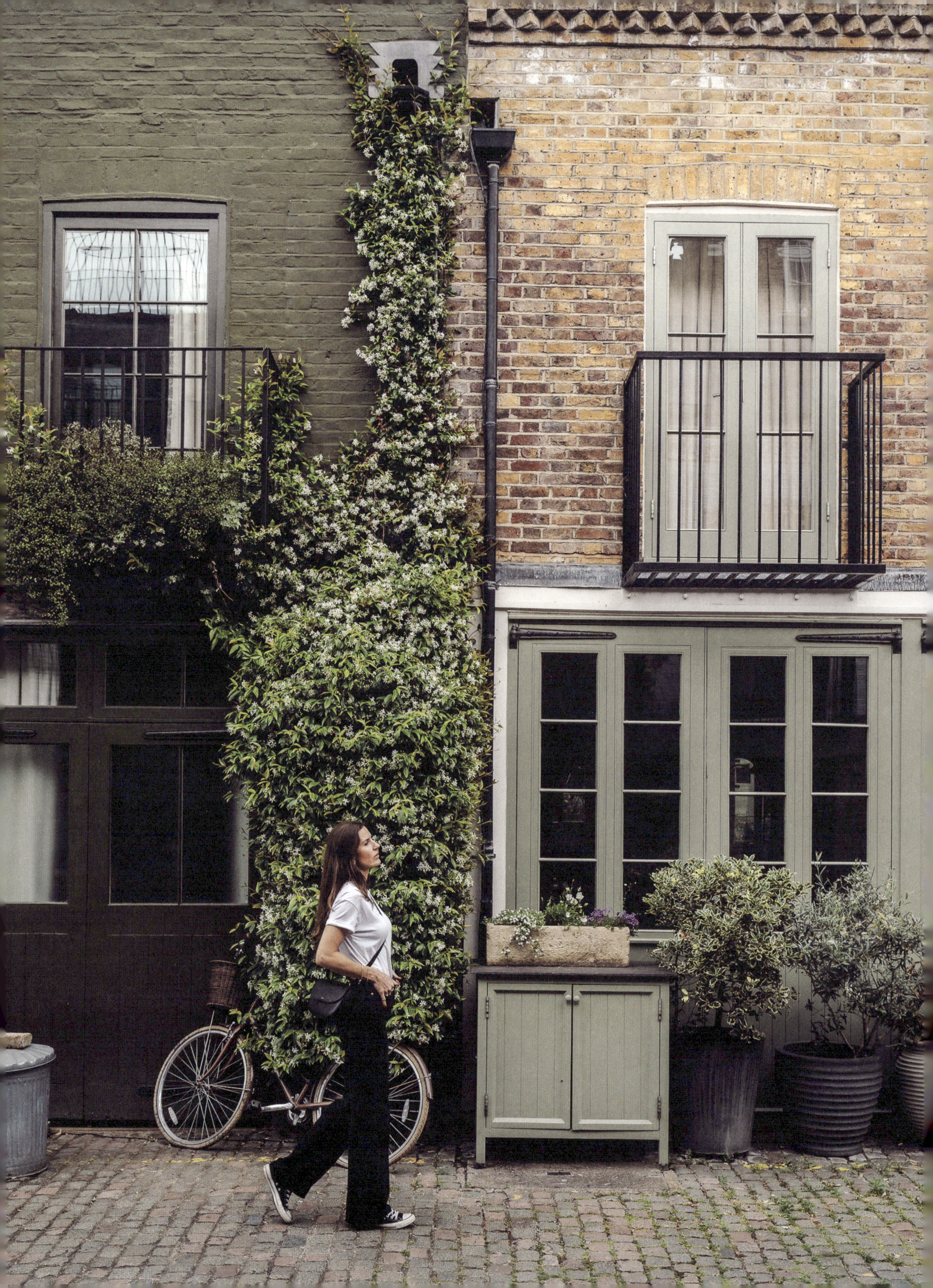

YOUR STORY, YOUR *STYLE*

I've never been entirely sure whether we're born with style, or whether it grows quietly through the years as we train and nurture it. For me at least, it was definitely the latter – a long, slightly drawn-out process of curiosity, trial, and error. Creativity has always been my natural language, but it took me years to realise I could build a life around it.

As a child, I was always making something or other – little dresses from scraps of fabric my mother had left over, papier-mâché creatures, endless scribbles of flowers, animals, and whatever else popped into my imagination. I was happiest with glue on my fingers and something half-finished on the table, or usually the floor. I was far from academic – my attention span was a short-lived thing that often floated right out the window like a butterfly sometime between long division and physics. The creative side of life was where I felt free.

After a rejected university application – by my parents I might add – I landed in property, letting properties in and around London for various agents. The one part of the job I loved, as well as meeting new people every day, was the opportunity to snoop around people's homes and gasp in delight – or horror – at the interiors. I quickly found myself offering unsolicited advice to the tenants about what they could do to improve their potential new homes. It became clear I might be in the wrong job...

With a bit of savings and some help from my father, I bought a small flat in north-west London from a developer. By some miracle of timing, the market was booming, and we flipped it before completion – making just enough to fund my place at KLC School of Design. For the first time, I found something that completely absorbed me. I threw myself in, worked my socks off, graduated, and landed my first design job working as a junior design assistant for a small studio in Chelsea. I was finally where I was supposed to be.

Nearly twenty years later, my style has evolved more times than I can count. In the early days, I worked under studios that had

← Strolling through a quiet mews in the heart of Notting Hill, home of House Nine Design's studio. The houses here are painted in every shade imaginable, and nowhere else am I more inspired by colour. My camera roll is always full from walks like this – whether it's the combinations of painted renders, the charm of the window details, or the beauty of the planting.

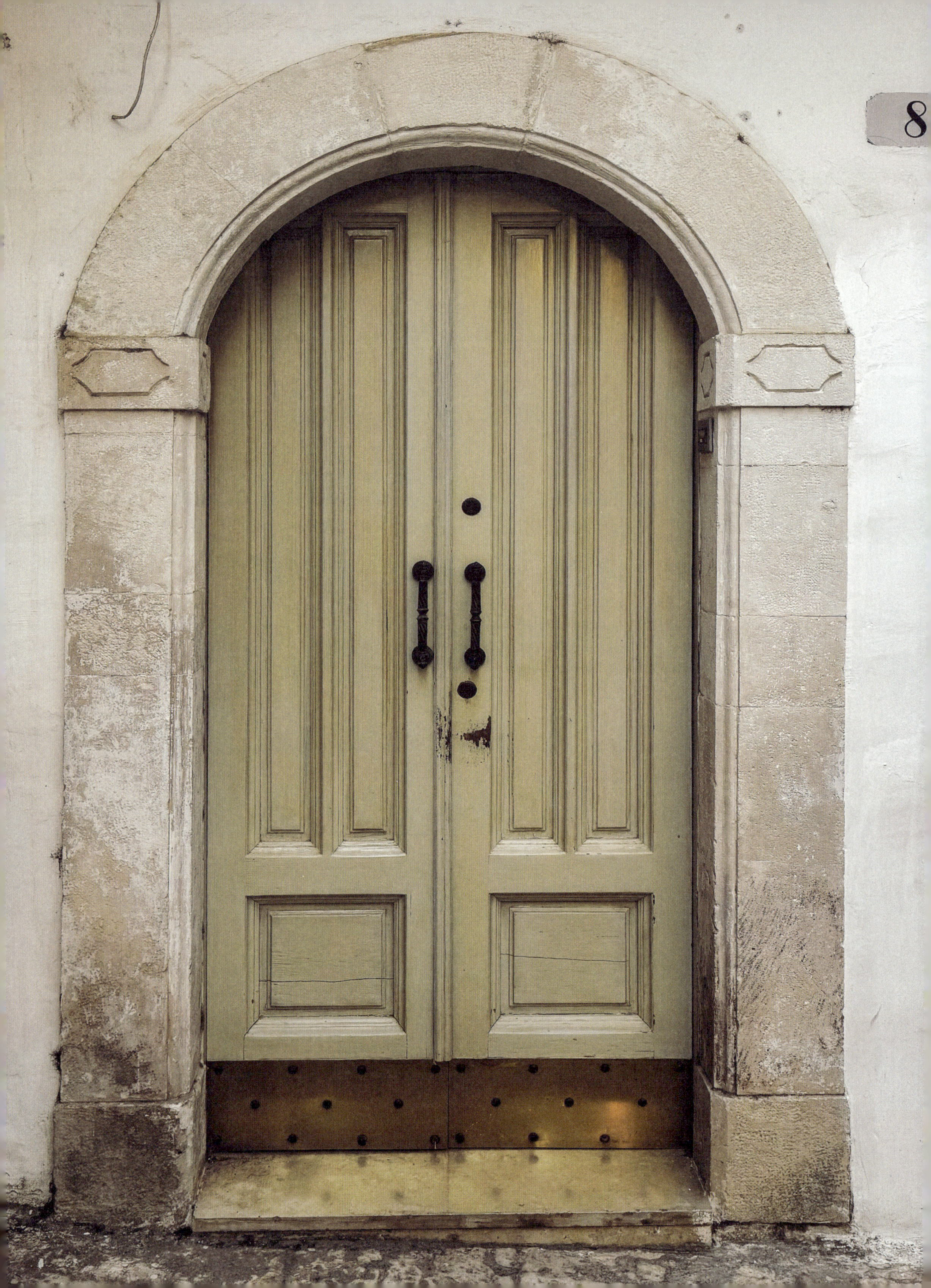
8

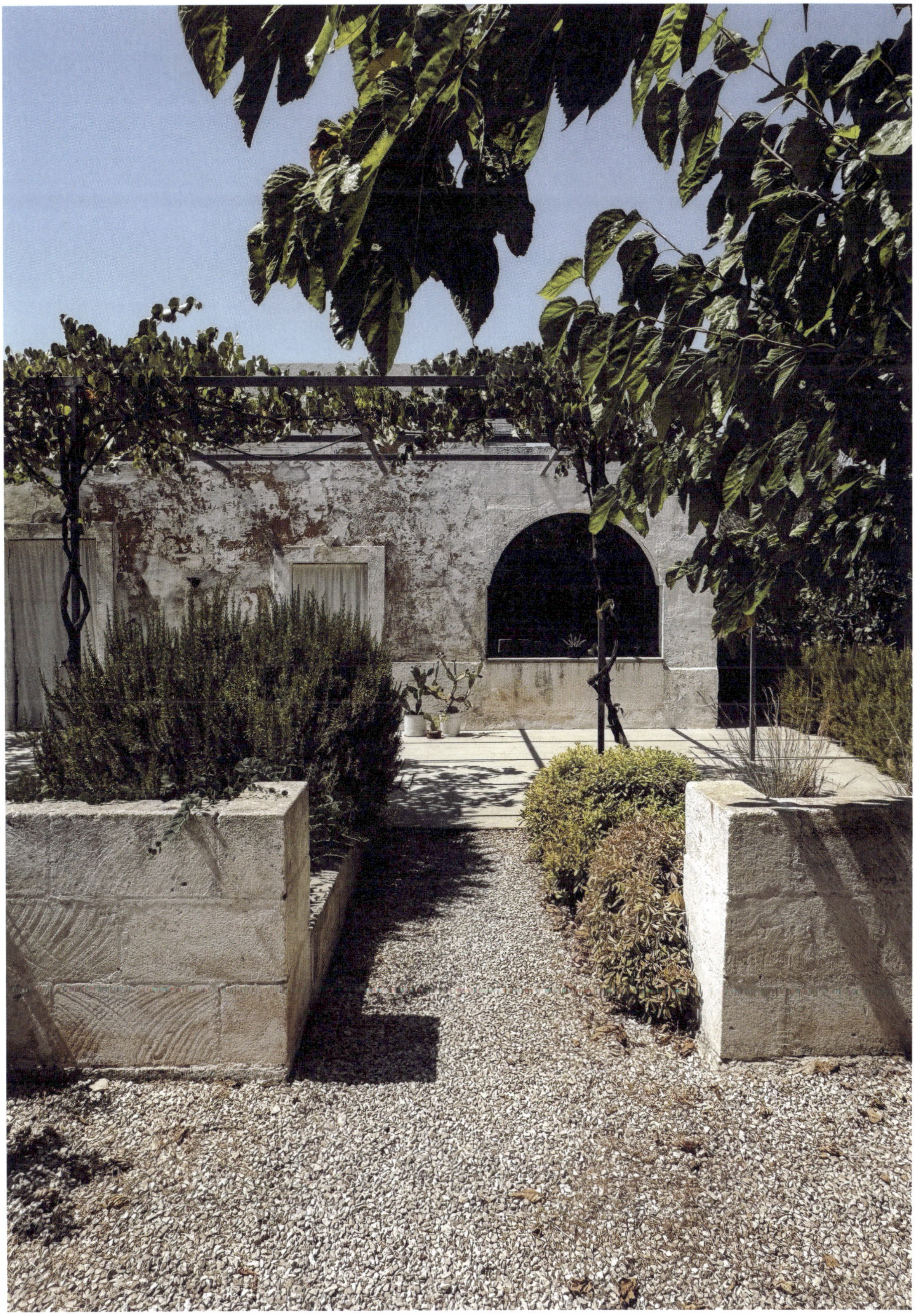

← A perfectly proportioned arch door in Ceglie Messapica, Puglia. The faded green paint against the stone architrave is ancient, worn, and utterly beautiful. I have a thing about doors, they set the tone for everything that follows.

↑ The villa we rented one summer in Cisternino. Imperfect in every way, and somehow all the better for it – unpolished, unpretentious, completely without agenda. My time in Puglia has found its way into our work in more ways than one, not least in my love of arches.

their own "house style". They were wonderful places to learn, but the style was never quite me. The best way I can describe this, is "stroking the dog the wrong way". It didn't feel right, but I did it anyway; it was part of finding my confidence, paying my dues, and learning the rules before I could bend them.

My first big design crush was Ralph Lauren – those timeless, white-boarded Connecticut houses, the effortless blend of masculine and feminine, the rich textures layered in a way that still felt lived in. I loved the sense of elegance that was soft but masculine at the same time. The combination felt grounded and homely. Perhaps that's what has always guided my taste – homes that feel real. I've always been drawn to English period properties – old beams, dark wood, and furniture with a history. Maybe it's because I'm an earth sign (you can call me woo-woo) or because I grew up in the countryside, but I've always needed a connection to nature. To things that have weight, patina, and history.

> *"Taste evolves; it should. Taste is a living, breathing thing."*

Art has always influenced how I see the world. When I paint, I'm not wild and abstract; I'm deliberate, measured, and fascinated by movement and tone. I used to worship the Impressionists, but over the years I've fallen for the boldness of modern brushstrokes and the power of simplicity. Taste evolves; it should. Taste is a living, breathing thing and it develops with age, maturity, and experience.

Travel, too, shapes how I see. I am happiest when lost wandering the streets of a European city. We spend a lot of time as a family in Puglia in southern Italy, and it's impossible not to fall in love with the architecture there – the soft, creamy-white limestone known as *tufo*, the sun-bleached walls, the quiet, humble confidence of age. I can walk the streets for hours; sometimes I have to physically stop myself from rubbing my hands along every surface I see, literally salivating with delight. It's also where my obsession with pots and ceramics has blossomed – those hand-painted, slightly imperfect pieces that each hold their own story.

I appreciate all styles of design – done well – and I've always had deep respect for designers whose work looks nothing like my own. I love seeing the world through someone else's lens. But it's worth pausing here to think about your lens too: the designers, artworks, places, and interiors that stop you in your tracks. Ten people can walk into the same empty room and create ten completely different results. The foundations of proportion, flow, and light may be shared, but what we build on top of them is deeply personal. We all have our own journeys. Interior design is an art form, the home our canvas, and there is no shortage of creativity, nor any need to compete.

That's why I want you to let go of the idea that there's a "right" way to design. There isn't. Inspiration is everywhere – it's how you filter it that matters. Take ideas from others, absolutely, but let them pass through you before they reach your home. The goal isn't to copy; it's to interpret. Your home should look like your life, not someone else's. Much like the bodies we live in, our homes hold us, protect us, and reflect who we are. They deserve our patience, not pressure.

So be kind to yourself, and be kind to your home. Inspiration doesn't come from following trends; it comes from paying attention to how you live, to what you love, to the things that quietly move you. That's where true style begins – not in imitation, but in understanding what makes you feel most you. Now let me help you find a little of that inspiration.

→ Early mornings in Puglia, before the heat sets in. We pull on our sandals and head out - markets spilling over with hand-thrown pottery, Baroque church domes, doorways so perfectly weathered you have to stop and stare. I am a culture vulture by nature, and I am raising my girls to be exactly the same. I never come home without a piece of local pottery either - something handmade and imperfect that earns its place on a shelf.

→ The *tufo* stone that builds these towns has a warmth no material can imitate - honey-coloured, ancient, porous. Arches, domes, carved stonework softened by centuries of sun and salt air. Beauty that seeps into you quietly, and finds its way into your work long after the holiday is over.

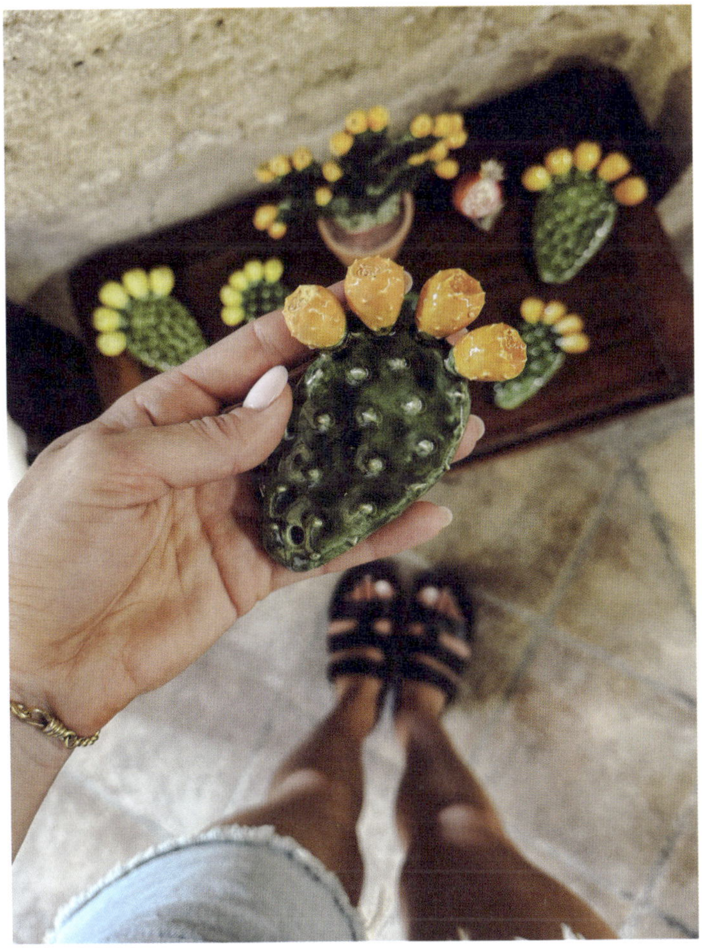

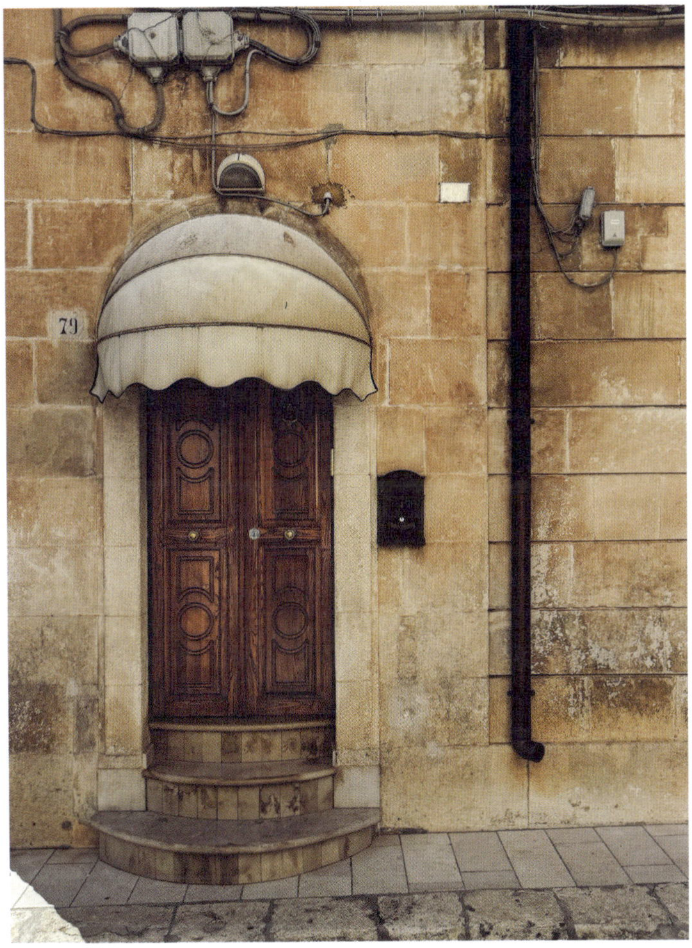

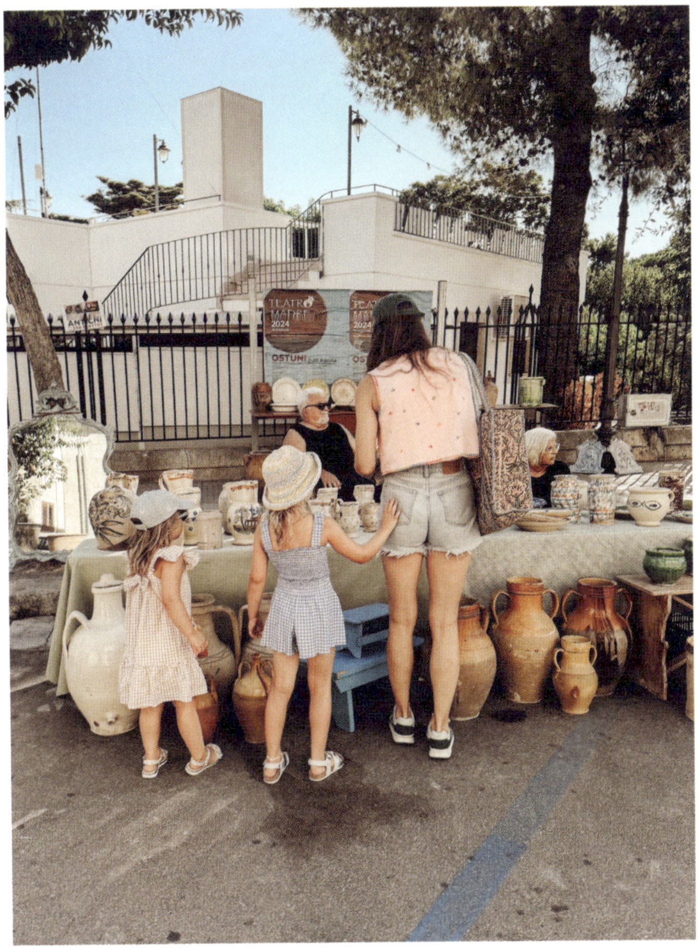

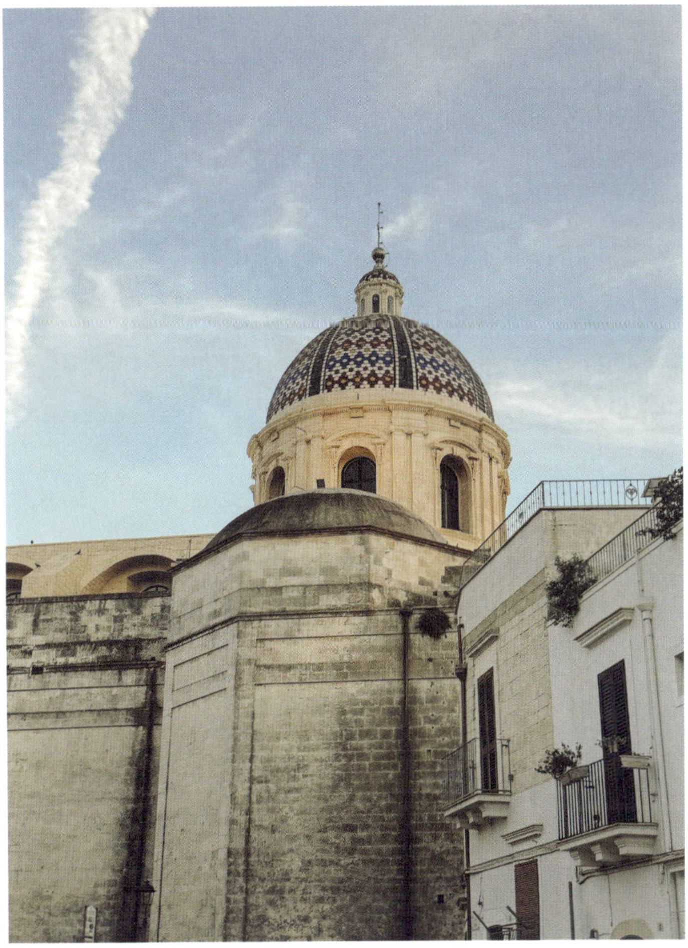

Finding Inspiration

Finding inspiration isn't about sitting around waiting for a lightning bolt of creativity to strike; it's about learning to notice. To slow down enough to see what moves you, what feels good, and what catches your eye. The best ideas rarely come from scrolling aimlessly through lifestyle websites or copying someone else's aesthetic; they come from curiosity and from paying attention to the world around you.

→ A mood board that almost put itself together. Tumbled limestone, soft muted plaster tones, and the loose, unhurried brushwork of a French oil painting – sometimes a collection of things simply belong in the same room and you feel it before you can explain it.

Start by looking at what draws you in over and over again. It might be a colour palette you always gravitate towards, a texture you can't stop touching, or a type of architecture that makes you feel instantly calm. These small preferences are the breadcrumbs of your style. Collect them, not in a perfectly curated Pinterest board (although that can help), but in a way that feels personal. Keep a folder on your phone, tear pages from magazines, or even start a physical scrapbook. Seeing everything together helps you recognise the common threads – the tones, materials, or moods that consistently draw you in.

Where travel might be one of my biggest sources of inspiration, I am not suggesting you have to hop on a plane to find yours. It might be a walk through your neighbourhood, a local café, a hotel lobby, or a museum. Pay attention to how certain spaces make you feel. Does it feel calm, grounded, joyful, or energizing? That emotional reaction is your design compass. When you start honing your style, don't panic if it feels inconsistent. Style evolves; it's supposed to. What you love at twenty-five won't necessarily be what you love at forty-five or sixty-five – you're growing, so your surroundings should too. The key is to keep the heart of it the same: choose what feels authentic, not what's trendy. If you only follow trends, you'll spend your life redecorating.

Look beyond interiors for ideas. Fashion, art, film, and nature all teach us about balance, proportion, texture, and colour – if we learn how to translate what we're seeing. Pay attention to the combinations that make you pause: a faded linen dress might become the inspiration for a pair of curtains; a sun-bleached terracotta pot might inspire the perfect limewash for a ceiling; the awning of a restaurant could spark a palette of burgundy, brass, and leather. Inspiration doesn't need to be copied or explained; it simply needs to be felt, then quietly reimagined within your own space.

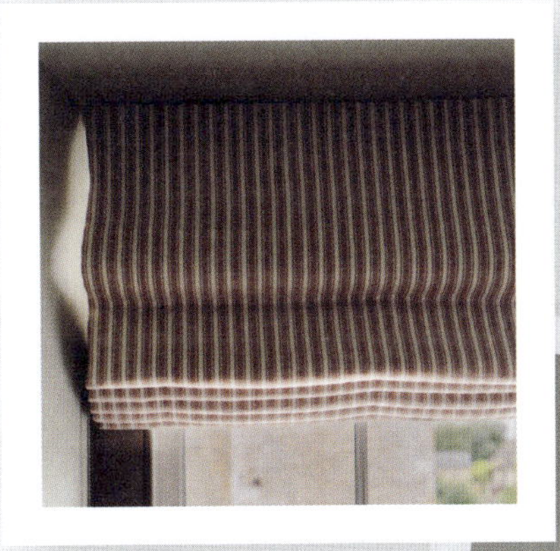

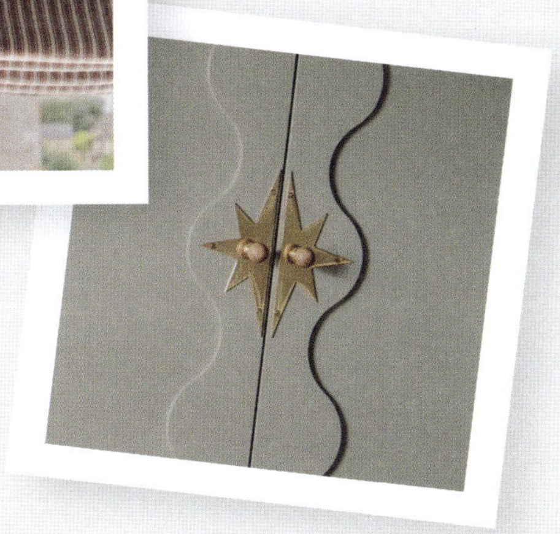

natural fibres

artwork

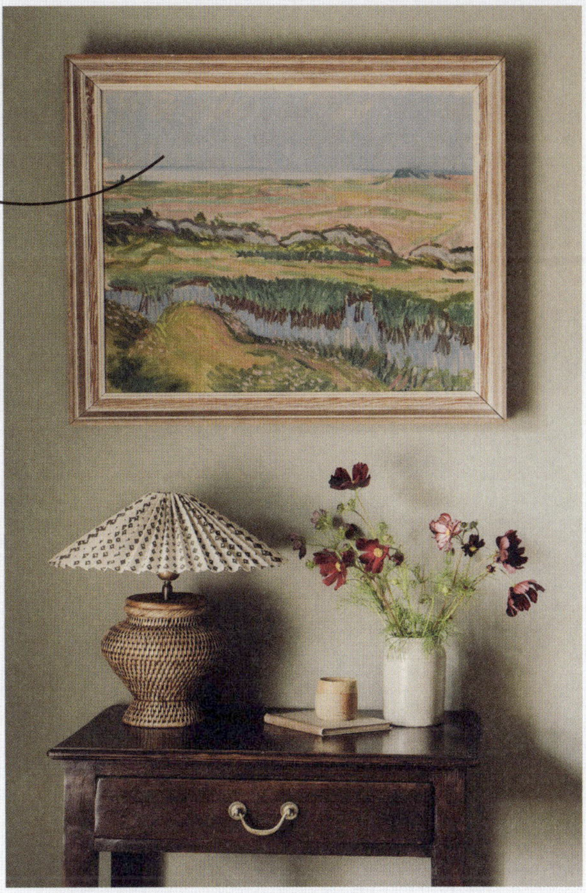

Inspire

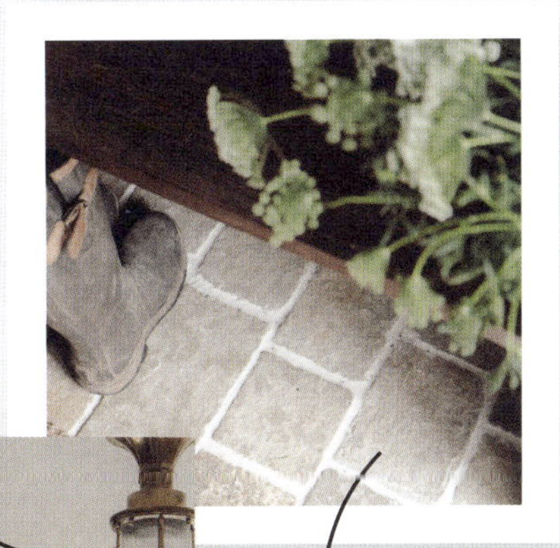

warm, timeless colours

green doors and brass drainpipes

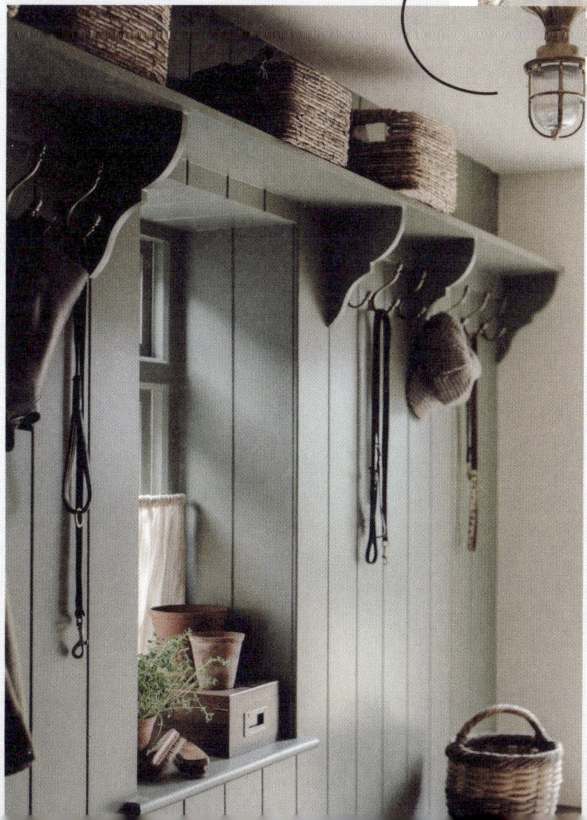

prints, fabrics, texture

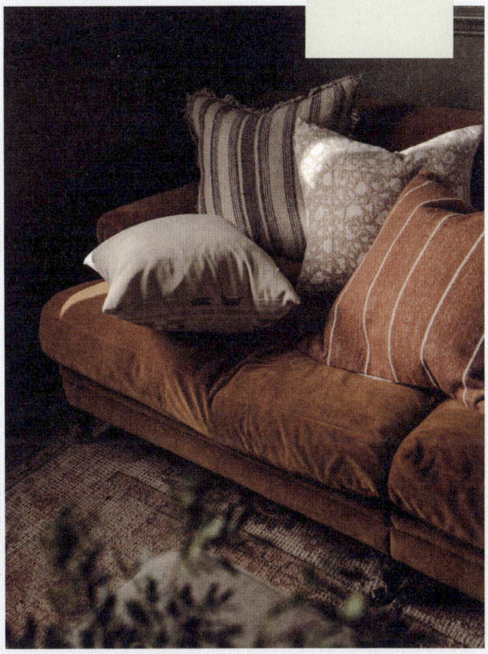

natural stone

And finally, give yourself permission to experiment. Try things. Move things around. Make mistakes. You can't find your voice if you never use it. Take inspiration, yes, but let your instincts lead. Your home should look like your life, not someone else's feed.

True inspiration doesn't come from copying; it comes from connecting. The more you notice what you're drawn to – the textures, tones, and moments that quietly resonate – the closer you get to your own signature style.

"Choose what feels authentic, not what's trendy."

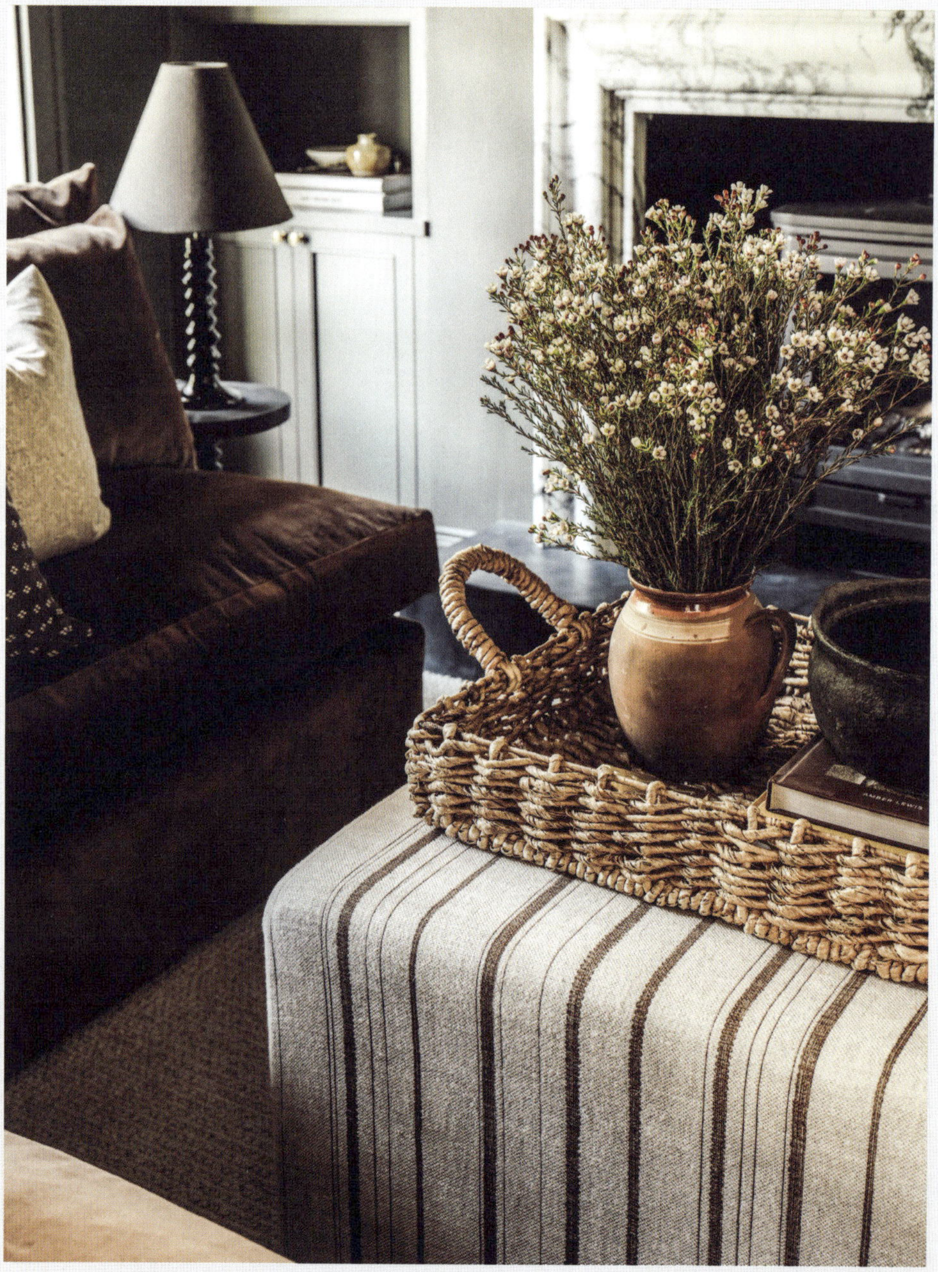

→ The snug at our Green Park Project in Dublin. This room carries so much of what has become a House Nine signature – earthy greens, striped linens, the Adley basket tray from our homewares store, and that mix of antiques layered in alongside the new. These are details you'll see running through many of our projects; our own quiet thread of consistency.

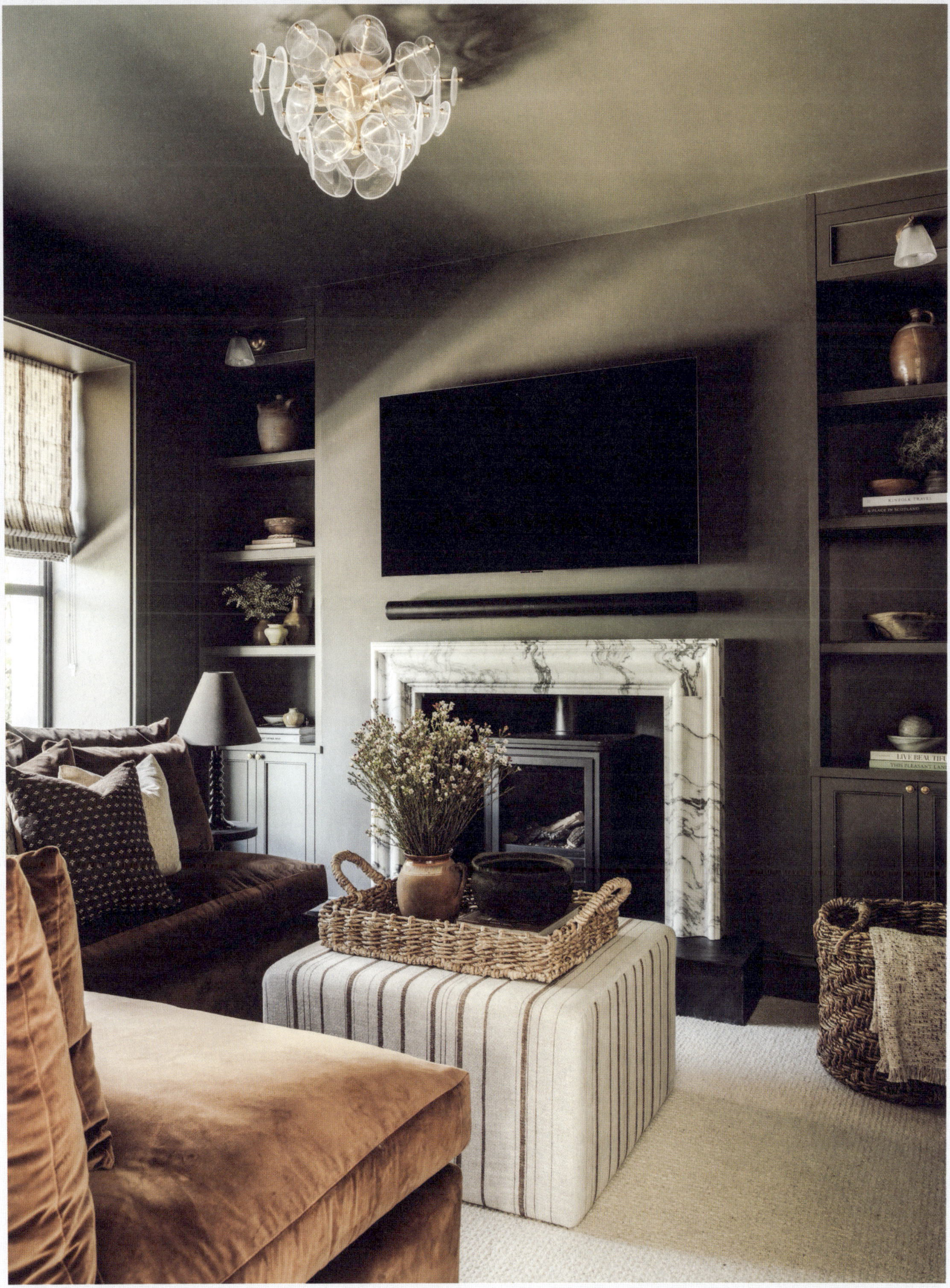
KINFOLK TRAVEL
A PLACE IN SCOTLAND

Using Mood & Vision Boards

Once you've gathered all that inspiration – the colours, textures, places, and feelings that speak to you – the next step is turning it into something you can actually see. That's where mood boards and vision boards come in.

A mood board is your creative playground. It's where you pull together the essence of what you want a room (or whole home) to feel like. Think of it as the visual version of an interior daydream: fabric swatches, paint chips, furniture, photography, art, architecture, and even fashion. Anything that captures the mood you're chasing belongs there. It's not about matching everything perfectly; it's about energy and connection. You're looking for threads – colours that speak to each other, textures that play nicely, tones that build a story.

A vision board sits one step higher; it's about your bigger picture. It might include lifestyle imagery, places that inspire you, or even snippets of writing that reflect how you want your home to make you feel. It's less about a specific design scheme and more about a mindset and what you want to draw in.

The trick is not to overthink it. Start broad, then refine. Don't curate as you go – collect first, edit later. I often find the most exciting ideas come from unexpected combinations, like an old oil painting next to a piece of modern joinery, or a colour pulled from the spine of an old book that jumps out at you.

Digital tools like Pinterest, Microsoft PowerPoint and Canva are all brilliant creative tools and where I tend to create for myself, but there's also a real magic in doing it by hand, especially when starting out. Printing, cutting, tearing, and sticking helps activate your senses. Touching materials changes how you think about them. When you can physically move pieces around, new ideas start to appear.

Most importantly, remember that your board isn't for anyone else to see. It's a visual conversation with yourself, a safe space to play and edit. Let it be messy, let it evolve, and let it tell your story. That's how inspiration becomes design.

→ The beginnings of a scheme for a guest shower room, laid out on my presentation board. Soft terracotta, handmade wall tiles, a nod to Delft, and a marble mosaic that will sit underfoot – already it has a story.

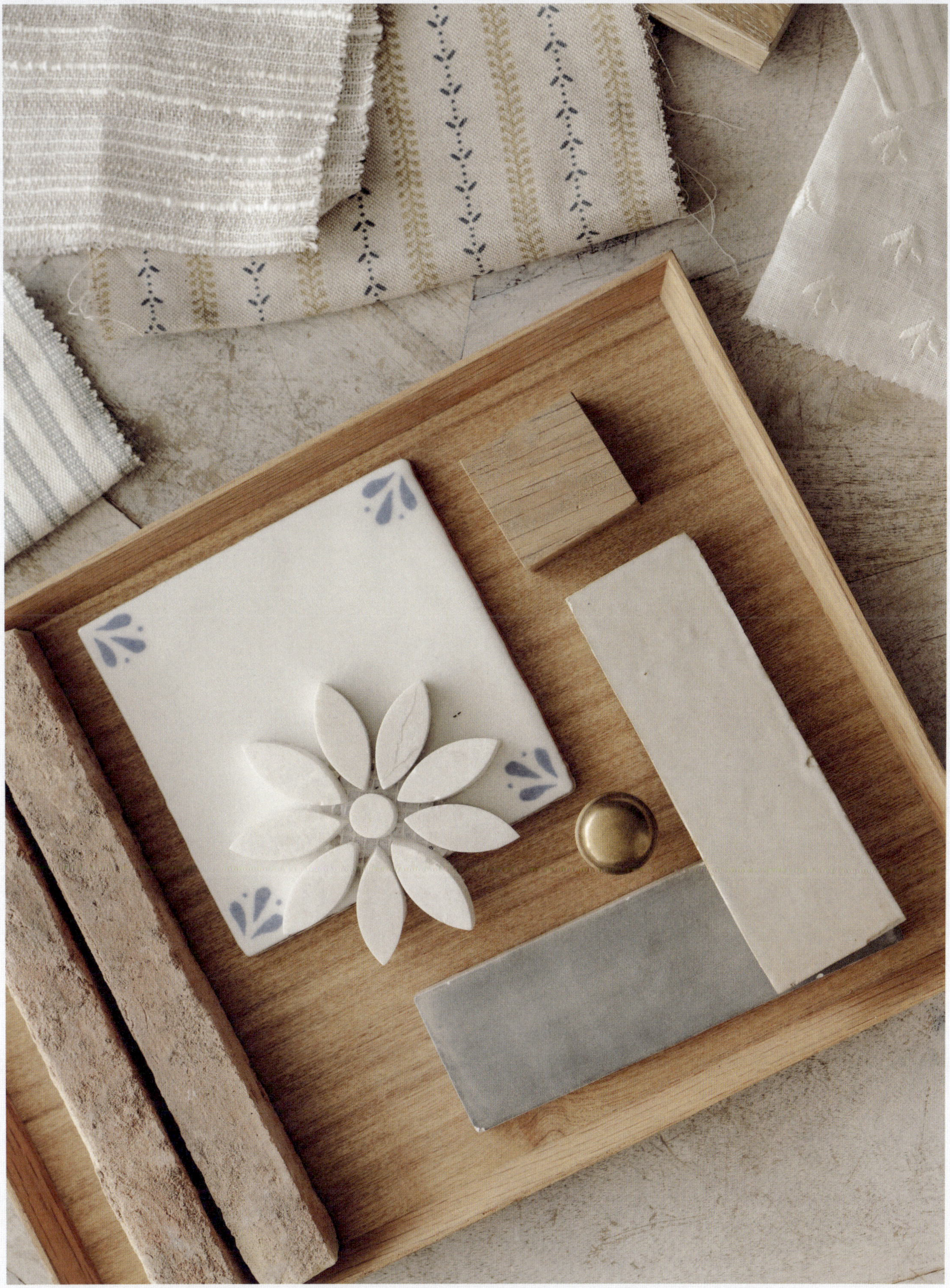

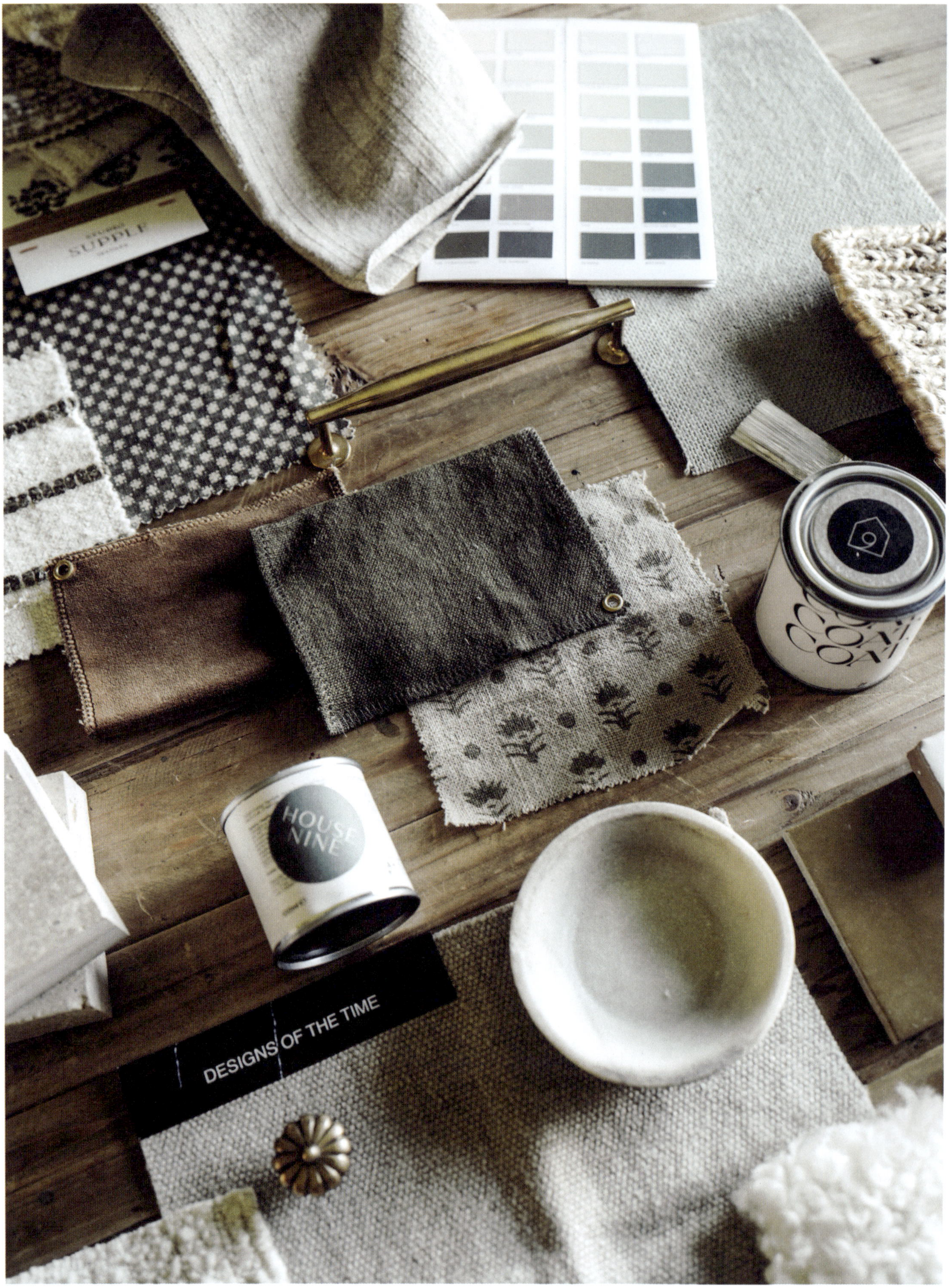
SUPPLE
HOUSE NINE
DESIGNS OF THE TIME

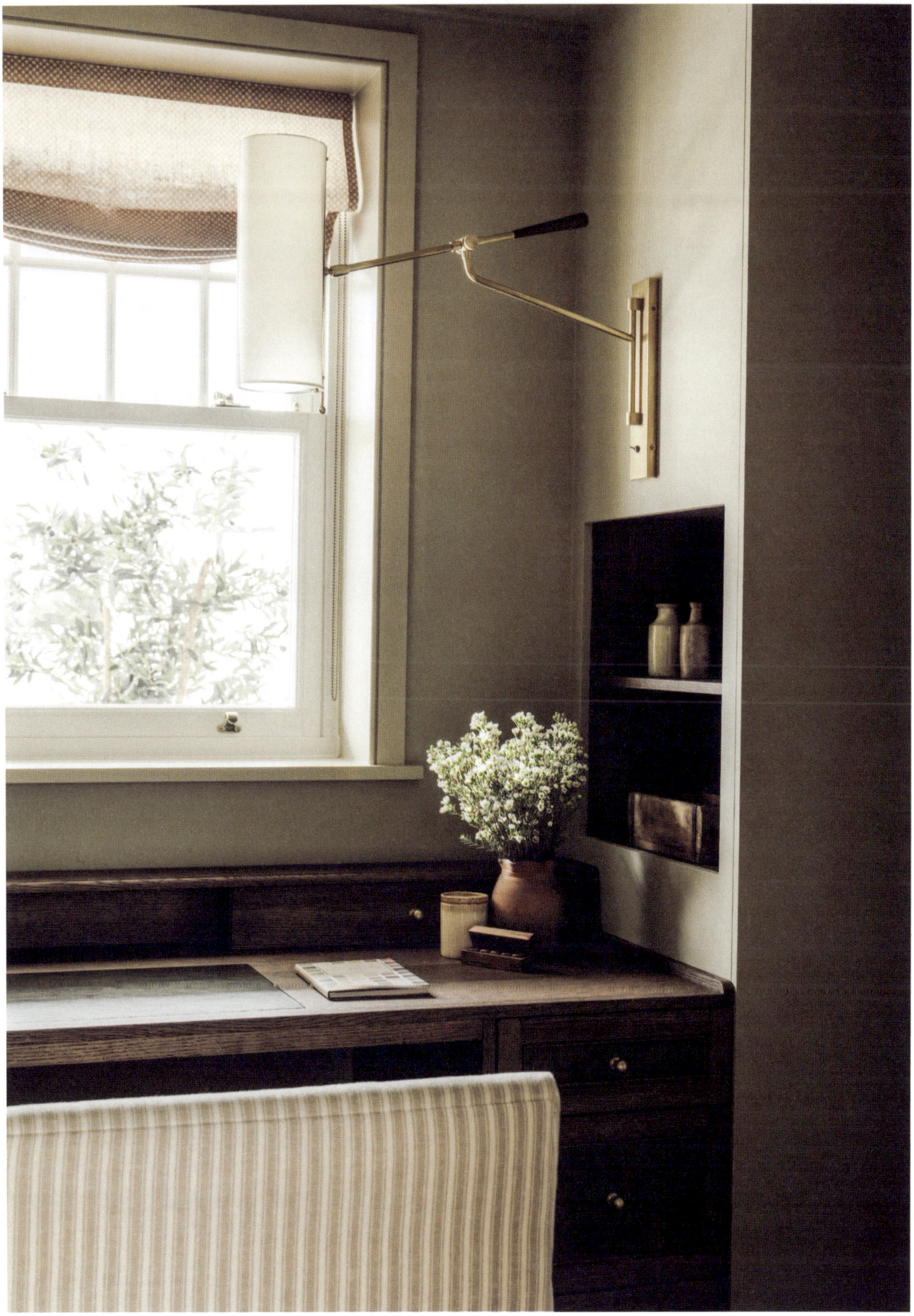

← A scheme taking shape. Linen and wool samples in sage, putty and warm taupe, a brass handle, a marble bowl, paint swatches pulled from the quieter end of the palette. This is where a project lives before it becomes a room – nudged around, edited down until everything earns its place.

↑ The home office at Project Sandbanks. Dark walnut joinery, striped linen, walls in a soft sage, and a brass articulated wall light doing quiet, considered work. A terracotta vase, a handful of white flowers – nothing more needed. Calm enough to think in, lovely enough to want to be in.

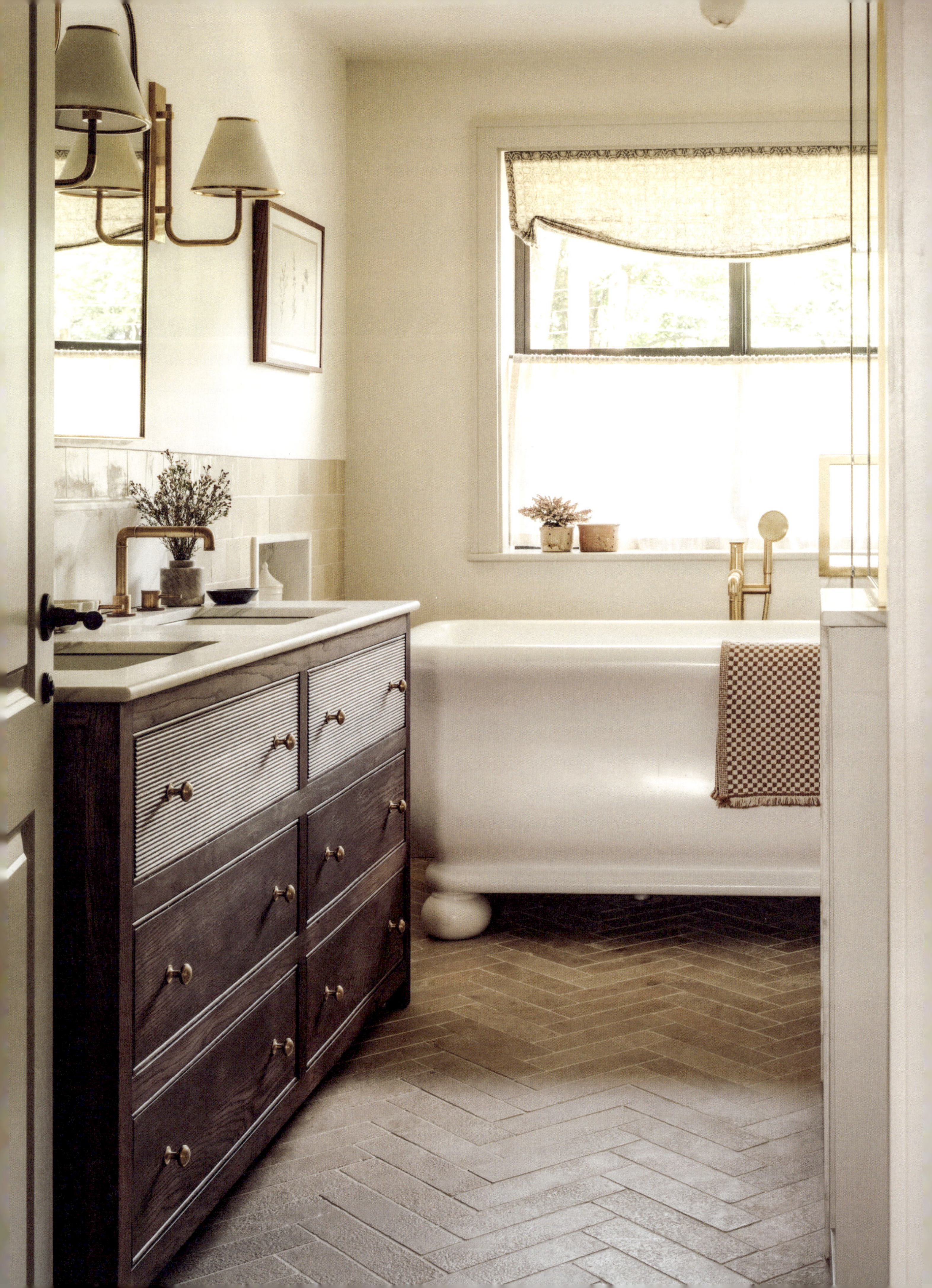

← The principal bathroom at Project Green Park, Dublin. Herringbone limestone floors, a dark walnut vanity with reeded drawer fronts, a freestanding bath, and brass fittings; every element chosen to feel collected rather than coordinated. This room began as a mood board not unlike the one on the previous page. A sliver of stone, a brass knob, a scrap of linen, a warm white paint swatch. Laid together they told a story before a single decision was made.

↓ Aged brass fittings, hand-glazed Zellige tiles, marble herringbone underfoot, and a niche carved in for the simple things. Small details like these are exactly what mood boards are built to capture: the texture of the tile, the warmth of the brass, the way light catches the marble long before a single piece is ever installed.

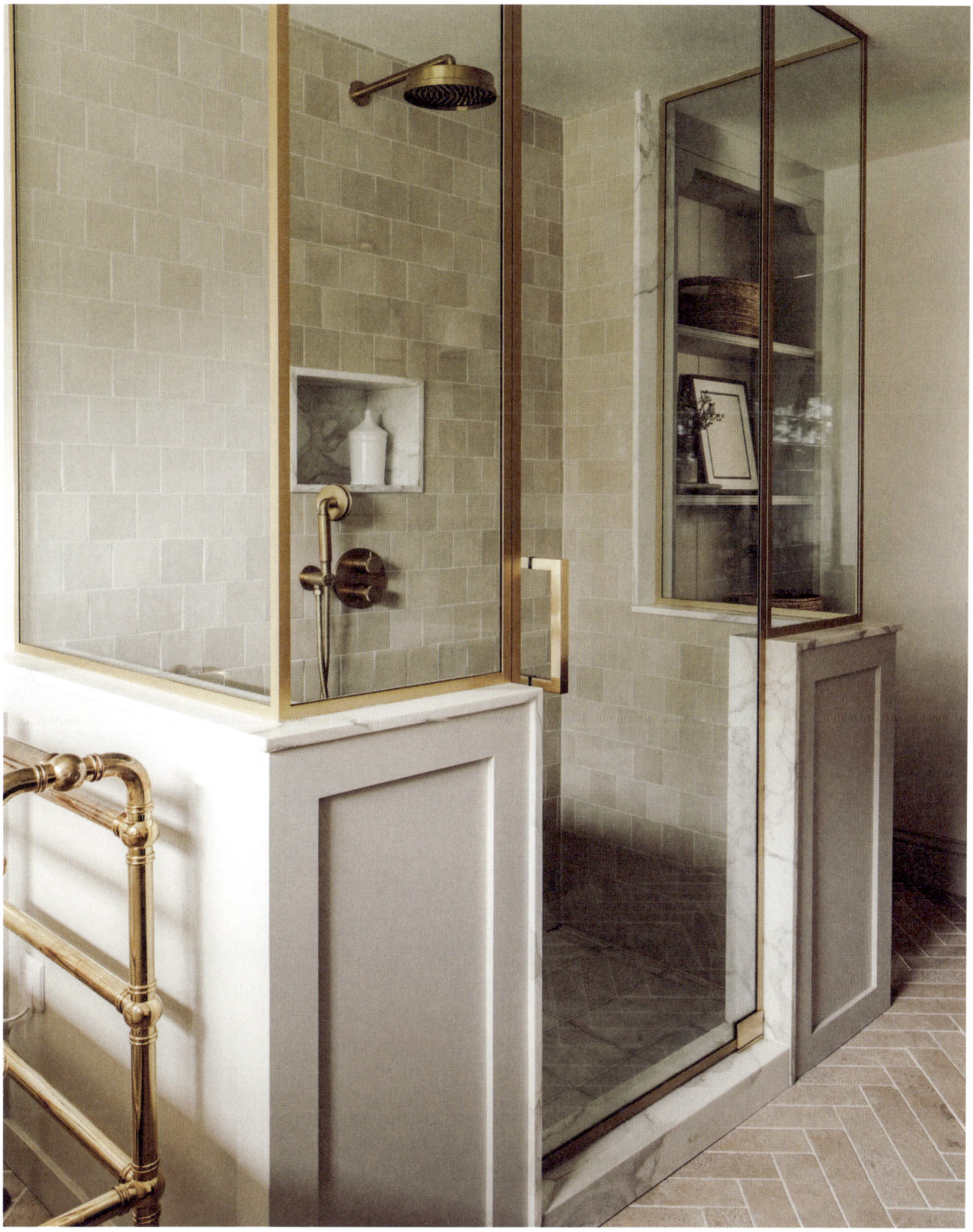

Gather Inspiration

A mood board is how inspiration stops floating around in your head and starts materializing into a plan. Once you have made one, you will start to notice your tastes sharpening and your confidence growing.

1. START WITH FEELING

Before you pin or print a single thing, ask yourself: "How do I want this space to feel? Calm, cosy, playful, bold, moody?" That one word becomes your filter for everything that follows.
Do this now: Choose one room (or even just a corner) and write down a single feeling word for it.

2. COLLECT FIRST, EDIT LATER

Don't overthink it. Spend a few days gathering anything that sparks something: screenshots, magazine clippings, fabric swatches, postcards, photos. Even if it feels random, let it in.
Rule of thumb: If it makes you smile or pause for a second, it goes in.

3. GO TACTILE WHERE YOU CAN

Screens are great, but texture tells you more than a phone ever could. Build a physical board if possible – swatches, ribbons, samples, torn pages, anything you can touch. Lay them out on a tray, pinboard, or just across the table.
Tip: Notice how materials feel together, not just how they look.

4. LAY IT ALL OUT AND SHUFFLE

Whether you're working on Pinterest, Canva or a kitchen table, get everything visible at once. Move things around – group by colour, texture or mood until something starts to click.
You're looking for that moment where you think: "Yes, that's it."

5. FIND YOUR RHYTHM

Look for patterns emerging: colours that repeat, textures that complement each other, materials that make sense together. This is your style, quietly revealing itself.
Ask yourself: "What keeps showing up? What am I clearly drawn to, even if I didn't realise it?"

6. PLAY WITH CONTRAST

A good mood board has range – rough and smooth, light and dark, warm and cool, matte and shiny. Character lives in the contrast, not in everything matching perfectly.
Try adding: One thing that feels a bit "too much" and one that's unusually calm. See how they change the energy.

7. STEP BACK AND EDIT

When you think you've nailed it, walk away. Come back with fresh eyes. What still excites you? What feels wrong, flat or out of place? Be ruthless, but not precious – this is where you start to see what really matters to you and to the space.

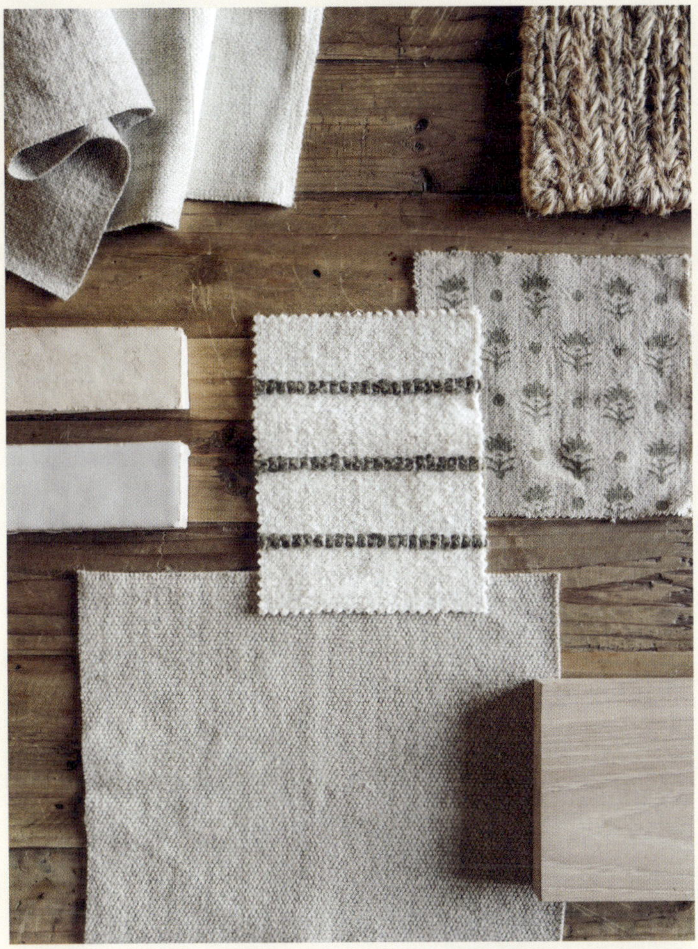

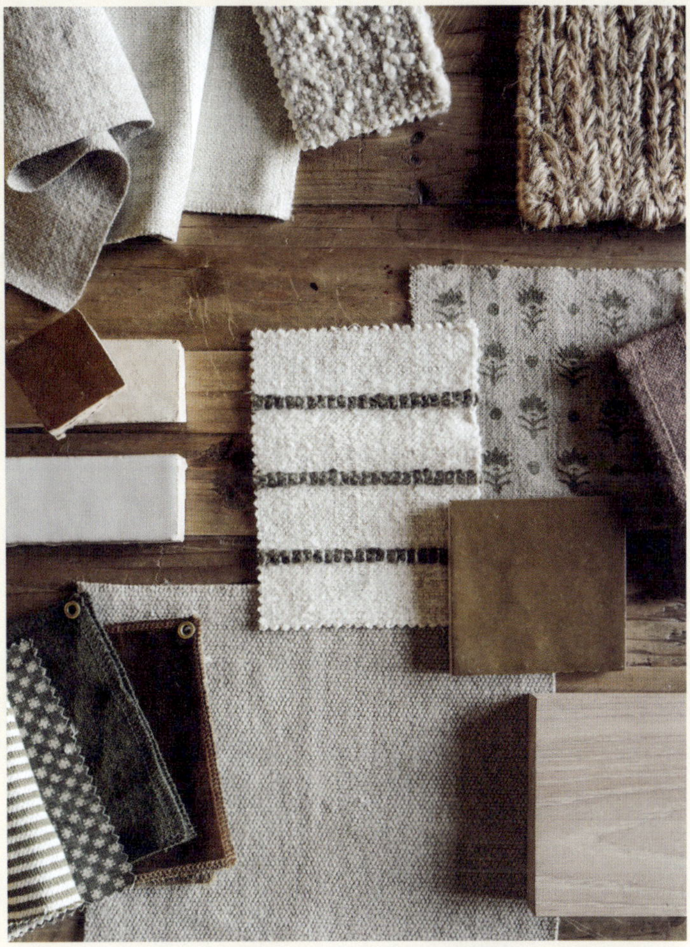

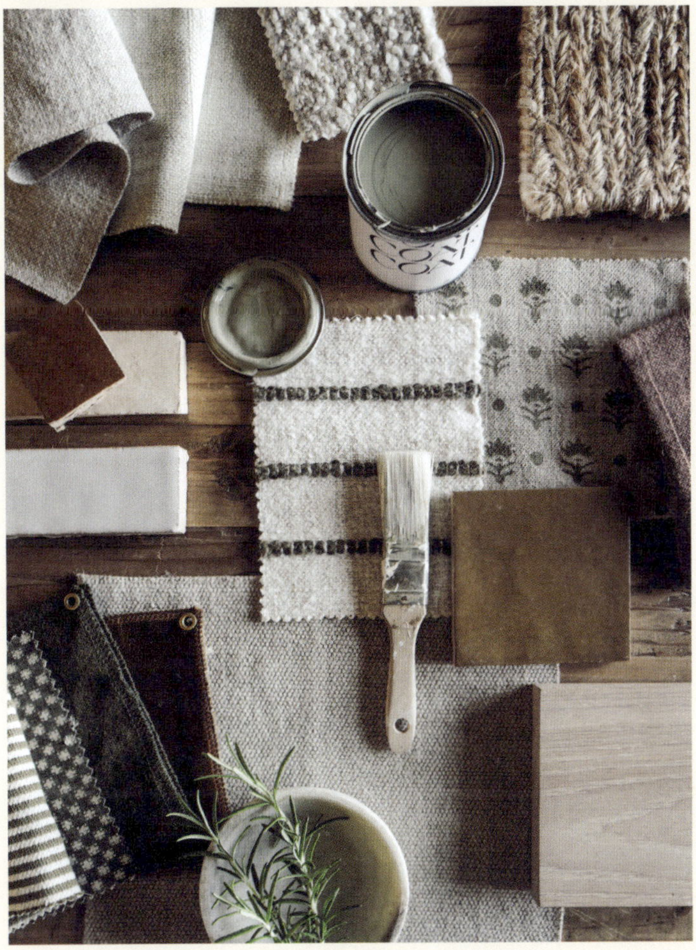

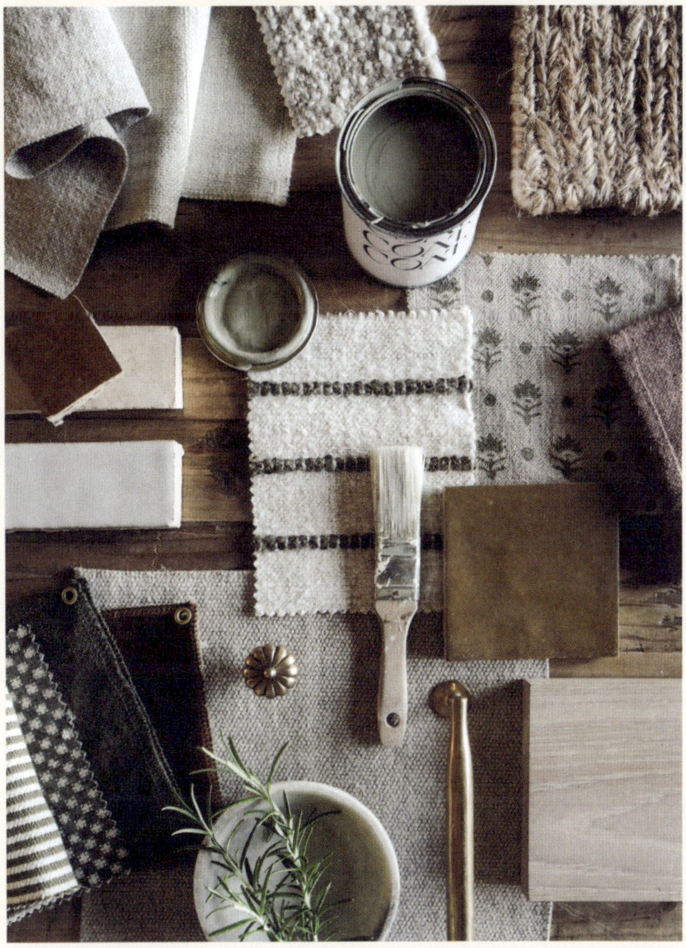

“*Details are not the details.*
They make the design.”

CHARLES EAMES

Refine

LAY THE FOUNDATIONS FOR SUCCESS

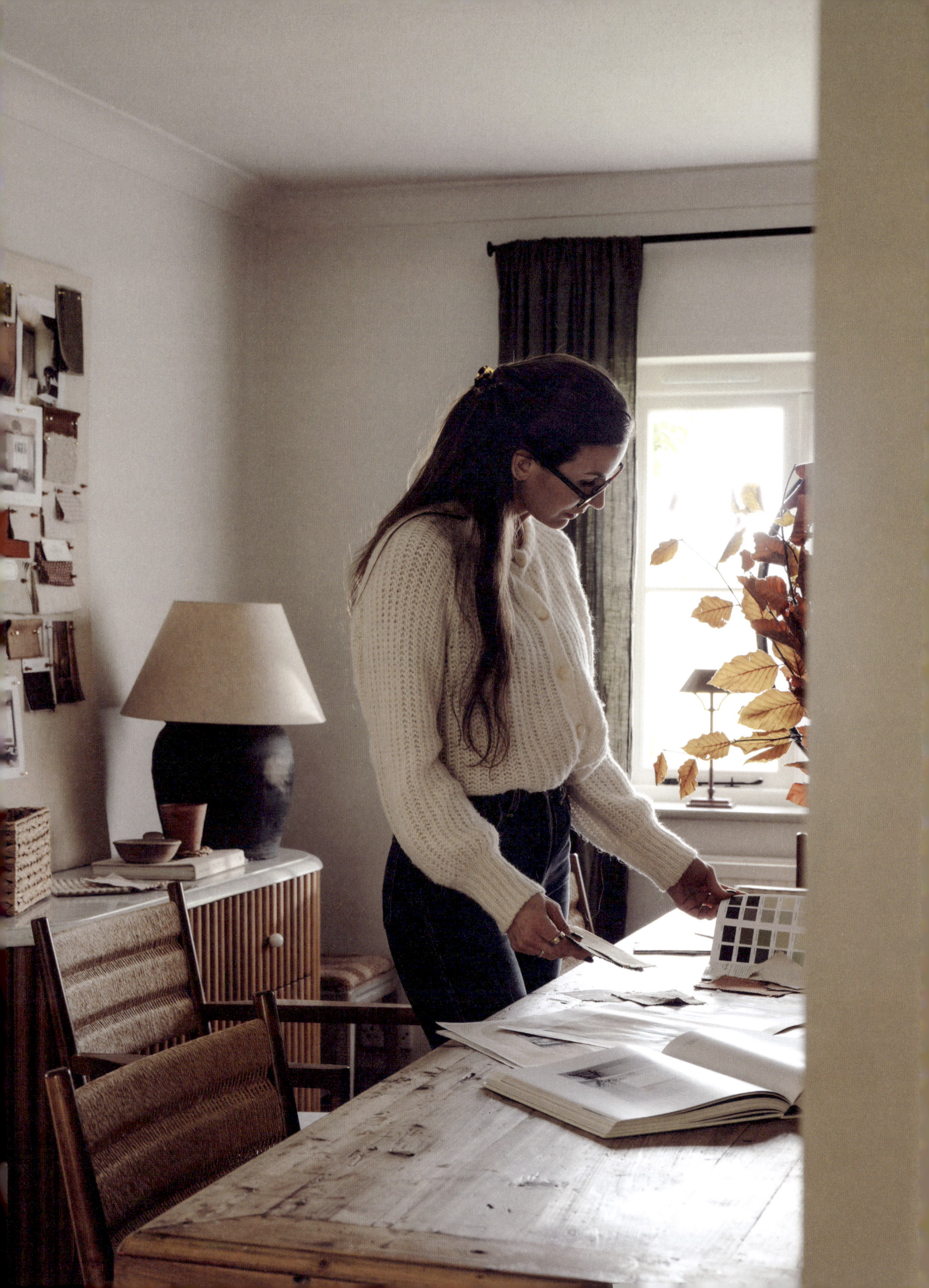

THE BEAUTY OF *FOCUS*

There comes a point in every project when the inspiration boards start to feel heavy – real heavy. I have been here many a time! At first, gathering ideas is thrilling – you're discovering what excites you, saving every single image that makes your heart skip a beat. But somewhere between the hundredth kitchen pin and the fifth saved living room board, the excitement turns into major overwhelm.

← At home, working through ideas for our own house. My home is honestly both the easiest and the hardest project – I know exactly what I want and yet the decisions feel weightier than any client brief. Refining my style has never been a single moment. It has happened slowly, over years – at this kitchen table, coffee going cold, turning over samples, editing things out, until what remains feels genuinely and unmistakably mine.

You are down a deep, deep Pinterest hole and everything begins to blur, and instead of clarity you feel utterly paralysed. Hello, decision paralysis! This is where refinement comes in. Refinement isn't about being ruthless; it's about being honest. It's the quiet moment when you stop collecting and start seeing. I've learned that the most beautiful homes aren't born from endless options; they tend to come from strong filters and a big old dose of focus. The people who design effortlessly aren't necessarily more creative, they're just better at saying no.

So, close the tabs. Step back. Take a breath, or a walk if you need to! Look at what you've already saved and ask yourself: "What's the thread that runs through all this?" Maybe it's a certain warmth in the materials, or the colours, a love of clean lines, or architectural detailing. That's the beginning of your point of view. Editing isn't about cutting things out for the sake of it, it's about recognizing patterns. Once you spot them, the rest should become a little easier. You start to see what belongs, what's a distraction, and what was never really "you" in the first place. The goal isn't a sterile board with three images and a caption that says "done". It's about tightening the story so your vision can breathe. Keep the pieces that feel timeless to you – the ones that make your shoulders drop when you look at them. Let go of the rest. I promise that soon you will forget they ever existed.

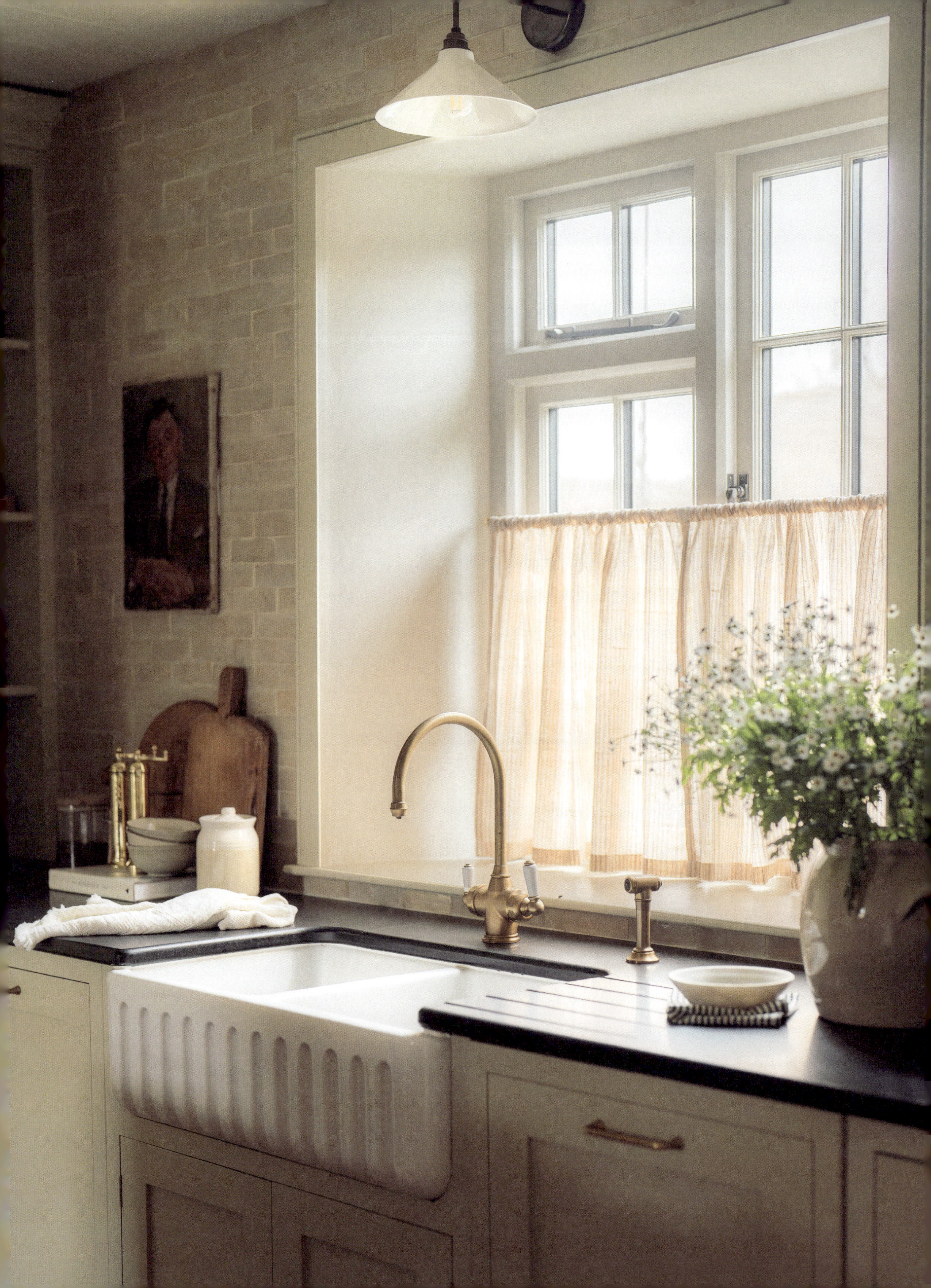

"Refinement isn't about being ruthless; it's about being honest."

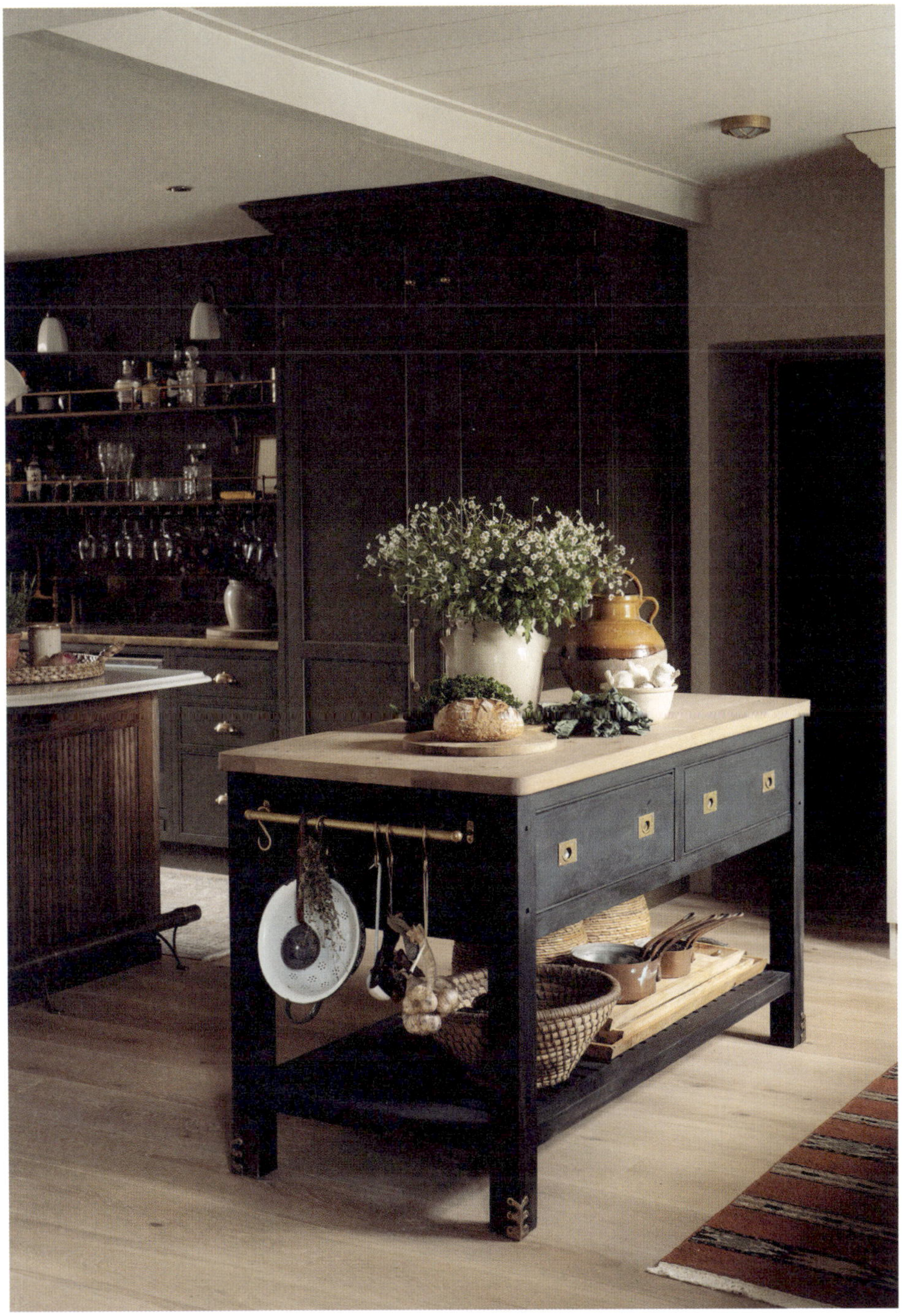

← One of my favourite projects to date – Hastings House. Not only for the interiors themselves but for the experience of working so closely with this client to really refine what she needed her home to be. The kitchen was designed for living in and for people in it – a true heart of the house. A double Belfast sink, brass fittings, shaker cabinetry in the softest warm putty, and a bespoke freestanding island that invites you to pull up a stool and stay. Nothing here is for show. Every decision was made in service of a home that works as hard as it is loved.

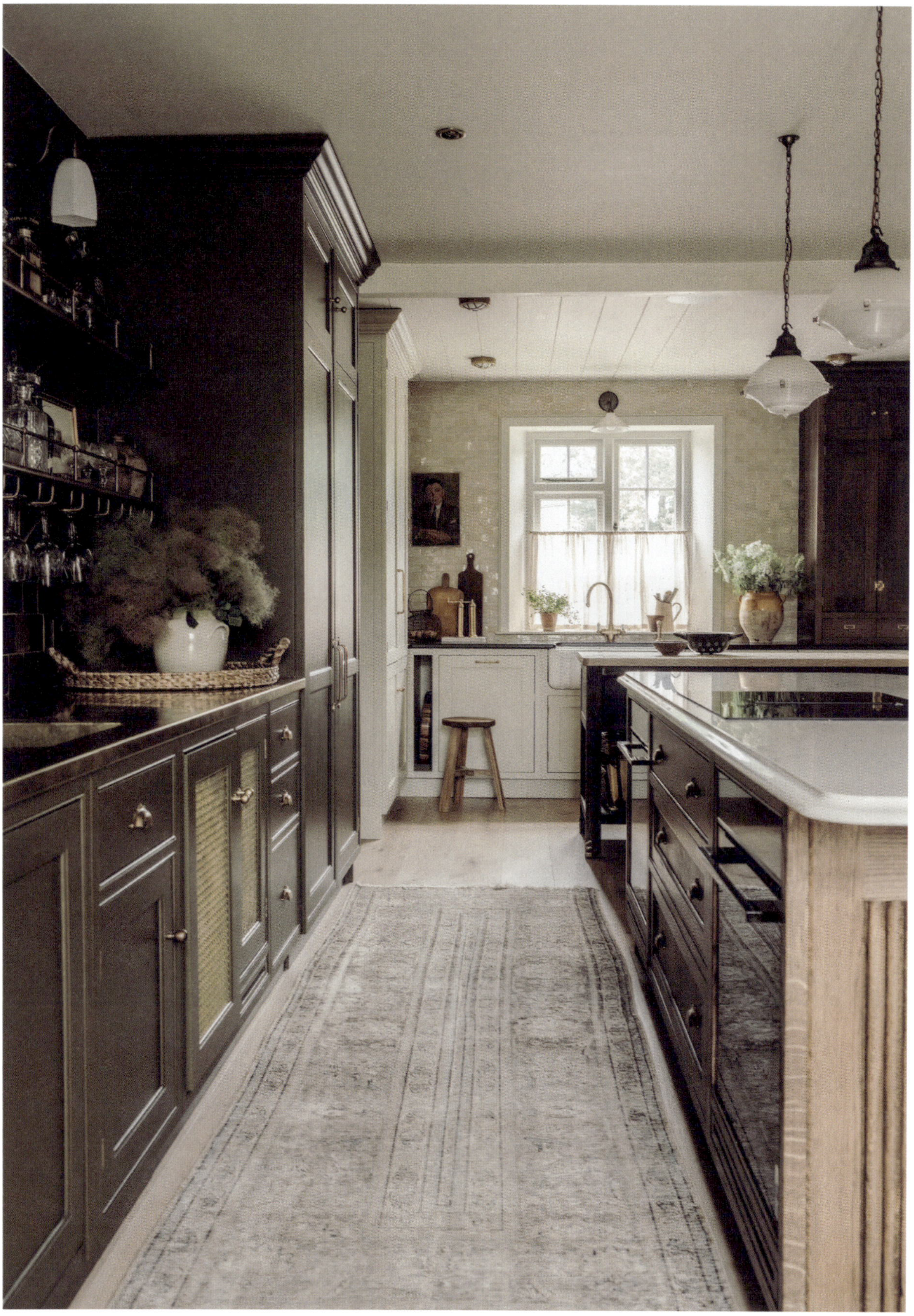

↑ Looking back through the kitchen from the garden end. This design came from the client – she works in pubs and wanted that same warmth. Deep earthy green, open shelving, brass fittings, and a faded runner. At the far end, a secondary kitchen in a softer, brighter tone for prepping. Two kitchens, two moods, one very considered home.

→ This was originally just a window and a walkway. We lowered the window, created a vestibule off the kitchen and made a proper place to store wine, hang coats, and pause to look out at the garden. The dark green carries through from the kitchen, grounding the space. And a little favourite House Nine signature - terracotta floors.

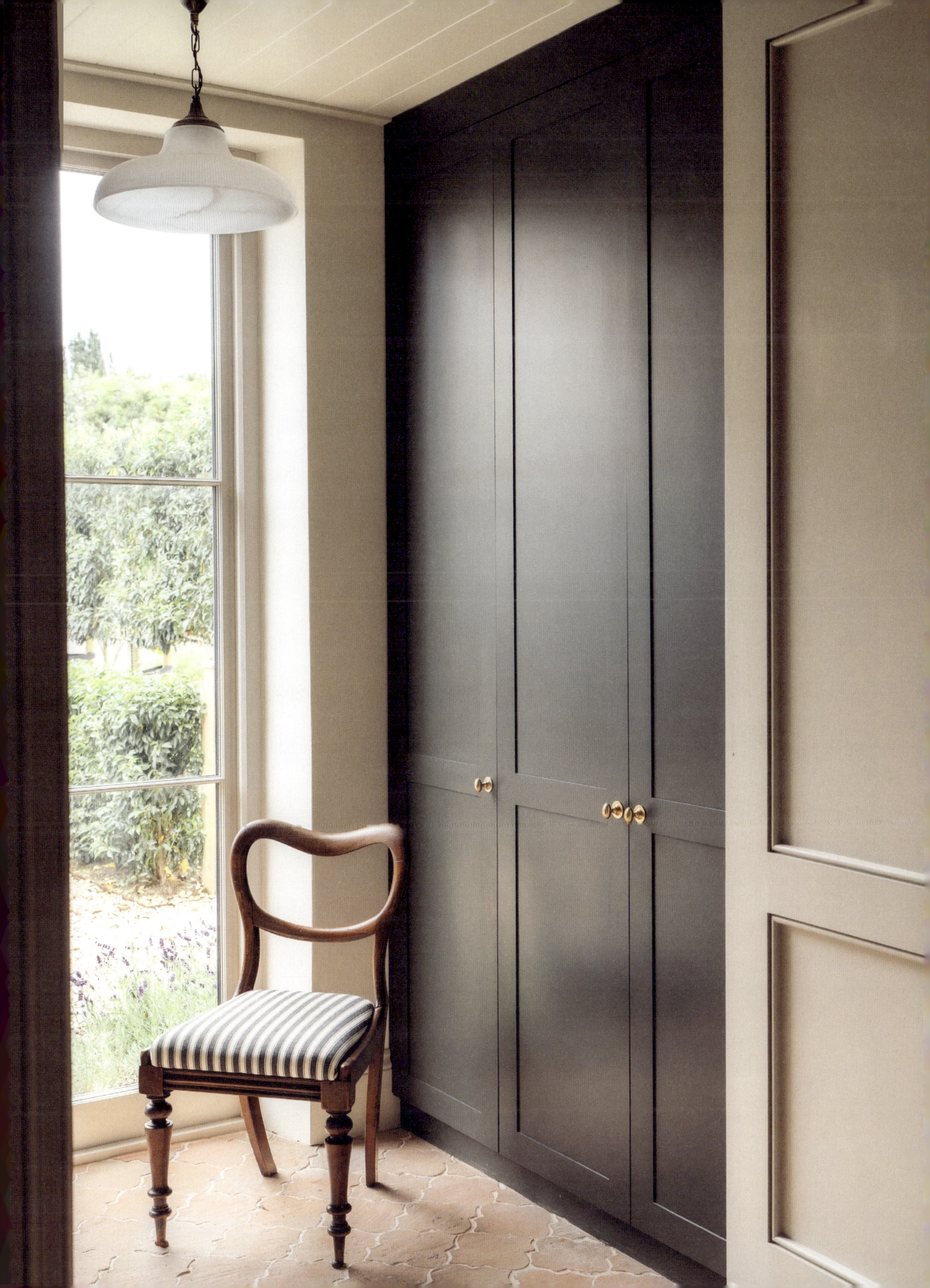

Decision Fatigue

→ A tray of metal finishes pulled together to see how they sit against one another. Brass, blackened steel, chrome, unlacquered copper. Placing them side by side is the only real way to judge tone, warmth, and whether they belong in the same room.

We live in an age of infinite choice. Every product, colour, and finish has twenty near-identical cousins. It's exhausting. Refinement is how you protect your energy – by making early calls on what truly matters.

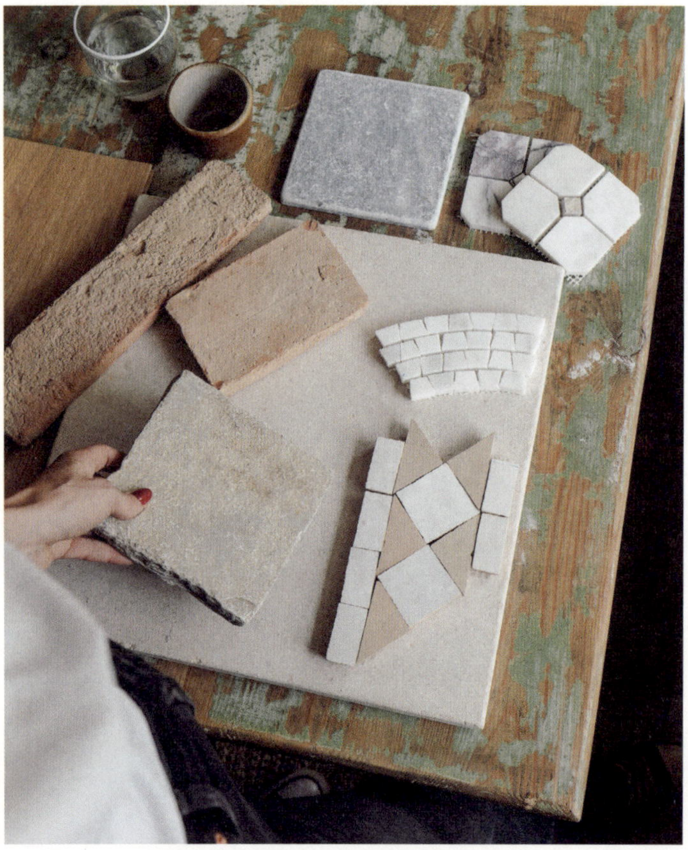

↑ Playing with hard finishes in the studio. Stone, tile, and timber samples laid out side by side. Selecting the flooring is usually one of the first decisions I make on a project; get it right and so much of what follows starts to fall into place.

In my early days of designing, I would spend hours debating various shades for a client's hallway. I would test them under every bulb and time of day, only to usually choose the one I liked in the very beginning. Refinement is mostly about trusting that first feeling and having the courage not to second-guess it. If you're hesitating between two ideas, you probably already know which one feels right. The instinctive one or the choice that feels a little too simple is almost always correct.

The way you edit says a lot about who you are. Are you drawn to contrast or calm? Do you crave order or spontaneity? Editing reveals your natural rhythm, your aesthetic fingerprint. When you strip away what's not essential, what remains is unmistakably yours.

For example, choose one or two metal tones and stick to it. Decide on your preferred timber finish. Settle on the palette of three or four base tones that can run throughout the house. These early, confident choices will free you later. There's nothing more liberating than realizing you don't have to look at another hardware brochure ever again.

There's also relief in limits. When you narrow the field, decisions start making themselves. The palette becomes clear, the materials make sense, and the boards begins to hum with coherence. Suddenly, what once felt overwhelming becomes instinctive.

Like in most walks of life, I always find a touch of humour helps. In this case, it makes editing easier. We all keep things we secretly know don't belong – a lamp that was too expensive to admit we don't love it, or a colour we chose because we thought we should be "brave". I'm here to tell you, you can be brave by admitting it was a mistake and in the words of Frozen's

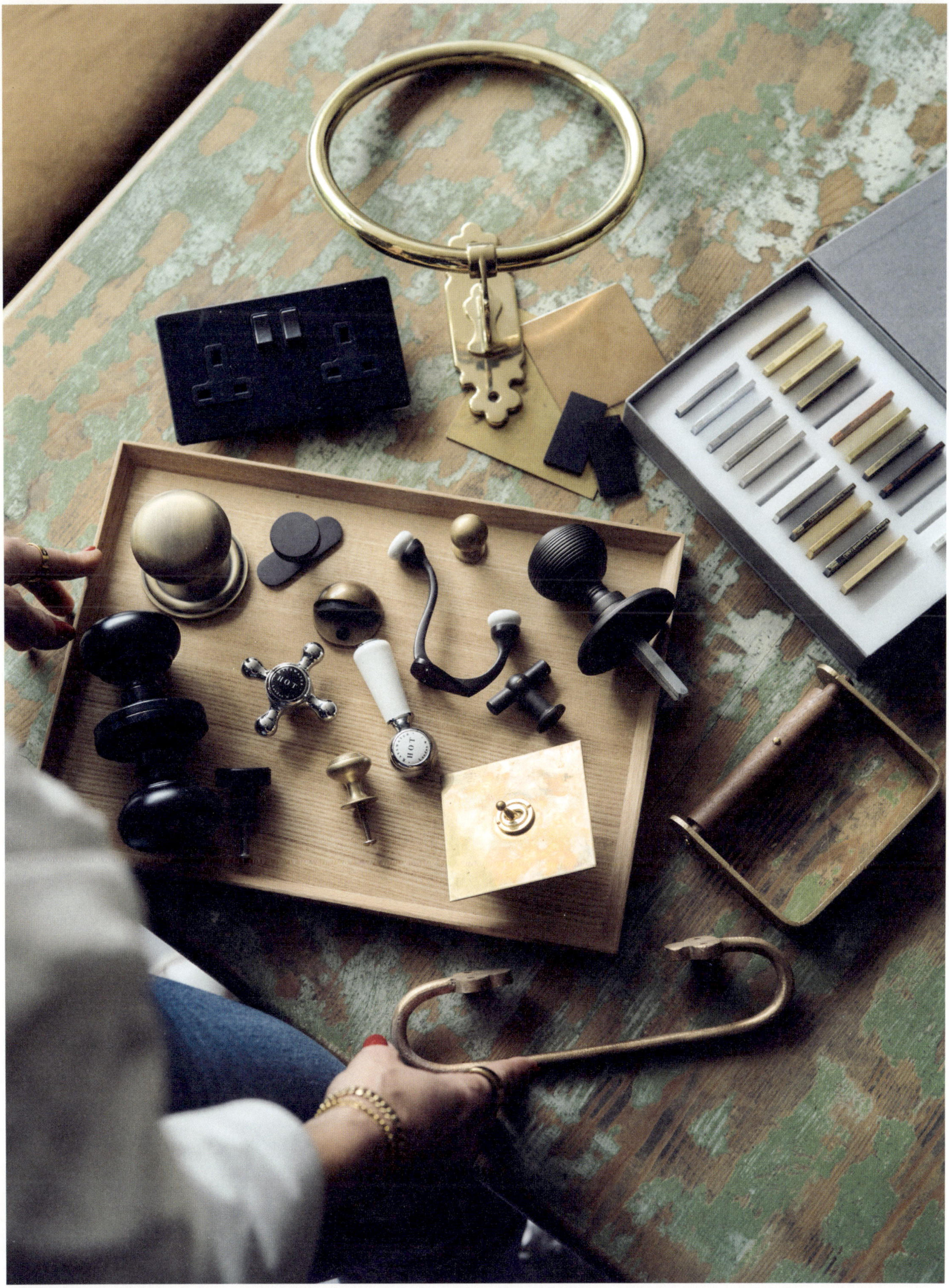
HOT
HOT

Elsa, simply "Let it Go". Refinement doesn't mean severe minimalization, it just means no more pretending you like something if you don't!

Editing isn't about having less; it's about giving shape to what matters. When you choose fewer things with more intention, the home starts to breathe. Space, light, and texture begin to work together instead of competing for attention.

So, before you move forward, pause here. Revisit your inspiration. Notice what keeps showing up. Keep what feels true and let the rest fall away. That's where refinement really begins, not with a spreadsheet of finishes or a mood board full of everything you've ever liked, but with the quiet confidence to say: "That is quite enough."

"When you narrow the field, decisions start making themselves."

→ Project Hastings House. I remember this room evolving rather than arriving. There was no single "hoorah" moment where it all clicked. It was slow, a colour adjusted here, a finish swapped there, until it simply felt right.

→ → Kitchen colours, and even the brassware, are usually the decisions our clients spend the longest deliberating over, and rightly so. It's the biggest expense in the house, and the one you'll live with longest. That's usually how the best rooms come together. Not a flash of inspiration, but patience, and the willingness to keep refining until it's unmistakably the one.

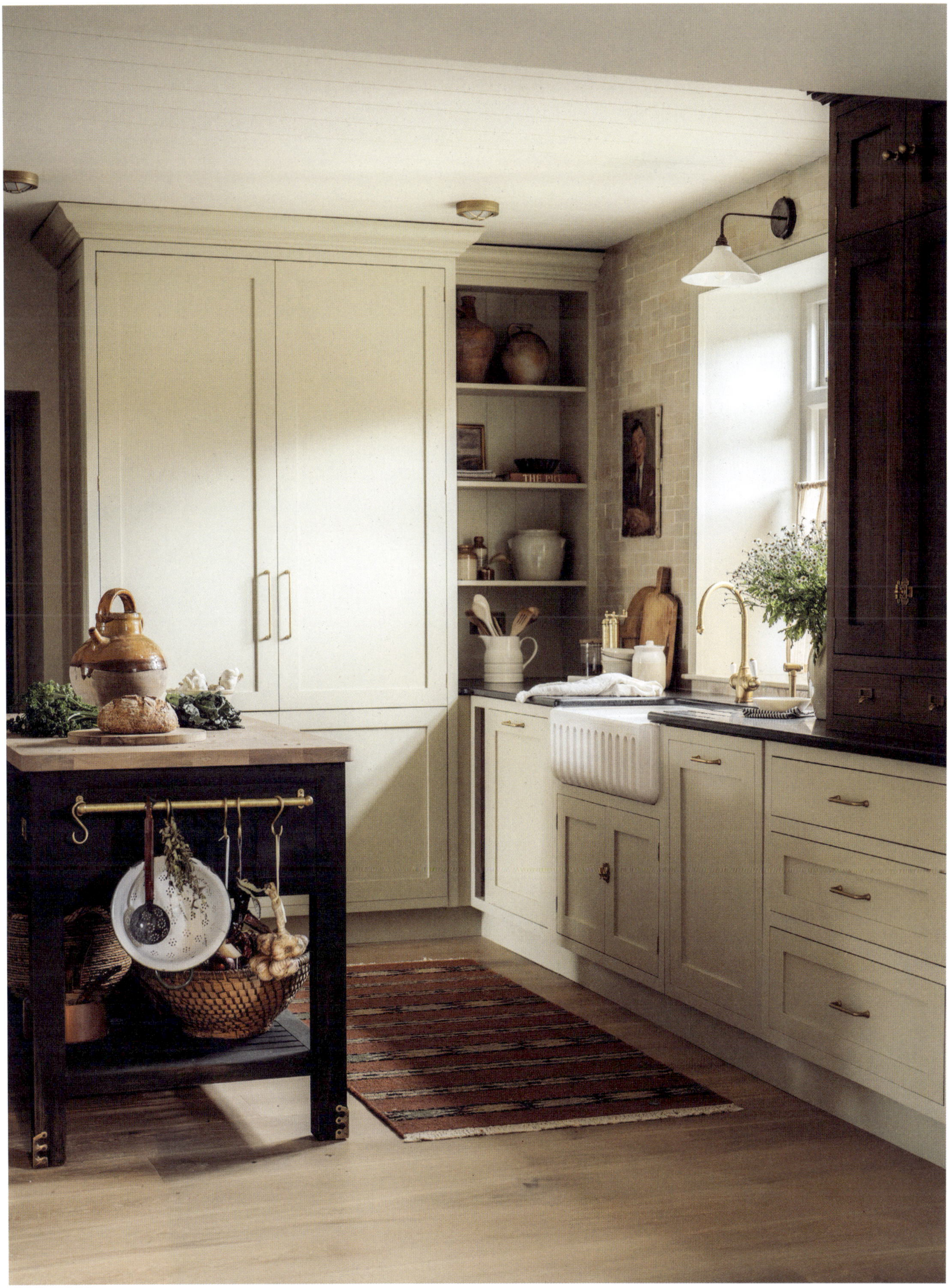

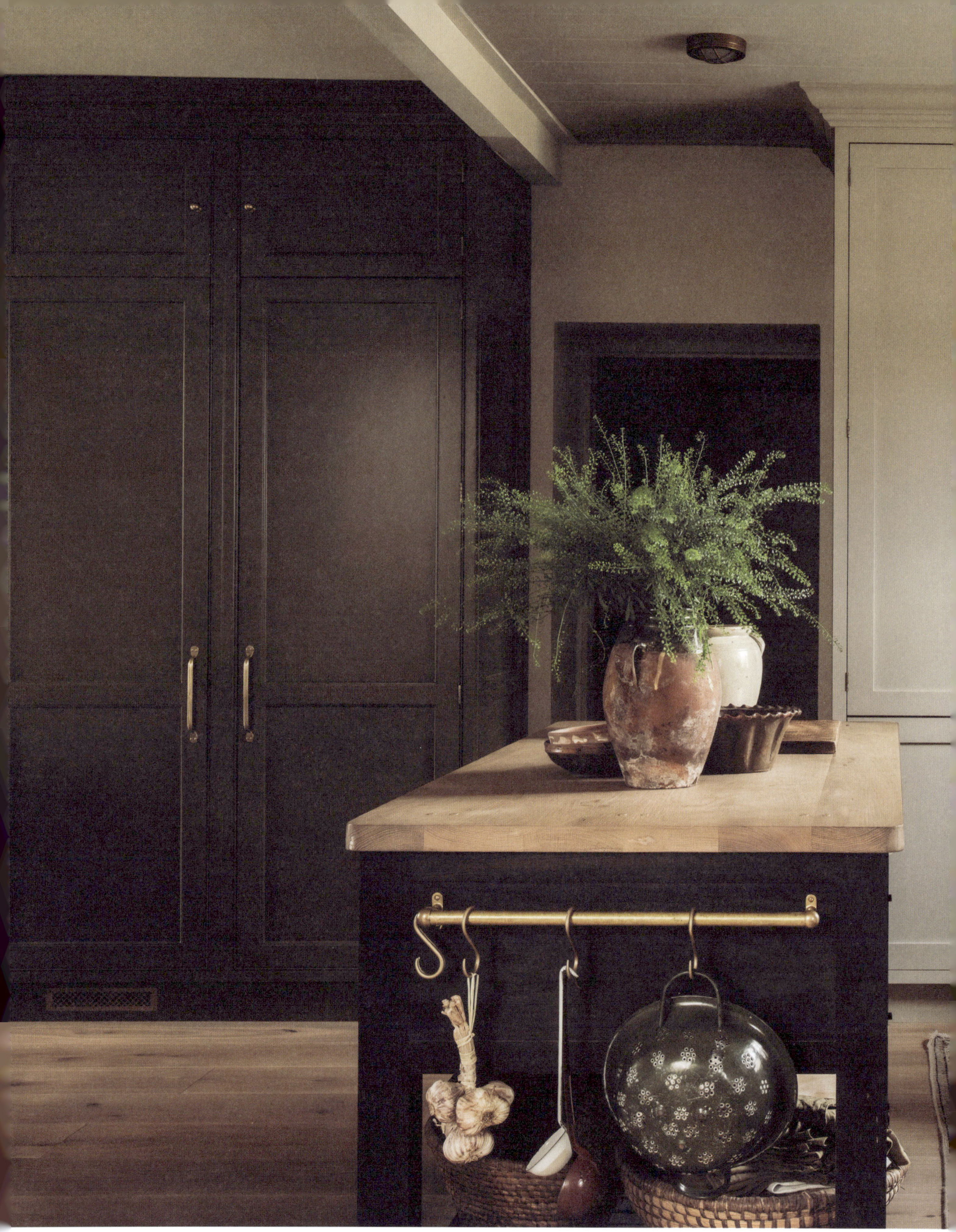

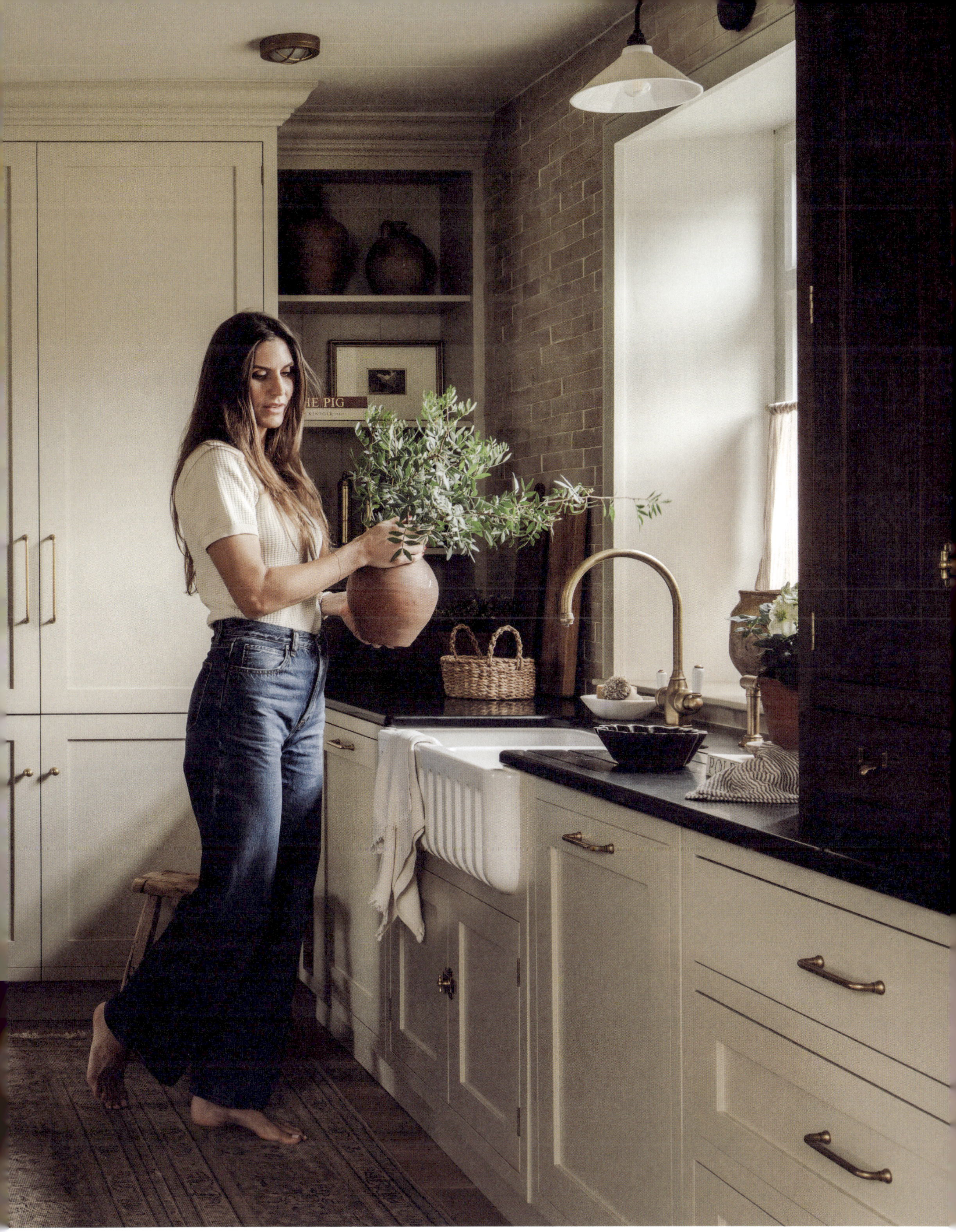

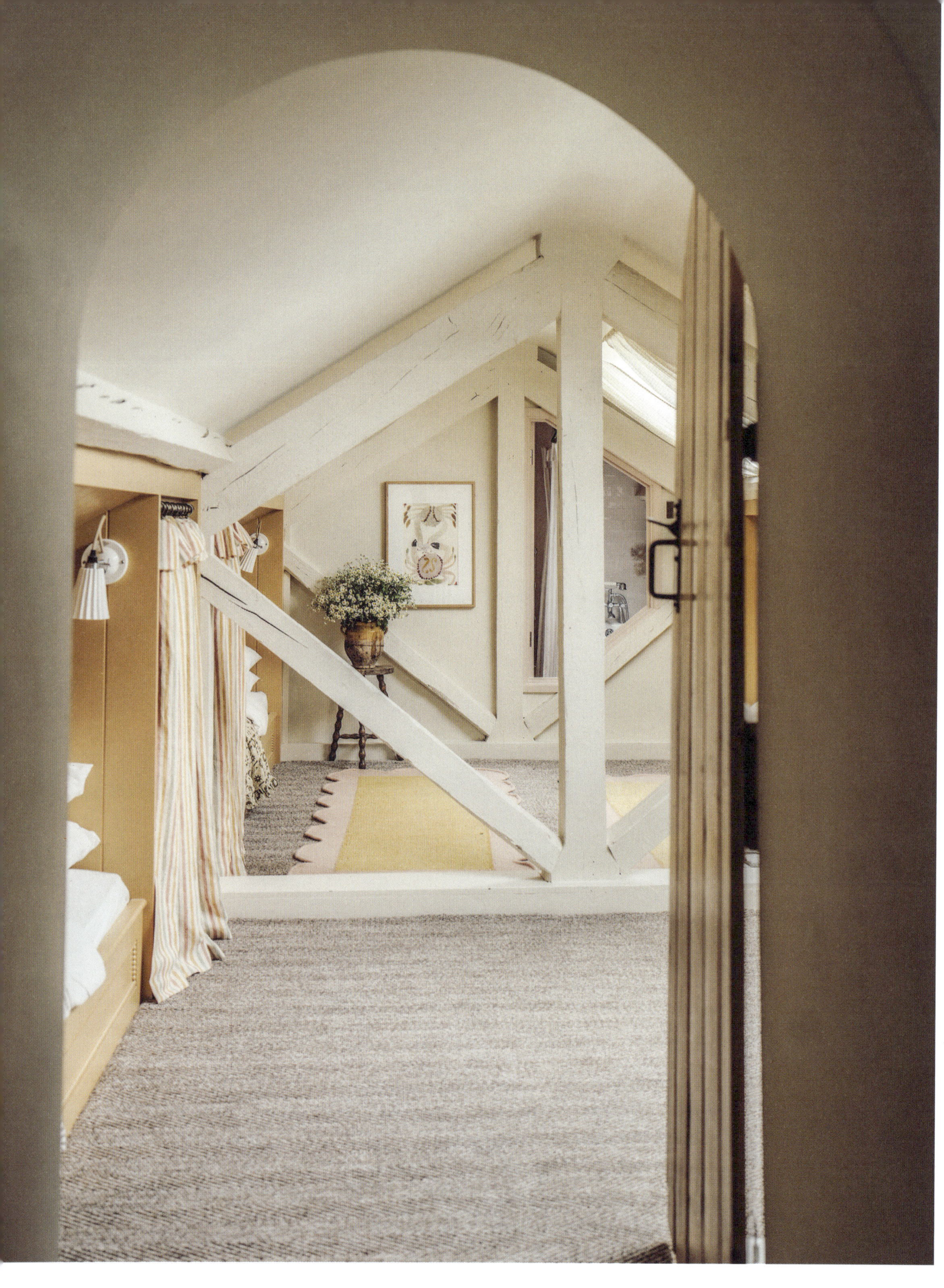

Colour and Light in Conversation

← The whimsical top bedroom in the eaves. This is one of our favourite rooms to design, complicated by a real criss-cross of beams and rafters, but there is so much fun to be had once you stop fighting the architecture and start working with it.

Refining a home is about paying attention to what's already there and making small, deliberate choices that elevate the whole. Colour is one of the most powerful tools in this stage. When considered alongside light, it helps clarify mood, sharpen atmosphere, and bring quiet cohesion to your spaces. Rather than adding more, this is about editing, adjusting, and allowing colour and light to work together to reveal a home that feels resolved, intentional, and lived in.

I like to start by thinking about emotion. Each tone carries its own energy: soft neutrals create stillness, dusty greens bring a sense of balance, deep blues or warm terracottas can anchor and cocoon a space. It won't be the first time I repeat this. But please don't worry too much about trends; instead focus on how you want to feel when you walk through your home. Colour, more than almost anything else, sets that emotional tone.

Light transforms colour constantly. A pale stone wall might appear almost white in morning sun but takes on a golden warmth by evening. Artificial light changes it again – cool bulbs can flatten colour, while warm lighting enhances its depth. That's why it's important to test colours at different times of day and under different lighting conditions. Let them live on the wall for a while before deciding. The right colour will feel calm in daylight and gentle under lamplight; balanced rather than busy.

Colour also depends on what sits beneath it. Flooring has a huge influence on how a tone reads. A cool, grey floor might make a wall colour feel crisp and contemporary; warm timber can soften it instantly. If your flooring varies throughout the house, consider how colours transition between spaces. Subtle shifts in tone can help create flow without every room feeling the same. When you're unsure where to begin, start small. Paint a door, a skirting board, or a single wall to see how it behaves in your light. You don't have to cover every surface; sometimes restraint is the most powerful choice. A neutral base allows you to introduce colour through art, textiles, or even the landscape seen through your windows.

"When you're unsure where to begin, start small."

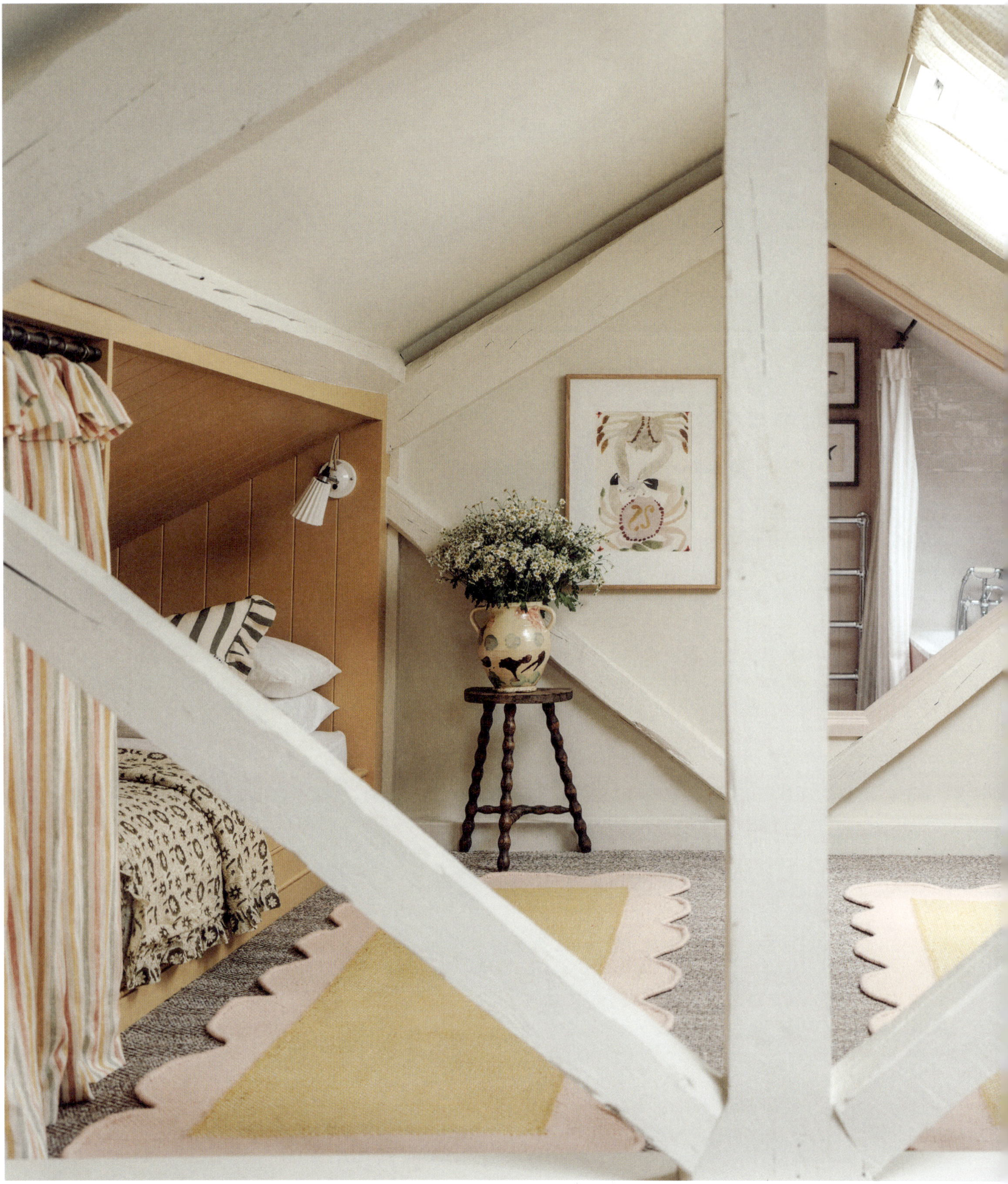

↑ Colour is what brings this room to life. Soft yellows and dusty pinks against warm timber, catching the light differently in every corner of the room throughout the day; exactly the kind of conversation between colour and light this chapter is about. Bright, playful, and full of air, even tucked right into the roofline.

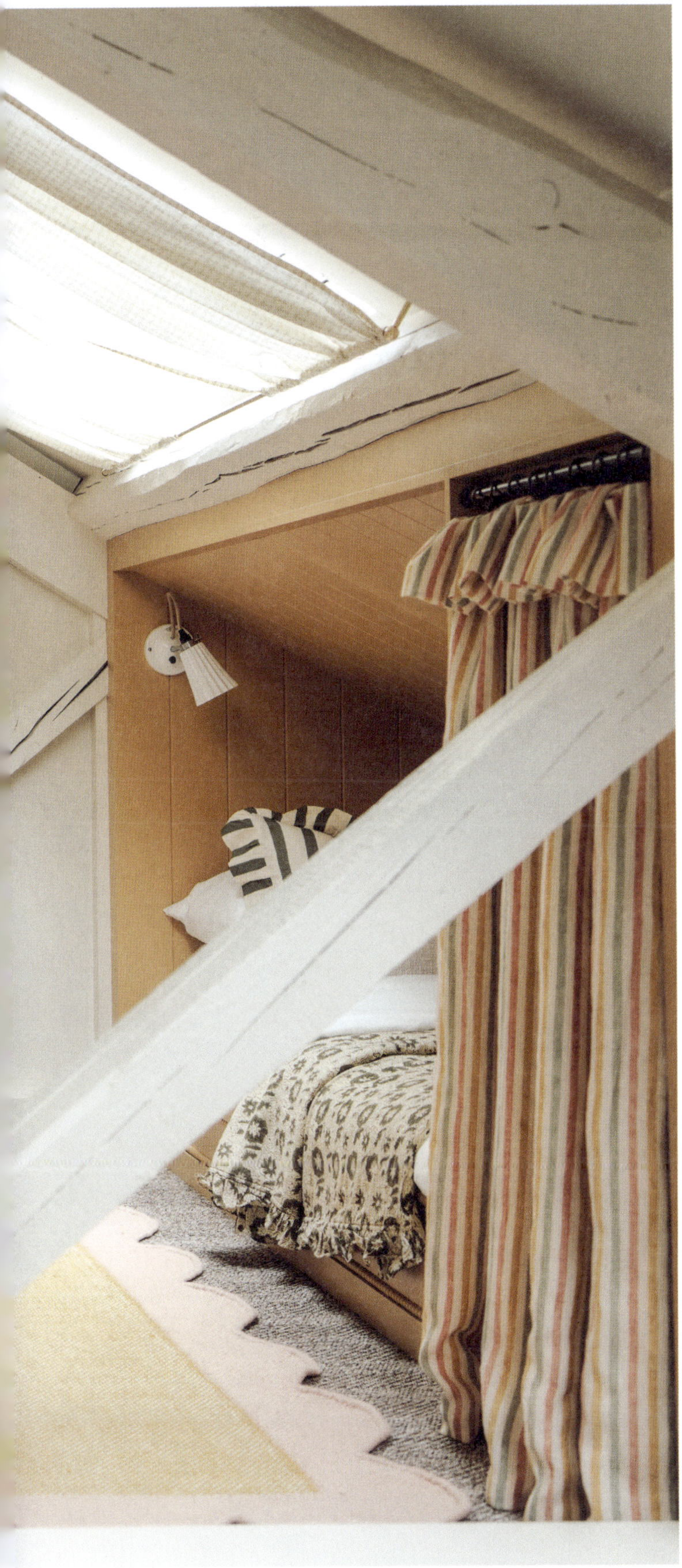

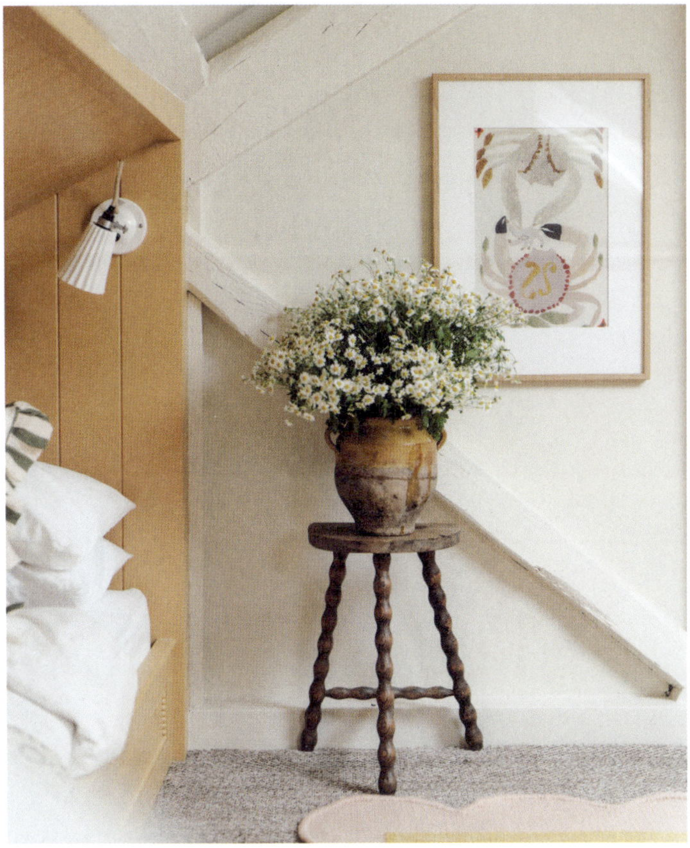

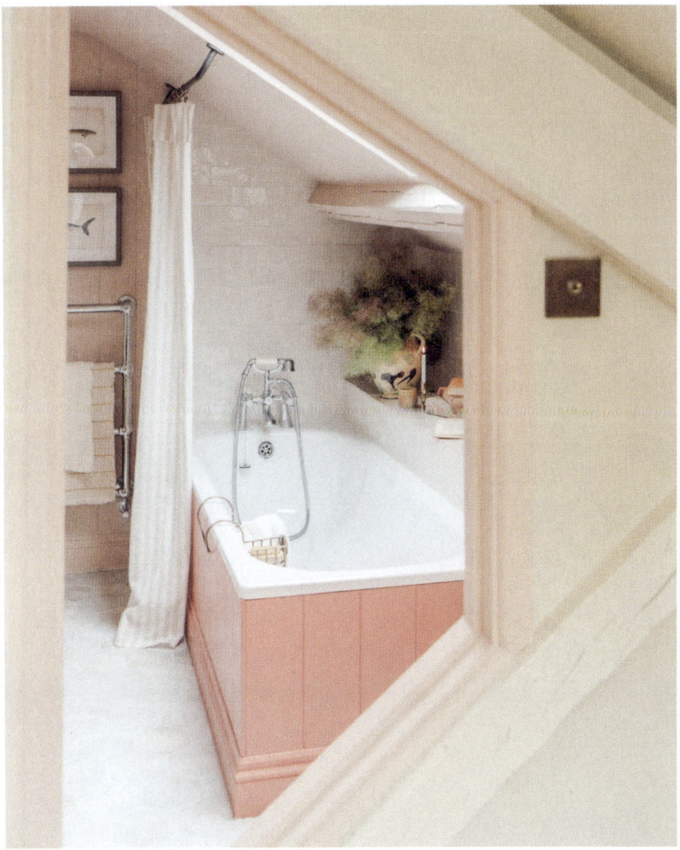

→ → In the studio, floor plans always sit alongside the mood board. While we're choosing colours and materials, we're constantly checking back against the plan - space, light, angles, flow - to make sure the scheme actually works in the room it's designed for.

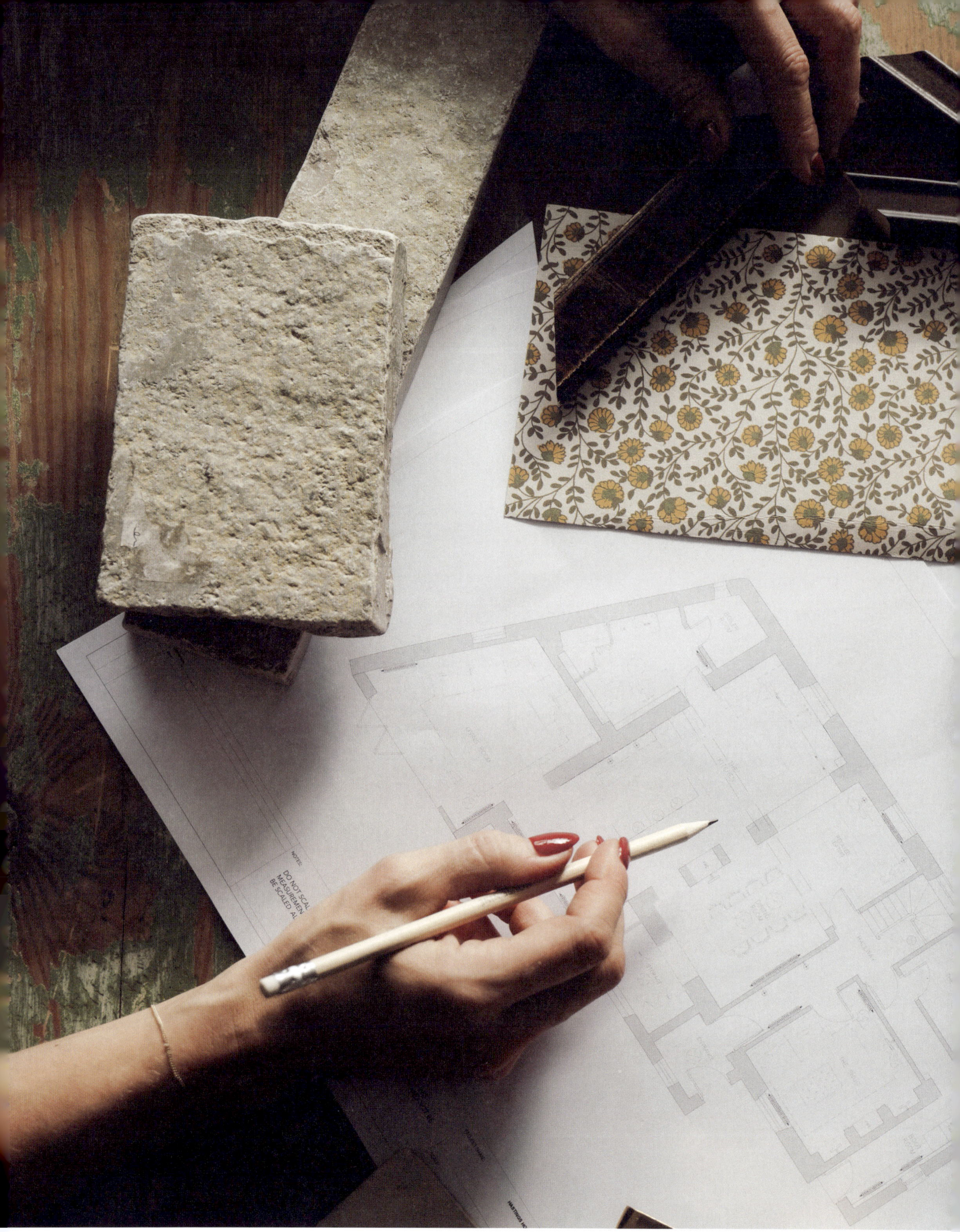

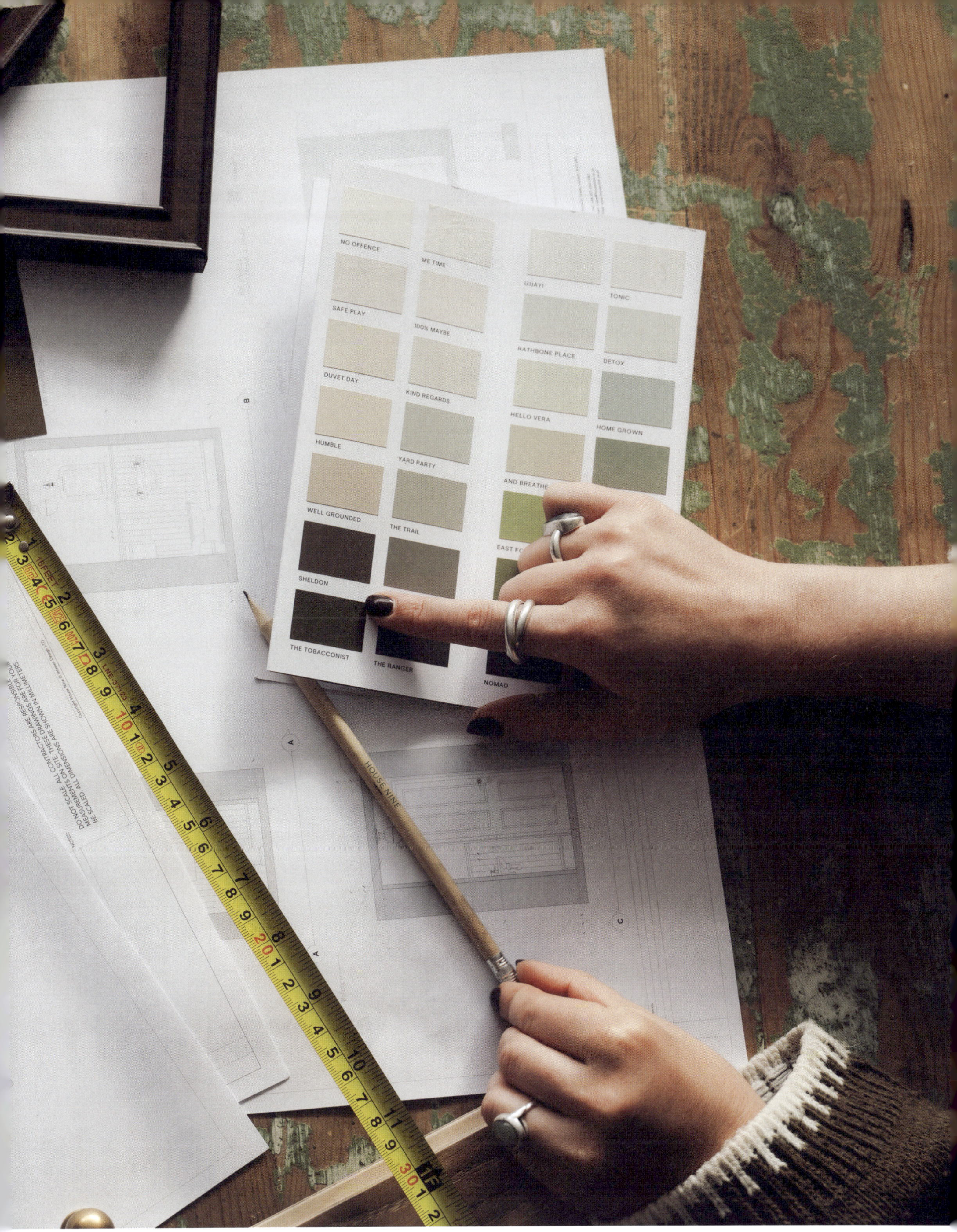
NO OFFENCE
ME TIME
UJJAYI
TONIC
SAFE PLAY
100% MAYBE
RATHBONE PLACE
DETOX
DUVET DAY
KIND REGARDS
HELLO VERA
HOME GROWN
HUMBLE
YARD PARTY
AND BREATHE
WELL GROUNDED
THE TRAIL
SHELDON
THE TOBACCONIST
THE RANGER
NOMAD
HOUSE NINE

The Art of Restraint

Refinement isn't about perfection; it's about clarity. Once you've set your foundations, the next step is to edit. This is where your home starts to take shape – not through what you add, but through what you choose to leave out.

Editing is one of the most powerful tools in design. It asks you to pause and look again, to question whether each element still serves your vision. A room that feels "off" often isn't missing something, it's holding too much. Simplifying allows space for the essentials to breathe and for the things you love to stand out.

Start by returning to your vision. Does every choice – colour, material, light – still align with how you want your home to feel? If something jars, remove it, even if it's beautiful on its own. Maybe there is a better place for it elsewhere. Refinement is about cohesion. When every element shares the same intent, the whole space feels balanced and calm.

Don't mistake simplicity for emptiness. A pared-back space isn't about doing less, it's about doing what matters most. Neutral backdrops, consistent materials, and subtle repetition of tone create a quiet rhythm that feels effortless. Give your rooms moments of pause: a clear surface, a stretch of wall, a space between objects. These small intervals allow the eye to rest and give meaning to everything around them. All of these elements I will go into in more detail in later chapters.

Editing also means trusting your instincts. You'll know when something doesn't feel right, like a bright rug that interrupts the flow, a too-large pendant that fights the architecture, or a colour that is too dominating. The more you refine, the more confident you become in what your home needs and what it doesn't.

There's also a quiet confidence in restraint. A home that's been edited with care feels grounded and intentional, not overdesigned. It holds warmth and character without shouting for attention. The best spaces are the ones that seem simple at first glance, but reveal their depth slowly; a texture here, a play of light there, a detail you notice only after living with it.

→ A bathroom built on restraint rather than addition. Checkerboard marble, a butter yellow vanity, brass fittings, and a single freestanding bath; nothing competing for attention. The window is left to do its job uninterrupted; a clear run of light across the floor, a moment of pause exactly where the room needs one.

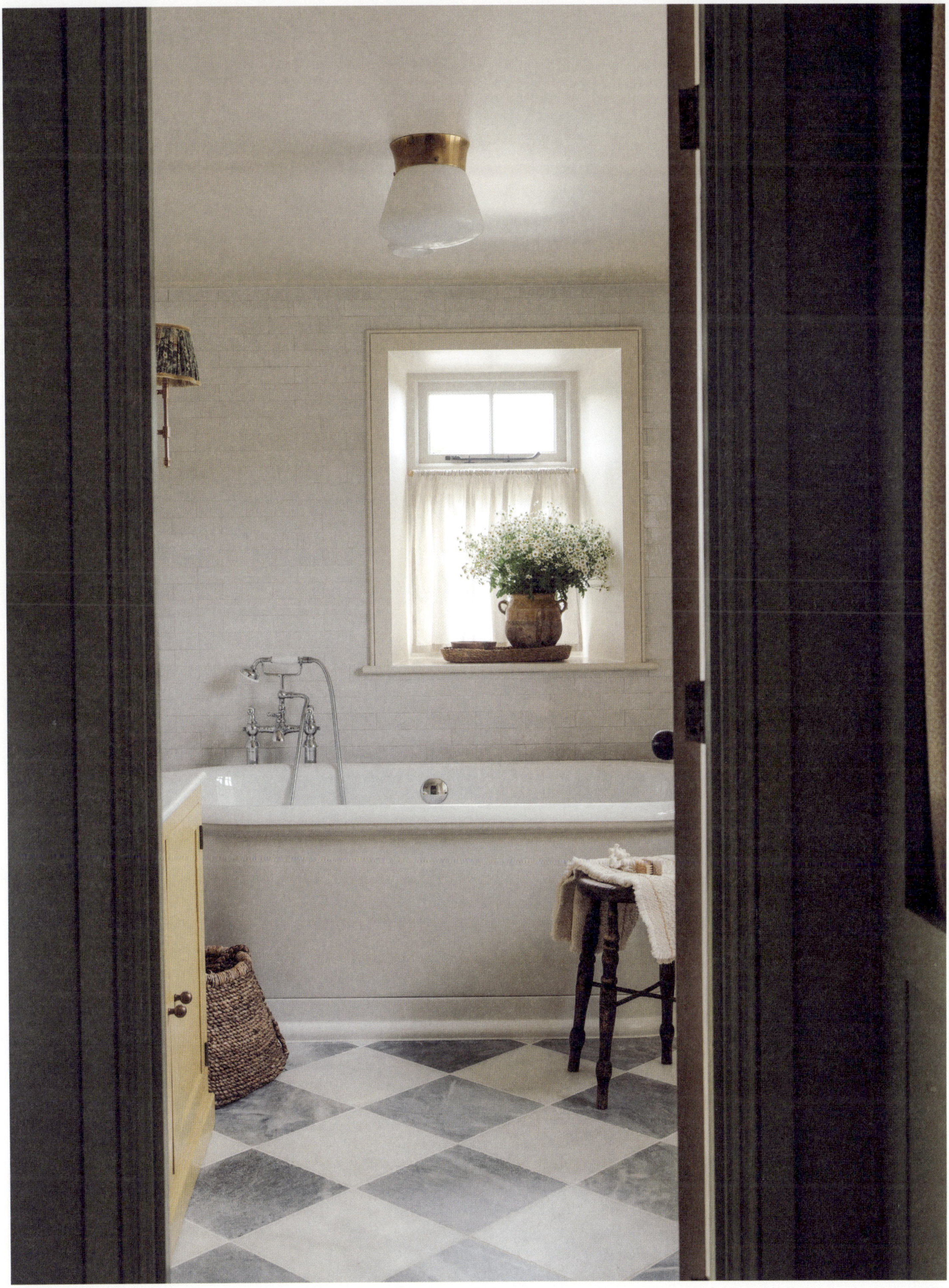

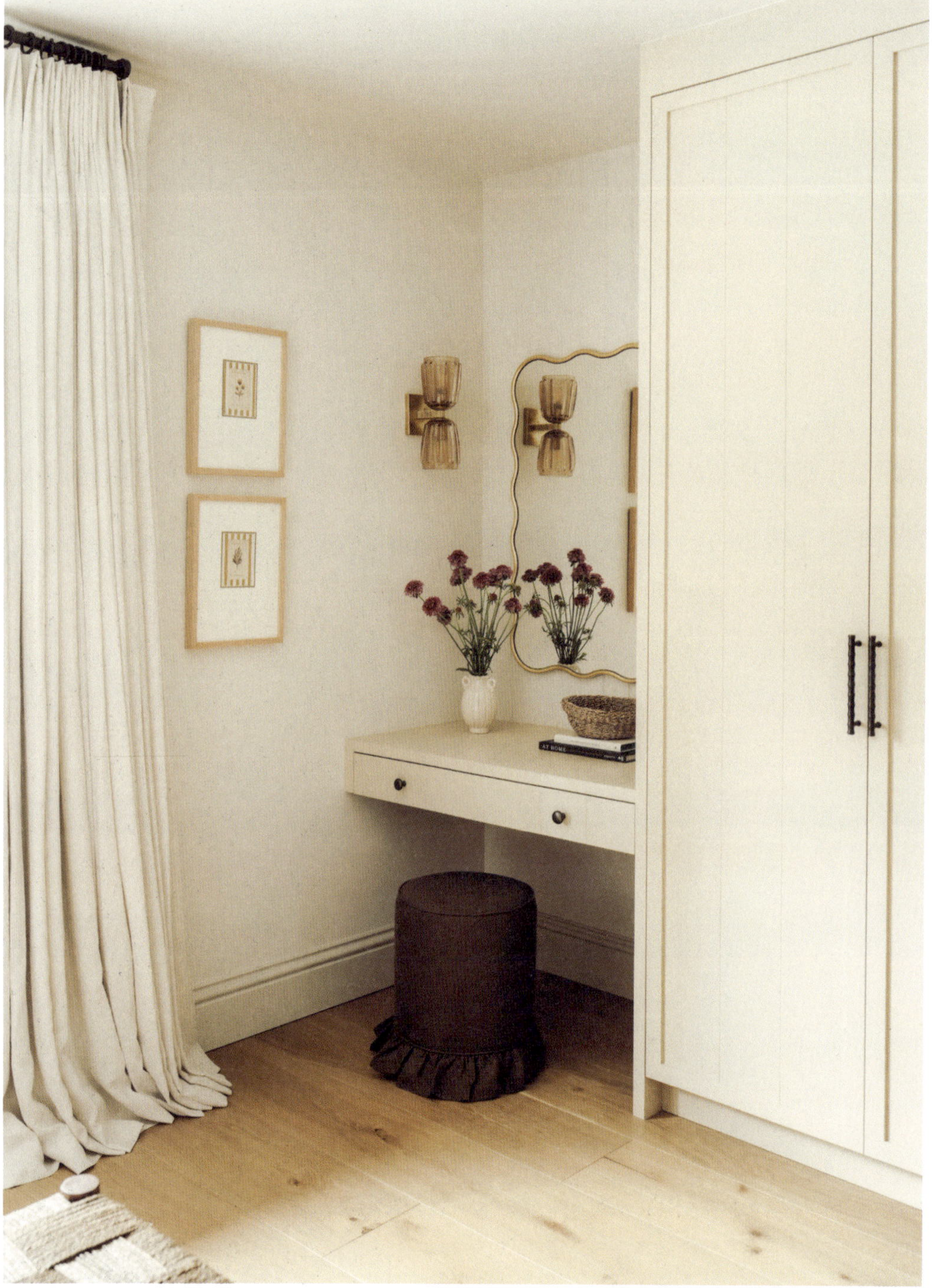

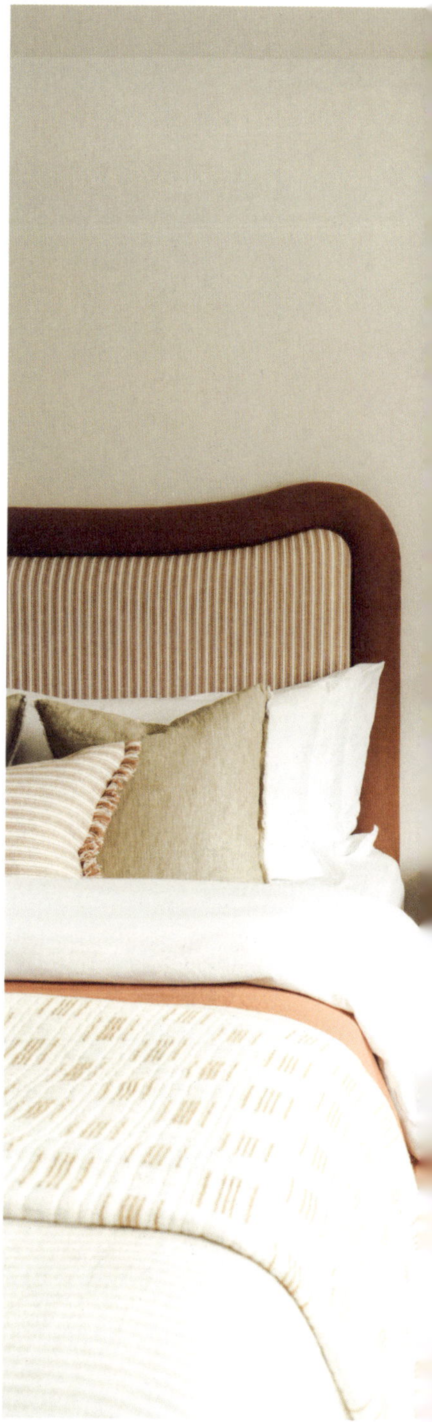

↑ The same quiet rhythm carried through a guest bedroom. A dressing corner, a bed, and its mirror on the other side of the room, all built from the same neutral backdrop, the same warm timber, the same restrained palette repeated rather than varied. We don't want bedrooms to shout. It's the consistency, the considered repetition of tone and material, that gives the room its calm.

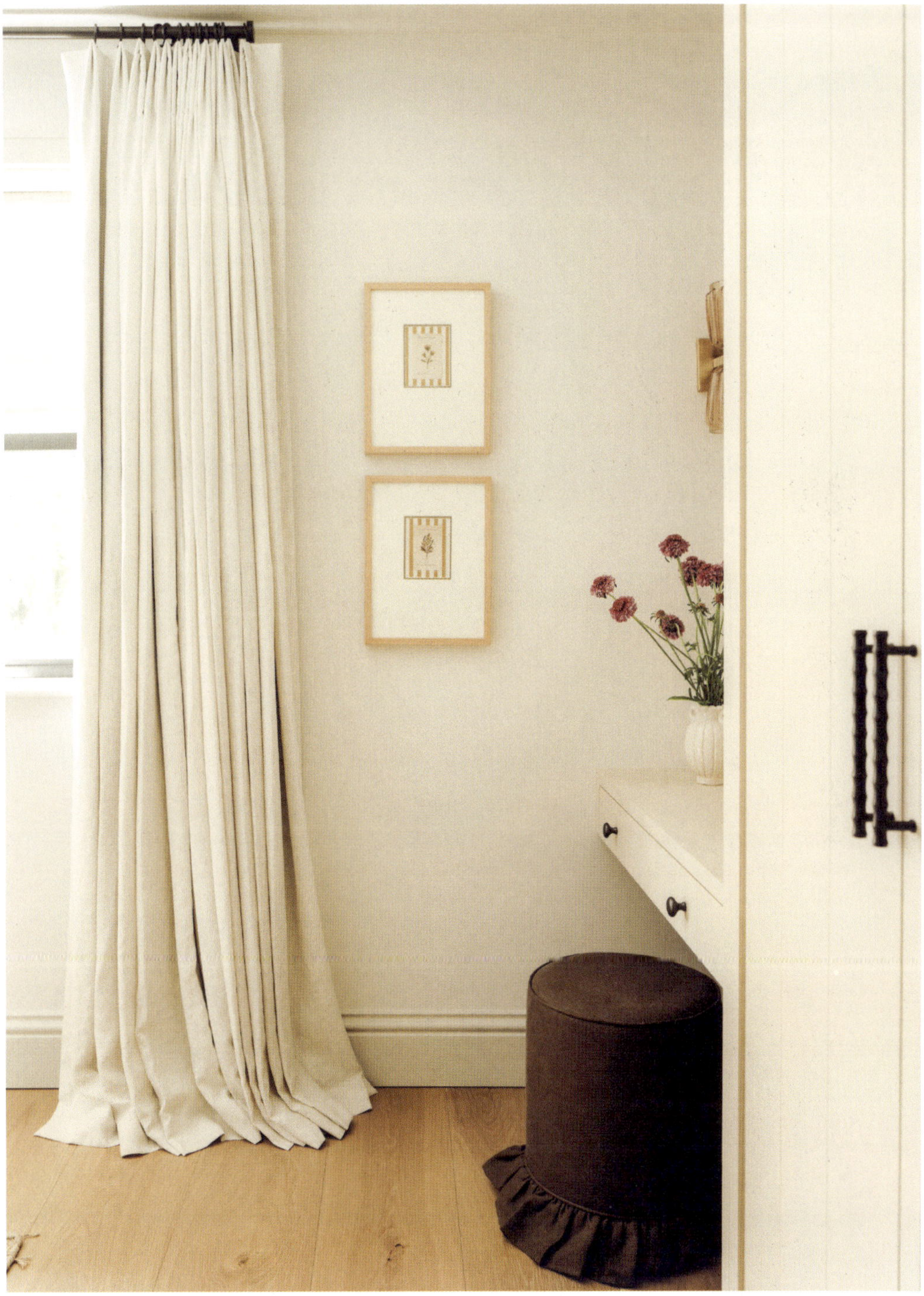

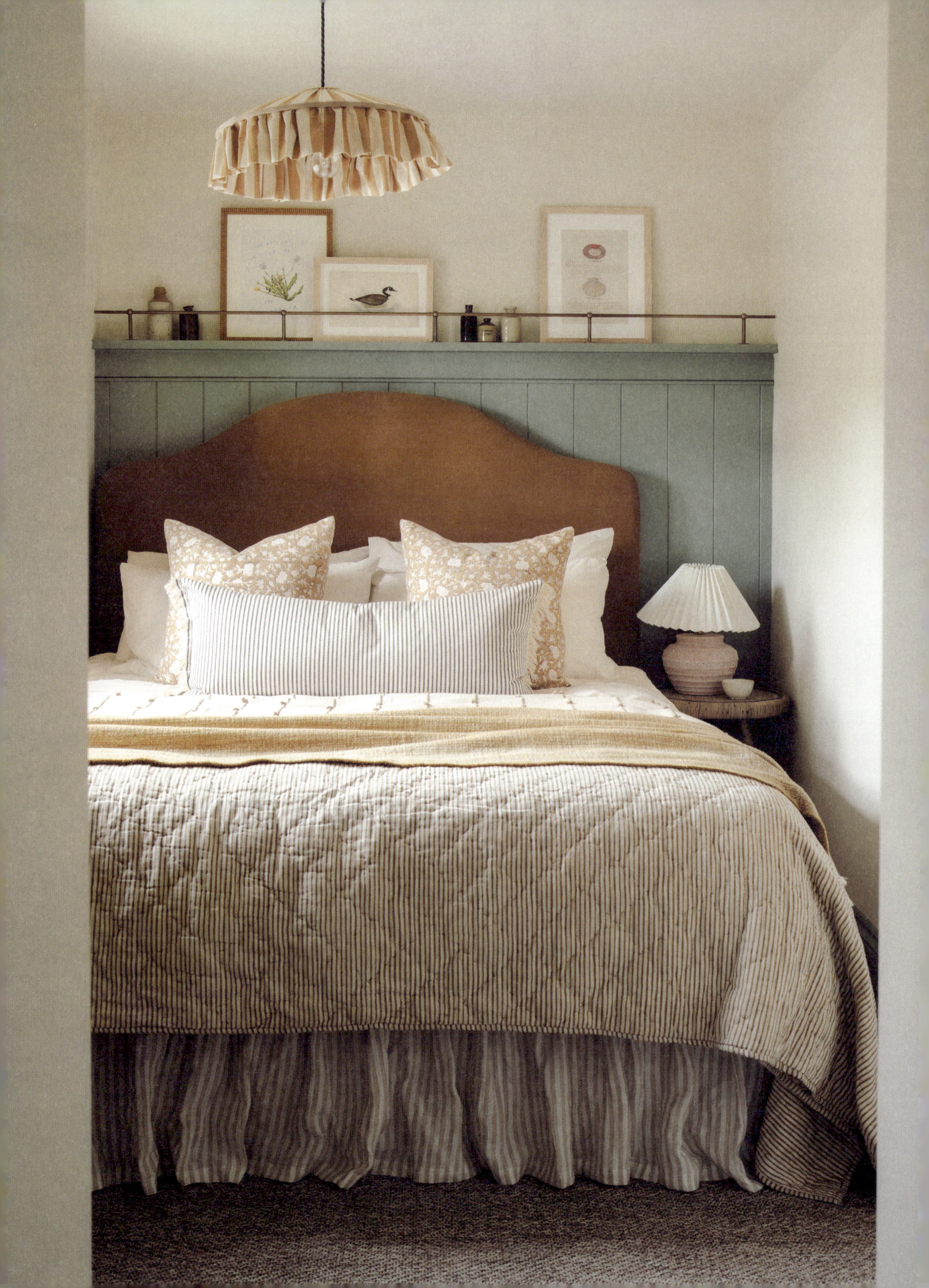

"Editing is one of the most powerful tools in design."

← This room was just about big enough to fit the bed. Our client wanted to maximise guest beds throughout the house, so instead of fighting the size, we leaned right into it and had some fun with the tight space. A panelled headboard wall in sage, a curved tan headboard, and a little picture rail above to hold favourite prints, all of it doing more with less. Sometimes the smallest rooms end up with the most character.

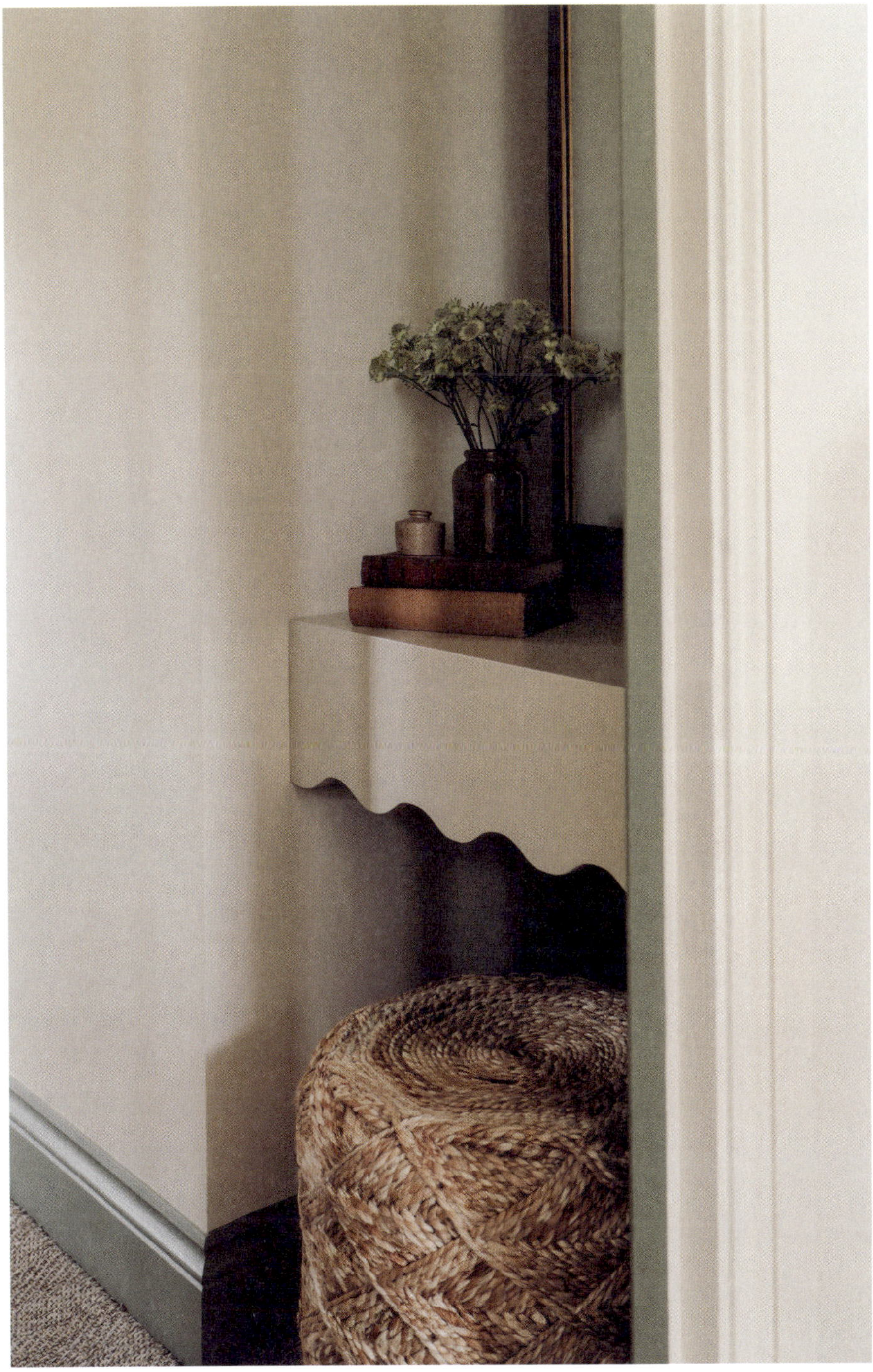

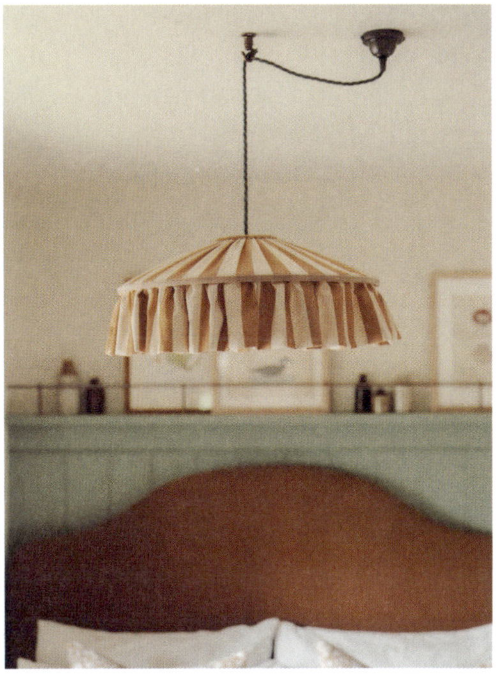

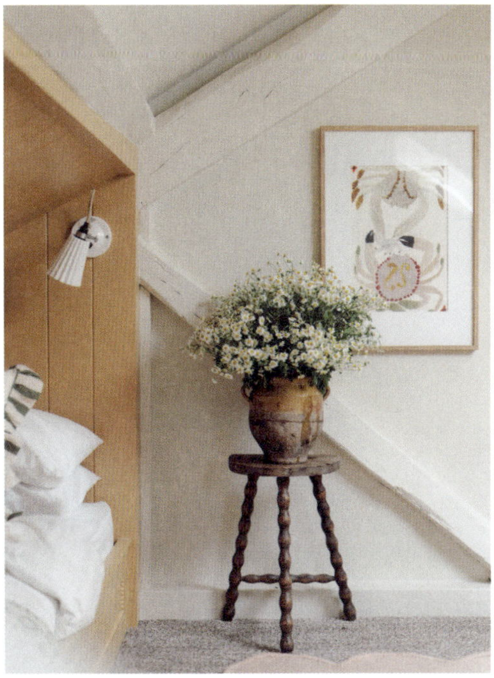

Refine with Purpose

DESIGN NOTES

The following are a few handy pointers for putting refinement into practice and making your home feel intentional.

1. OBSERVE THE LIGHT

Spend a full day watching how light moves through your home – where it lands, where it hides, where it feels alive. Light quietly tells you how a space wants to be treated.

Do this now: Pick a room. Note how it looks at three moments today: morning, afternoon, evening.

2. CREATE YOUR FOUNDATION PALETTE

Gather a small set of samples that speak directly to your vision – paint, flooring, fabrics, textures. Keep it tight: five or six at most. You're defining tone, not perfection.

Tip: Lay them together; you'll feel immediately when something's off.

3. TEST COLOUR WITH INTENTION

Paint swatches on different walls and watch them shift throughout the day, from morning glow to evening shadow. The right colour won't just look good, it will feel calm in every light.

Ask yourself: "When does this colour feel most like 'me'? When does it feel strained?"

4. EDIT ONE SPACE

Choose a surface, a corner, or an entire room and simplify it. Remove what doesn't belong and let it breathe. Notice how the energy changes when space is allowed to exist unfilled.

Try this: Remove five things. Then put back only the ones that genuinely matter.

5. REFLECT

Step back and sense what feels inevitable; what feels as though it has always belonged. That is the essence of refinement: knowing when enough is exactly right.

Note it down: What felt essential? What felt unnecessary? This becomes your compass for the rest of the home

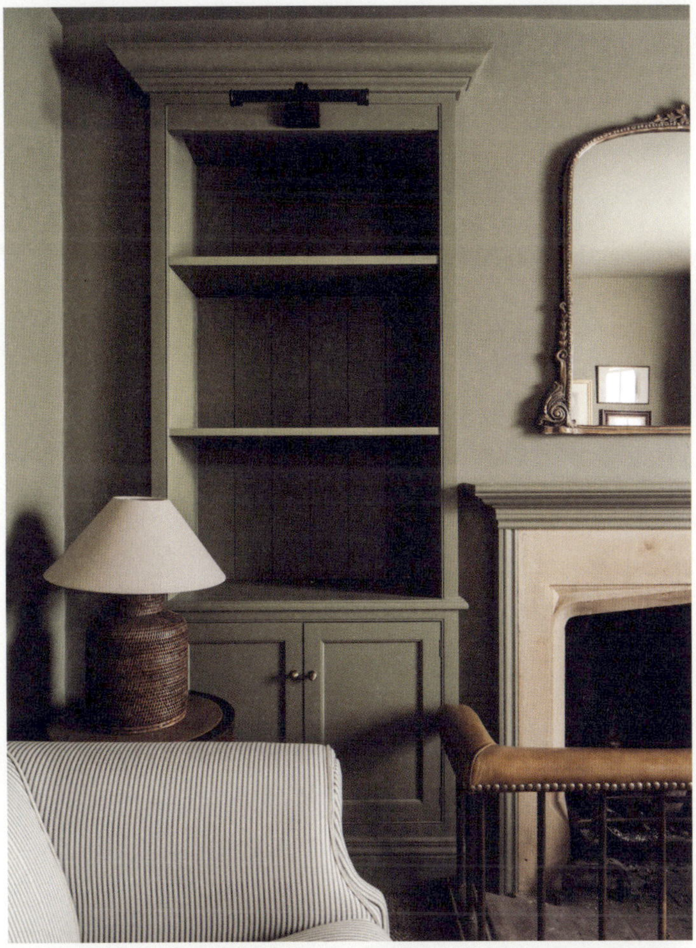

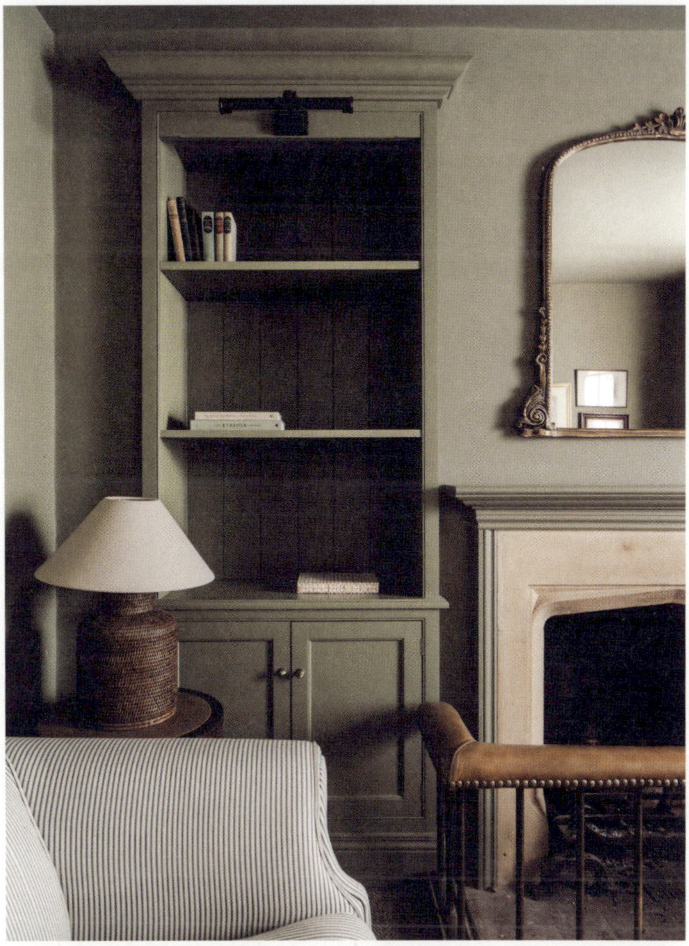

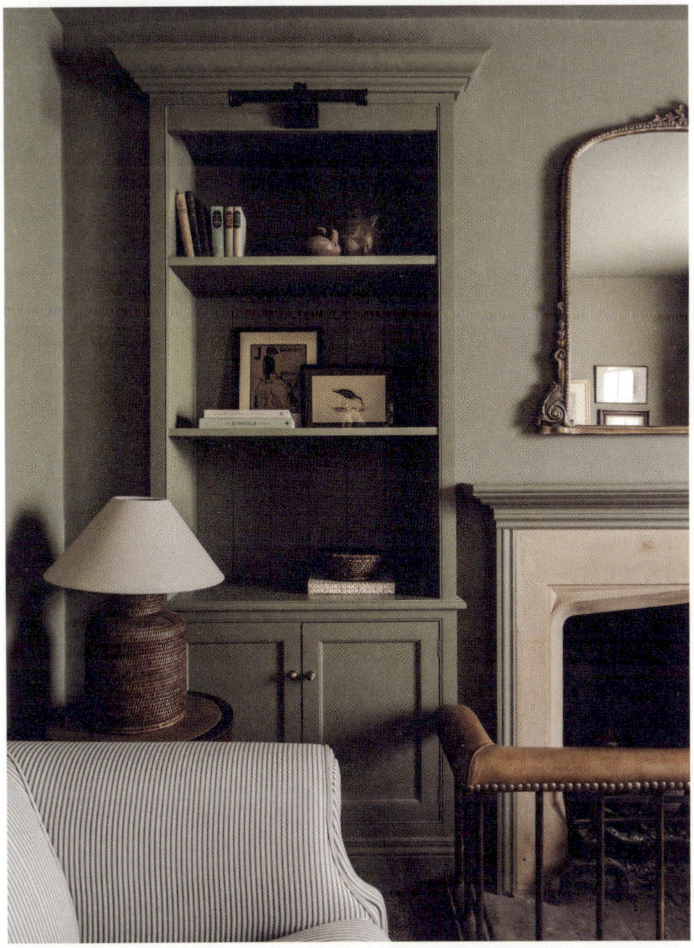

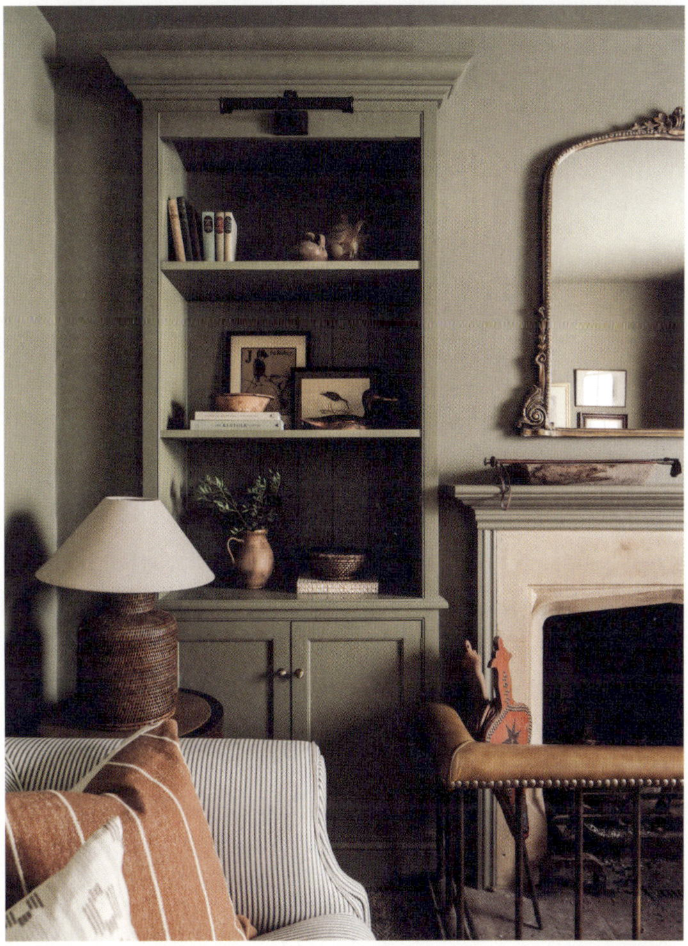

"Eventually everything connects – people, ideas, objects... the quality of the connections is the key to quality."

CHARLES EAMES

Flow

CREATE HARMONY BETWEEN ROOMS

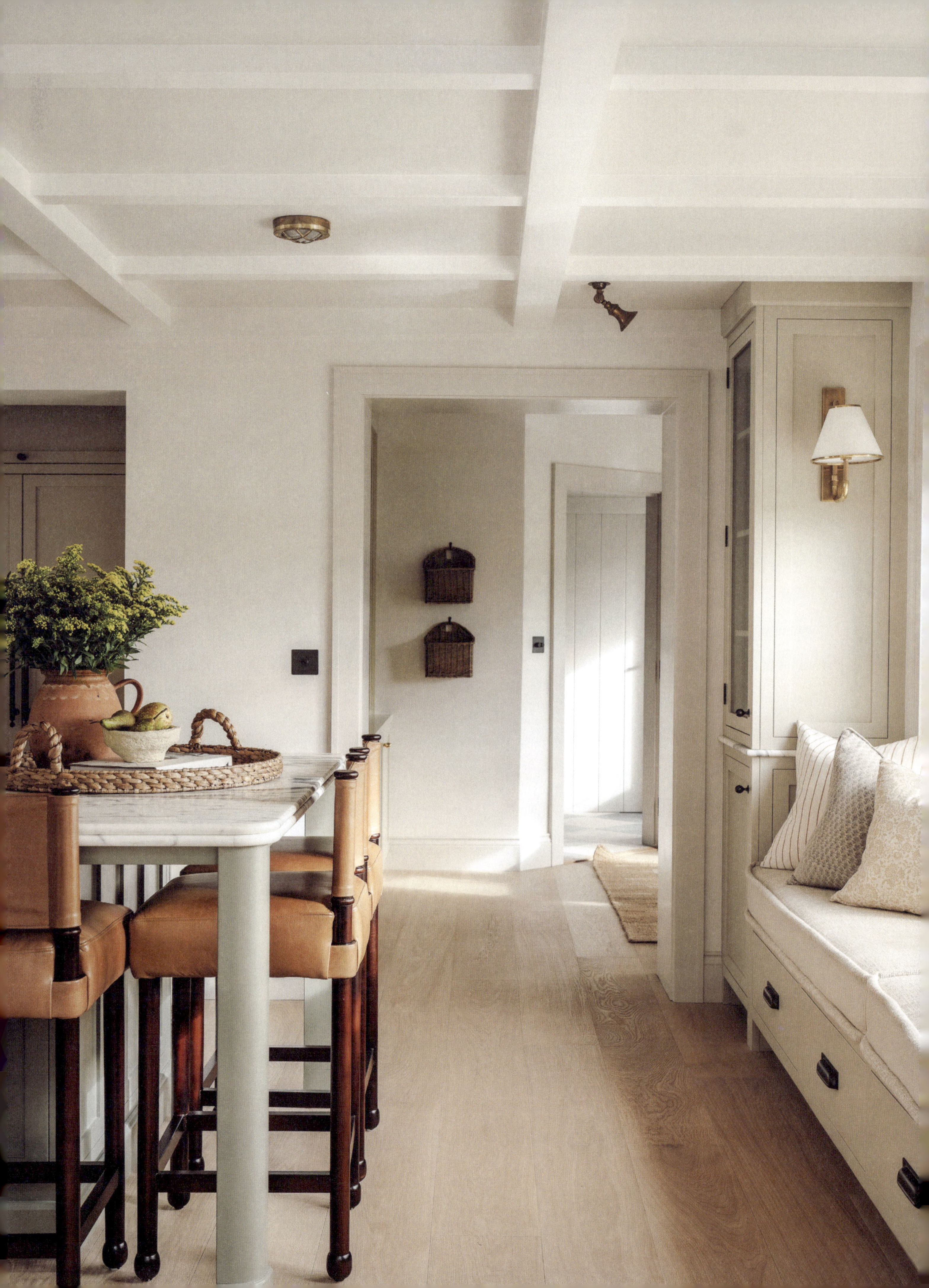

A COMMON *THREAD*

Moving through a home should feel easy and enjoyable, almost like the house is showing you the way. When the flow works, you don't have to think about it, you are just gently pulled along. When it doesn't, you notice. A too-tight hallway, a door that opens the wrong way, or a landing that feels like a cupboard – these missteps can interrupt your home's natural rhythm, and yours, too.

When I walk through an existing house for the first time, I always pay close attention to how it feels to move through the space. Does the circulation flow naturally, or do I find myself taking awkward detours just to reach the loo, and then struggling to find my way back again? We've all been there. That tiny moment of confusion says a lot about how well a home has been planned. Do the rooms connect in a way that feels open and intuitive, or are they cut off from one another, forcing a sense of interruption with every turn?

Often, the difference comes down to something deceptively simple and might involve just rejigging a few pieces of furniture; other times it might need a little more thought, and sorry to say, maybe a little structural work.

Clear pathways are essential. Think of them as giving the house its "dance floor". You need room to move without bumping into chairs or zig-zagging around obstacles. When circulation is done right, you're simply carried forward, almost without realizing. Flow is what makes a home feel cohesive rather than a collection of separate rooms – it's the invisible thread that ties everything together.

Light has this wonderful way of guiding you. Morning sunshine in the kitchen practically yells "coffee!" while golden evening light tempts you towards that armchair with a book, perhaps this time whispering "wine". A window at the end of a hallway can feel like a little "ta-da!" moment that pulls you towards it.

Before materials or colour palettes come into play, I imagine how rooms will function, how people will move, where they'll

← Project Springbank, York. The invisible thread at work here with a considered palette of naturals and brass accents that let the light do the guiding, connecting kitchen to hallway and beyond.

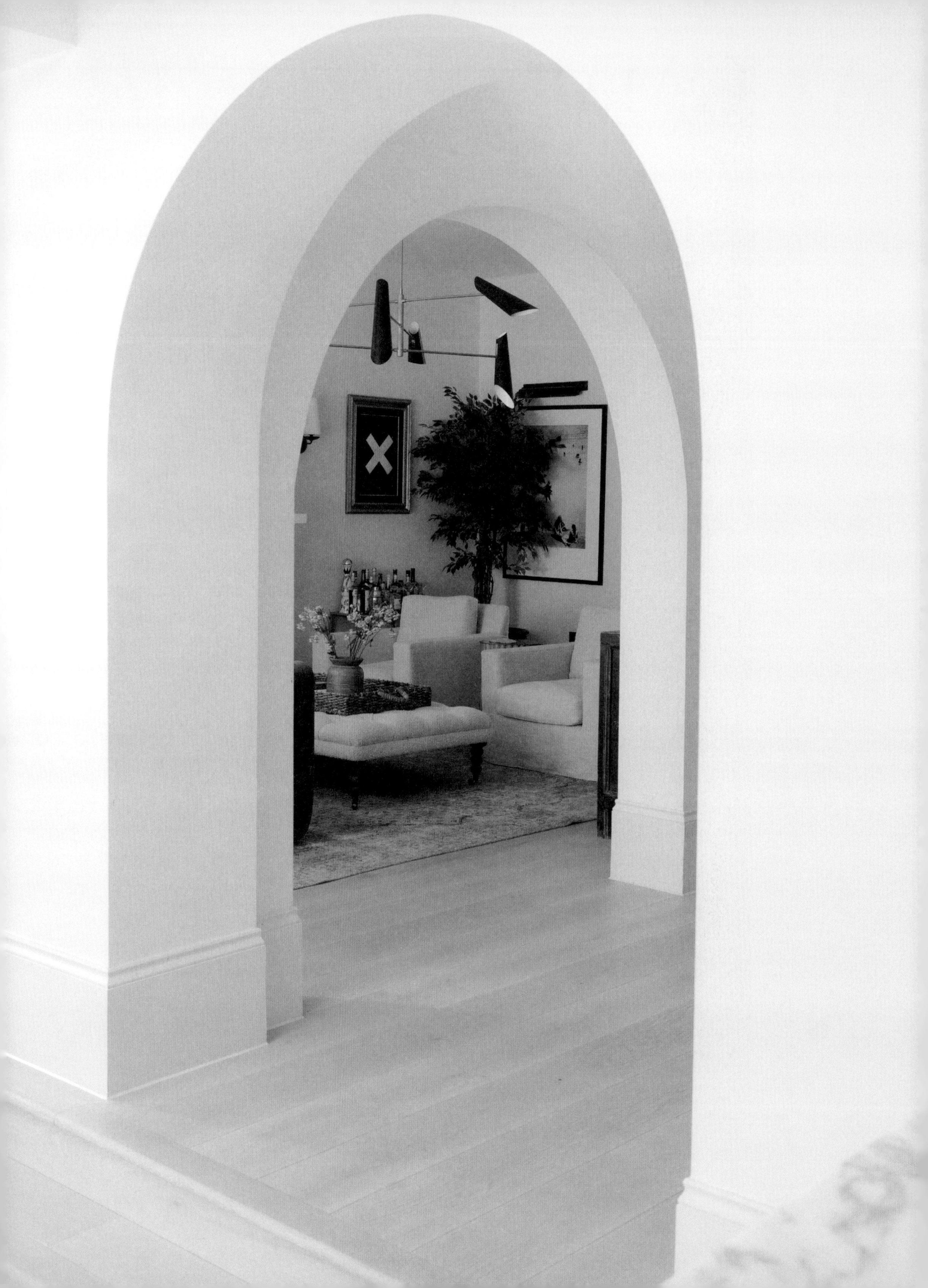

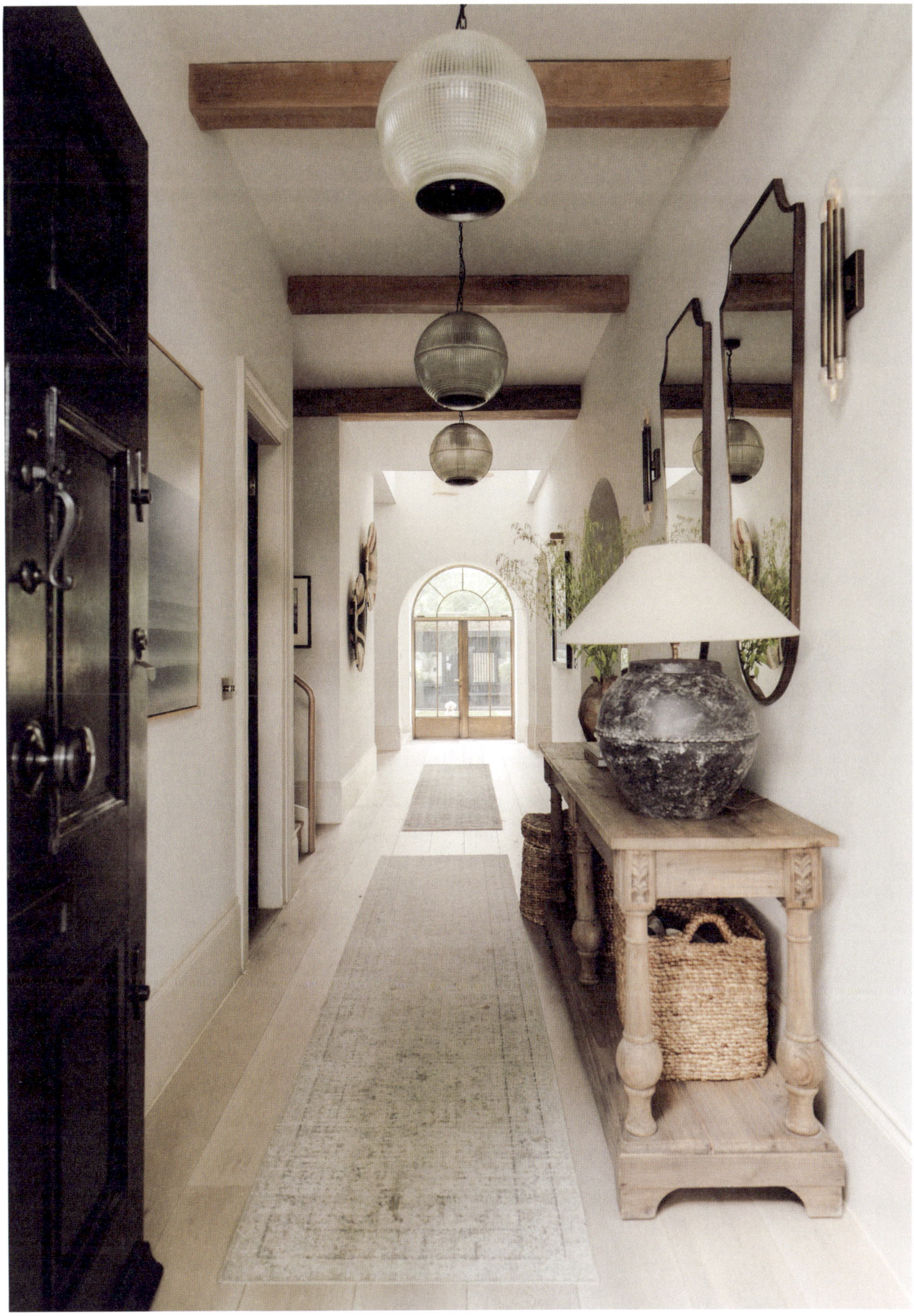

← An arched doorway pulling you straight through to the room beyond. This is flow at its simplest; an opening shaped to draw the eye, and the body, onwards without a second thought.

↑ Looking from the front door towards the garden beyond. The repetition of arches creates a soft, natural pull through the hallway, no hard corners or abrupt turns, just one gentle threshold leading to the next, all the way out to the light at the far end. It's exactly why we lean on arches throughout so many of our projects.

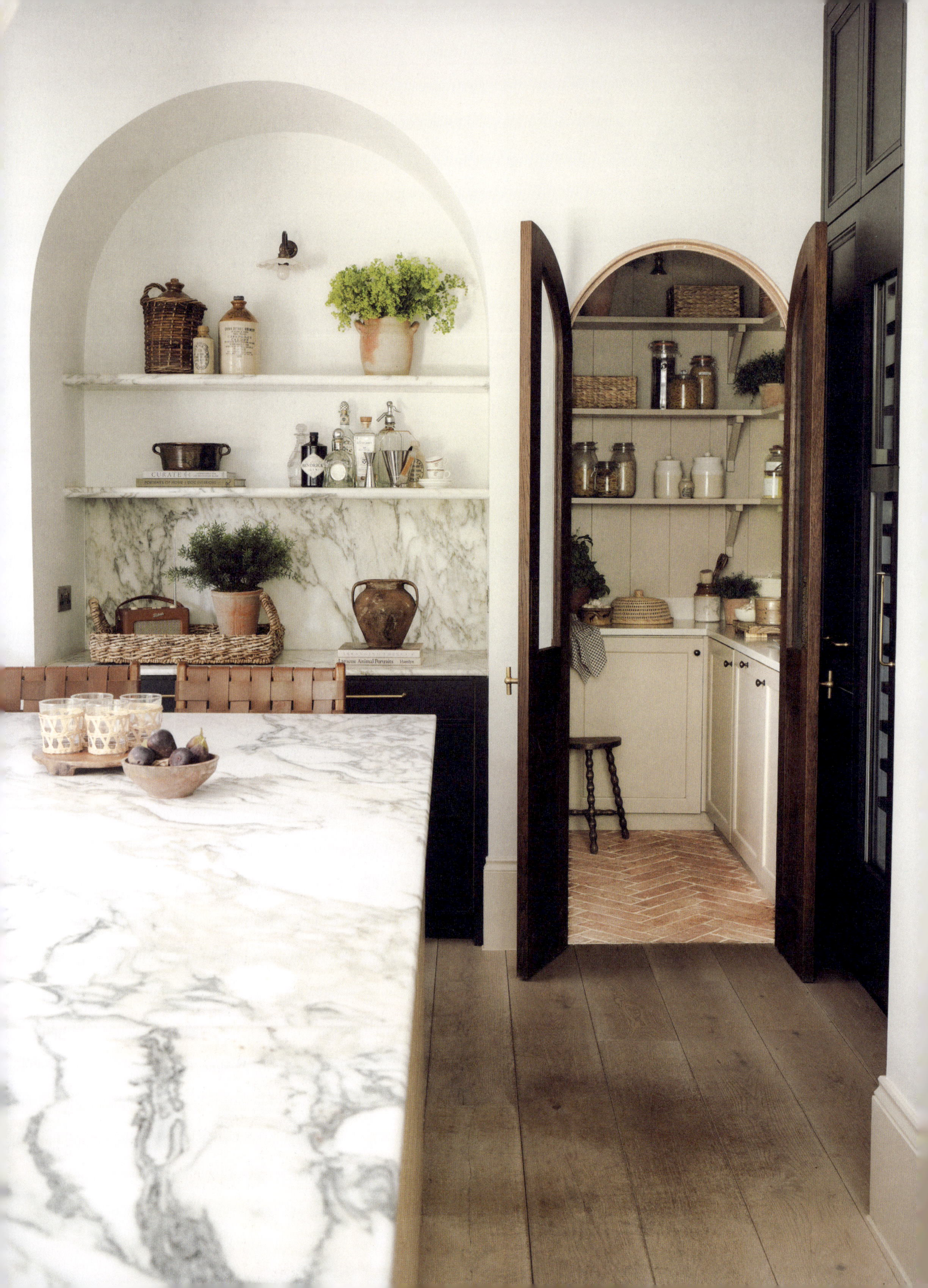
CURATE
Animal Portraits

> “Each room deserves its own character; that’s what makes a home feel alive and have soul.”

pause, and how light will carry them from one space to another. A home should be a lived experience, not a static composition. The in-between spaces – hallways, staircases, landings – are the unsung heroes. They’re the palate cleansers between courses; the little breaths between rooms. A landing with a window can hold a small chair or plant, a favourite print, or a feature light that gives the space character. At home, I have a little porthole window at the top of my stairs that always makes me pause and observe what’s happening outside. These small touches transform dead space into connecting moments. And here’s the magic bit. When flow is achieved well, no one points it out. Your guests won’t say, “Oh, how clever, the hallway lines up with the garden view!” They’ll simply feel it. Flow isn’t about perfection; it’s about ease, belonging, and those little moments of joy as you move through your home.

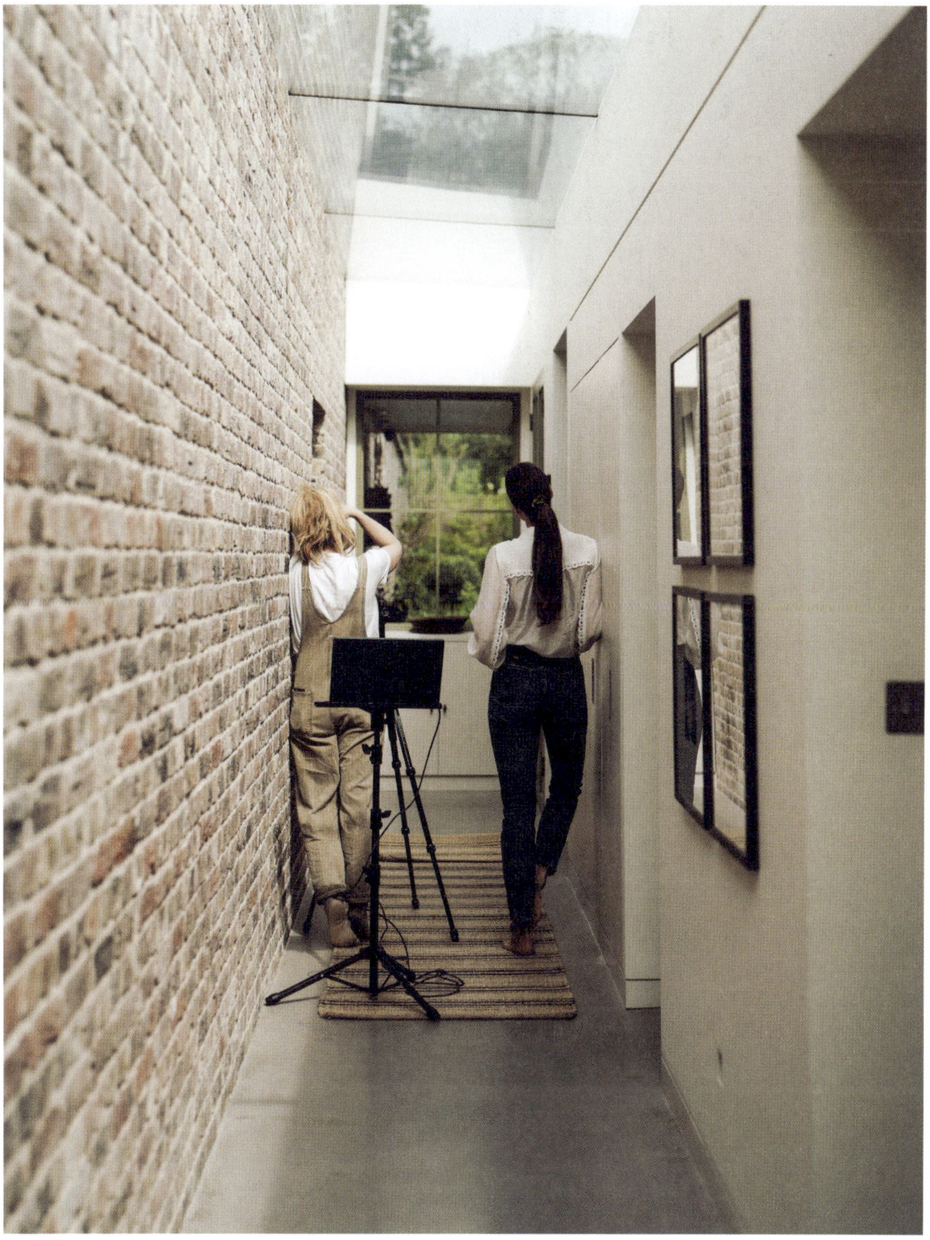

→ Joey and I capturing the hallway through to the garden at our Garden House project in Sussex, an architectural treat of cleverly connected spaces. That exposed brick wall and run of skylights turn what could have been a dead corridor into one of the best moments in the house.

← This image went viral, and I understand why. Instead of a large downstairs loo, we halved it and stole the space back into the kitchen to create this clever little pantry. Clients always dream of having a pantry, so we will always try and find a way to bring one in, even when the house hasn't really left room for it. The arch is doing a lot of the work here, drawing you in rather than letting it feel like what it really is - a cupboard. Proof that flow isn't only about hallways and landings; it can transform the smallest, most unlikely spaces too.

Purpose & Personality

Every room should have its own purpose and personality. A home isn't a hotel lobby where everything "needs to be" coordinated within an inch of its life. Each room deserves its own character, that's what makes a home feel alive and have soul.

When I design, I start by asking what a room needs to be. The kitchen is where energy gathers – practical and hardworking, but also warm and welcoming, hence why it's often known as "the heart of the home". The living room might want to exhale a little more, with softer textures and intimate lighting; a space that invites you to curl up with a cup of tea (or, in my case, a large glass of red after seven attempts at finally getting the kids to bed).

One way to balance individuality with flow is the 60–30–10 rule: 60 per cent dominant colour, 30 per cent secondary colour, 10 per cent accent. This creates harmony even when rooms have different moods. The 60 per cent might be a soft neutral across most rooms, including the walls, floors, and larger furniture. The 30 per cent is often a warmer natural tone, like timber or stone. Then comes the fun bit, the 10 per cent where personality shines: a deep green on bookcase joinery, ditsy wallpaper, rust-red cushions, or patterned tiles in the bathroom.

This approach gives freedom rather than restriction. When you set that common thread through colour ratios or material choices, you can layer personality without losing cohesion. Purpose gives a room its reason for being, personality gives it charm, and the thread of connection makes it all flow.

→ The hallway at Project Springbank. Soft neutrals form the base here, panelled walls, a stone-tiled floor, framed in muted tones, exactly the 60 per cent this chapter talks about. Character was always going to come later, in the small things: a worn antique bench, gathered botanicals in an urn, an old gallery wall hung with real intention. Purpose first, personality after. It's a quiet hallway with plenty to say.

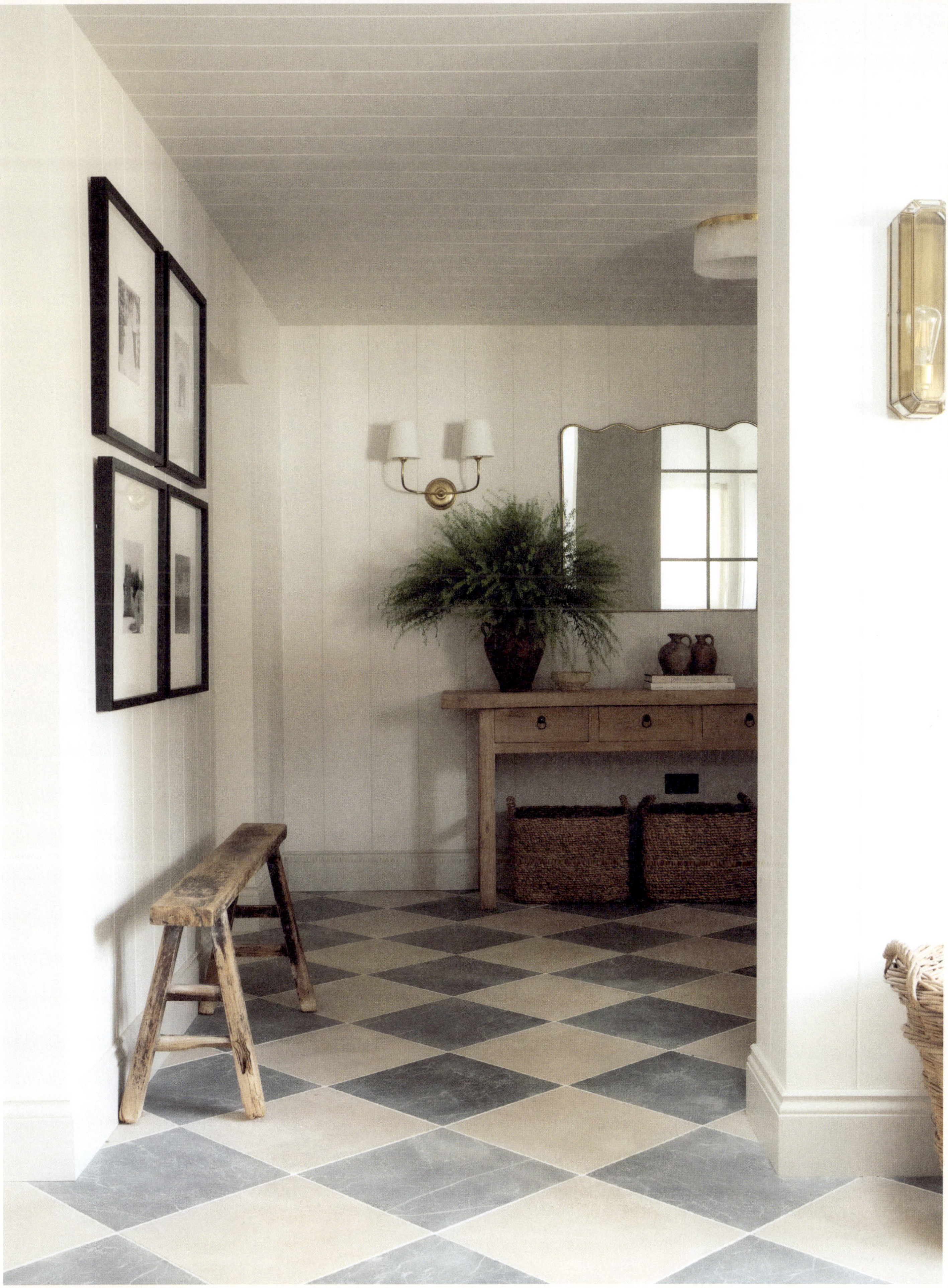

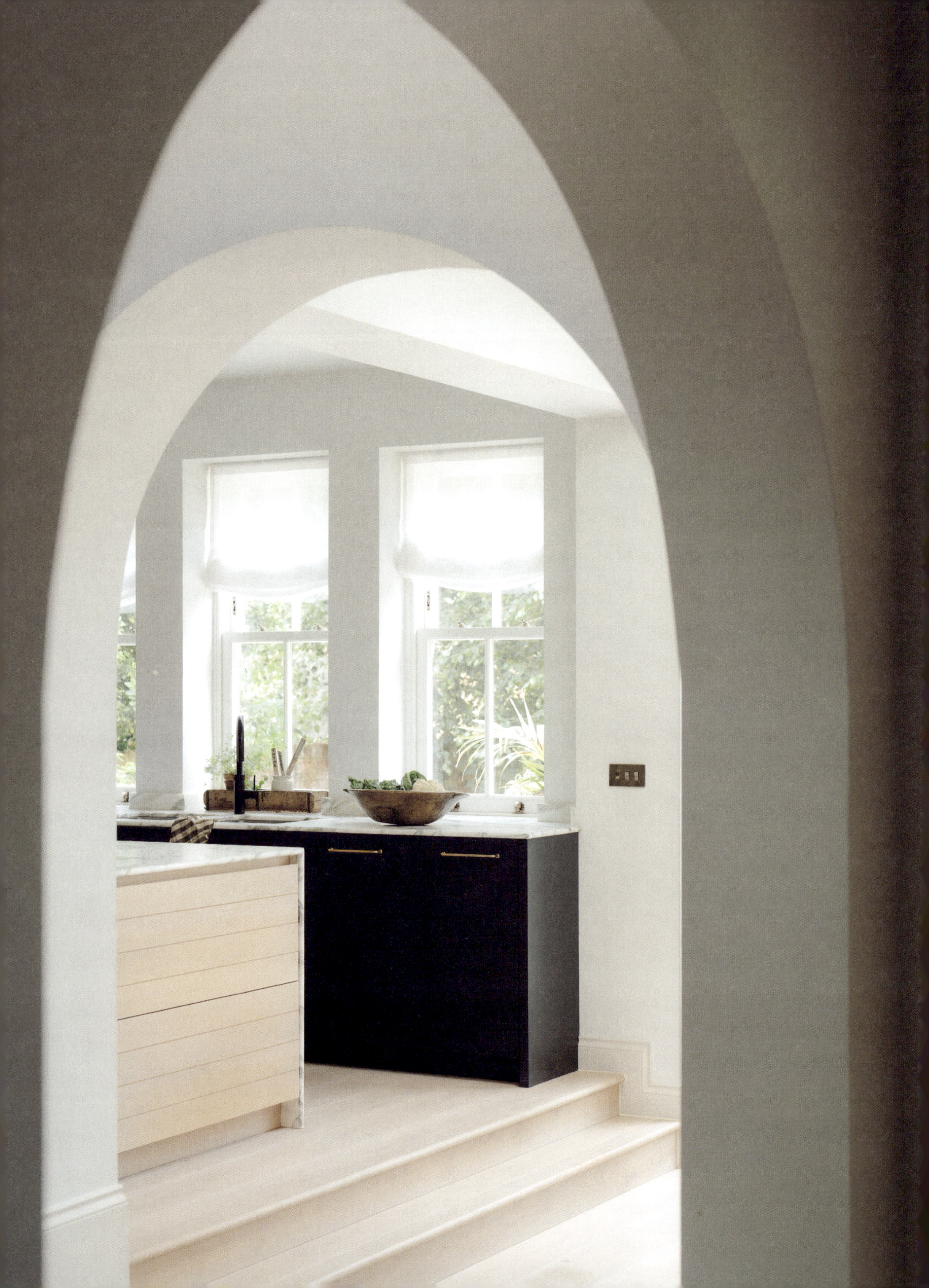

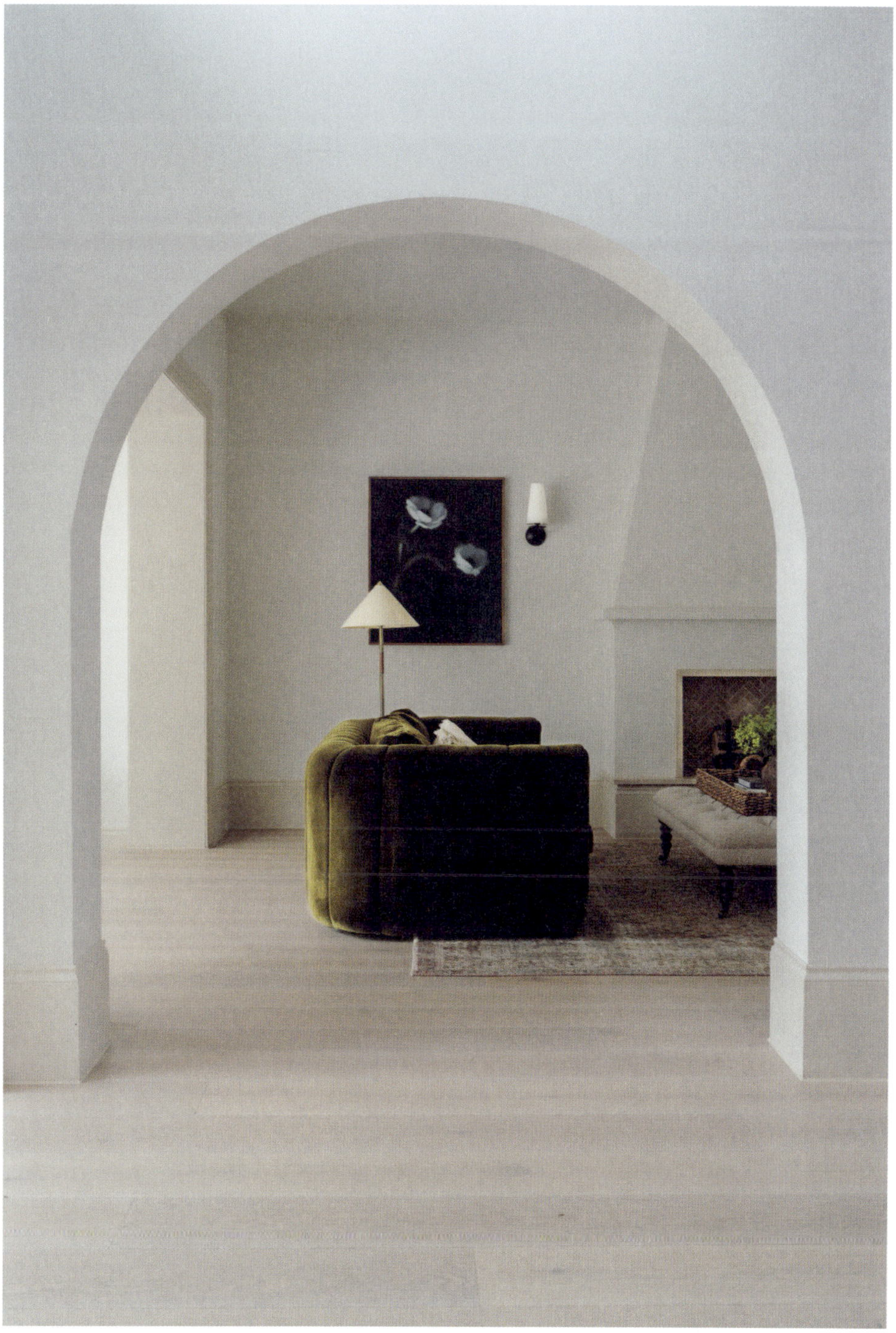

← The softness of these arches gently pulls you in, then the black-painted cabinetry stops your eyeline right where it should. I always love that play of masculine and feminine energy in design, and this is one of my favourite examples of it, with soft curves meeting hard, graphic colour. My client actually called me mid-build in a panic, worried there were too many arches and it would end up feeling like a church! I won't lie, it made me question myself for a moment, but I stood firm, and to this day I am so glad we did.

↑ The same arch language carried through to the living room, framing the space perfectly from the hallway. Olive velvet, soft plaster walls, and pale timber floors sit calmly within it, proof that a good archway doesn't just connect rooms; it composes them.

→ → This kitchen feels calm and grounded the moment you step into it. Pale timber, soft marble veining, brushed brass, and that black runs through it all without ever feeling heavy. Every colour, shape and material is connected; the common thread that makes a room feel resolved rather than simply decorated.

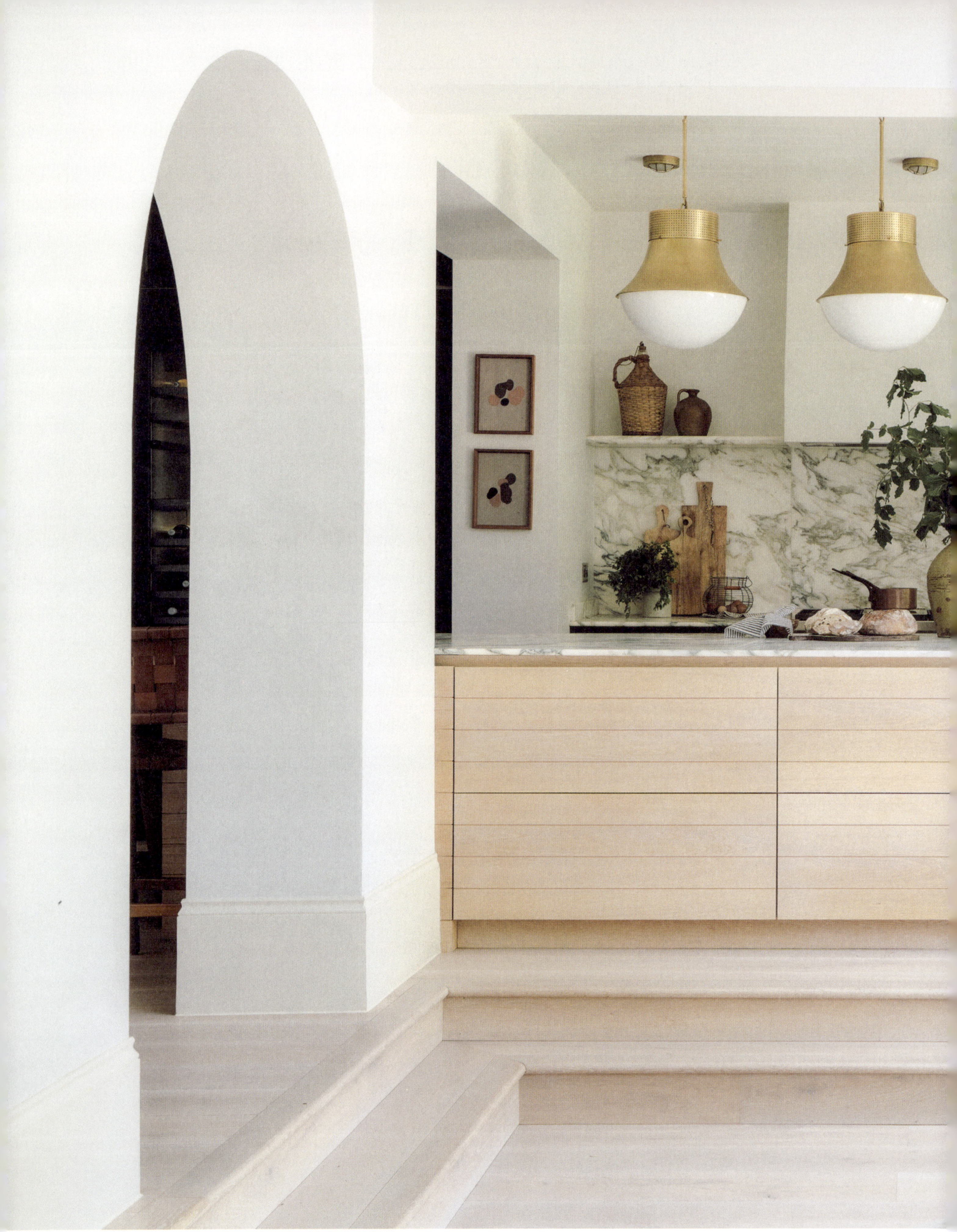

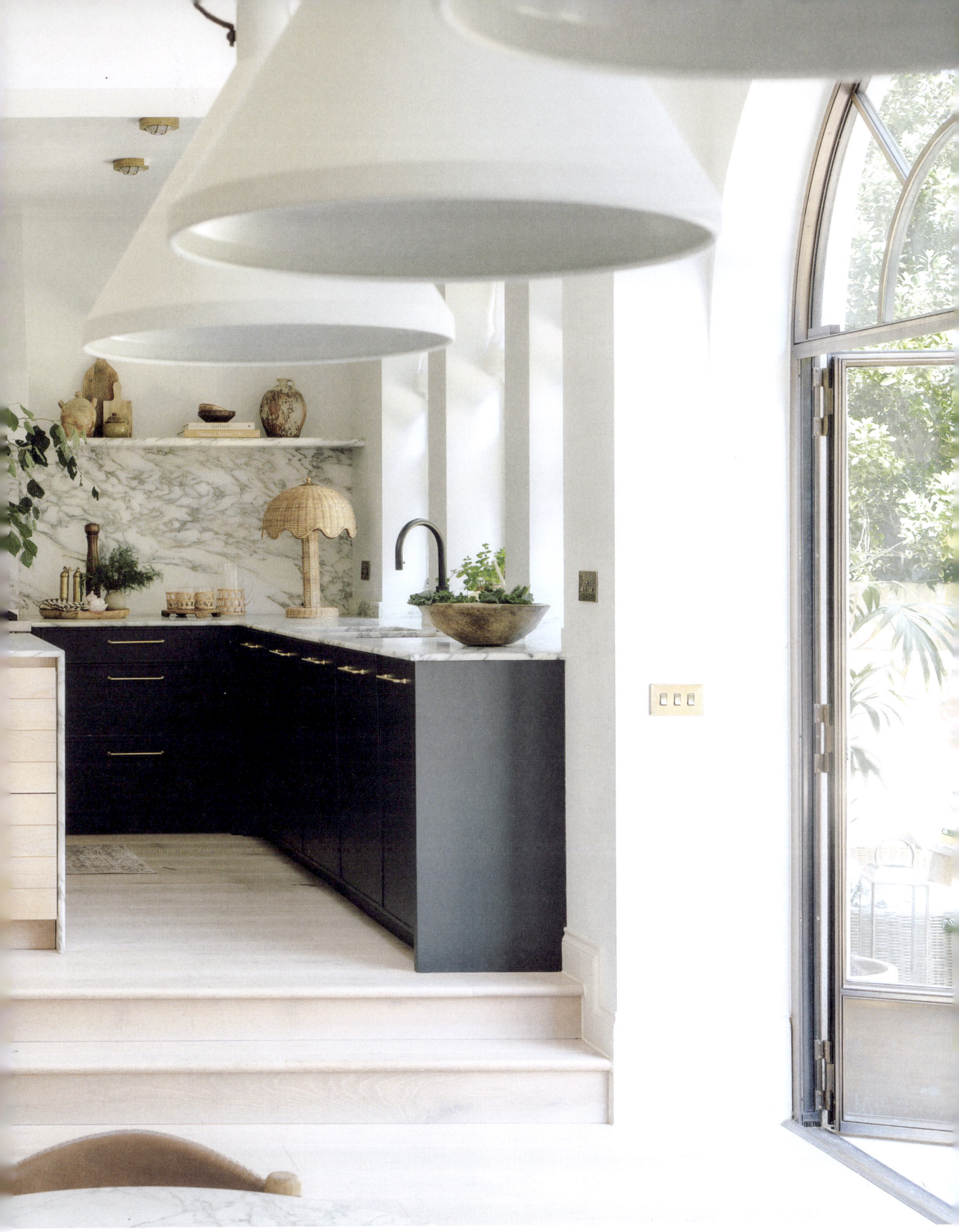

Practical Flow

Traffic flow is about instinctive, friction-free movement. It's never accidental; it's the result of deliberate spatial planning. My core principle is to minimise congestion and eliminate dead ends. Areas where people converge should feel generous, particularly in high-traffic zones like hallways and kitchens. Zoning helps too. By clearly defining where you cook, relax, eat, and work, a home becomes easier to navigate. Each space should have its own identity, but transitions should feel natural.

A common challenge is houses that have grown over time with extensions bolted on without thought to how they connect. Realigning doorways or opening sightlines and continuing flooring can instantly restore calm or indeed give more purpose to rooms..

Arches are one of my favourite ways to encourage flow. There's something instinctive about how a curve draws you forward. Unlike a sharp-edged doorway, an arch softens transitions and adds rhythm. They catch light beautifully too, the curve shifting with shadows through the day.

→ The dining room sits just off the kitchen, down a two-step level change. That shift was important to get right; it had to feel purposeful, not like an afterthought, especially as this was an extension to the original house. The arch frames the room beautifully from the kitchen, drawing you forward and down rather than letting the change in level feel like an interruption. Sometimes the trick to making an extension feel original isn't disguising it, it's giving the transition real intention.

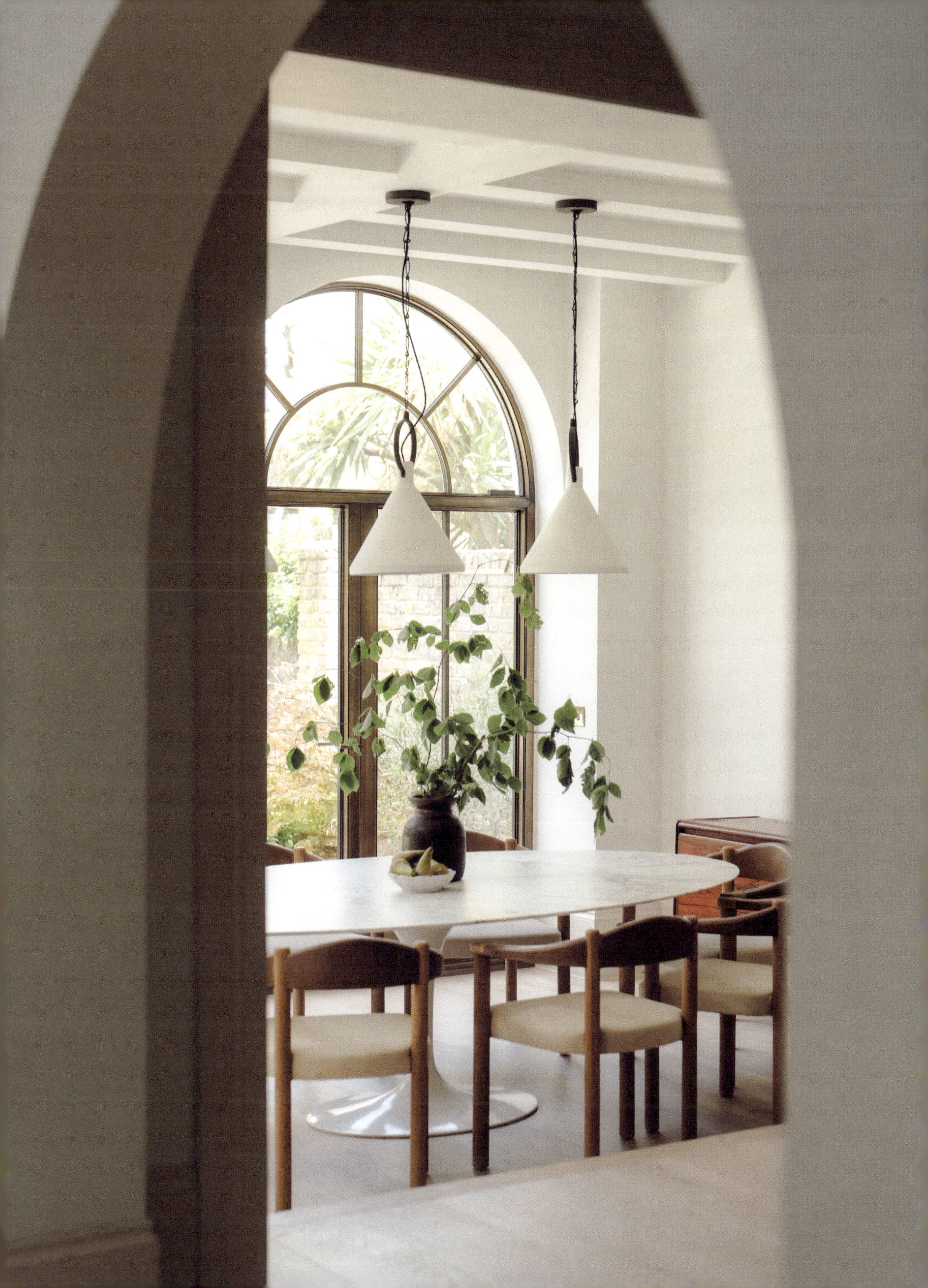

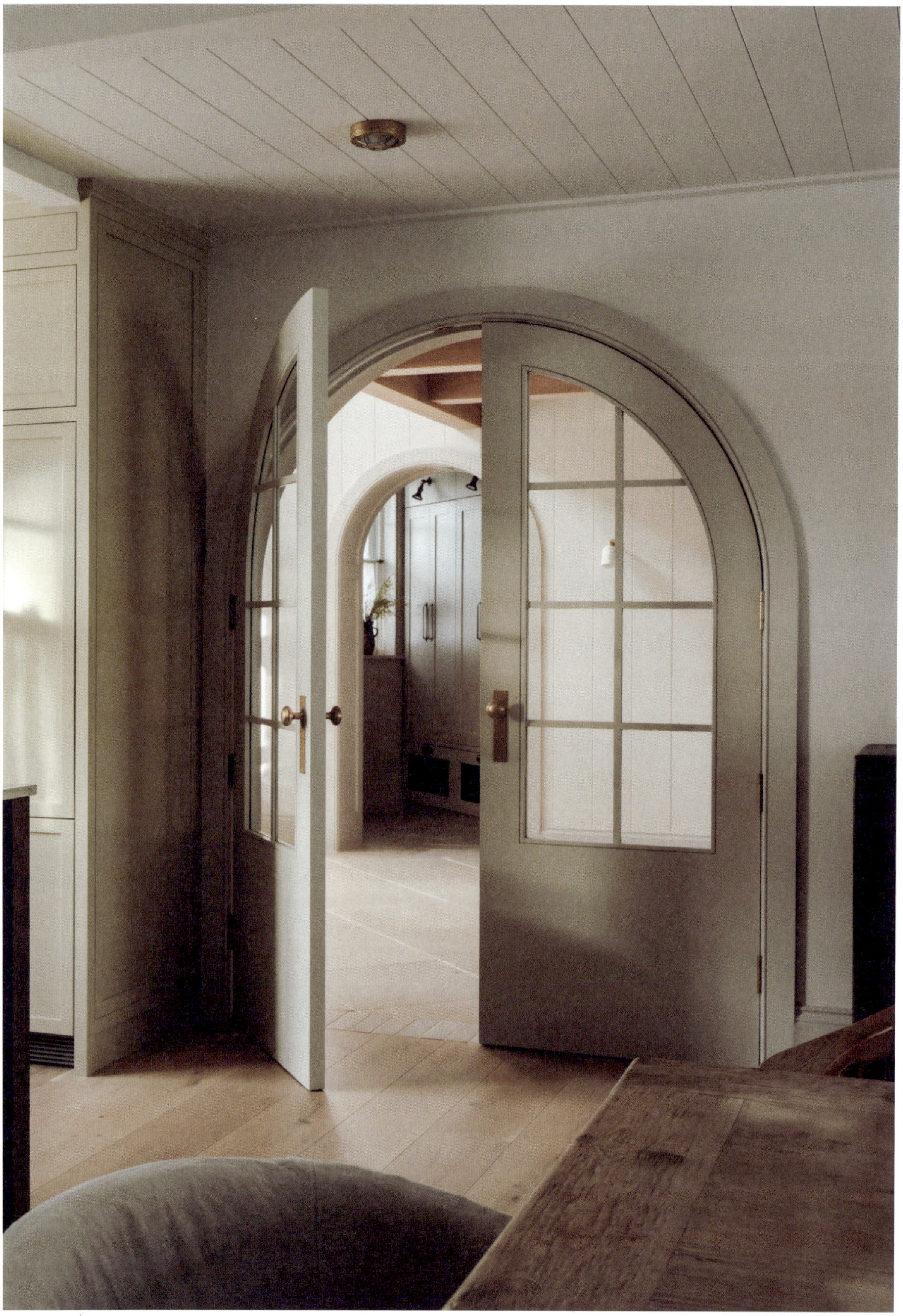

↑ Another moment of flow at Project Sandbanks. This client specifically asked us to bring arches into the design, and we were only too happy to oblige. These glazed doors connect the hallway through to the kitchen, the curve softening the transition and pulling you forward into the next space.

→ Notice the threshold here – the flooring changes format as you step through into the boot room, but stays within the same colour family, so the two spaces feel connected rather than abruptly divided. It's this kind of consideration that keeps a home feeling cohesive room to room.

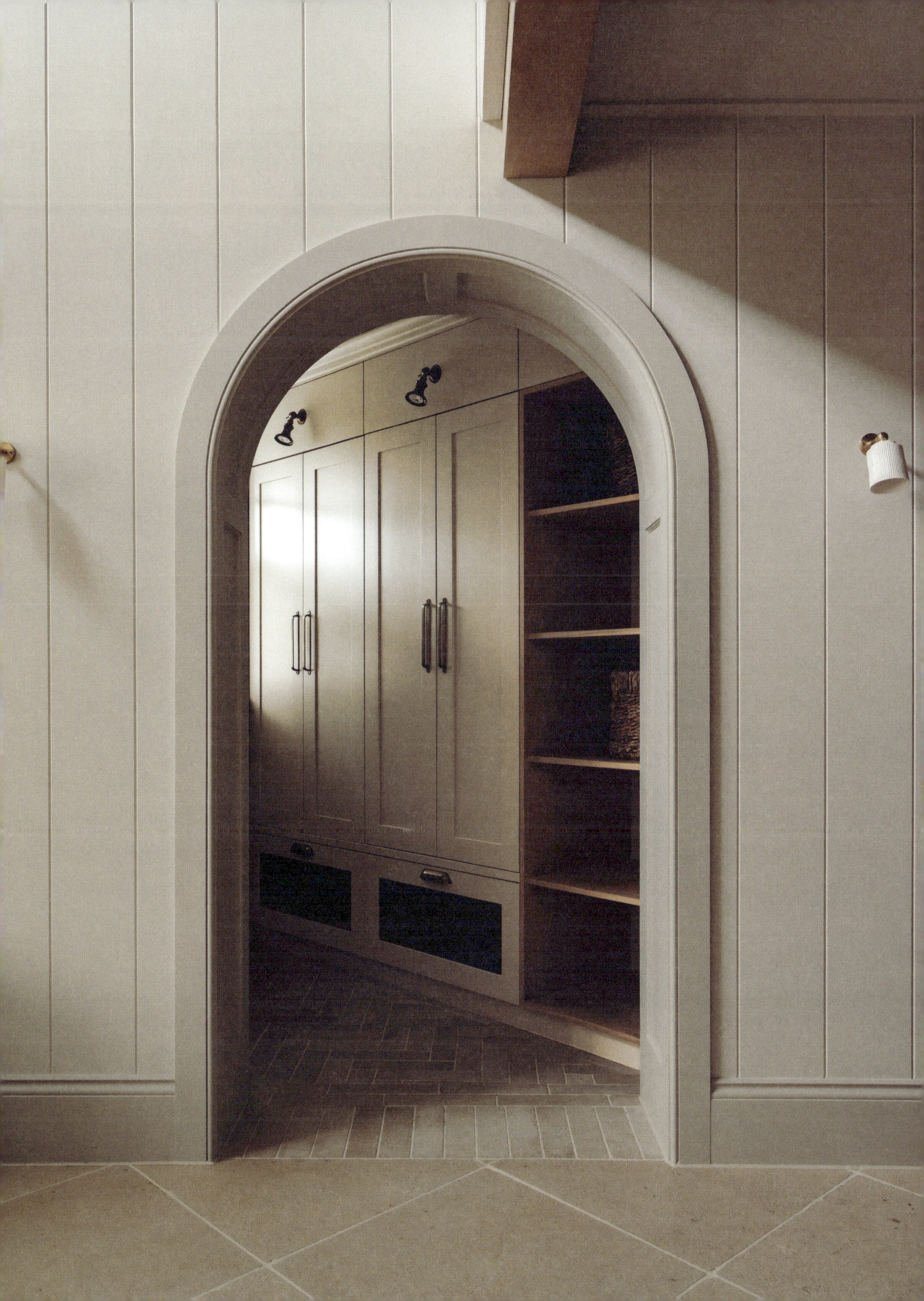

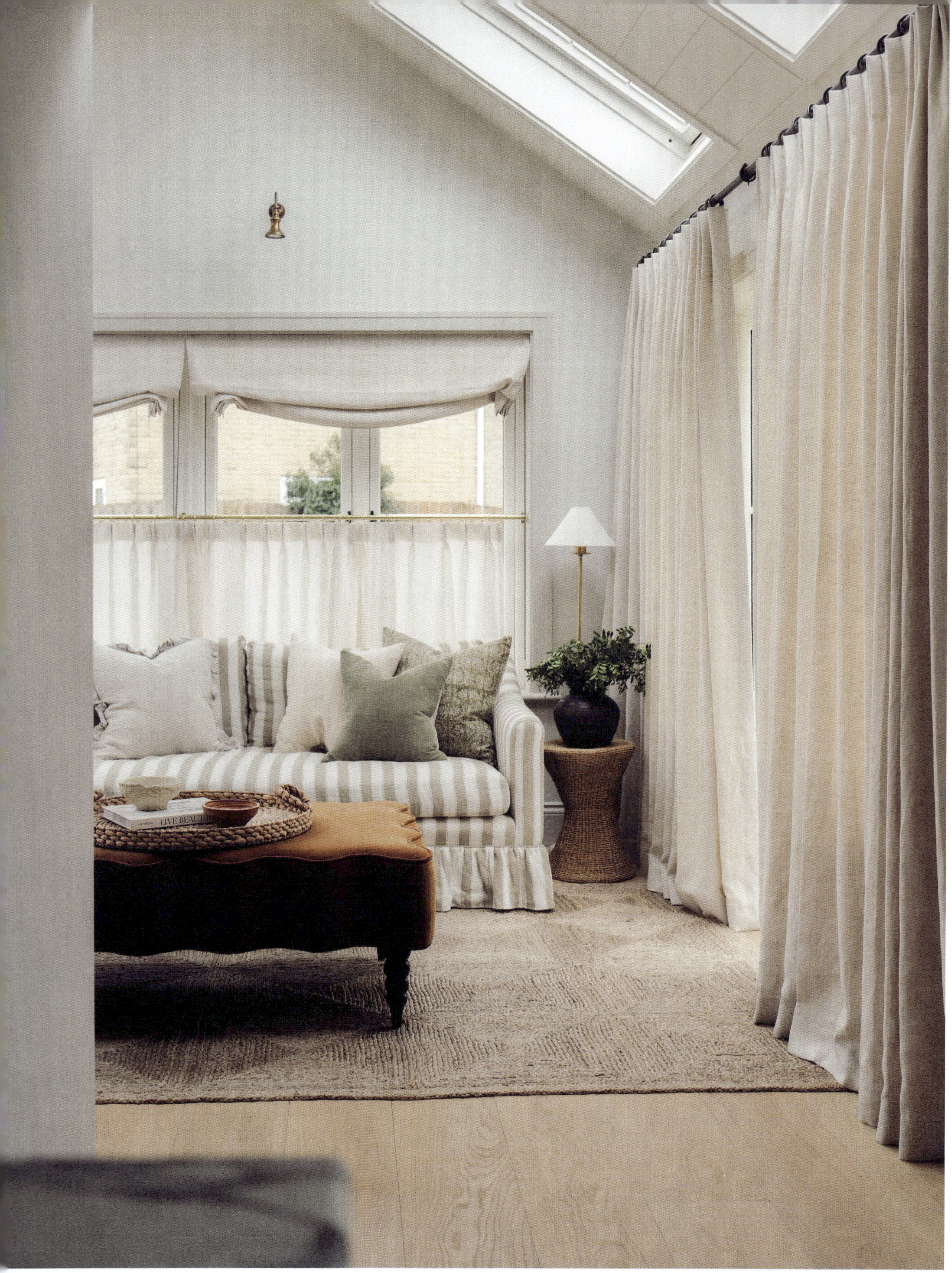

Placement of Furniture

Once architectural details and traffic patterns are established, furniture should support that rhythm. Each piece should feel intentionally placed, helping you glide through a space rather than blocking your way. Sofas shouldn't cut across sightlines or back onto doorways like bouncers guarding an entrance. Dining chairs need space to pull out freely.

> *"Each space should have its own identity, but transitions should feel natural."*

Placement is a dance between usability and breathing space. A coffee table close enough to reach without stretching, but not so close you might accidentally shin yourself when walking past; a footstool positioned where you can prop your feet up, yet let others pass; an armchair angled towards a fireplace, inviting you to sit down. A low console can define a zone without closing it off, while open shelving keeps a space feeling light and connected. These decisions make a home feel considered and comfortable.

Proximity matters as much as position. Allow around 45–60cm (17.7–23.6in) between a sofa and coffee table, and at least 90cm (35.4in) for a main walkway. In kitchens, aim for about 1m (3.3ft) between an island and opposite units. Storage pieces play a crucial role, too.

Rugs anchor seating zones or direct paths through open-plan spaces. Lighting does the same – a pendant draws you to a table, a floor lamp invites you into a corner, and wall lights lead you down a hallway. A mirror at the end of a corridor extends flow, drawing the eye forward and makes the space feel longer. A painting anchors the view and creates a natural pause; a quiet full stop that invites you to pause and appreciate the moment. In simple terms, a mirror says "keep going", while a painting says, "you have arrived!"

← The garden room at Project Springbank with a wonderful vaulted ceiling, and furniture placed to support its natural rhythm rather than work against it. The sofa angles towards the windows rather than blocking the path through, the footstool sits low enough to prop your feet up without obstructing anyone passing, and that round console table defines the seating zone without closing the room off. Nothing here is placed by accident. It's that same dance between usability and breathing space, proximity considered as carefully as proportion, so the room feels easy to move through and easy to settle into all at once.

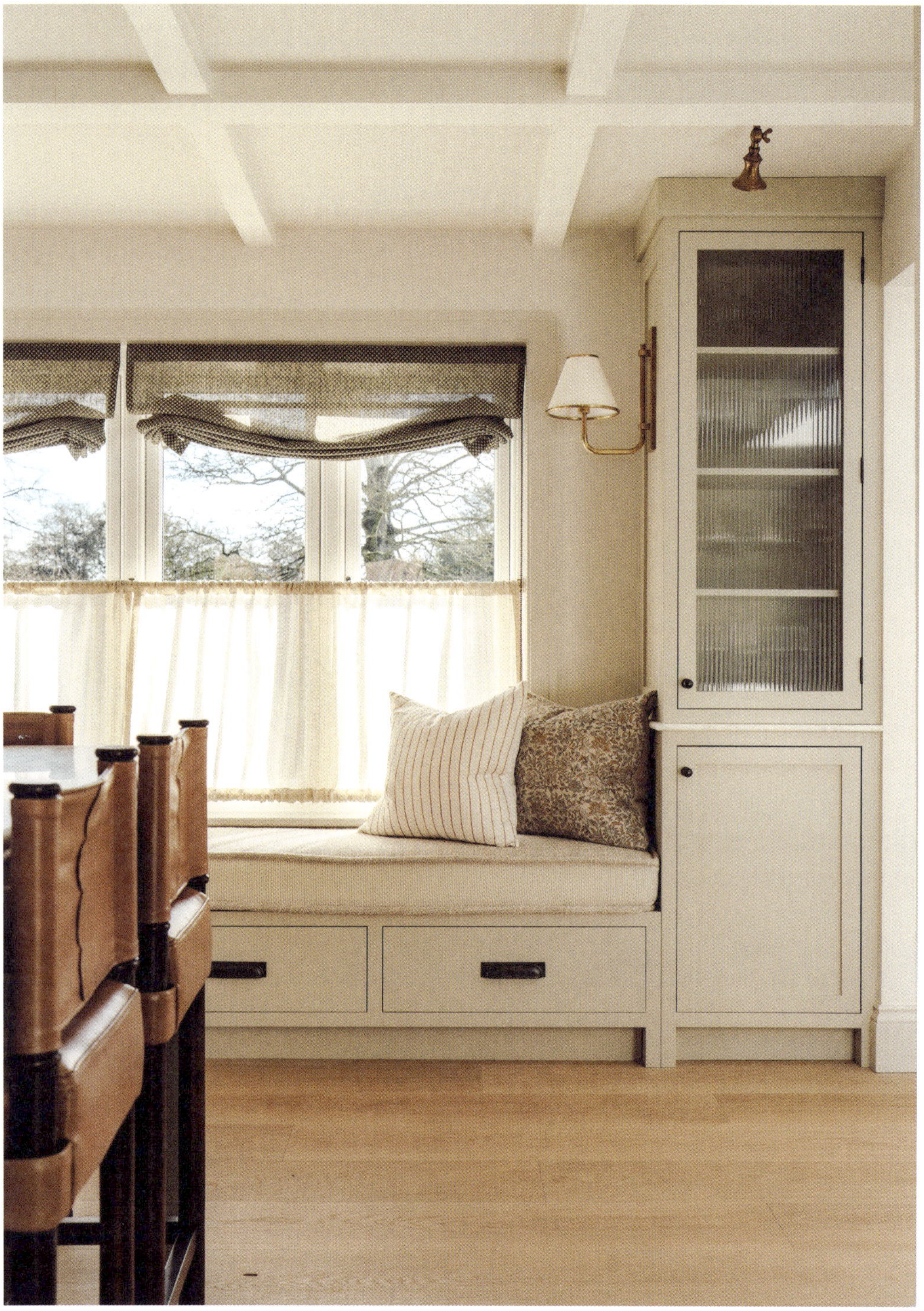

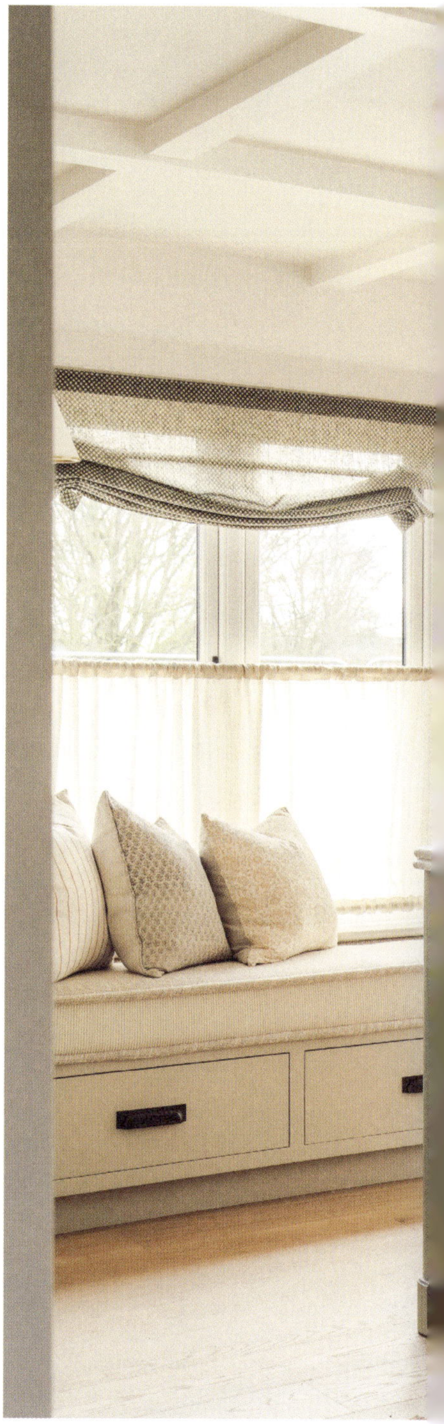

↑ This room will always hold a special place. The coffered ceiling does so much of the work here, adding real visual interest overhead, so the rest of the room can stay calm and considered. We designed the window seat to be generous; somewhere our client would actually want to use, not just perch. The island anchors it all, that statement range and reclaimed timber shelf giving the sage green cabinetry something to play against. Even the small things connect – the leather on the stools, the brass pendant echoing the wall lights by the window. A kitchen built for cooking and for lingering in equally.

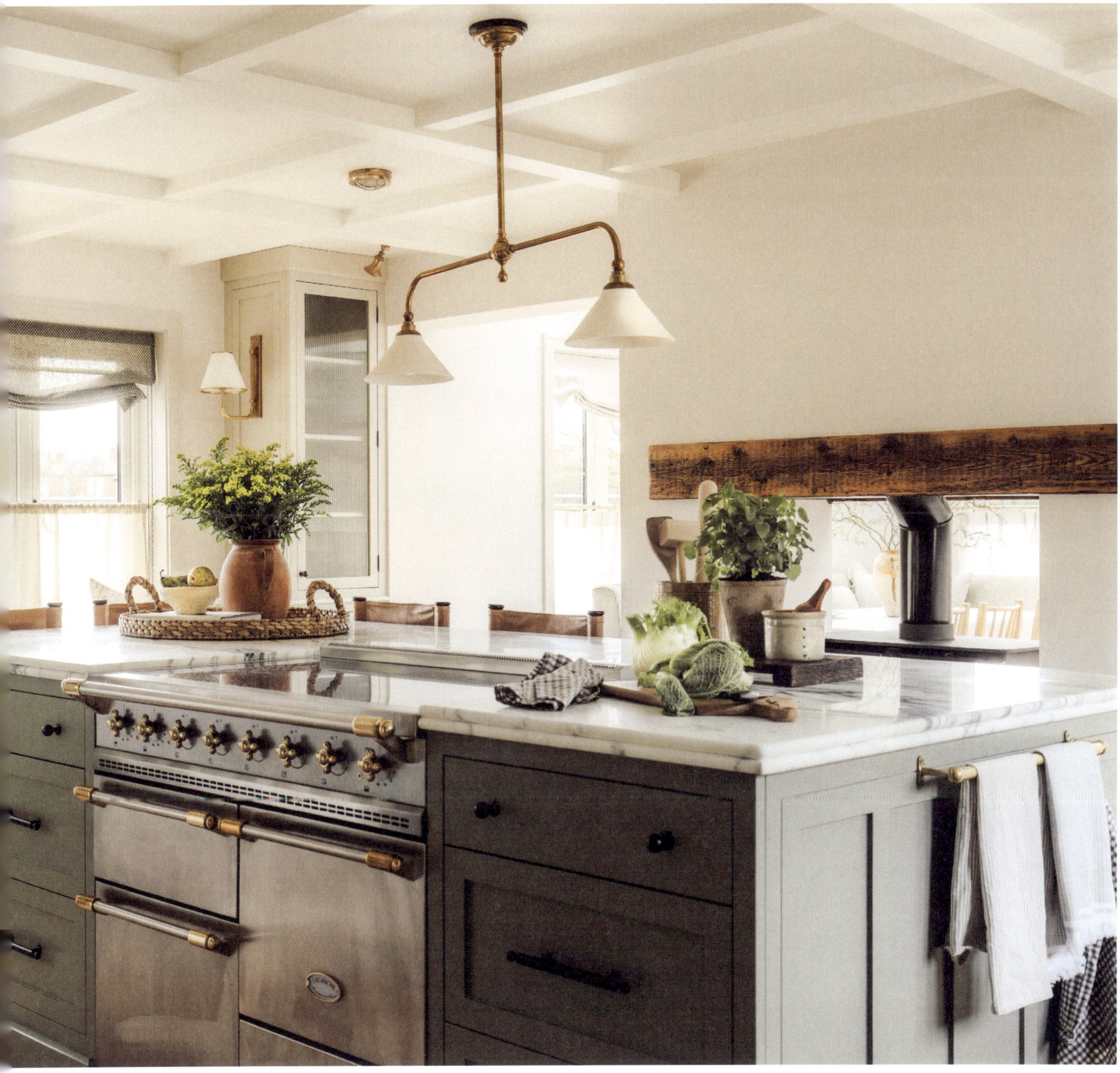

Light in Motion

Light is one of the most powerful tools for creating flow. It doesn't just shape how a space looks, it determines how you feel when you move through it. When light flows, so do you.

Bright morning sunlight spilling across the kitchen invites you to start the day; warm evening light pooling softly in a reading corner tells you it's time to slow down. Our bodies respond to these natural cues through our circadian rhythm. Bright daylight energises, while warm light signals rest and calm.

Artificial light should follow this same flow. Layering ambient, task, and accent lighting allows a space to evolve throughout the day – bright and clear when you need to work, soft and golden when it's time to relax. Dim, heavy lighting can make a room feel stagnant, while harsh glare can jar the senses. The key is balance: light that changes with the hours, flowing naturally through the home, alive but never overpowering.

"When light flows, so do you."

→ Bright morning sunlight spilling across the kitchen; exactly the kind of light that invites you to start the day. The veined honed marble worktops catch it beautifully, bronze and brass fittings warming under it, every surface alive with the hour rather than fixed in one mood. This is what light in motion looks like; a room that changes character through the day, energising at breakfast, softening by evening.

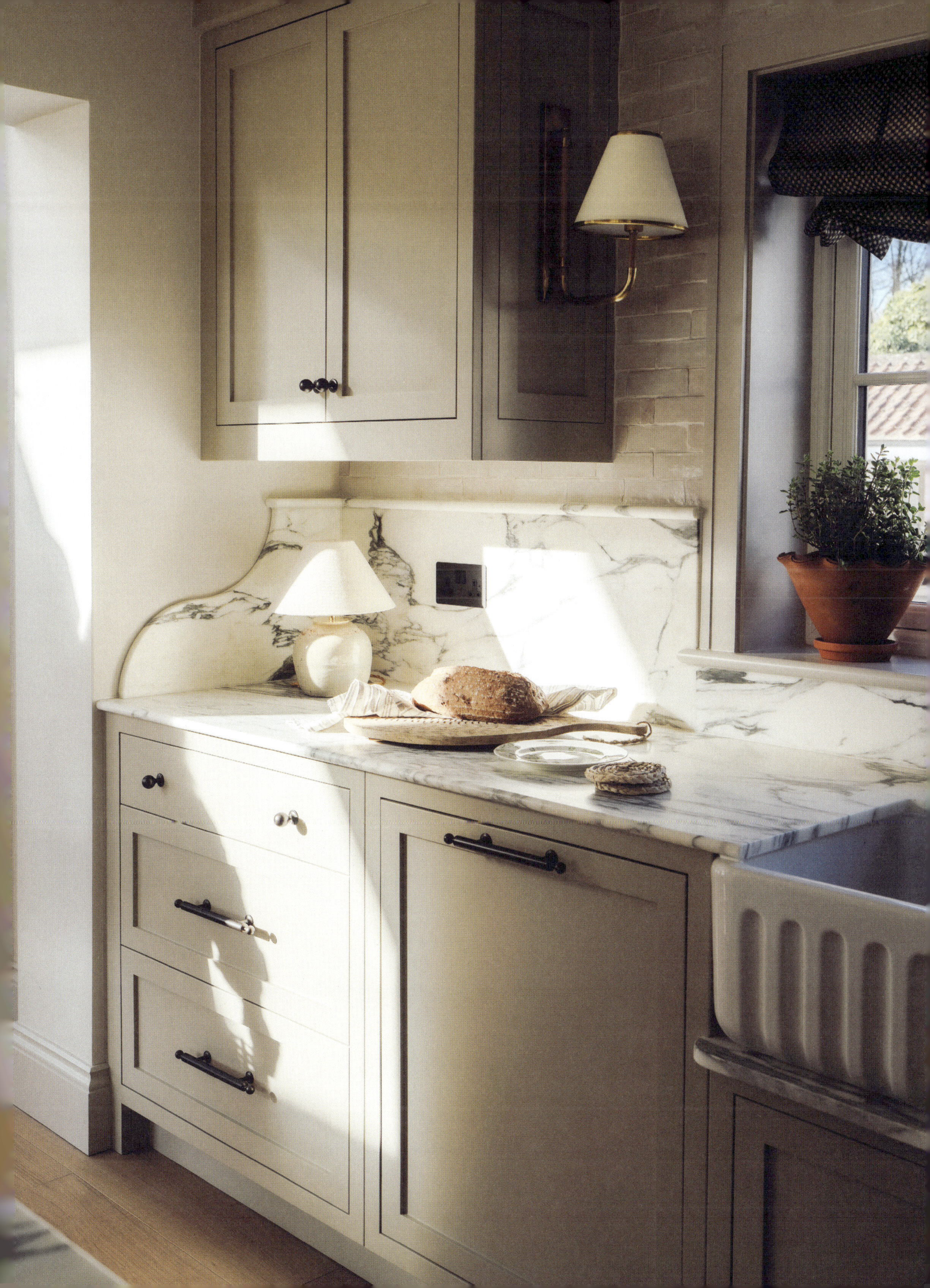

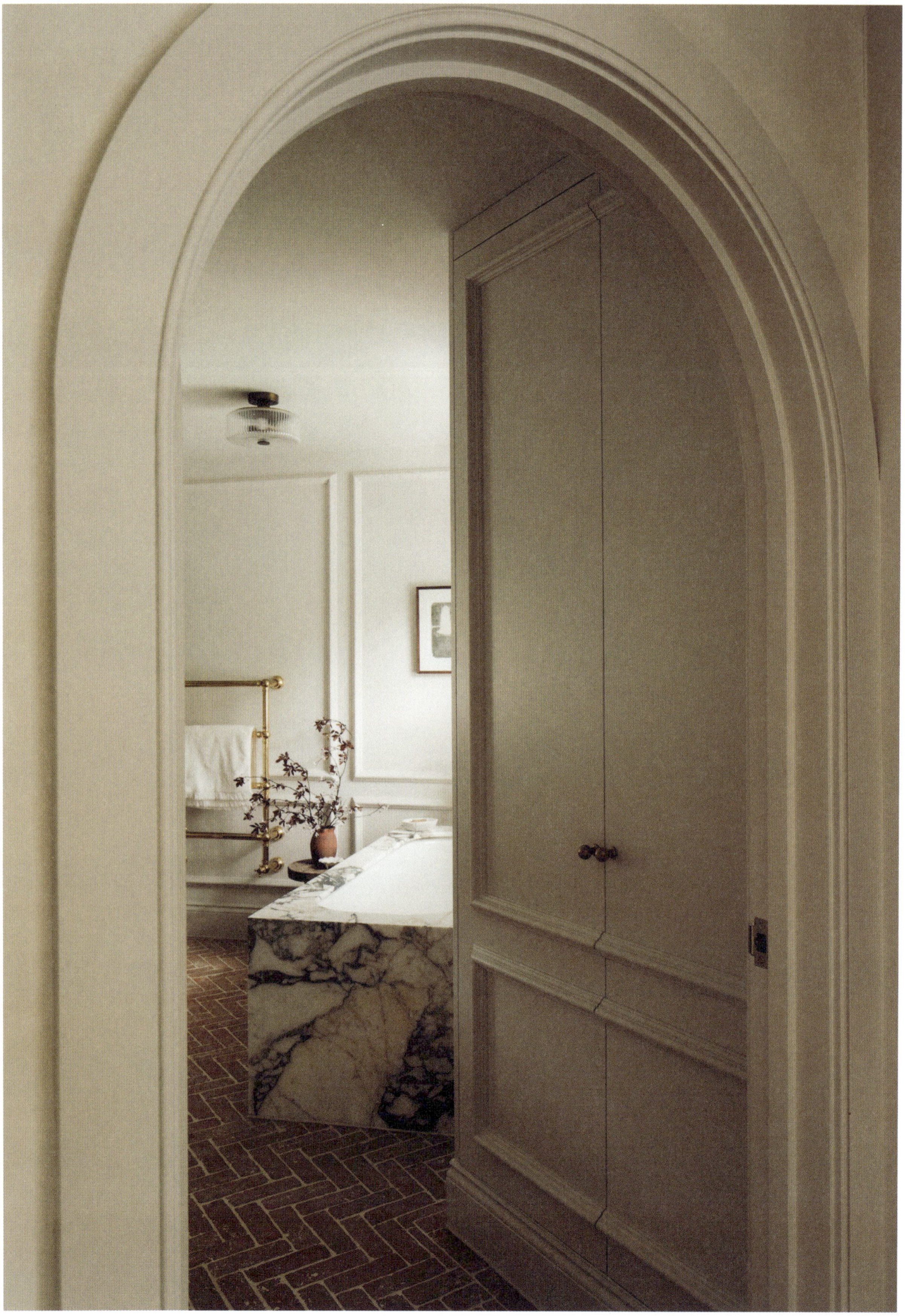

↑ Project Sandbanks. Even glimpsed through a doorway, you can see how the light moves through this room, soft and warm across the marble bath, catching the warm terracotta below. When light flows, so do you, and this room proves it before you've even stepped inside.

→ Light pooling across the marble, brass fittings warming under it. This is the kind of light that shifts the whole feel of a room through the day, bright and clear for getting ready, soft and golden once the bath is run and it's time to slow down. What a treat to bathe here!

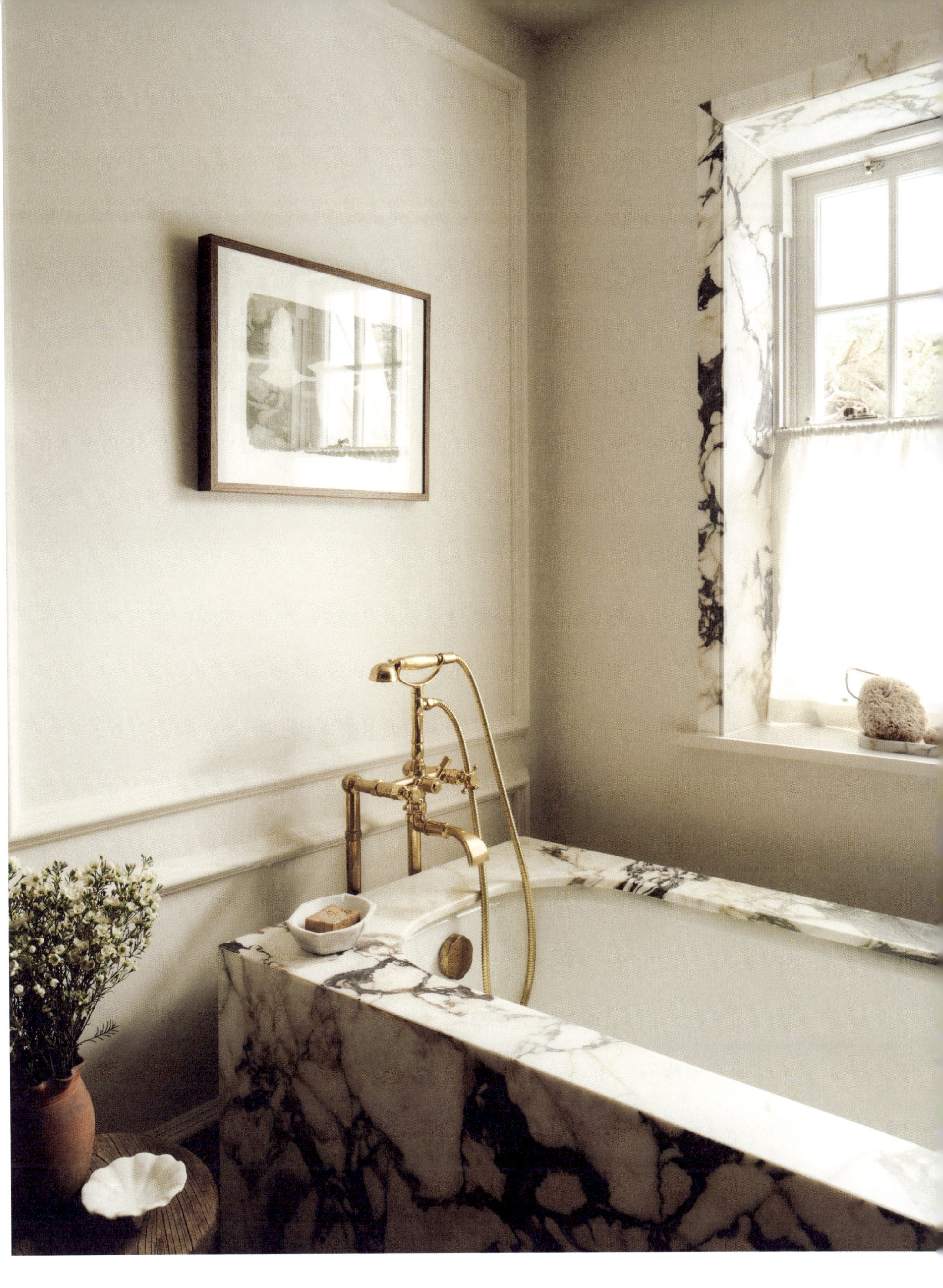

Colour as Continuity

Colour is one of the easiest ways to make – or break – flow. It sets the tone, mood, and pace of how the whole house feels. Understanding hue, shade, and tint keeps things cohesive. Layering variations of the same hue – say a deep olive in the hallway fading to a soft sage in the living room – creates a journey that feels calm and connected. The eye glides rather than jolts.

Colour has its own rhythm. Bright, crisp tones energise and sharpen us, while warmer, muted shades slow the pace and invite us to linger. A home that flows well often mirrors this progression: lighter shades where the day begins, deeper ones where it ends.

Tone and undertone are the secret glue. Tone is lightness or darkness, undertone reveals temperature – warm or cool. Rooms that share tonal values will always feel related, even if their colours differ entirely. A deep olive and muted terracotta work beautifully together because they share grounded warmth; throw in an icy emerald blue and the flow stops dead.

Small echoes of colour keep a palette alive: a hint of terracotta in a vase that resurfaces as a cushion, a brass detail echoed across rooms. Materiality strengthens the story. Colour behaves differently depending on surface and texture, too: limewash absorbs light softly, polished stone bounces it, and timber grounds it. When colour, texture, and tone align, a home immediately feels more balanced and lived in, with character that doesn't have to shout. The transitions between rooms become like turning the pages of a really good book, each chapter distinct, yet unmistakably part of the same story.

→ A dressing room where we made every echo of colour intentional. Warm terracotta on the upholstered bench, picked up again in the flowers, the brass wall light catching the same warmth, the timber panelling grounding it all. Nothing here is matched exactly, but everything is related. This is colour as continuity in practise, tone, and undertone working together so the room feels balanced and lived in; character that never has to shout to be felt.

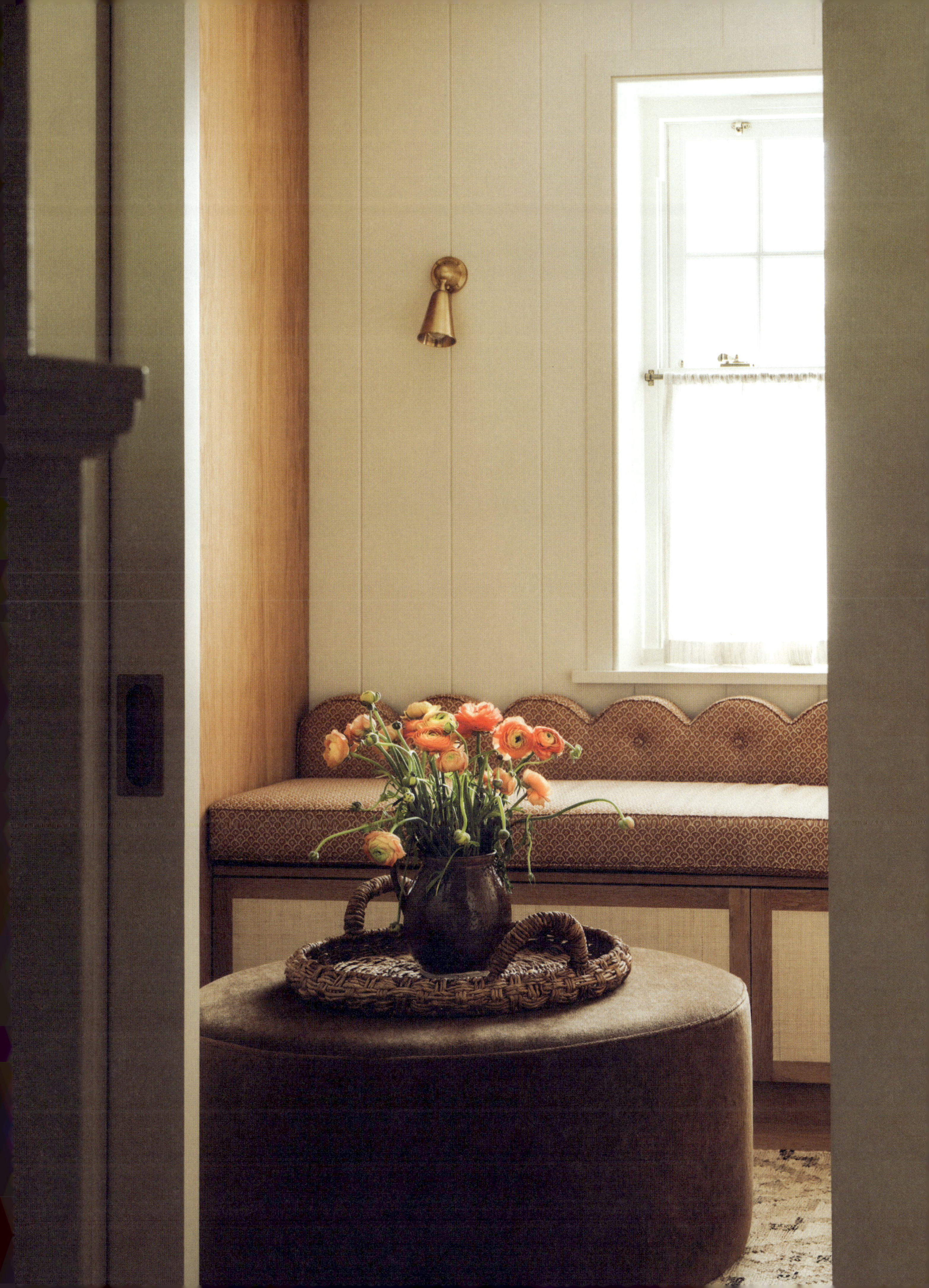

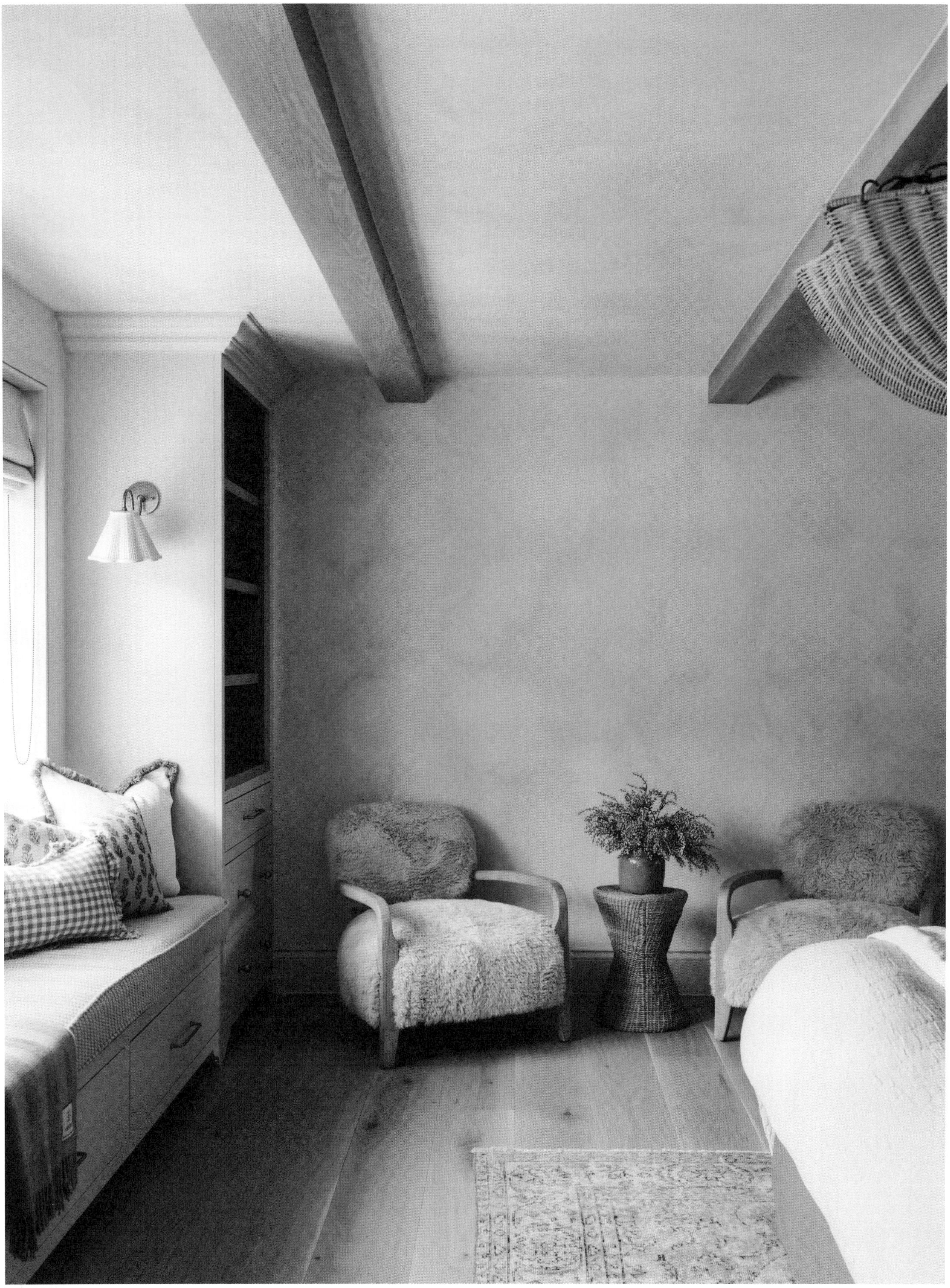

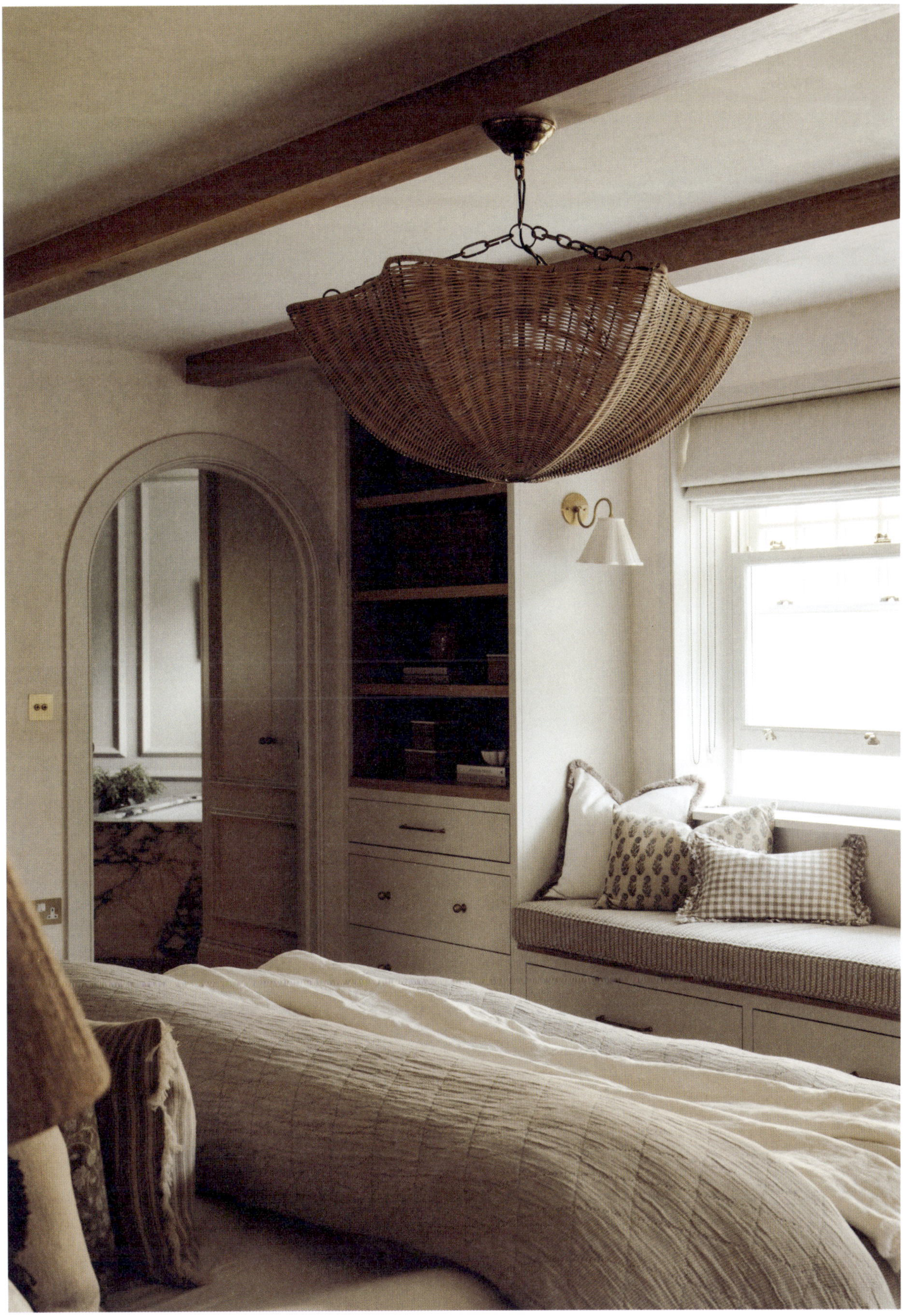

← The principal bedroom, off the previous bathroom you've just seen. We used Bauwerk chalk paint on the walls here, as that gentle movement and softness it gives is exactly what a bedroom asks for. Sheepskin armchairs, woven textures, and warm timber against it create a real sanctuary.

↑ The same room, looking through towards the arched doorway and a window seat tucked beneath the eaves. Chalk paint walls, natural linens, and that woven pendant keep everything grounded in texture; the kind of layering that makes a bedroom feel like a calm retreat.

Move Through Your Home

DESIGN NOTES

Below are some ideas to help you see how you move through your home, and how small shifts in layout, light, or colour can create a calmer, more natural flow.

1. FLOW IS ABOUT MOVEMENT

It's how the body, the eye, and the light travel through a space; that feeling that one room leads naturally into the next.

Try this: Take a slow walk around your home as if you're a guest. Notice where you pause, zig-zag, or squeeze past something. Map your path. A few small tweaks, such as shifting a chair, rethinking a doorway, or adding a rug, can change everything.

---

2. START WITH STRUCTURE

Flow begins with the bones. Let the architecture guide you first; decoration comes later.

Practise: Sketch a quick floor plan. Mark your main walking routes. Are they smooth? Interrupted? This will tell you more about flow than any trend ever will.

---

3. USE REPETITION TO CONNECT

Repeated materials, tones, or details quietly link one room to another.

Mini exercise: Pick one element – a metal finish, a wood tone, a colour – and echo it twice elsewhere. Small echoes create big calm.

---

4. MIND YOUR TRANSITIONS

Flow doesn't mean sameness; it's about gentle change. Each room can have its own personality while still belonging to the same home.

Try this: Notice where one room shifts into the next. Add a small change in texture, tone, or light to mark the transition, like turning the page of a new chapter.

---

5. COLOUR CREATES RHYTHM

A consistent palette lets the eye move through the home without stumbling.

Practise: Use the 60–30–10 rule to find your rhythm:

- 60 per cent dominant colour (walls, large furniture)
- 30 per cent secondary colour (timber, stone)
- 10 per cent accent (details, accessories)

Start by identifying your 60 per cent. Feeling bold? Let your 10 per cent accent lead the way in one small space for a controlled hit of personality.

---

6. LIGHT LEADS THE WAY

Light pulls you forward and shadow slows you down. Flow often shifts with the sun.

Try this: Follow the light for a day. See where it lands first, where it lingers, and where it disappears. If a room feels dull, borrow light from somewhere – angle a mirror to bounce it in another direction, or add a soft pool lamp to gently draw you in.

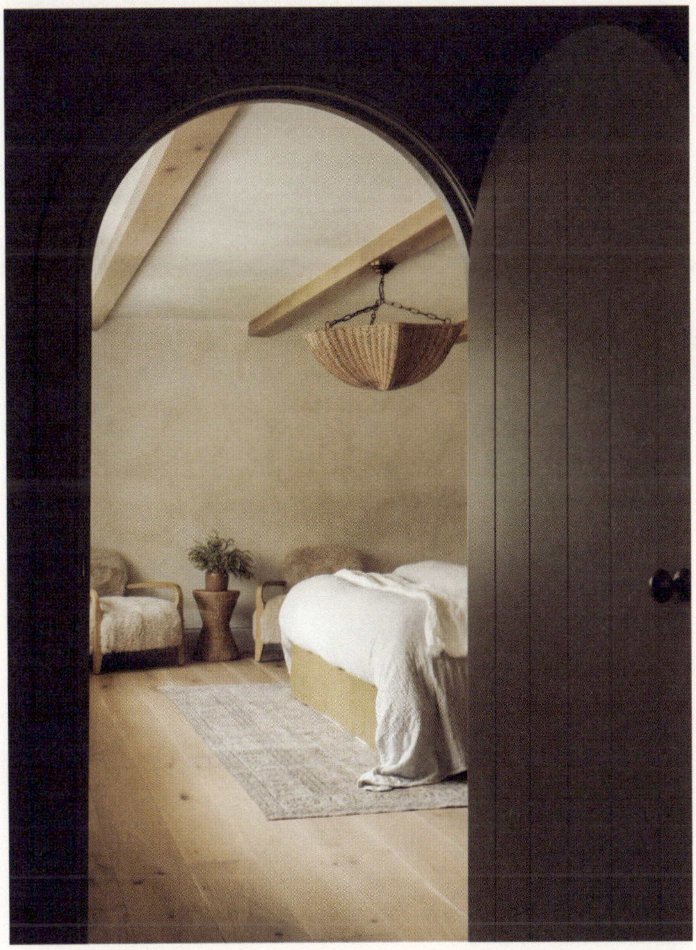

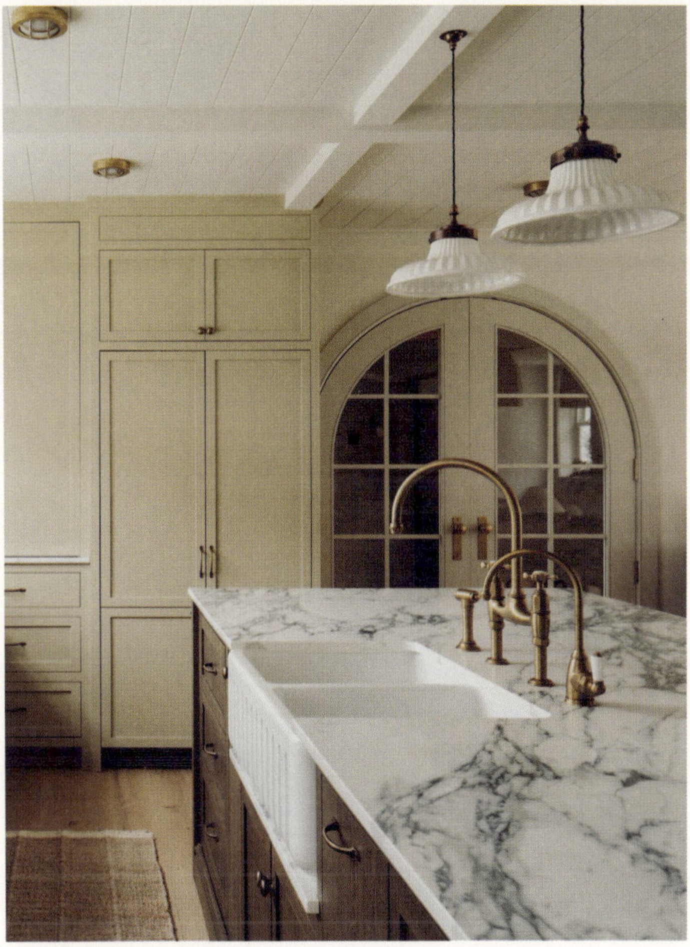

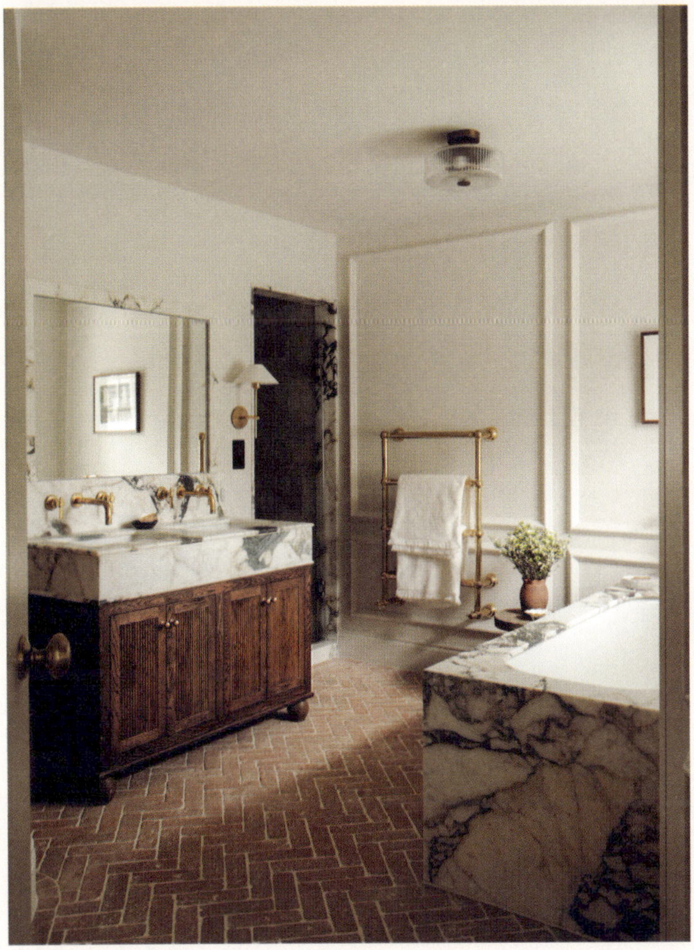

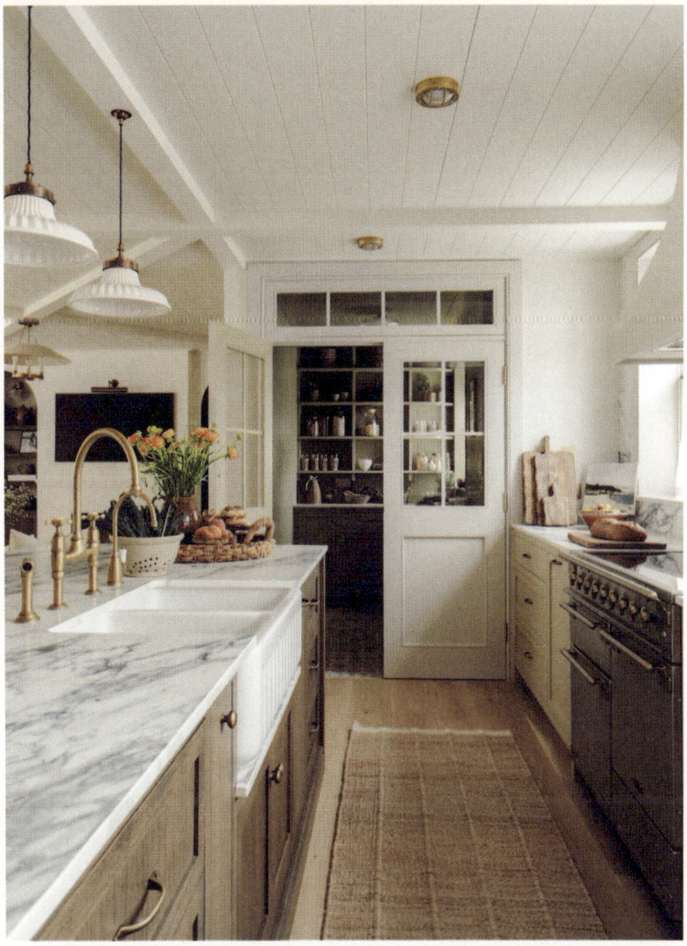

“*Balance is not something you find, it’s something you create.*”

JANE KINGSFORD

Balance

WHERE FUNCTION MEETS BEAUTY

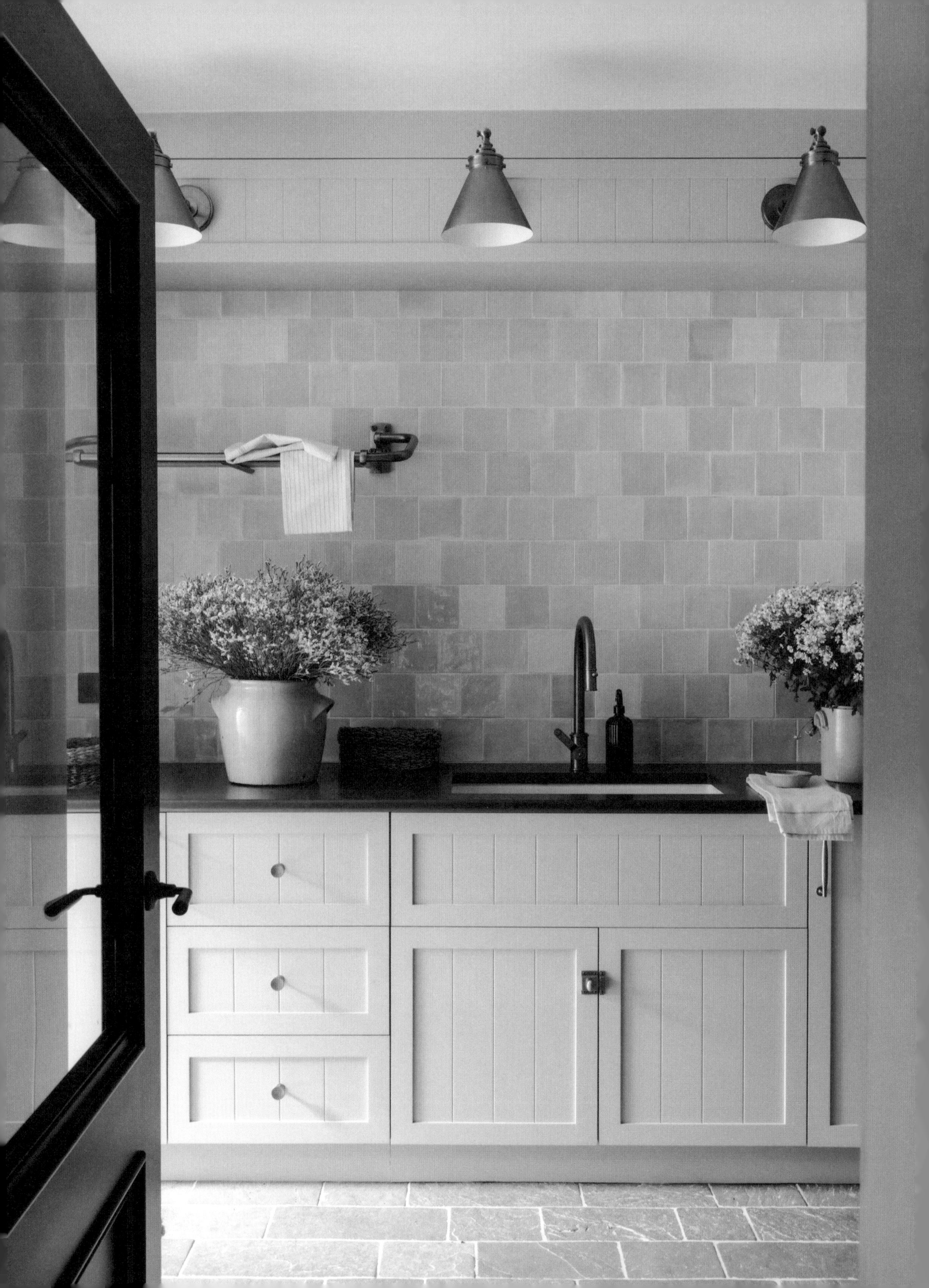

BALANCING PURPOSE WITH *CHARM*

A well-balanced home has very little to do with perfect symmetry – and thank goodness for that, because I've never met a real home that presents that neatly. Balance is far more instinctive than that. Much like with flow, a room either settles you or unsettles you. And believe me, I've walked into enough homes – including my own, mid-project – to know when something is leaning too far one way or the other.

You've probably felt it too – a living room where all the furniture huddles nervously against one wall while the opposite side sits awkwardly empty, like it's waiting for someone to ask it to dance. Or a giant modular sofa taking over one corner of a room, leaving the rest feeling slightly abandoned and unsure of its purpose. These spaces feel lopsided because, quite literally, they are.

Balance is about how furniture, décor, lighting, and colour are arranged so that a space feels stable and comfortable rather than tilted or tense. And here's the reassuring bit: you don't need to be a designer to sense it. Our bodies notice balance long before our brains catch up. We feel where we can move easily, where we hesitate, and where our eyes naturally come to rest. That quiet, internal "ooh, this feels right" – that's balance at work, doing its best impression of intuition.

In my experience, good balance happens when boldness is tempered with calm, when practicality is softened with charm, and when no single piece takes itself too seriously. A dramatic marble fireplace becomes far more welcoming when paired with a couple of simple, unfussy soft linen chairs. Even the unglamorous bits – hooks, baskets, cupboard handles – can support balance when they work with the room instead of shouting over it.

Negative space plays its part too. An empty stretch of wall or floor can be just as powerful as the pieces in the room, giving everything else room to breathe. Light does this beautifully as well – a pool of shadow can make a lamp glow more warmly, and daylight can soften the strength of deeper colours.

← The boot room scullery, or "bootility", at Project Green Park, Dublin where we leaned on balance as much as any living space. It's that quiet sense of stability you feel before you can explain it, with balance doing its best impression of intuition.

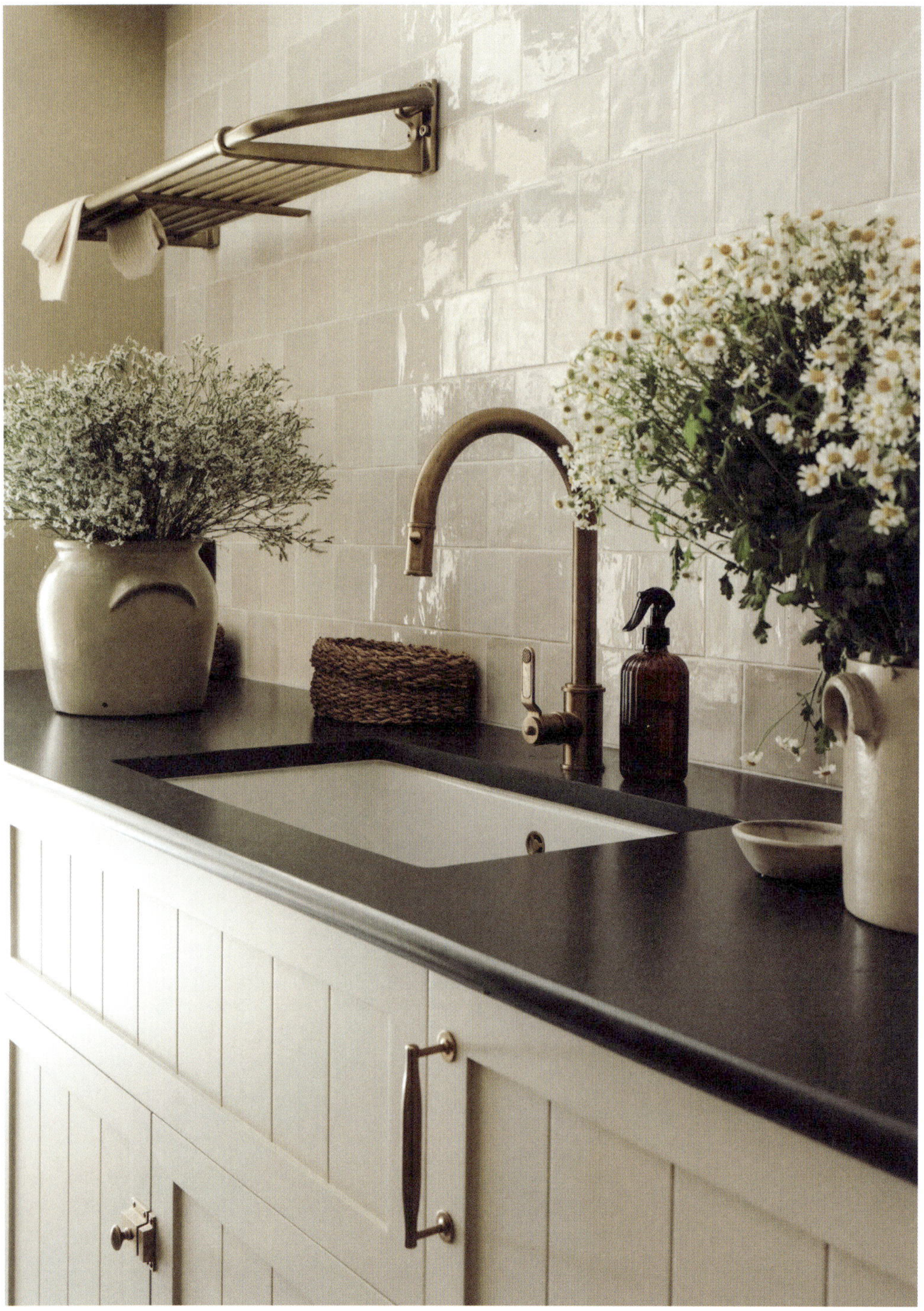

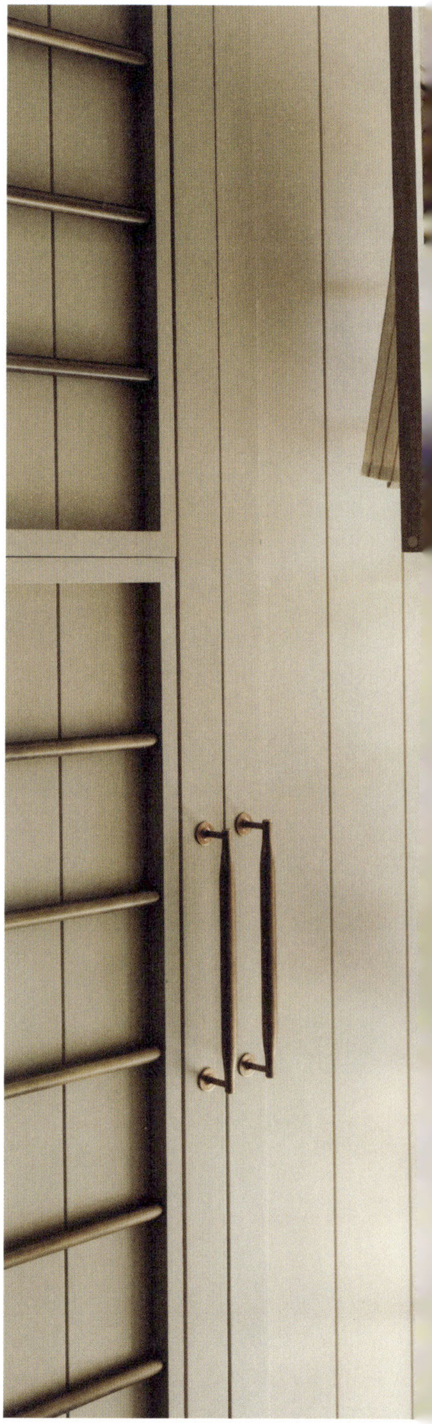

↑ Rows of brass wall lights repeat steadily overhead, Zellige tiles bring a soft, irregular pattern, and dark stone flooring grounds it all. Nothing here is shouting - the paint, the hooks, the handles, even the taps are all working with the room rather than over it.

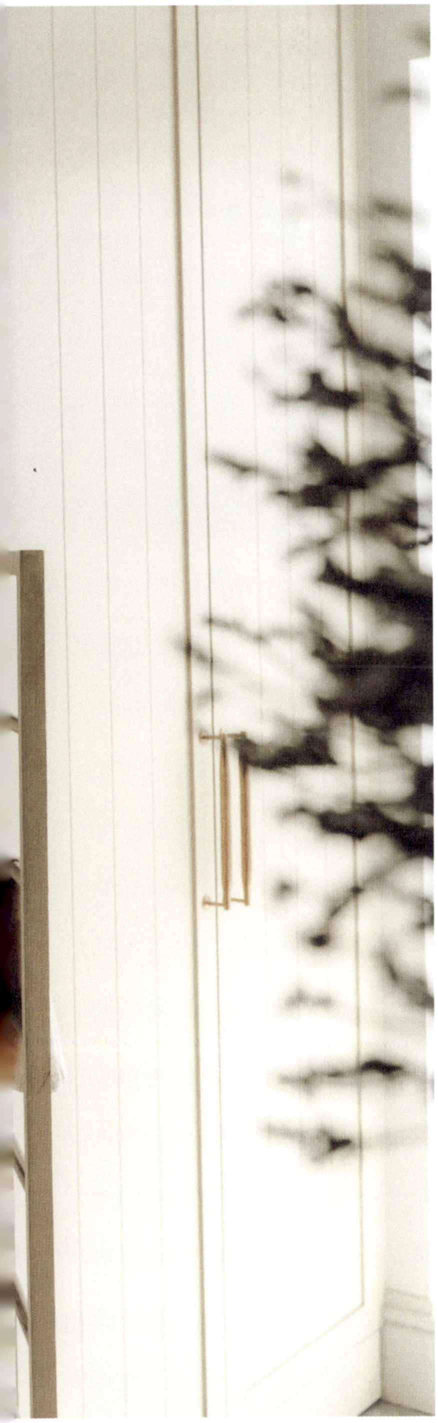

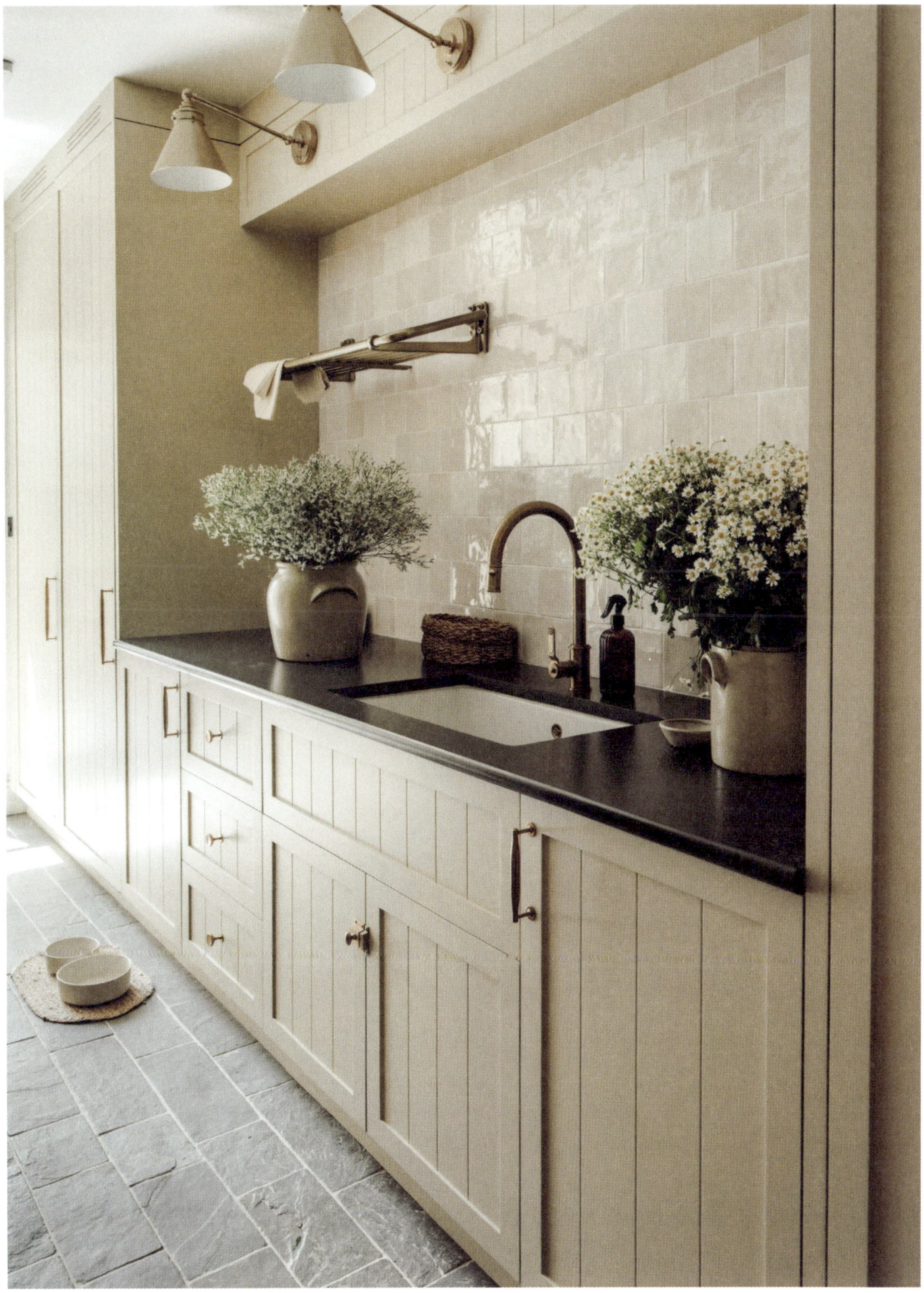

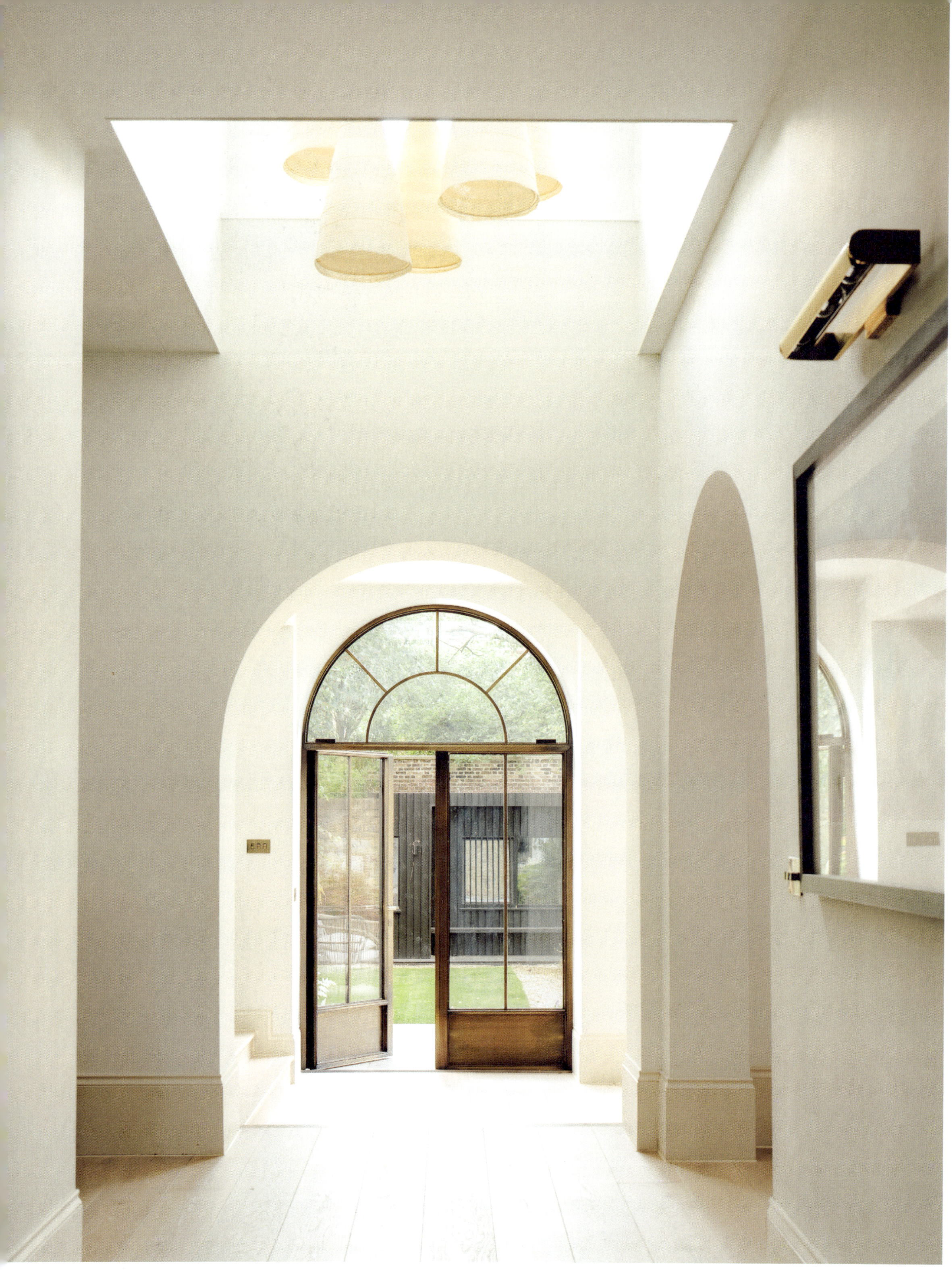

What I've learned over years of stepping into homes (and rearranging half the furniture before my clients have even offered me a cup of tea) is that balance thrives on imperfection. It isn't about erasing contrast, but orchestrating it. It allows a home to hold both energy and rest, practicality and beauty, quiet and playfulness in gentle conversation.

Ultimately, balance is a series of subtle relationships working together to make a room feel right. I am writing this book because I want you to pull these threads apart: how scale and proportion shape how we move; how form and silhouette give character; how colour, tone, and light create atmosphere; how texture, material, and even empty space add depth.

Together, these elements create the rhythm of your home – that soft back-and-forth between calm and energy that makes a space not just beautiful, but deeply human.

"Good balance happens when boldness is tempered with calm."

← With ceilings this high, I knew restraint wasn't the answer - scale was. We let the oversized pendant fill the volume above, chose a wide-arched doorway to pull your eye straight through to the garden, and made sure nothing here felt small or apologetic. For me, balance in this hallway meant being bold enough to match the room.

The Balance of Scale

Scale and proportion are the backbone of balance. They're what make a room feel cohesive and comfortable to move through, even before you've noticed why. Scale relates to the size of individual elements, while proportion is about the relationship between them. Together, they decide whether a space feels harmonious or slightly off; whether a chair sits comfortably beside a table, or a pendant light hangs at just the right height above it.

A common mistake is choosing pieces in isolation, without considering how they'll sit within the architecture of the room. There are times, of course, where this can work and, again, I don't want to be too dictatorial here. But a common mistake I so often see are sofas so large that they block circulation and dominate the space, and others so small they seem to float, leaving the room feeling hollow. When furniture doesn't relate to ceiling height, window scale, or light levels, the sense of balance slips away.

Proportion is what holds everything together. It's the subtle art of ensuring each piece feels in conversation with the others. A small rug beneath a large dining table makes the setting top-heavy, while a tall lamp can balance the height of a window or high ceiling by drawing the eye up. When scale and mass echo one another, the room feels settled and calm.

In the studio, we often mark out furniture footprints on the floor with masking tape before ordering anything. It's a simple exercise, but it reveals how pieces will breathe within the space, and prevents costly mistakes.

Scale also governs rhythm – how the eye moves around the room. Varying heights and proportions create movement without chaos, giving the space a quiet sense of order. You can have perfect colours and beautiful materials, but if the proportions are wrong, a room will never quite rest. When they're right, everything clicks – the architecture, the furniture, and the feeling of home itself.

→ At Project Ziggy Rocks, this kitchen is scale and proportion doing their quiet work. We varied the pendant heights deliberately over the island - that rhythm draws the eye along the run without it ever feeling chaotic. The marble waterfall island anchors the space, but we balanced its weight with the warmth of timber drawers and brass hardware, so nothing feels too heavy or too cold. Even the run of cabinetry was scaled to the ceiling height, so the whole room breathes rather than crowds.

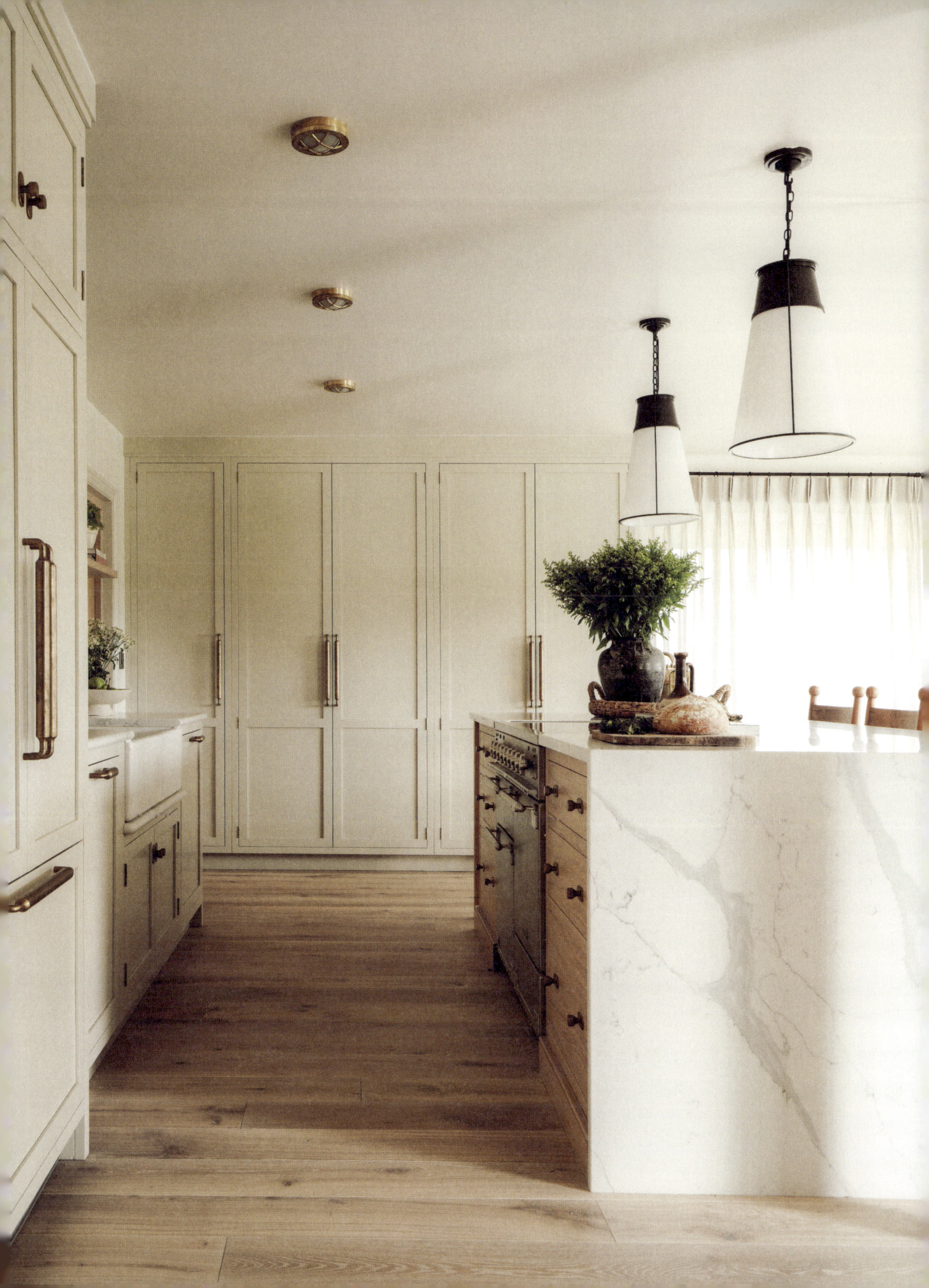

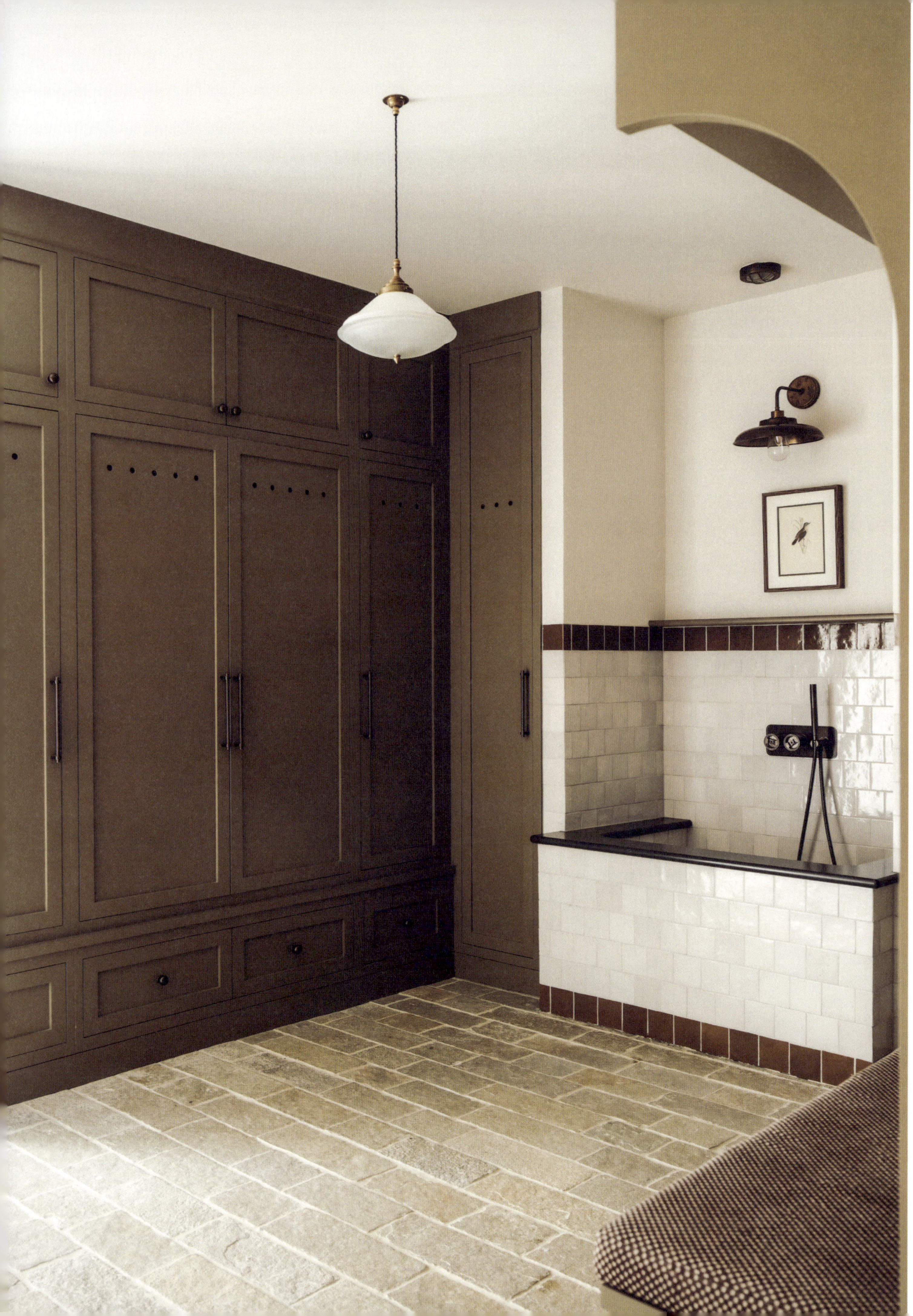

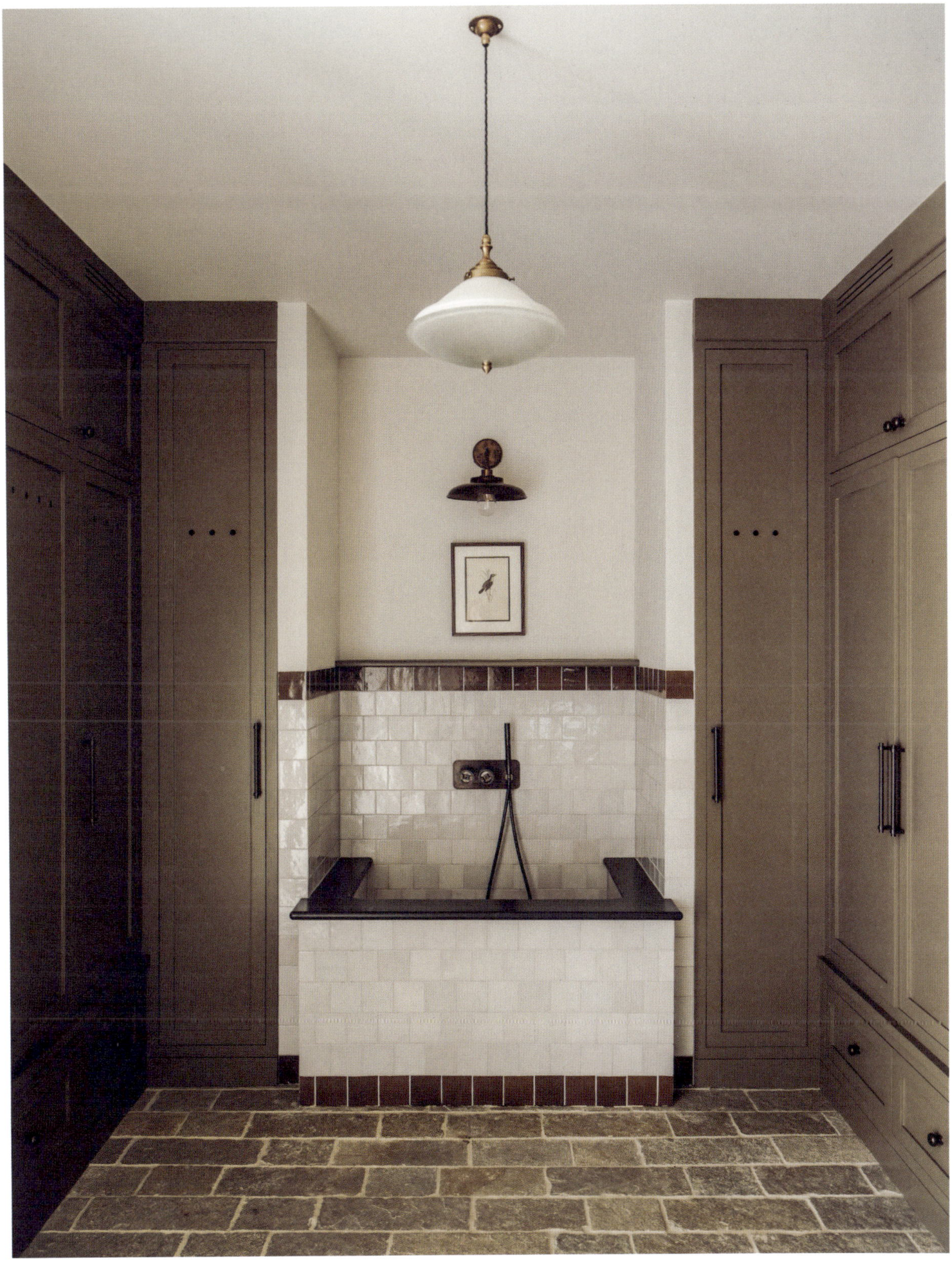

←↑ Deep olive cabinetry wraps this boot room floor to ceiling, with a dedicated dog wash designed for our client placed right into the centre of the scheme. Bright and centred, it becomes a focal point rather than an afterthought - the white tile and black tap catching the light against all that deep olive. Rust-toned trim and a warm brass pendant lift the room from purely functional to genuinely considered, proof that even the practical spaces deserve to be seen.

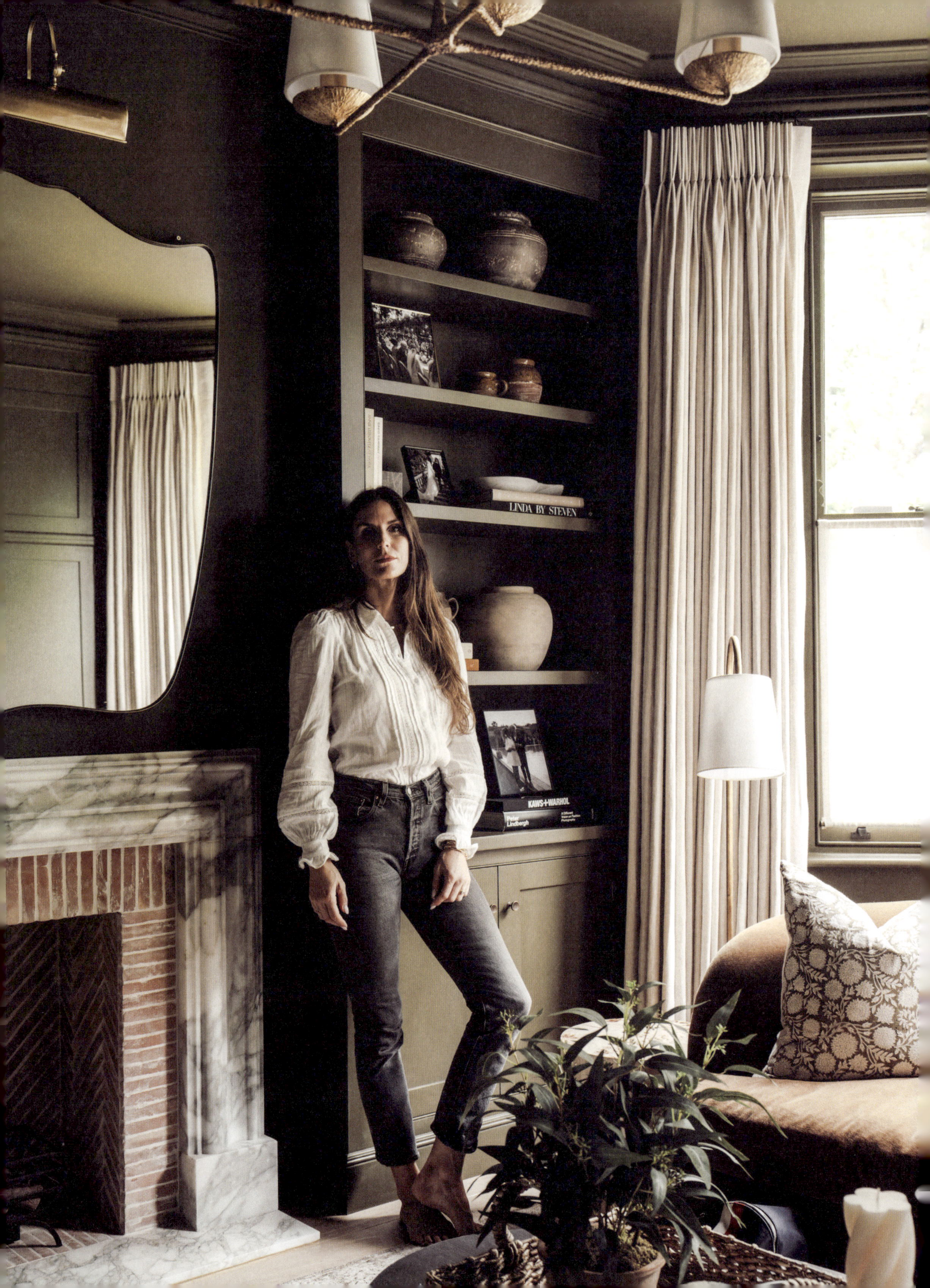
LINDA BY STEVEN
KAWS+WARHOL
Peter Lindbergh

← Me, in the front room of our Notting Hill townhouse project. We colour-drenched the whole room in Rocky, one of our own paints with COAT - the perfect backdrop to display all the furniture and accessories we sourced.

↓ The armchair we designed to be made bespoke, made using English sheepskin, deeply comfortable, and those slender curved legs stop it from feeling too bulky.

The Shape of Things

If scale and proportion define size, then shape and form define character. They give a space its personality – the mix of softness and structure that makes a room feel balanced and alive. Every object carries a kind of geometry: straight lines bring order and clarity, while curves introduce movement and ease. A room filled only with right angles can feel rigid; one with nothing but curves can drift without focus. True equilibrium comes from the conversation between the two.

Architecture often dictates where that balance begins. In a room with strong linear bones –panelled walls, square windows, or beamed ceilings – rounded forms can soften the rhythm. Consider a curved sofa, an arched mirror, or a circular dining table. In more organic or irregular spaces, adding structure through clean, angular lines brings grounding and calm.

Repetition is a simple way to tie shapes together. When forms subtly reappear – be it a curve mirrored in a light fitting, a table edge, or the back of a chair – the eye recognises a pattern and the room feels composed without being predictable.

Shape and scale work hand in hand. A large, square coffee table carries visual weight; a round one with slender legs feels lighter. Balancing forms keeps the room from tipping too far in one direction. Even light interacts with shape; where curved surfaces catch and soften it, flat ones will sharpen and define it, giving a space depth and rhythm throughout the day. Ultimately, shape and form are about movement – how the eye travels and how the body feels in the room. When lines and curves are in dialogue, a space becomes both sculptural and welcoming, balanced by the subtle tensions between softness and structure.

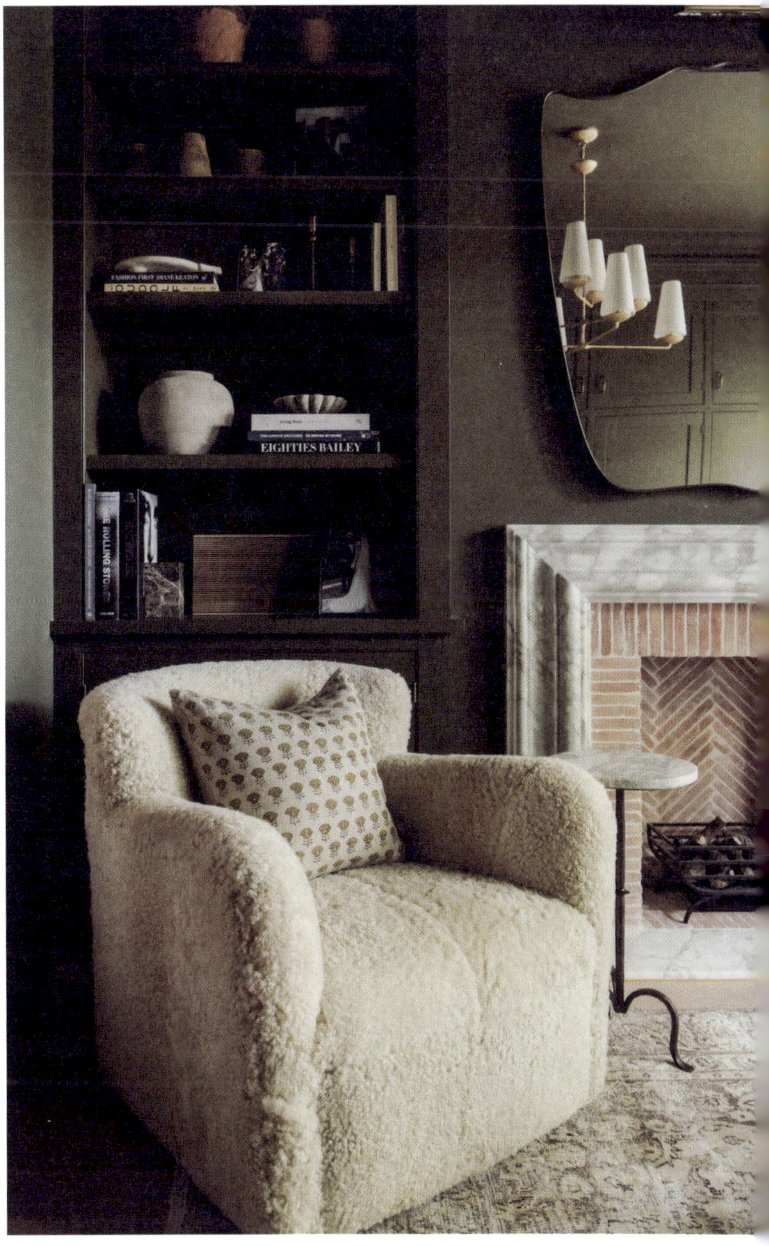

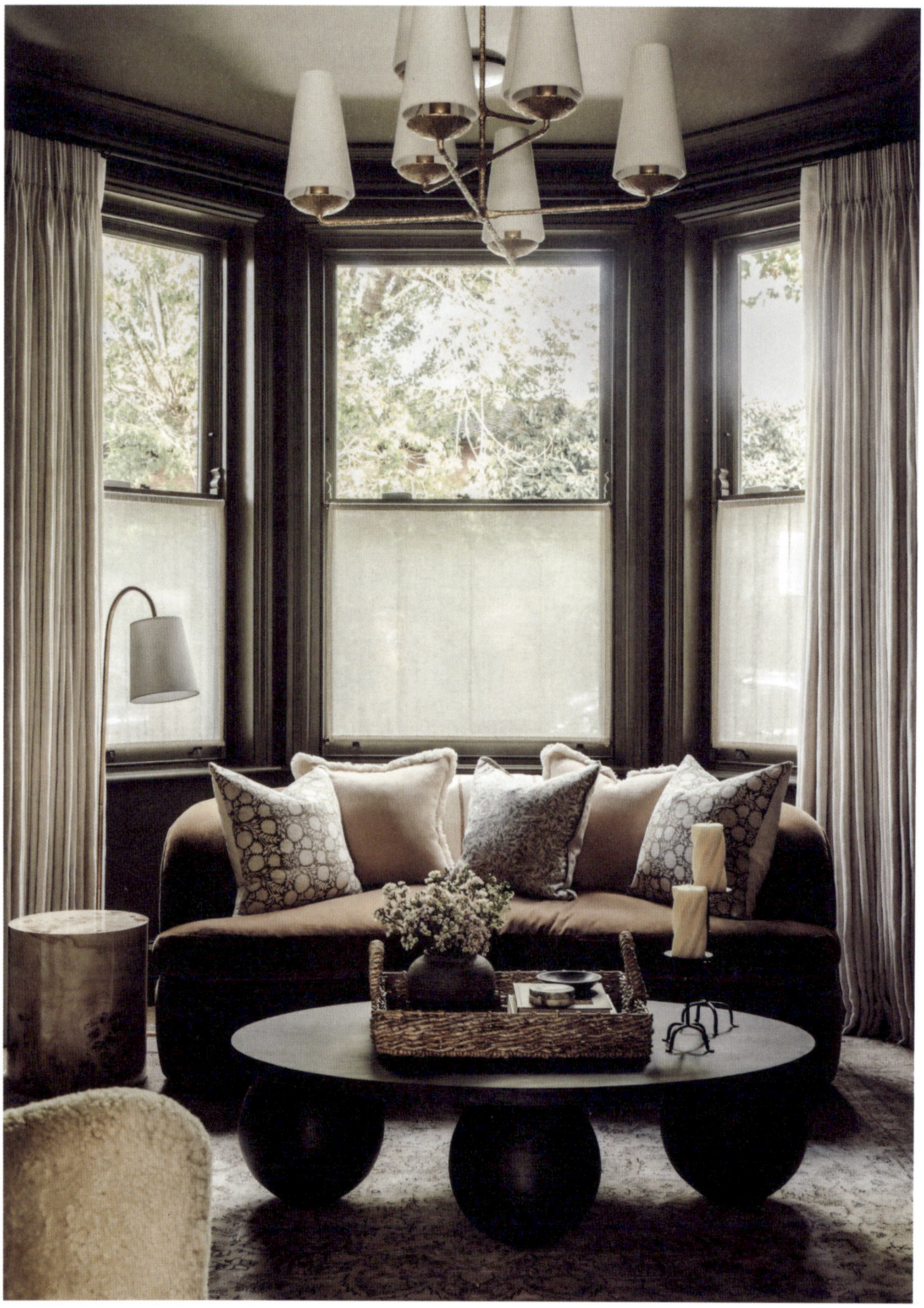

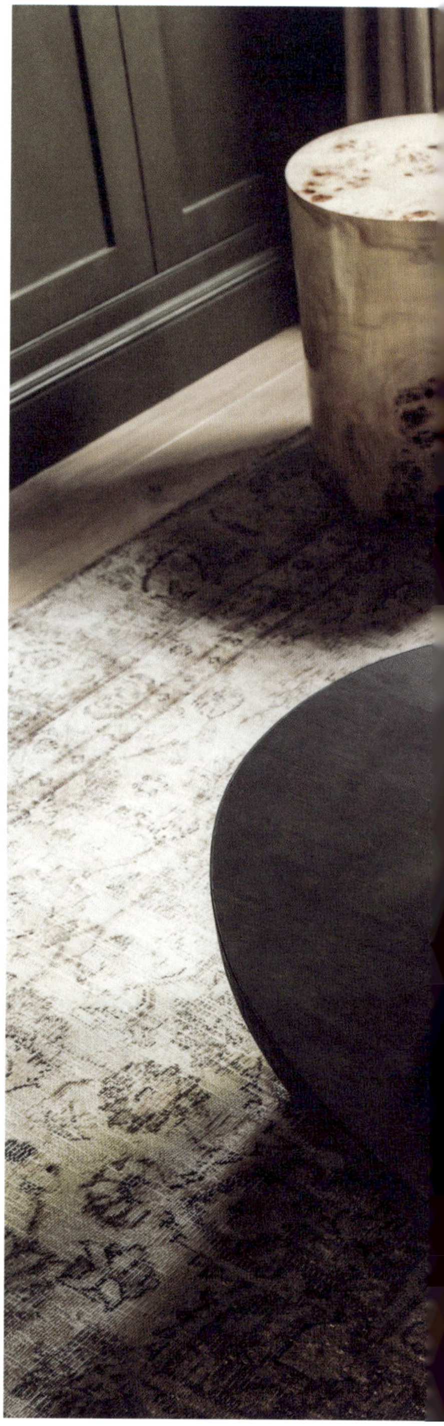

↑ Three corners of the same front room – proof that a dark, colour-drenched space can still feel warm. The oval coffee table, with its sphere base and the weathered stone vase, is offset against the softness of velvet, sheepskin, linens, and patterned scatters on the sofa. I love the texture mix here: wicker, antique Persian rug, raw wood, honed marble, all sitting comfortably against that deep olive panelling. Nothing in this room is shouting, but everything has been chosen with real intention.

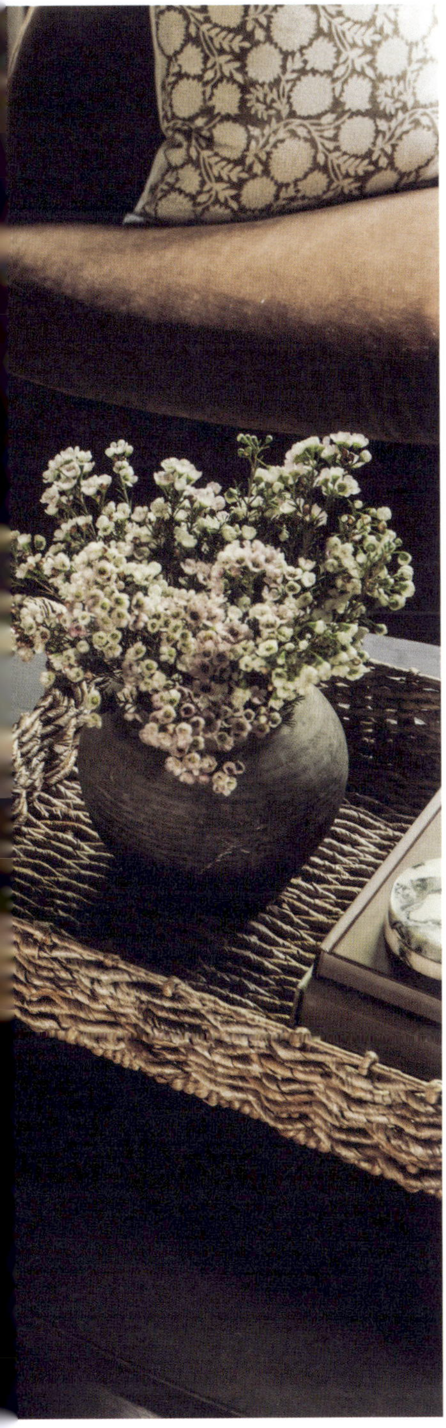

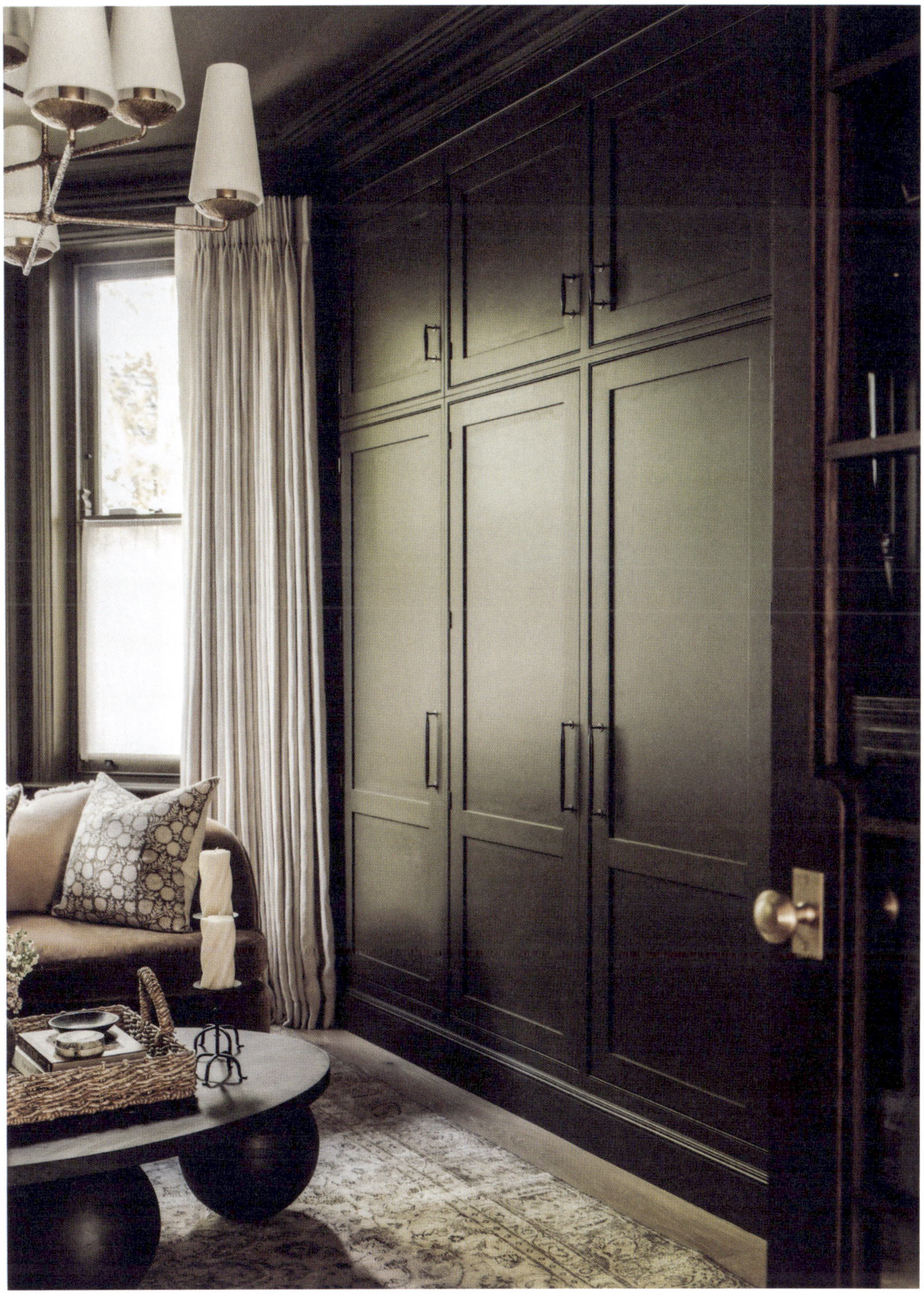

Colour in Balance

→ This room is a good example of colour setting the mood before you even notice the furniture - the dusty rose linen sofa brings warmth and softness, while the leopard print ottoman adds a little energy without ever tipping into busy. The commissioned gallery wall layers in even more personality. Warmth to make it inviting, a little edge to keep it interesting and cool - that's the balance our client was after.

Colour has an extraordinary influence on balance. I could talk about it endlessly; it never stops fascinating me. I'm always exploring how colour behaves; how subtle shifts in tone can completely transform a space. It's the first thing we register when we enter a room, but its impact runs far deeper than decoration. Before we even notice the furniture, the lighting, or the architecture, our brains have already responded. We process colour faster than form – it's essentially our body's shorthand for atmosphere. In an instant, colour tells us what kind of room we're in, be it calm or lively, cool or warm, welcoming or withdrawn. It sets the emotional temperature before our minds have time to catch up. It's a wonder!

Again, colour can make a room feel open and expansive, or intimate and cocooning. When it works, it creates quiet cohesion; when it doesn't, you sense the imbalance immediately. Tone – the depth or lightness of a colour – is where that balance truly lies. Deep, saturated hues anchor a room and give it weight; lighter tones will lift and soften it. The most successful interiors hold both – the grounding and the air – playing one gently against the other. A dark wall balanced by pale upholstery, or warm timber set against cool stone, creates dynamic harmony. Temperature adds another layer to colour balance. Warm hues such as ochre, rust, and blush bring energy and familiarity; cooler tones like slate, sage, and chalky white bring stillness and clarity. A room being used for the every day usually needs a little of both: warmth to make it inviting, coolness to keep it calm and composed.

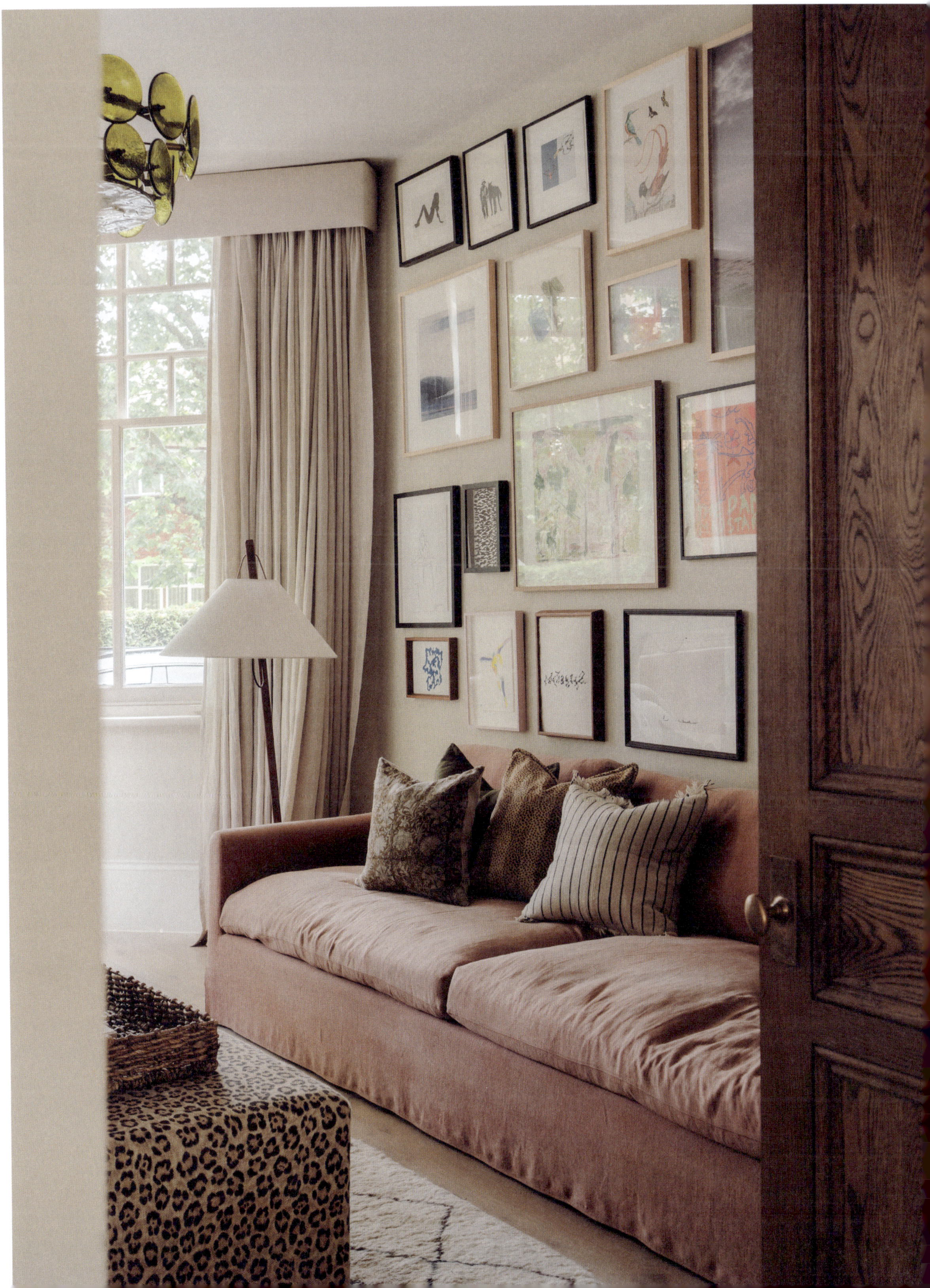

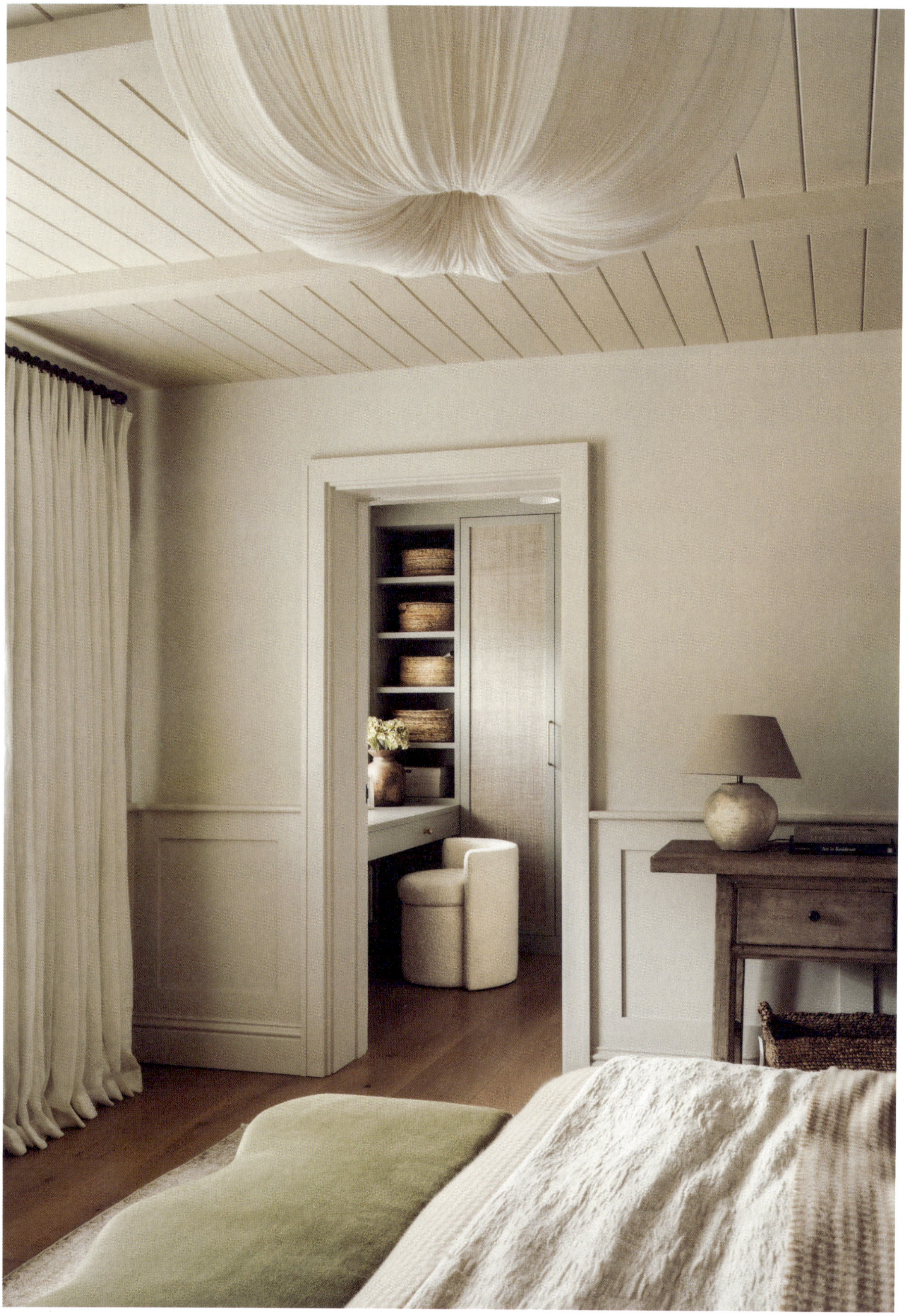

↑ Warm timber floors, a soft oversized ceiling pendant overhead, and a soft Persian rug underfoot - we kept this principal bedroom tonal and textural. A sanctuary of calm.

→ Textured wallpaper-fronted wardrobes, woven baskets, and a bouclé stool against soft sage cabinetry. This dressing room holds warmth and calm in equal measure.

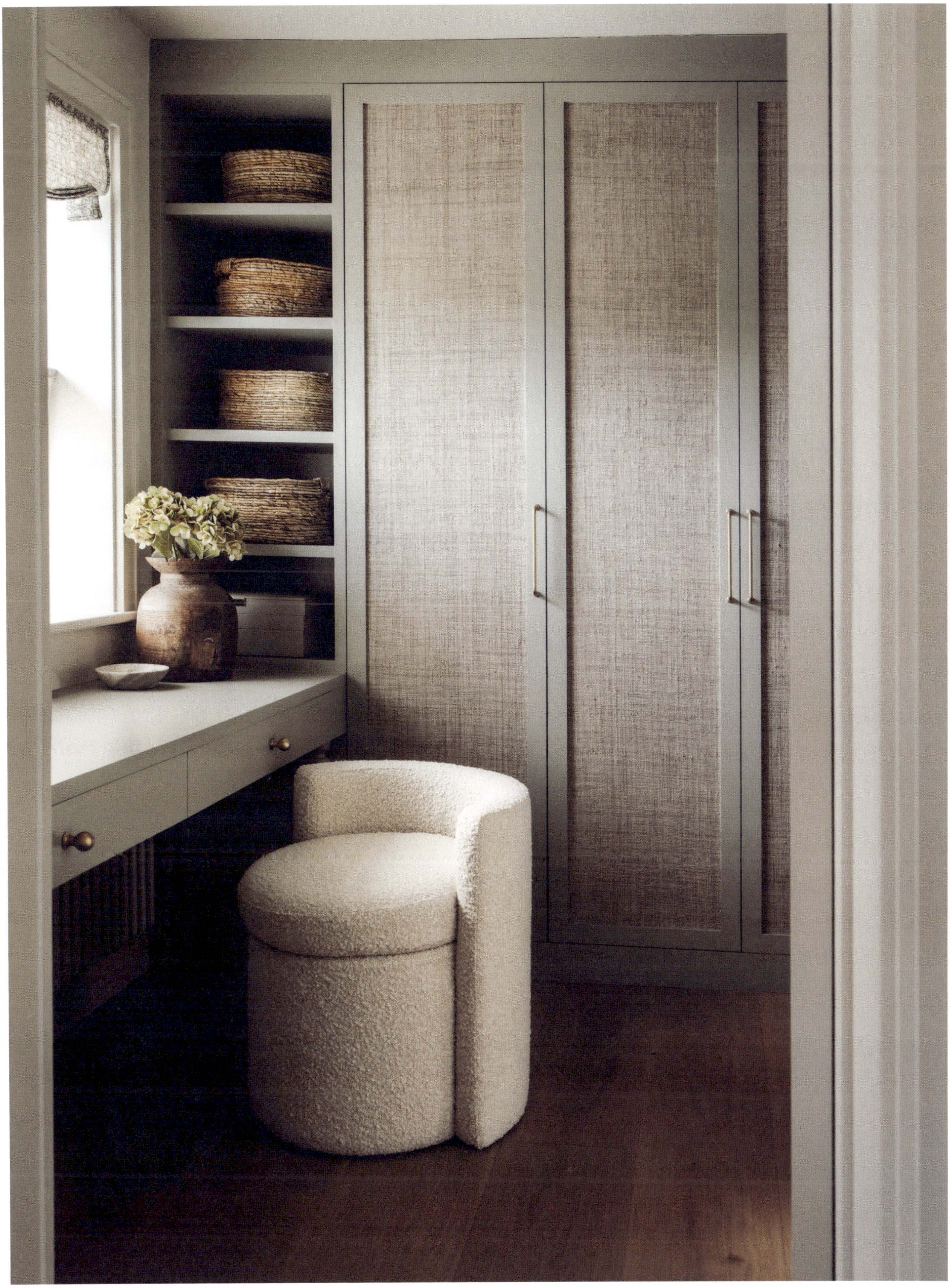

Balancing Light and Shadow

And then there's light – the ultimate mediator! As touched on in the previous chapter, light has an extraordinary effect on us because it's inseparable from how we live and feel. Long before we designed homes, light dictated our rhythm – waking, working, and resting. That connection is still instinctive. Bright, clear light lifts our energy; softer light slows us down. It's the body's natural response – our pupils contract, breathing deepens, our mood shifts. Light is what brings a room to life. It shapes how we see colour, how we read proportion, and ultimately, how we feel. I always think of light as the great editor, revealing what needs attention and softening what doesn't!

Daylight regulates our internal clock, setting the pace for alertness and rest. Morning light raises serotonin, bringing focus and vitality, while evening light encourages the melatonin that tells us it's time to unwind. It's no wonder that rooms flooded with natural light feel so energizing, while lamplight and candles at dusk feel comforting. Our bodies are naturally tuned to those changes.

This is why balance in light matters so much at home. Too much brightness and a space can feel exposed and restless; too little and it becomes heavy, the edges unclear. The art lies in the knowing where to let daylight flood in, and where to soften it. A shaft of sun across a wooden floor can bring joy, but it needs somewhere to rest – we don't want the entire room flooded with light or it will feel overexposed. This is why I find south-facing rooms the most challenging. Because south light doesn't gently arrive; it moves in, unpacking its bags for the day. You get full sun for hours, which means the colours shift dramatically between morning and late afternoon; whites can glare, whilst dark colours can look dusty, and mid-tones can bleach or flatten. Creating areas of shade will allow for shadow to calm the eye. Shadows give contrast and depth, allowing the room to breathe and be still.

Artificial lighting extends this rhythm after sunset. A well-balanced room holds both clarity and calm – ceiling lights for energy, lamps for intimacy, wall lights for warmth. It's never about the light itself, but the atmosphere it creates.

When light and shadow are in balance, a home feels alive. It responds to the time of day – the weather, the mood – shifting gently, just like we do.

→ We designed this playroom to grow with the family over time. The arched alcoves and built-in shelving give it a sense of permanence, while everything inside can change as the children grow. I love how the shadow in those recesses gives the shelves depth, letting the photo frames and baskets sit forward in the light rather than disappearing into the wall. It's a room built to flex, but never to feel temporary.

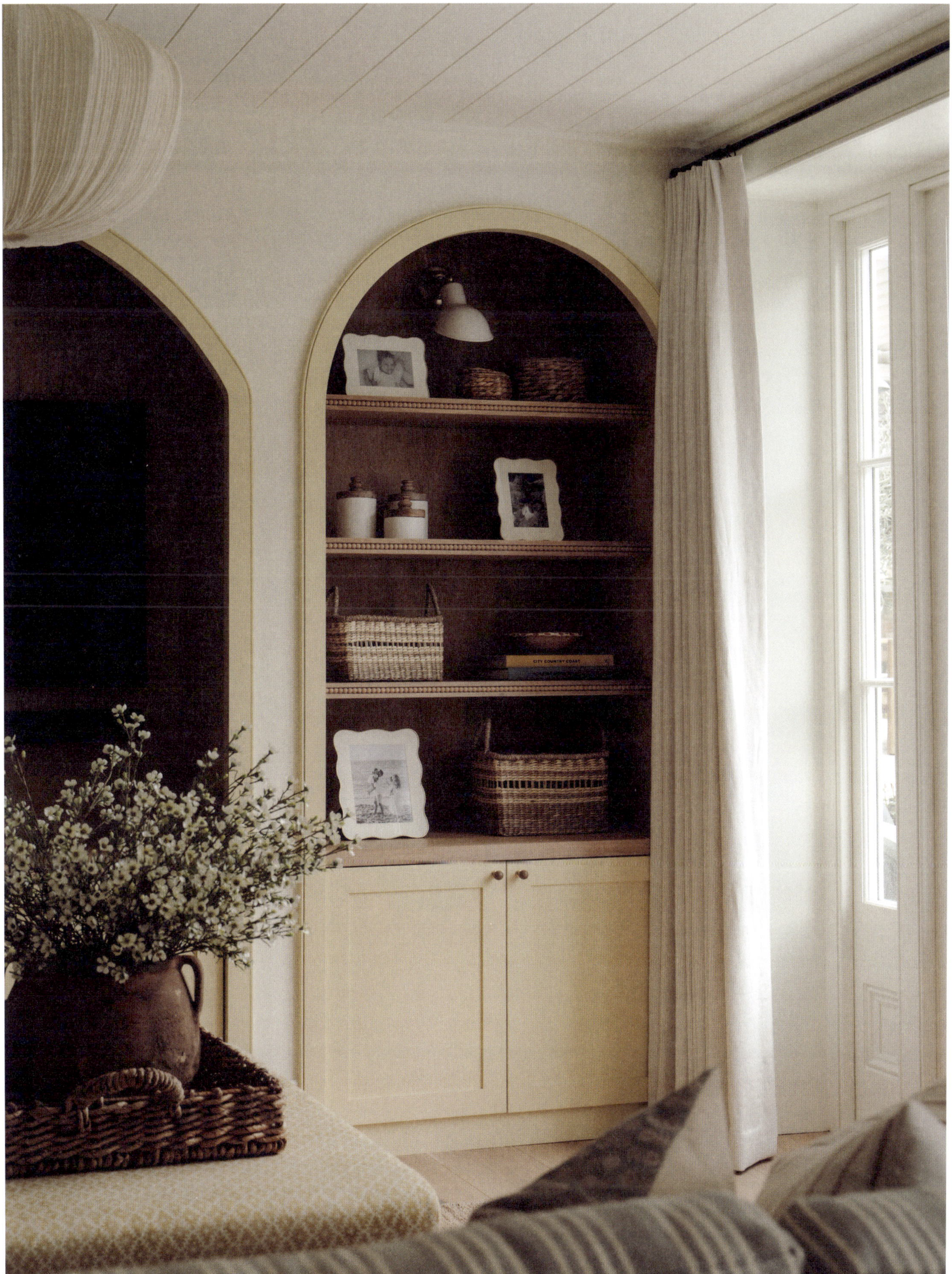

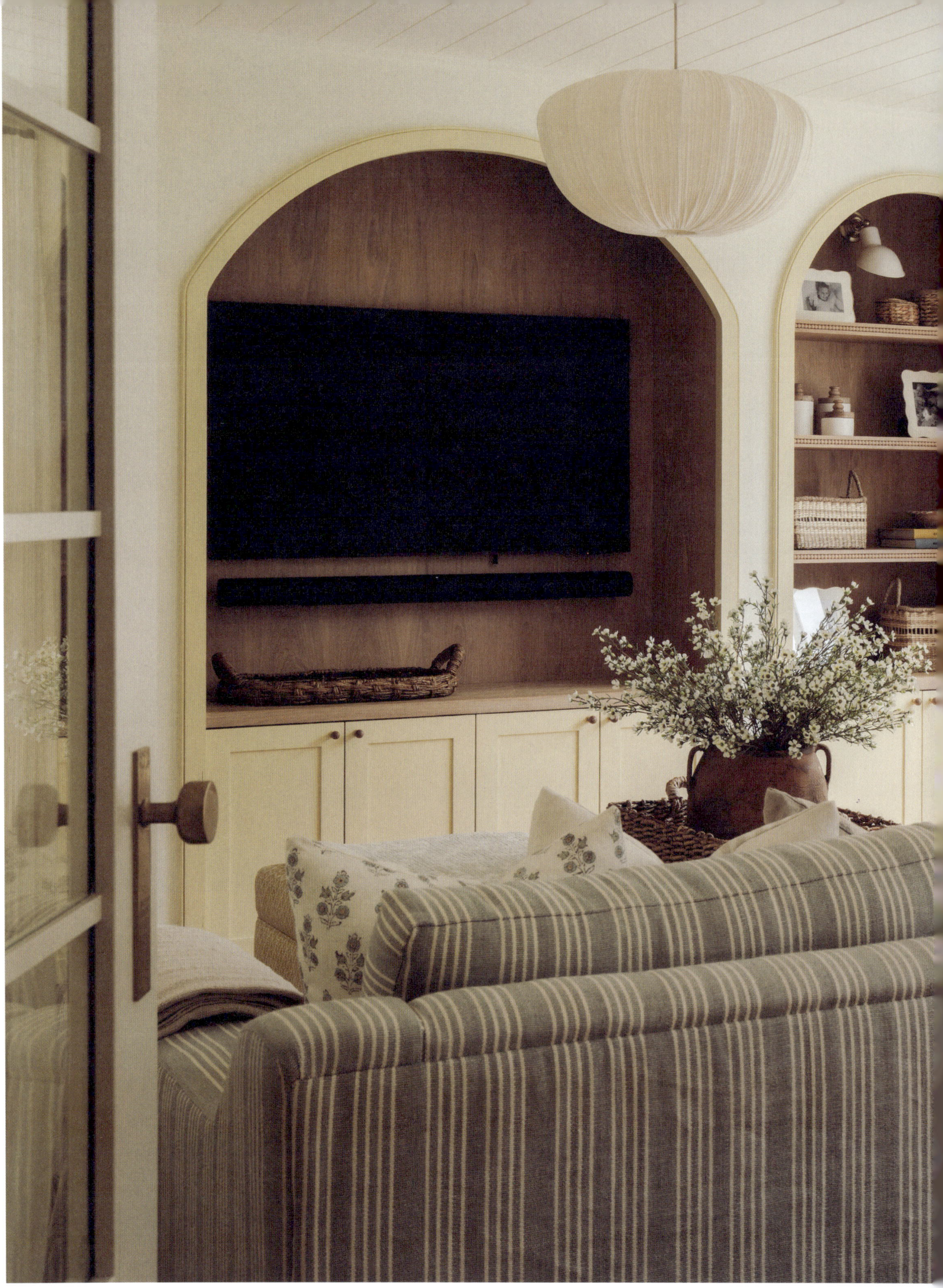

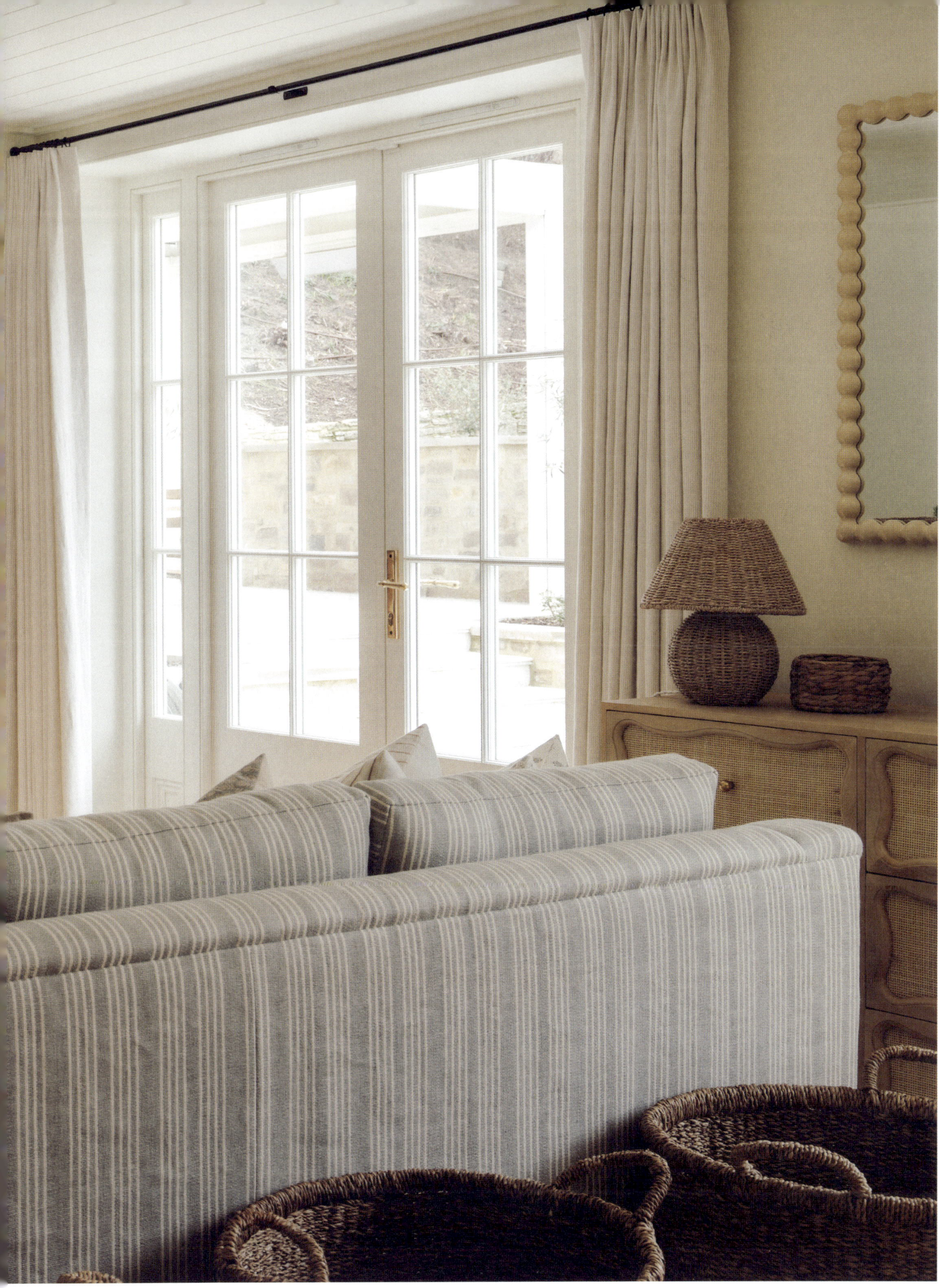

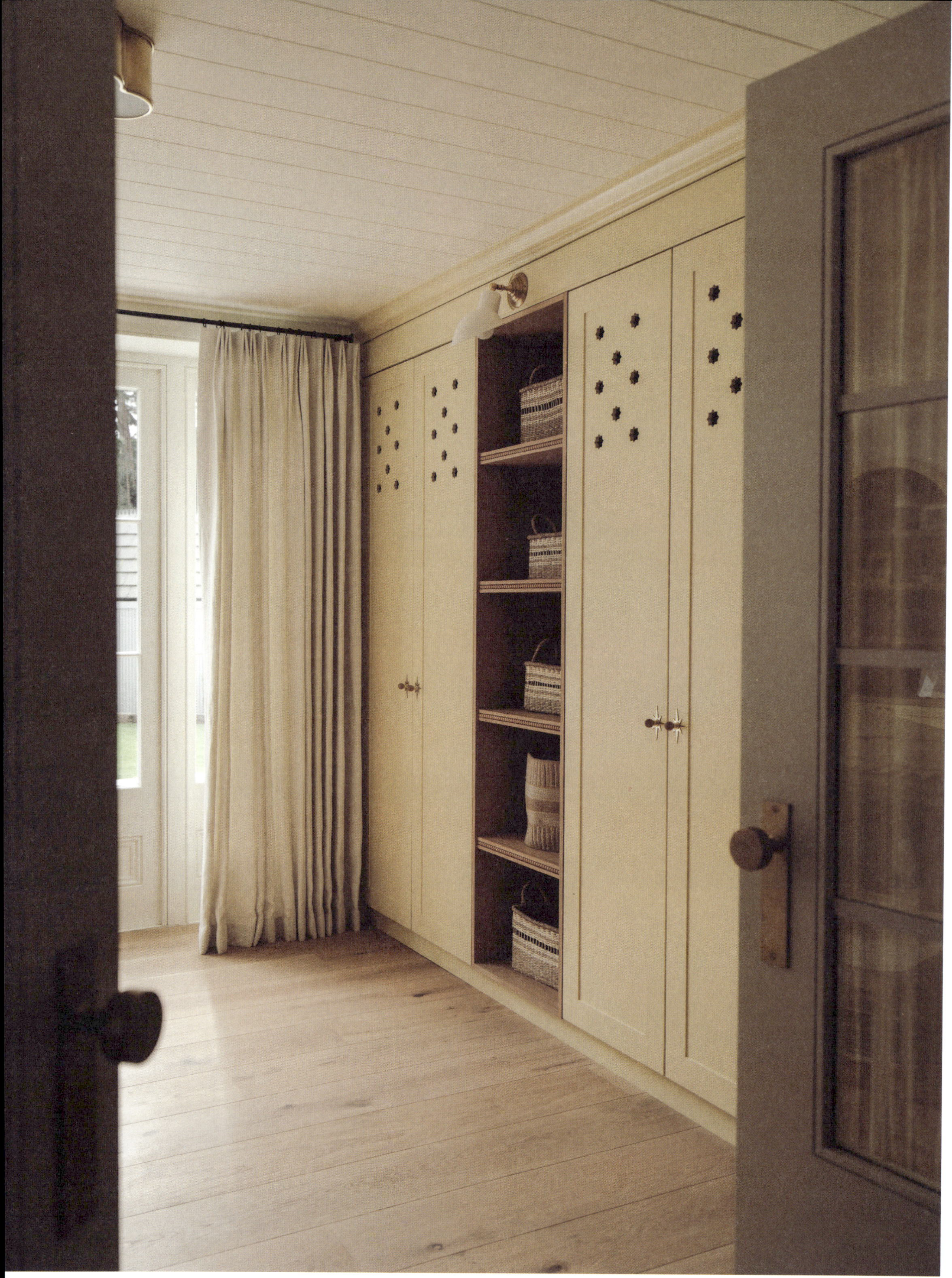

The Weight of Texture

> *"Light is what brings a room to life."*

Texture is what turns a room from something seen into something felt. It's the bridge between the visual and the physical – how surfaces meet the hand, how fabrics drape, how materials age over time. We often talk about colour or light when describing atmosphere, but I think it's texture that truly gives a home its depth. It's the element that makes a space feel lived in, layered, and tangibly real.

Every material carries its own kind of weight. Smooth marble, metal, or glass feels cool and refined; wool, linen, and timber bring warmth and softness. When everything is too polished, a room can feel sterile; when everything is rough or matte, it can feel heavy and dull. Balance's sweet spot lies in the contrast – gloss against matte, hard against soft, natural against man-made. These opposites allow each texture to heighten the other.

I love how texture changes and ages with time. I've had many a friendly tug-of-war with clients over choosing natural materials like marble or unlacquered brass, because sometimes you just have to abandon the quest for absolute practicality. Timber that grows warmer with age, honed marble that softens around the edges, linen that happily creases, metal that develops a quiet little patina – these are the beautiful signs of a home being lived in, not preserved. Perfection can feel a bit flat; character comes from materials that evolve, shift, and tell their own story. Embrace the imperfections – they're what make a space feel loved, lived-with, and wonderfully human.

Lighting also plays its role with texture. A slant of daylight across plaster, or lamplight catching the weave of a fabric, gives depth and life to a room. Texture also invites subtle shadow – it creates the quiet interplay between roughness and reflection that keeps a room visually grounded.

Ultimately, balance in texture is about feeling. You can sense when a room is too smooth or too busy, just as you can sense when it's right. A mix of materials that speak to one another – wool beside stone, brass near oak – bring softness, rhythm, and a grounded calm. It's the tactility of home, the comfort of surfaces that invite us to touch, and the beauty of those that bear the marks of time.

Balance is never something you achieve once and for all. Much like life, it's a careful and constant juggling act, something we keep on tuning as the years unfold. Furniture grows tired, seasons changes, families grow, and then they shrink – the house evolves with change and our changing needs. What remains constant is the feeling and that quiet sense of ease when everything sits just as it should. A balanced home doesn't ask for attention; it simply supports you, gently, and without fuss every changing day.

← Texture does a lot of the talking in this room. I love the contrast between the smooth, buttery yellow cabinetry with timber shelving and the rough weave of the baskets tucked inside - hard against soft.

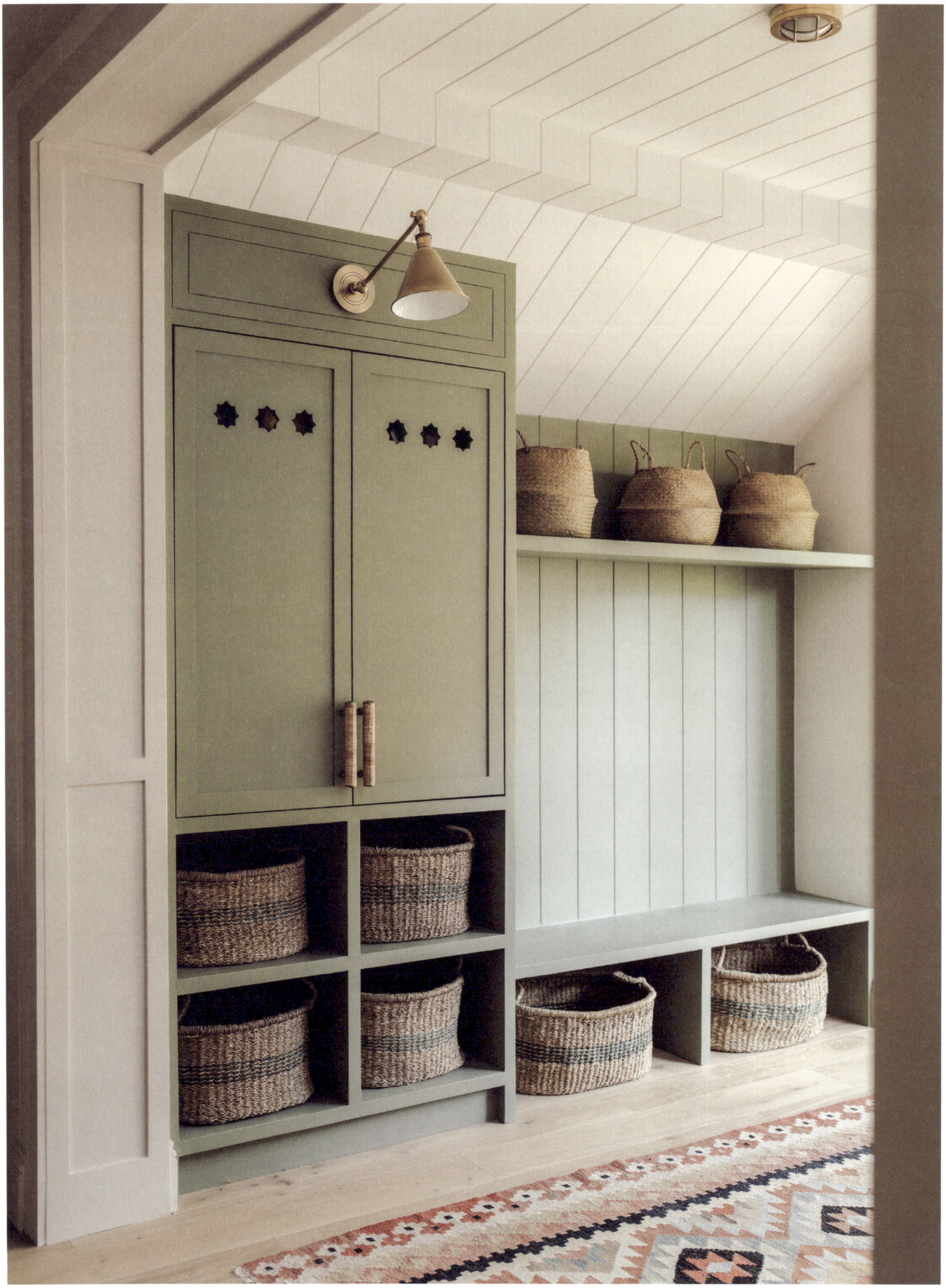

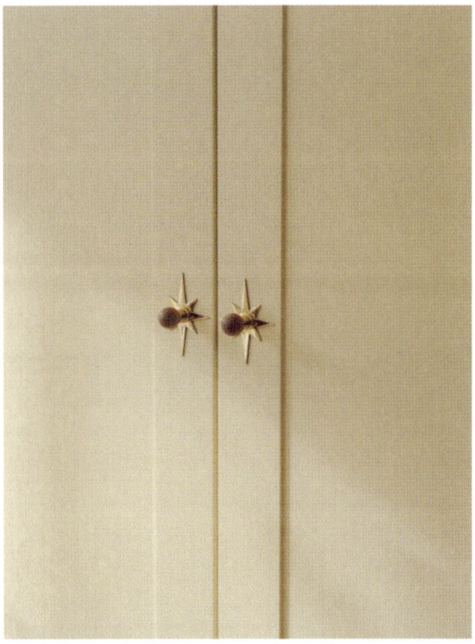

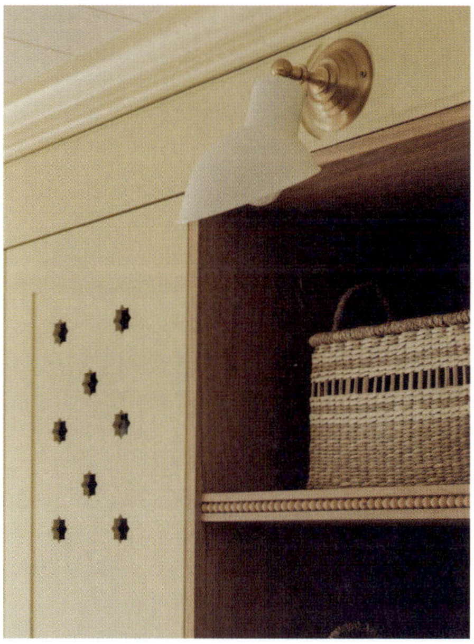

← Rarely will you catch one of my designs without a basket or two. They're the perfect, affordable way to bring in texture.

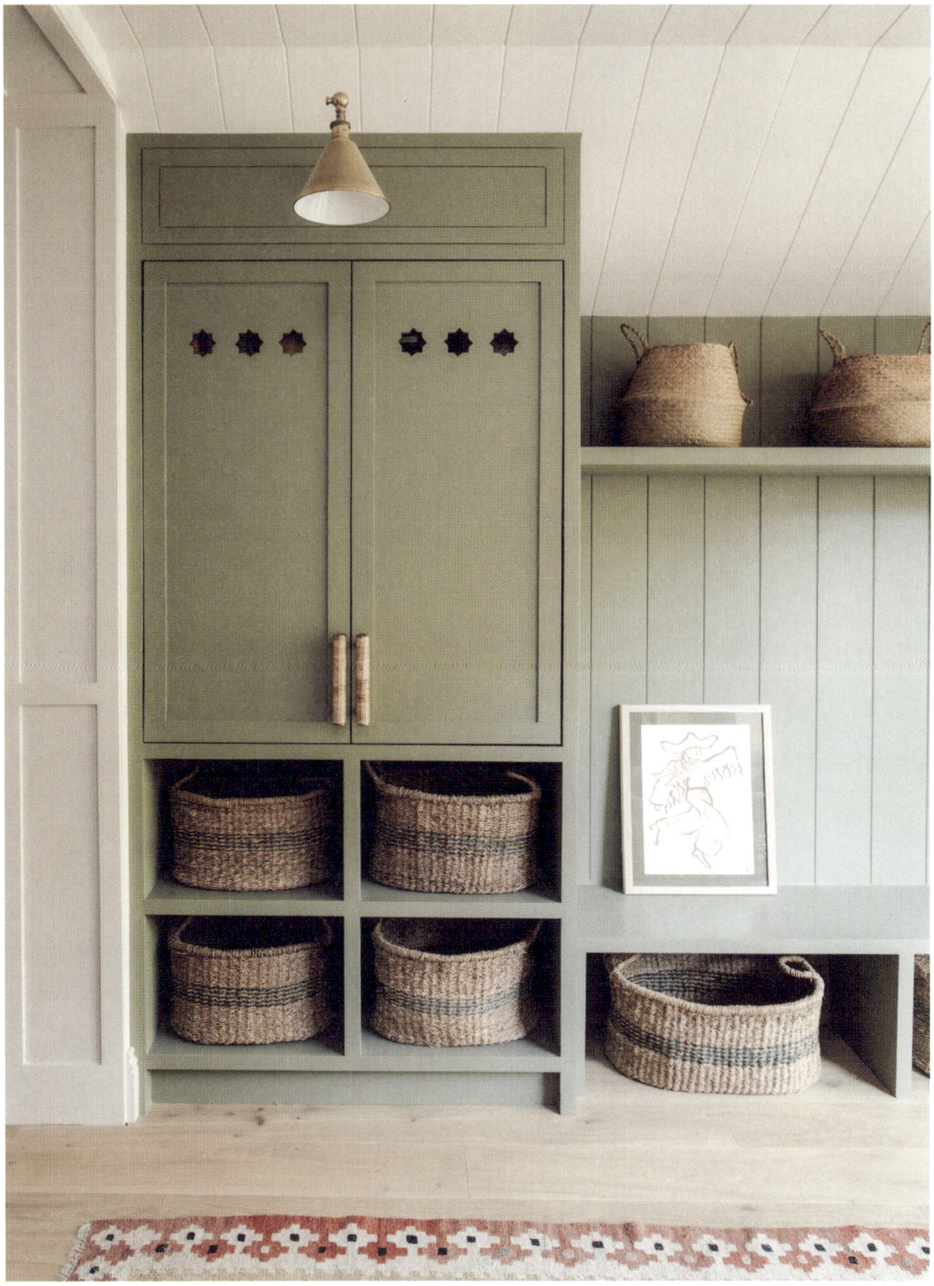

"It's texture that truly gives a home its depth."

← A little detail I'm especially fond of: star cut-outs on the joinery in both playrooms. They catch the light differently throughout the day, so the room never feels static, and they bring a sense of fun to all that practical storage.

Restore a Sense of Ease

Follow these easy prompts to help you see where balance might be missing, and how small shifts in scale, light, or placement can restore a sense of ease and stability.

1. BALANCE IS A FEELING, NOT A FORMULA

You sense it before you can explain it, that quiet "ah, yes" when a room just settles.
Try this: Stand in the doorway of each room. Does anything feel too heavy on one side? Too empty on another? A simple shift – moving a chest of drawers, a lamp, swapping cushions, or removing a piece of artwork – can bring the whole room back into alignment.

---

2. START WITH PROPORTION

Balance begins with how your furniture and objects relate to the architecture around them.
Practise: Grab some masking tape and map out the footprint of the main furniture. Are they too large, too small? Adjust the layout until your body moves easily and the room feels calmer.

---

3. OPPOSITES BRING HARMONY

Straight lines need curves; chunky shapes need something slender; soft textures need structure.
Mini exercise: Do a quick "shape audit". If everything feels square or solid, add one curved or lighter piece. If the room feels too soft, introduce something with a cleaner, more defined line.

---

4. COLOUR CARRIES WEIGHT

Dark tones anchor; light tones lift; warm and cool tones balance each other beautifully.
Try this: Choose one room that feels a little flat. Add a grounding tone (a deeper rug or darker timber accent) if it feels floaty, or lighten something (a throw or a lampshade) if it feels heavy.

---

5. LET LIGHT BE YOUR GUIDE

Balance shifts with the sun – too much light feels exposed, too little feels murky.
Practise: Spend five minutes in the room in the morning, afternoon, and evening. Notice where light floods and where it disappears. Add a sheer curtain or reposition a mirror to even things out.

---

6. TEXTURE STABILISES A SPACE

Smooth needs rough; matte needs gloss; natural textures need something refined.
Try this: Touch everything. If the room feels too sleek or one-note, add one contrasting material – a woven basket, a wool throw, a timber bowl. See how quickly the space settles.

---

7. LEAVE ROOM TO BREATHE.

Empty space isn't always missing something; it's giving the eye a place to rest.
Do this: Clear one surface – a side table, windowsill, or mantle – and live with it for forty-eight hours. Feel how that single moment of stillness balances the energy of the entire room.

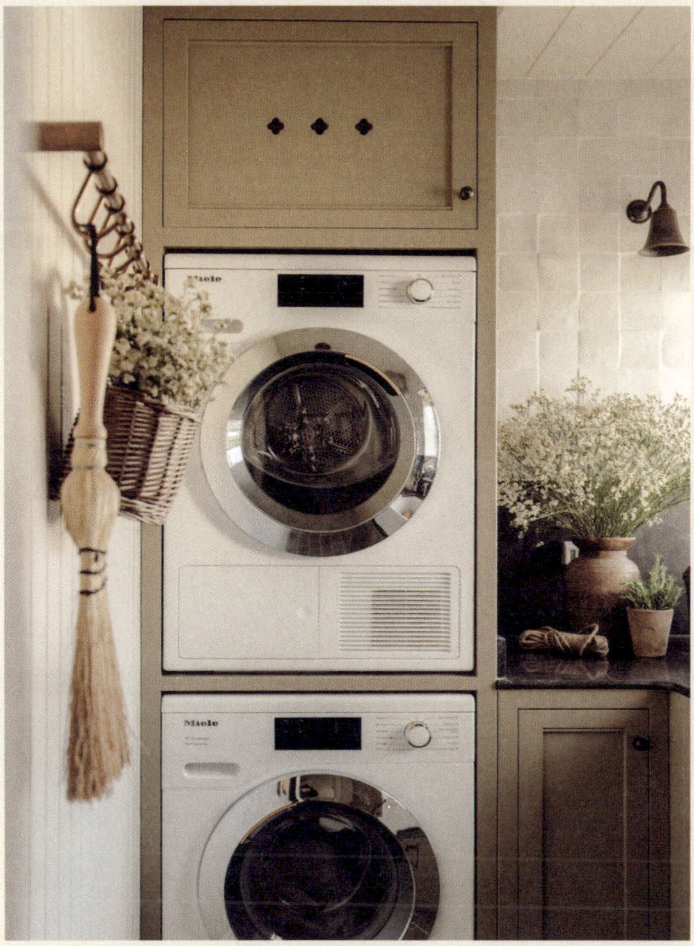
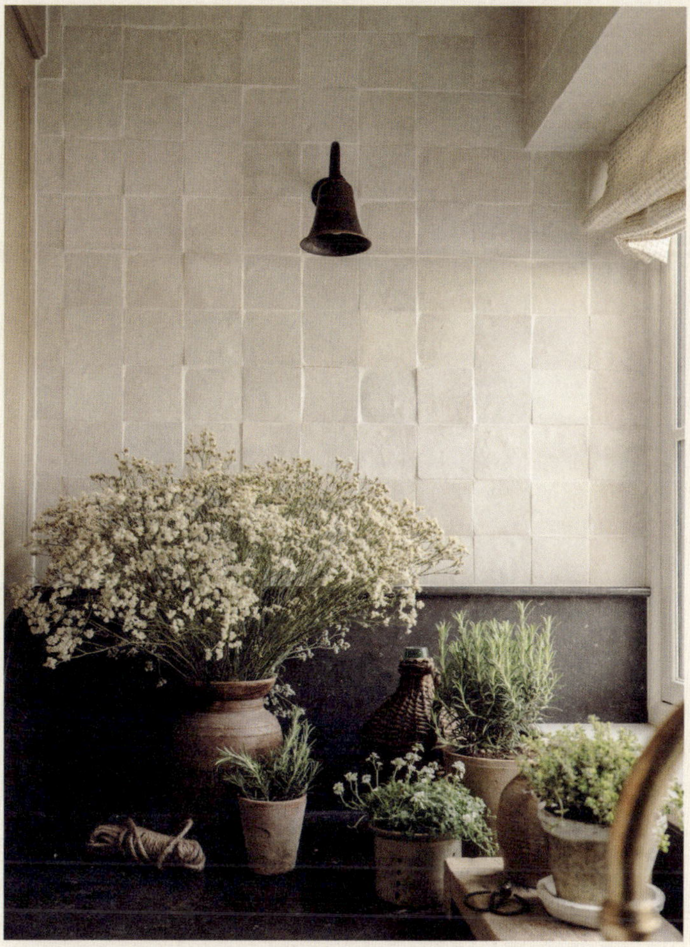
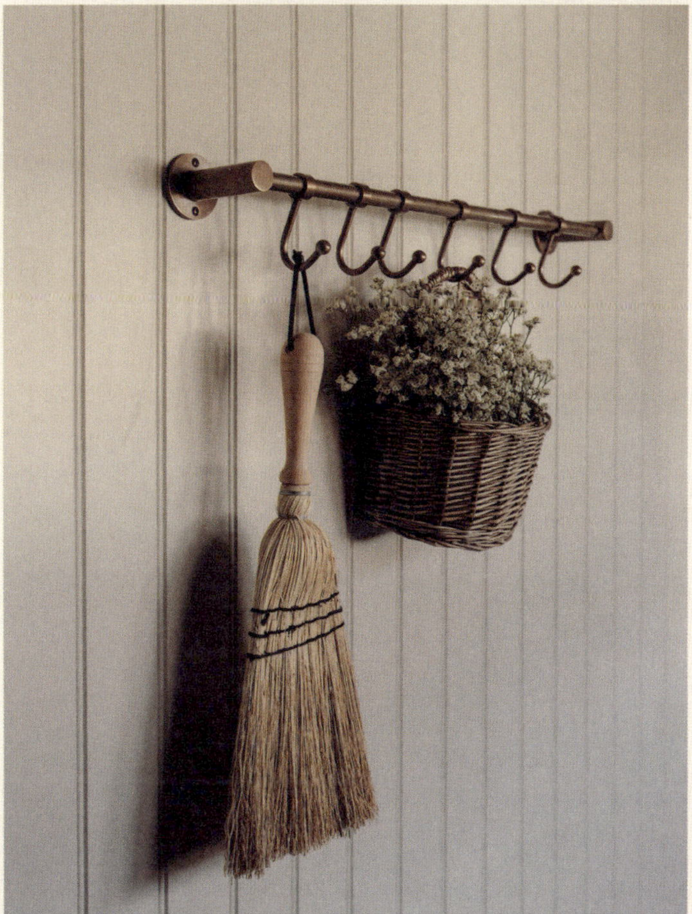
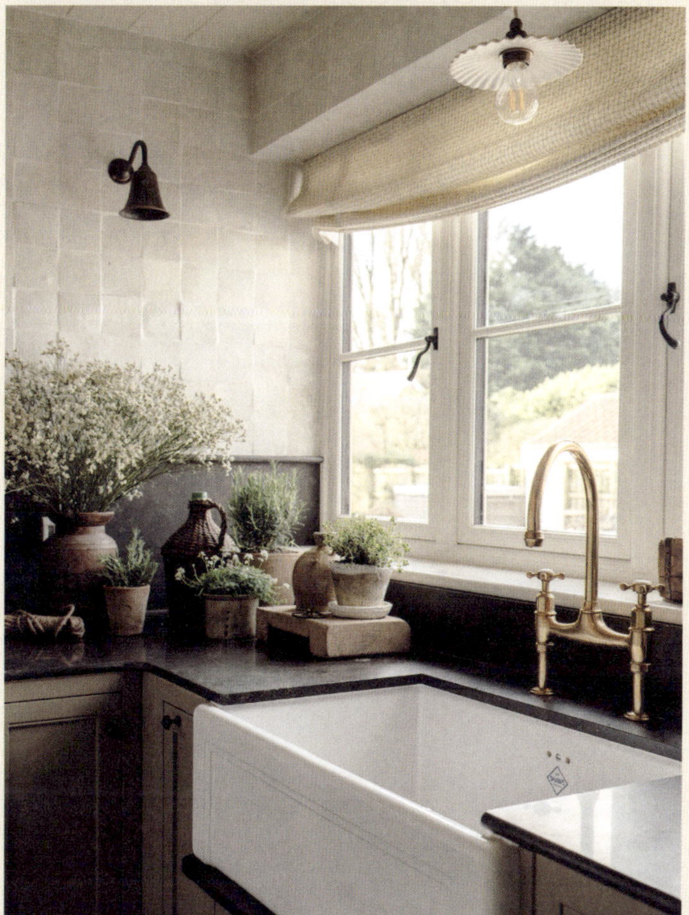

“Layering in different patterns will keep things from appearing too studied.”

NATE BERKUS

Layer

ADD DEPTH AND WARMTH

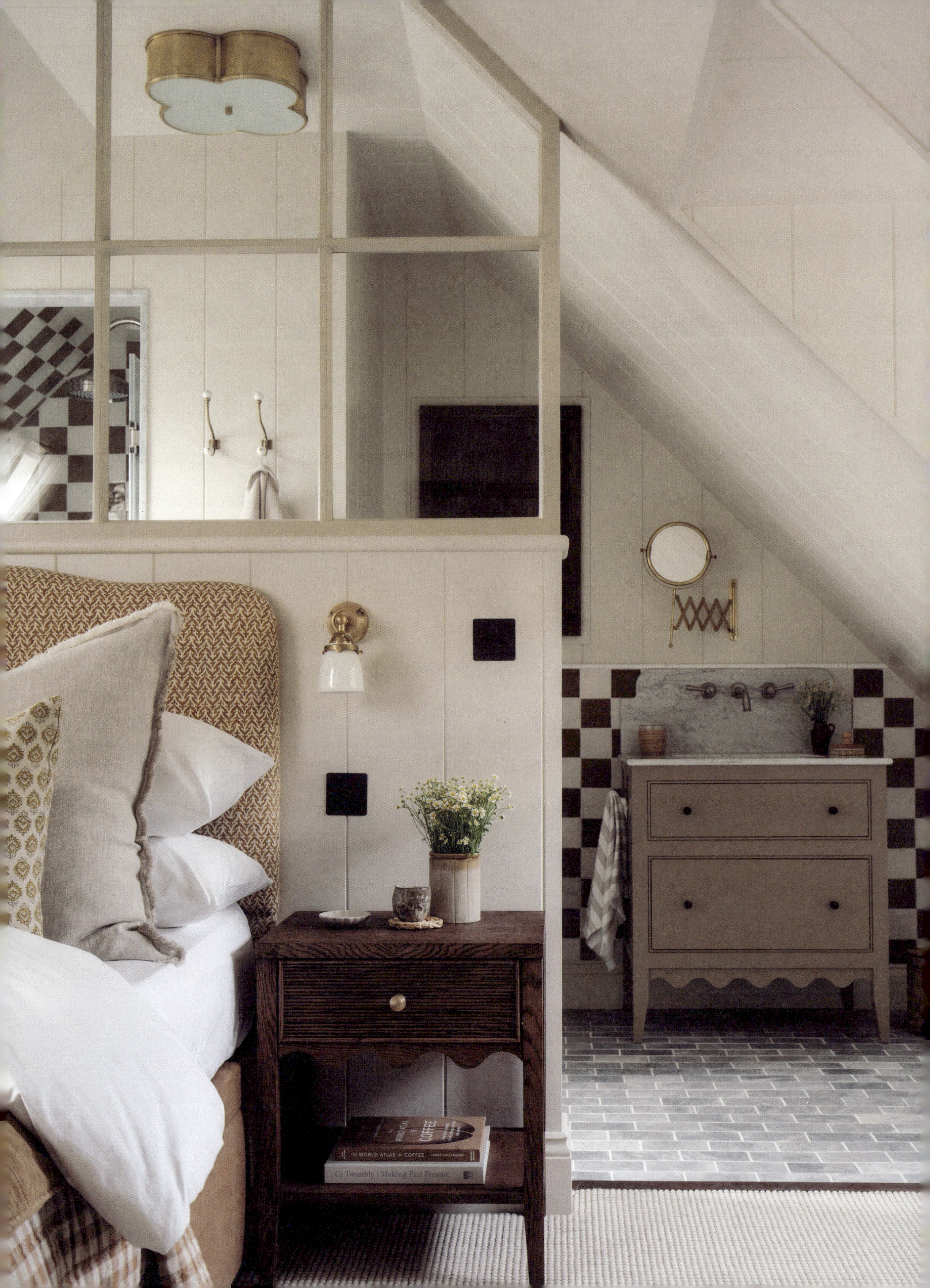
THE WORLD ATLAS OF COFFEE JAMES HOFFMANN
Cy Twombly | Making Past Present

THE ART OF *LAYERING*

A home without layers is like a flat white with no velvety top – fine, but missing the "Mmmmm". It's the same feeling I get when I walk into a flat room. A room needs depth, softness, contrast – the things that make you want to reach out and touch. Layering is what turns a good room into a great one. It's what makes a house feel lived in, not just looked at.

← This guest loft bedroom at Project Springbank is layering in action. The herringbone headboard, the scalloped edge of the bedside table, the checkerboard tile in the ensuite, nothing here is matching for the sake of it, and that's exactly the point. Every material brings its own texture, each one creating a little friction with the next. It's the kind of room you can't quite put your finger on why it works; you just know you don't want to leave.

People always ask what makes a room feel "House Nine". I talk about proportion, light, and flow – but really, it's the throw that does it. And the baskets, of course. And the cushions. And the books, and the candles, and the pots of all different shapes, ages, and sizes. Layering is our secret sauce. It's what makes a home feel warm, tactile, and just the right side of imperfect.

Layering is what draws you to sink into a sofa rather than just admire it. It's the weight of a linen throw at the end of the bed, the softness of a couple of velvet cushions, or a stack of books with a trinket dish and a candle on top. I like to think it's what we're known for at House Nine – those extra touches that create familiarity and soul and make a home feel not just lived in, but unique. I love to create rooms where you can't quite put your finger on why it feels so inviting; you just know you don't want to leave.

It begins with tone and texture. Just as colour carries emotion, texture carries temperature. Coarse slubby linen, smooth characterful oak, honed marble with its unique veining, raw nubby jute – each one creates subtle shifts in our atmosphere. You can have a perfectly balanced palette, but without tactile depth, it will always feel a little "Meh". Layering introduces a kind of friction – the good kind – where something rough meets something soft, or something old sits beside something new. It's this interplay that creates visual comfort and complexity, a subtle richness and depth that draws you in.

Tone is the quiet teacher in all this. It's what keeps everything playing nicely together. In good design, tones should be layered in the same way a musician builds a track – some light, some

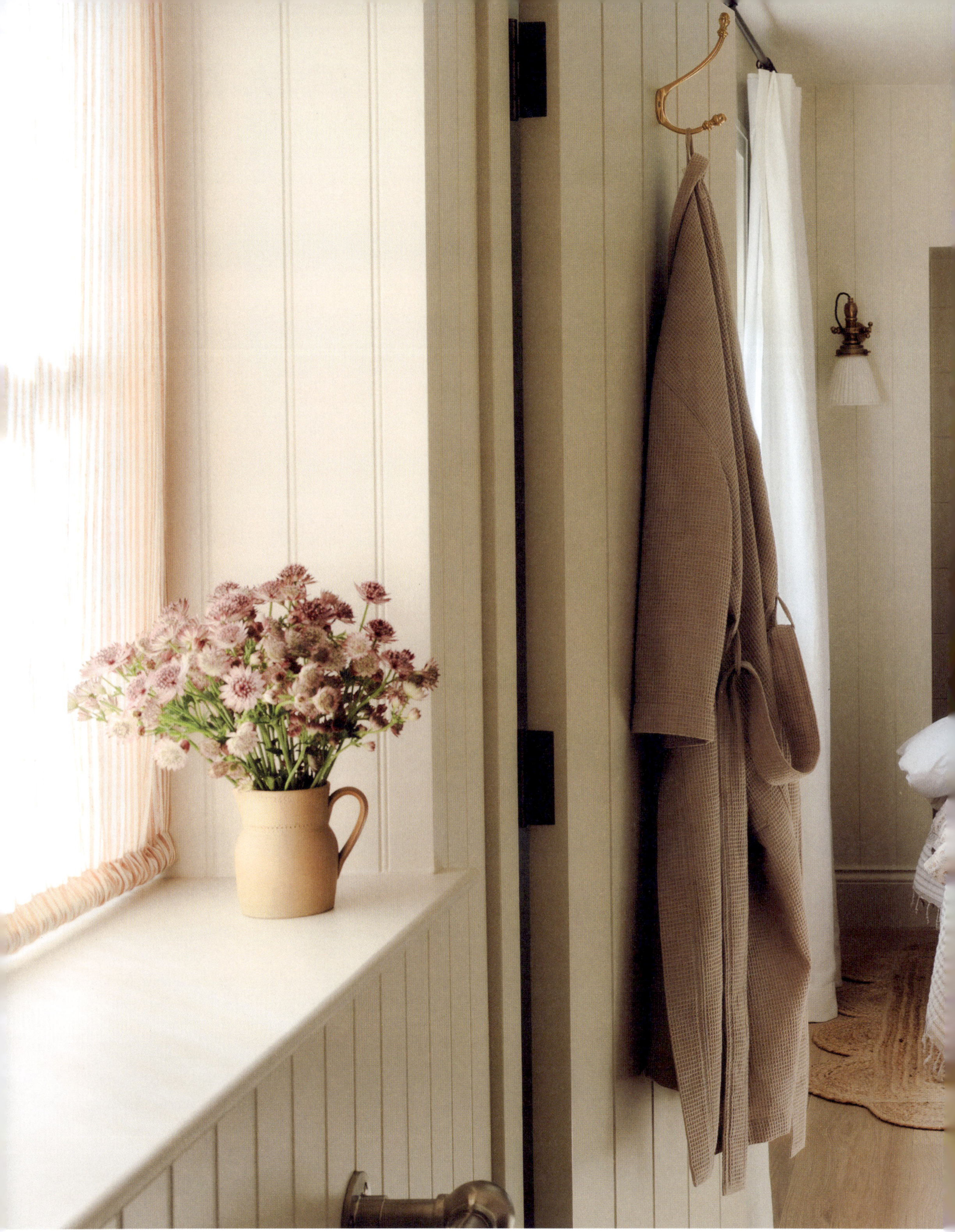

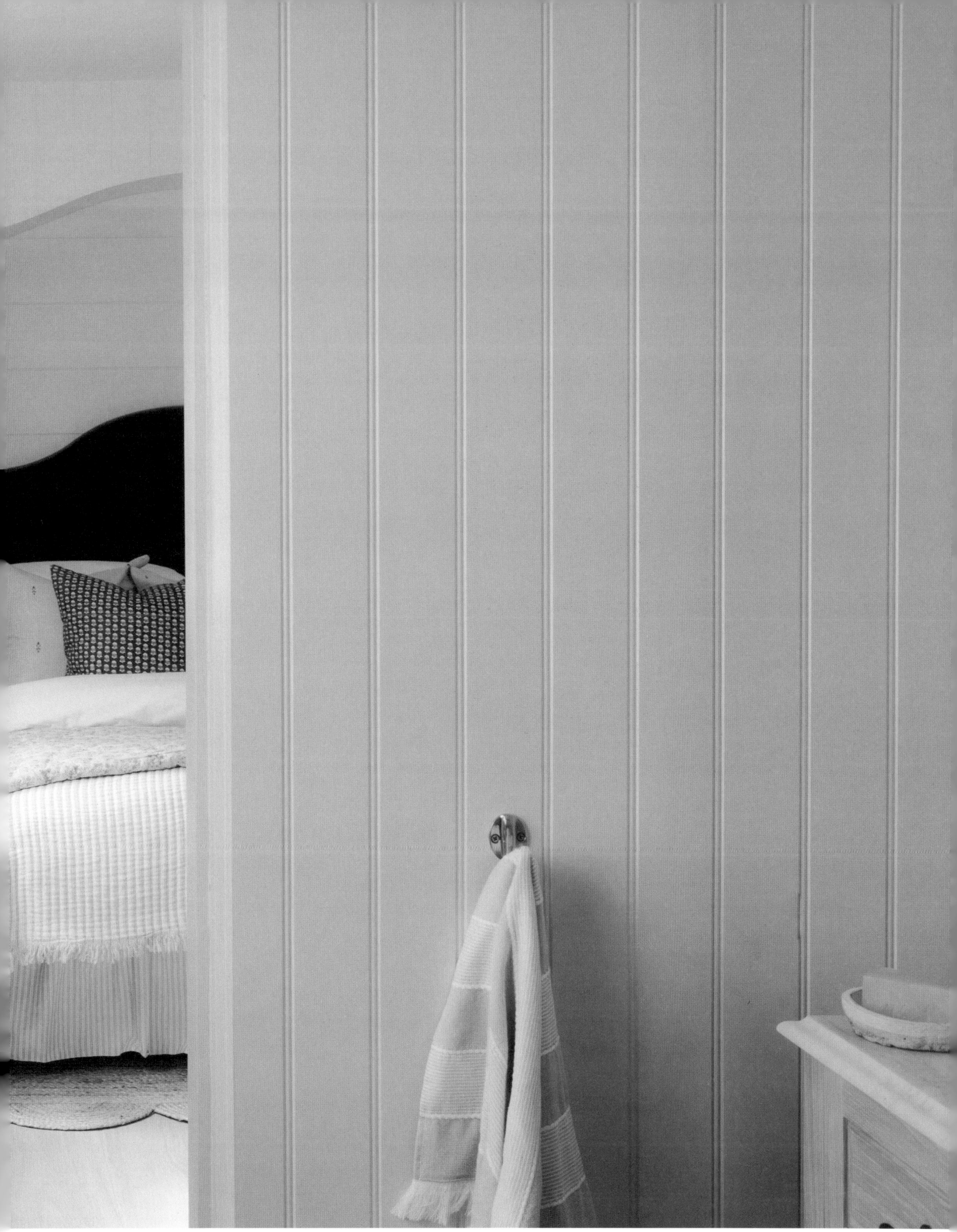

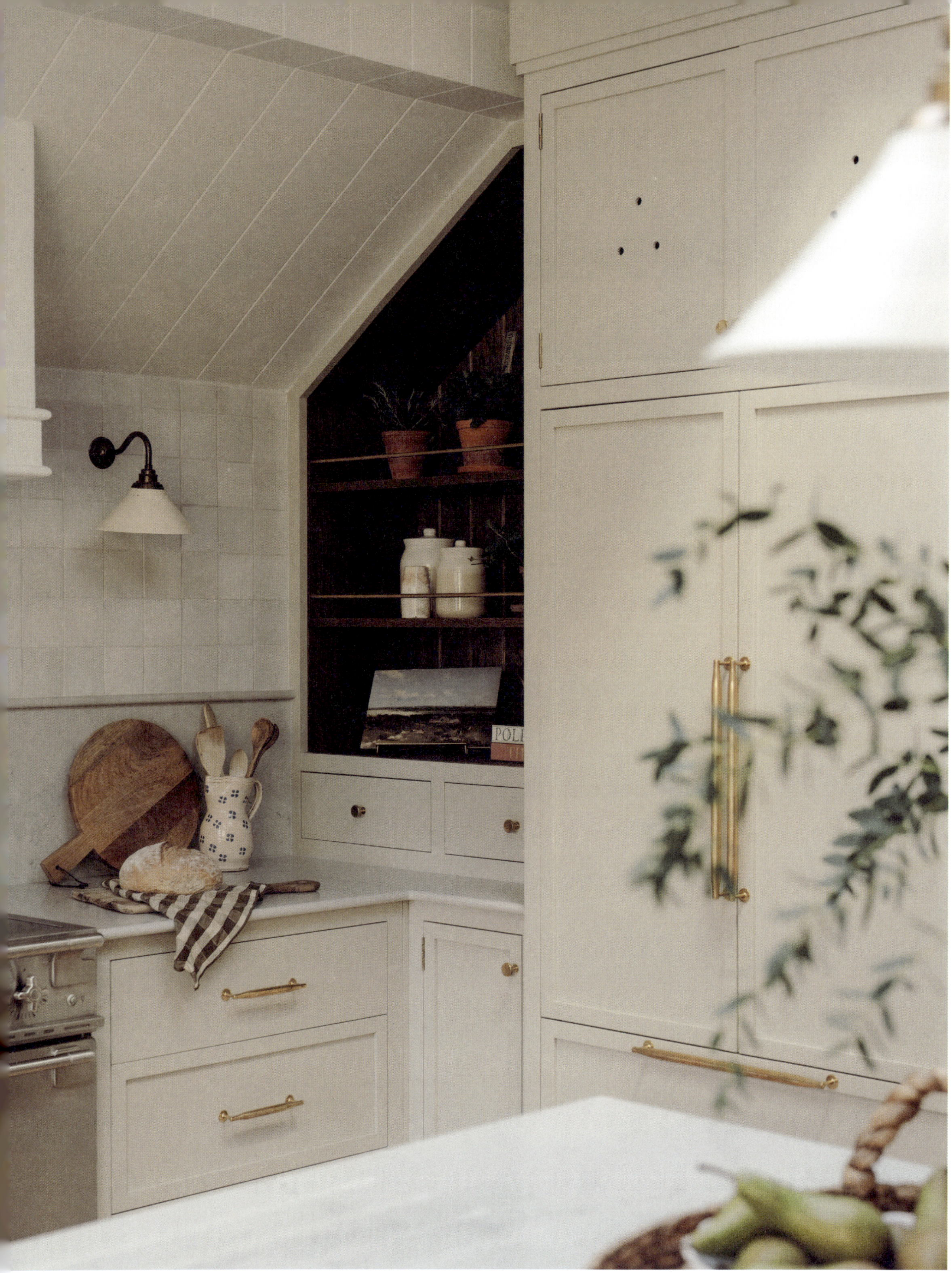

deep, some barely there but vital to the whole mix. The soft chalkiness of a wall colour, the muted patina of brass, the grounding feeling of a woven rug underfoot – they all add depth without shouting for attention.

There's also something so deeply human about layering. We layer naturally in all walks of our life, be it in our clothes in winter, the ingredients we use in cooking, plants in the garden throughout the seasons. A well-layered home tells a story of the people who live there. Layering doesn't mean mess, it just says: "Life happens here." These layers build connection. They soften the edges of design and replace perfection with personality.

Much like our clothes, I'm a firm believer in changing layers with the seasons. In summer, you can strip off – linen covers, light cottons, fewer cushions, open shelves. Come autumn, the textures deepen again – wool, mohair, heavier weaves. Candles come out, blankets pile up, and the palette feels warmer and cosier. These small, tactile changes make the home feel in tune with nature, responsive rather than static – and they also stop you from getting bored with the things you own. Pack them away in a box or drawer and you'll look forward to seeing them again, much like your Christmas decorations.

The hardest part of layering? Stopping. Once you start, it's addictive – one more cushion here, a candle there, a bowl that suddenly feels necessary. But layering isn't about quantity; it's about balance. If you can remove a few things and the room still feels complete, you've nailed it. The goal is for your home to feel relaxed, not rehearsed – like it's been built up naturally over time, not styled within an inch of its life.

Really, the best-layered homes aren't the ones with the most stuff – they're the ones that feel most like you. There's no one-size-fits-all when it comes to layering; every home, like every person, has its own rhythm. What follows isn't a rulebook as such, just my own advice into how I like to approach layering, with a few gentle pointers drawn from years of playing with tone, texture, and balance. We'll wander through the bedroom, living room, and kitchen together – the spaces that work the hardest – and hopefully you'll find a few ideas to make your own along the way.

"Layering is what turns a good room into a great one."

← This kitchen, in our Project All About You, is a good example of layering that tells a story rather than just decorating a wall. The open shelving holds the things this family actually uses: plants, jars, a stack of cookbooks. The brass hardware repeats throughout, tying it all together without ever feeling matched. It's a kitchen that looks like it's been built up naturally over time.

The Bedroom

> *"The goal is softness and ease, not perfection."*

Bedrooms should feel calm and cocooning places to rest. I'm a firm believer that the bedroom should be our private sanctuary (sometimes reluctantly shared with another), so everything in it should make you exhale a little. The goal is softness and ease, not perfection. I always think of the bed as our nest – somewhere to burrow into and pretend the outside world doesn't exist. In feng shui, bedrooms are all about flow, so to avoid clutter and let the bedroom breathe, keep surfaces simple, choose natural materials that feel grounding, and use light that flatters rather than floods.

In spring and summer, it's time to ease up on the layers. The light changes, the air shifts, and your bedding should follow suit. Swap heavier duvets for breathable linen or crisp cotton – natural fibres that feel fresh against the skin. Keep the layers lighter and cut back on the cushions – no one wants to fight through a mountain of them when it's 25°C (77°F) at midnight. Keep it simple, fresh, and cool.

This is also the time to play with softer colour. Leaning on nature again for inspiration, opt for brighter whites, soft yellows, gentle greens, or those small hints of blue that make everything feel light and open. Even a simple stripe can give a fresh relaxed feel; there is something so timeless and nostalgic about stripes. The idea is to make the bedroom feel airy, calm, and restful, like it's just opened the windows and invited the sunshine in. Come autumn and winter, it's a different story. This is where layering really earns its place. Lean into those delicious autumnal shades. Bring in the heavier bedspreads, thick throws, and yes, all the cushions. Now's the time for depth and warmth, when we turn to our homes for comfort and hibernation.

I love a full, generous bed that makes you want to climb in and disappear for a solid eight plus hours. Add texture with wool, mohair, or velvet, and break up big blocks of colour with a lighter throw draped across the top. It gives the bed movement and stops it feeling heavy.

As for bedside tables, they're your business. I have no hard and fast styling advice here – they should hold whatever makes you sleep well and wake up happy. The book you're halfway through, your favourite candle, a glass of water, your mobile phone – no judgment here. These aren't mini design moments; they're small, personal stations for comfort.

Even with all that comfort, a bedroom should still feel calm. Keep the palette soft, the lighting warm, and let the fabrics do most of the talking. When a room feels restful before you've even turned the light off – that's when you've layered it right.

→ A bed you want to disappear into is usually always the goal. This burnt red velvet headboard in the Project Hastings House guest bedroom brings warmth and a little fun, softened by layers of colour, pattern, and texture in the cushions and throw, and down onto the sisal carpet. The rattan bedside table holds exactly what it should: a lamp, a book, fresh flowers.

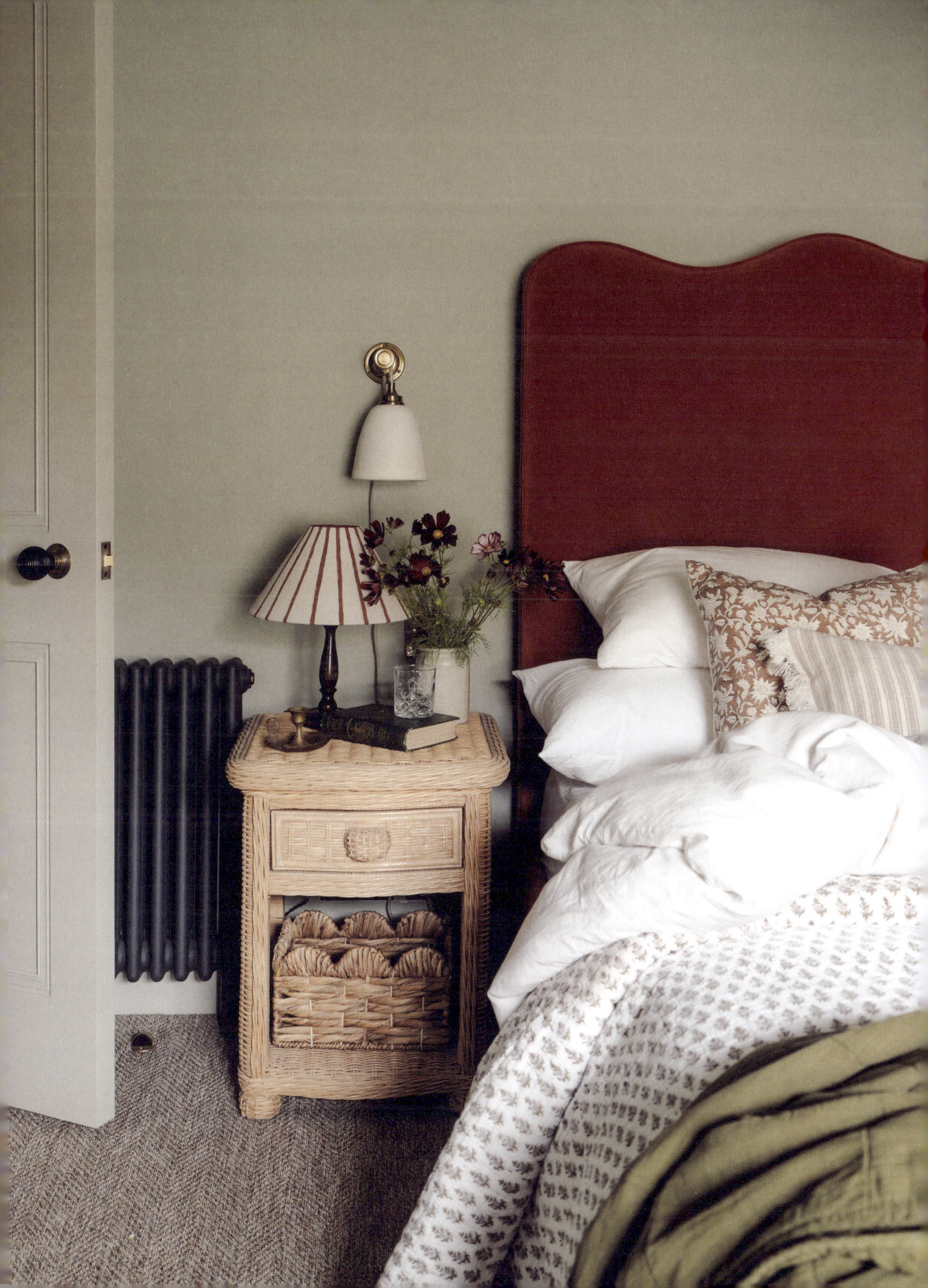

↓ → The guest bedrooms at Project Ziggy Rocks are layering at its most restful. Nothing jars against the view out of the window. Striped bed skirts, checked curtains, scalloped pelmets – nothing matches exactly, but everything sits in the same soft, earthy family of tone. I love a bed dressed like this, duvets and throws folded back, cushions plumped and layered in different patterns, room left for guests to climb in and make it their own.

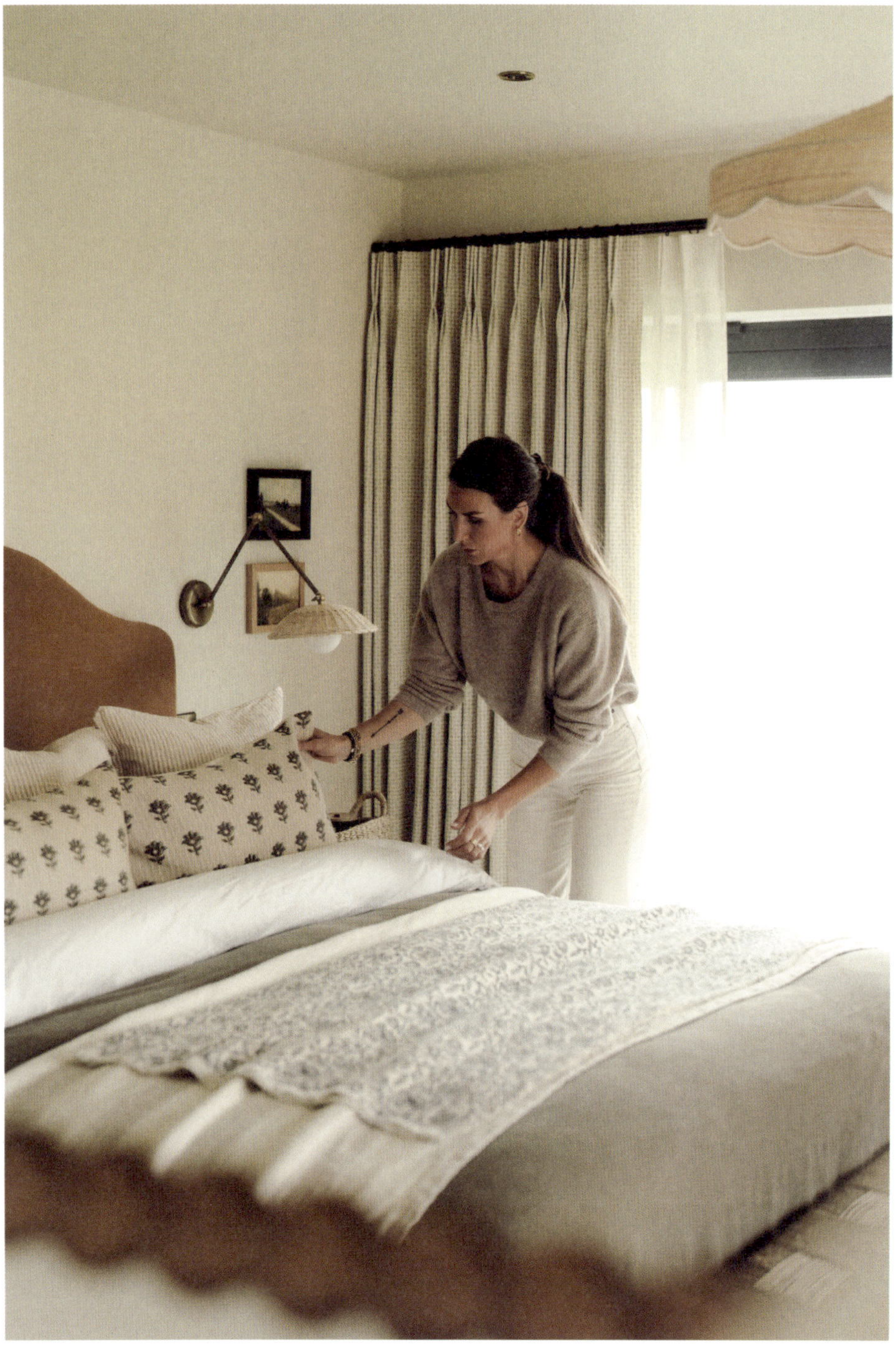

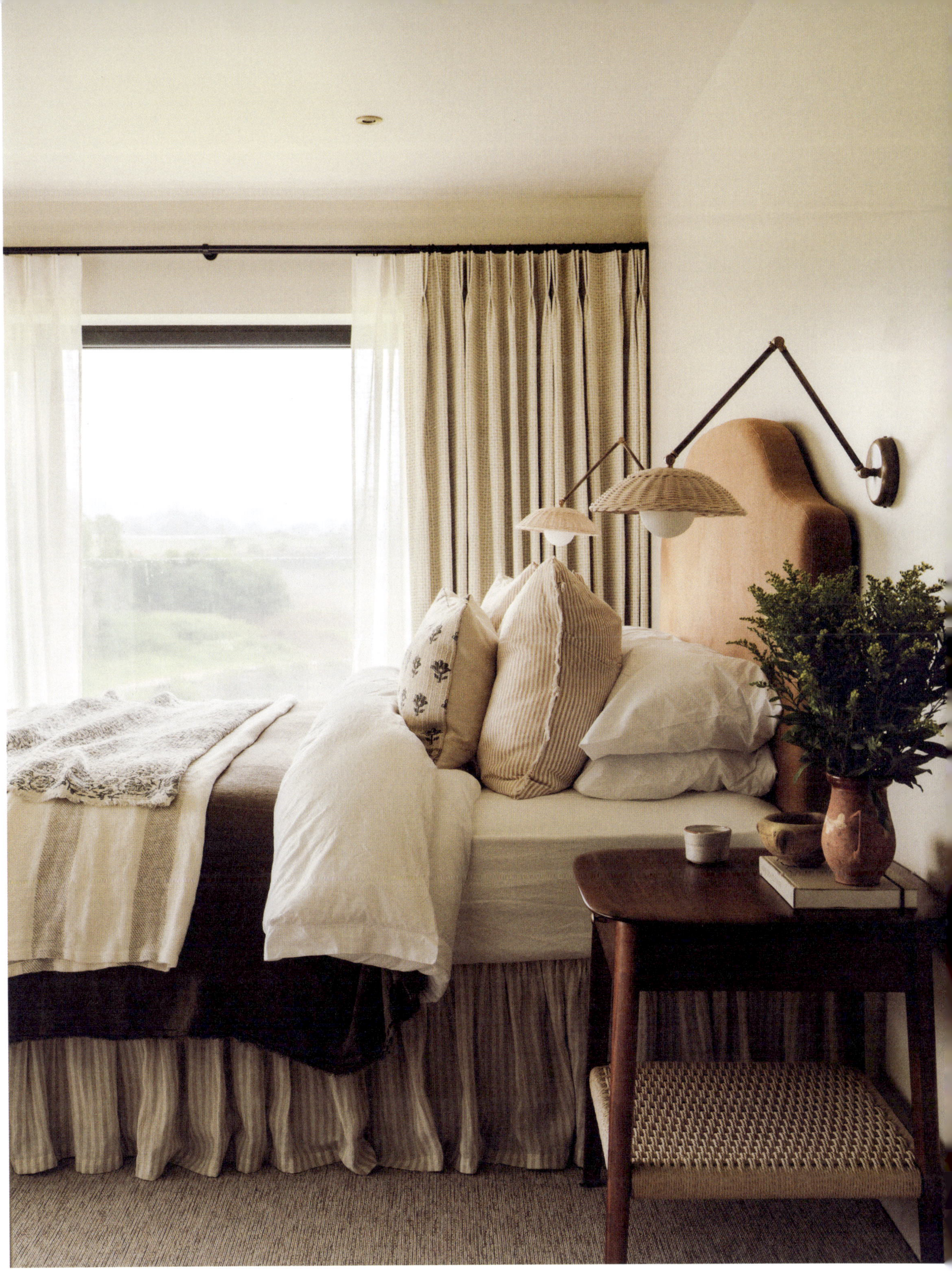

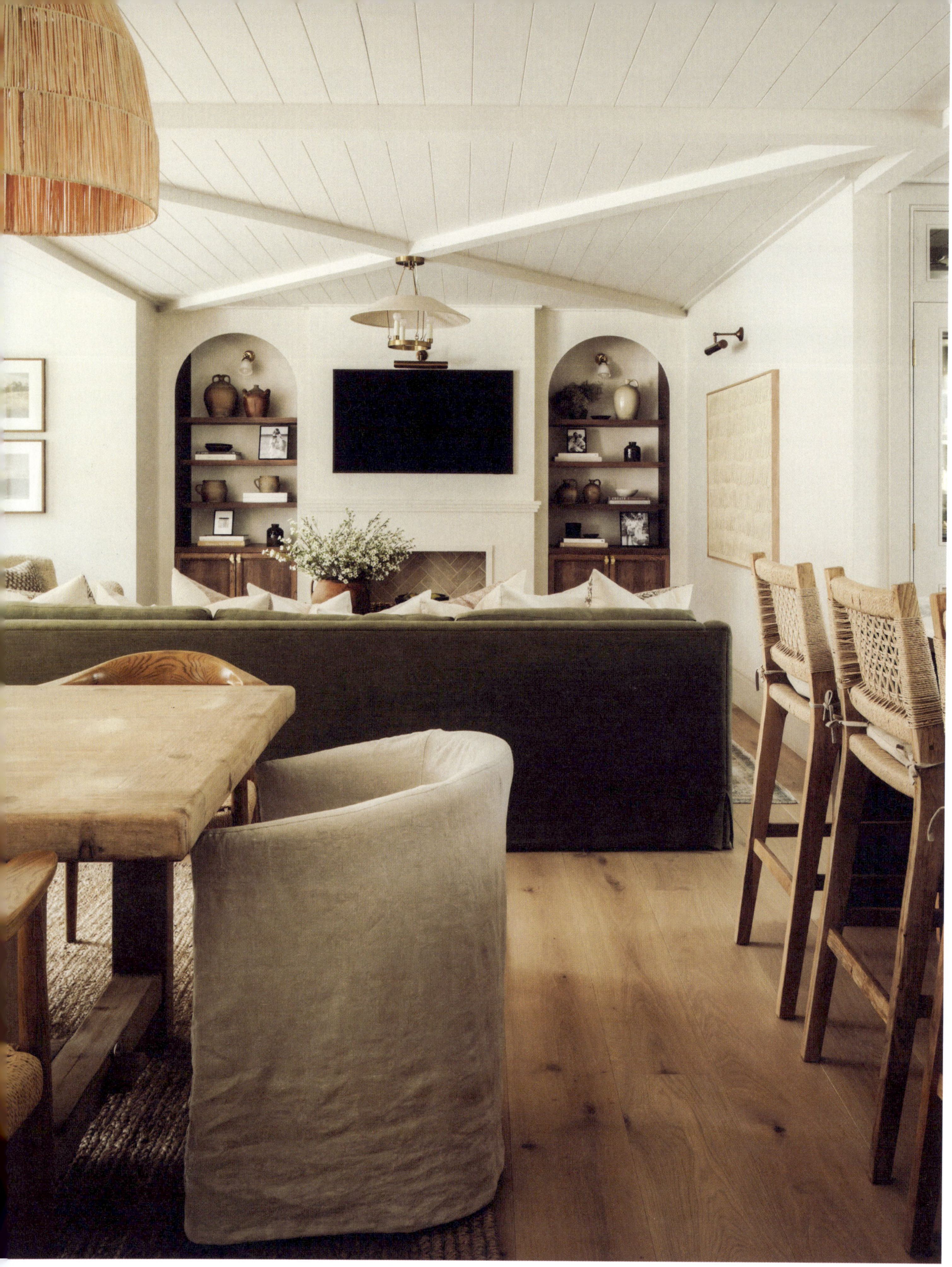

← The living room at Project Sandbanks is gently layered from the ceiling down. This was a new build, but the architectural details don't let you believe it. The green sofa anchors the space, while books and pots are layered evenly across the arched alcoves. A mix of pendant and wall lighting throughout the room keeps it warm from every angle, comfortable, collected, and quietly under control.

→ → The living room at Project Springbank shows what happens when you build slowly, one layer at a time. All furnishings are anchored on a large Persian rug. The bouclé armchairs in front of the window and that deep rust sofa sit in conversation rather than competition, with a brass drum side table bridging the two.

The Living Room

The living room wears a lot of hats. It's where we rest, socialise, watch TV, and play with the kids – sometimes all at once. It needs to feel relaxed enough to kick your shoes off, but still put together for our own sanity – or when someone unexpectantly drops by. That's where layering earns its keep.

Start with the big pieces. Think about your furniture first – the sofa, the armchairs, and the coffee table. These are your anchors, so remember, we want these to feel balanced in the space to ensure the scale works. A room instantly feels off if everything sits to one side or the rug is the wrong size. (Pro tip: rugs should always be large enough to let at least the front legs of your furniture sit on them – it grounds the space and makes it feel pulled together.)

Once the main furniture feels right, move on to your objects. Look at your largest decorative pieces – books, trays, baskets – and work your way down in scale. Spread the weight around the room so the eye moves evenly. If all your darker or heavier items sit in one corner, the room will feel lopsided. Disperse them, then fill the gaps with smaller, lighter touches: a stack of books, a bowl, a favourite find. Build slowly, one layer at a time. And if it doesn't feel right, strip it back and start again. Don't panic, it's not surgery – just shuffle until it feels balanced.

Lighting is another layer entirely. A good living room needs more than one source – a mix of table lamps, floor lamps, wall lights, and a pendant overhead. This creates depth and atmosphere. Harsh overhead lighting kills a mood faster than you can say "dimmer switch". Keep it low, warm, and inviting. A coffee table tray is my best friend in living-room design. In fact, I'd challenge you to find a project of mine that doesn't have one. It's the ultimate grounding piece, an organic texture that pulls everything together and makes sense of the surface chaos. It gives shape to the sprawl, so you can pile on the good stuff – books, bowls, candles, flowers. It's the stylish version of a landing pad, and once you've used one, you'll wonder how you ever lived without it.

And let's talk baskets, the unsung heroes of real life. A log basket beside the fireplace instantly softens all those hard edges, and if you have kids, extra baskets are non-negotiable. They're where the toys disappear to when you're too tired to care where anything goes. Just keep your textures consistent – if your palette is warm and biscuit-toned, stick with natural fibres. A random grey basket will throw off the whole balance..

Finally, keep mantles and windowsills clear of mini mountains of tiny trinkets and photo frames. A pair of candlesticks is plenty. Layering isn't about excess; it's about balance – areas of richness offset by moments of quiet where the eyes can rest. A well-layered living room should look lived-in but considered – comfortable, collected, and quietly under control.

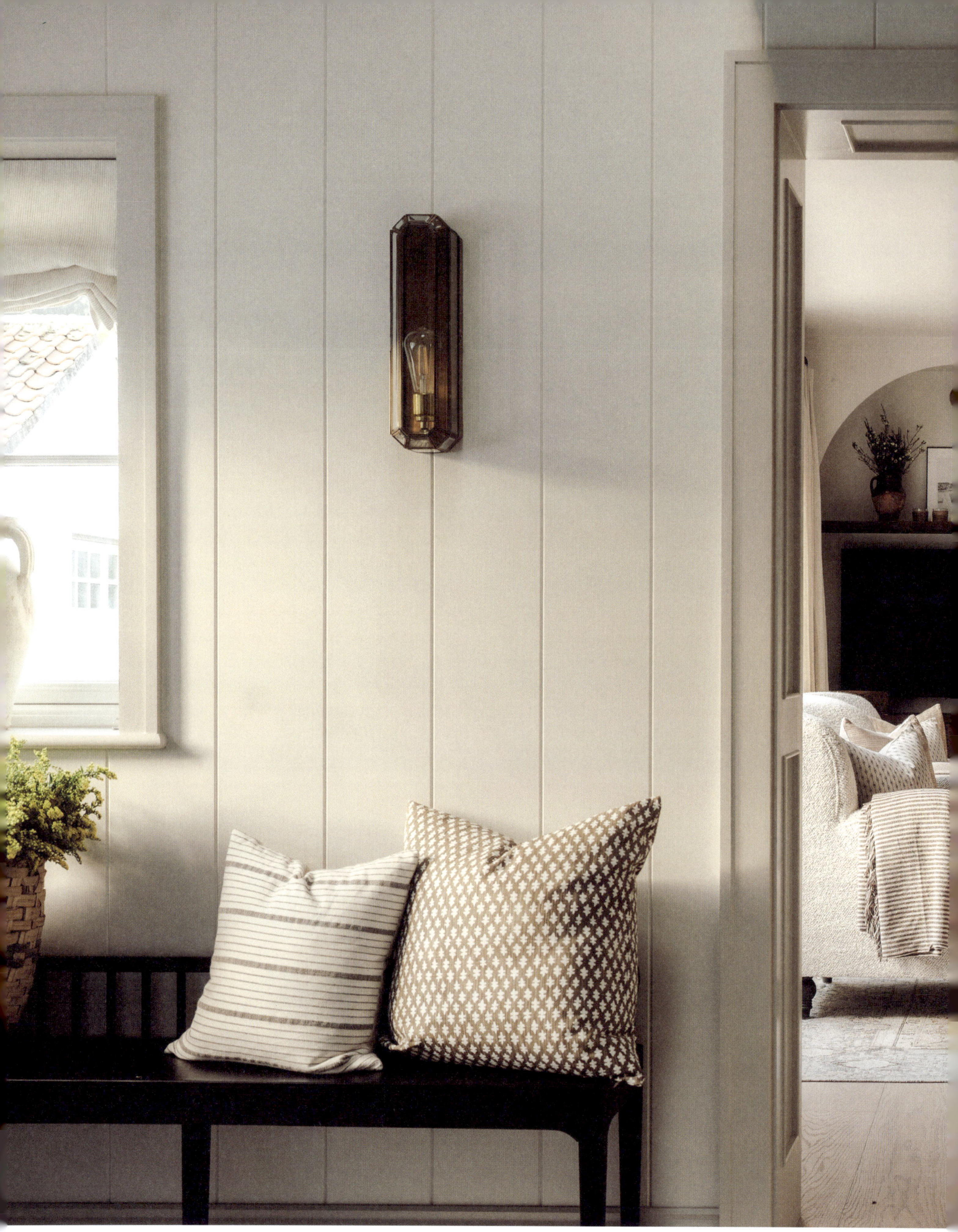

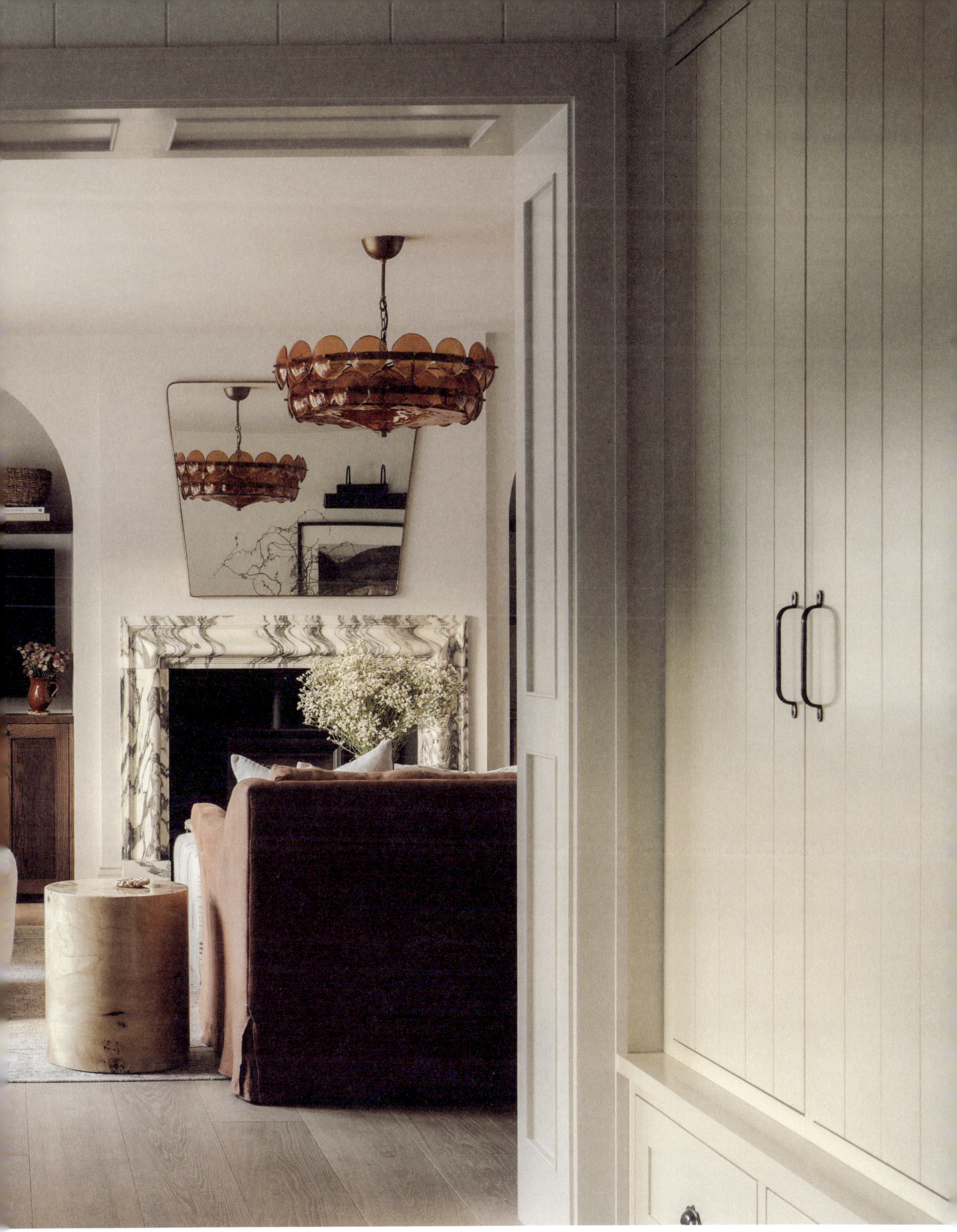

The Kitchen

→ A well-layered kitchen works hard without losing its warmth. We packed the kitchen at Project Sandbanks with character, detail, and charm. It's the final layer of dressing that really makes it feel like a home.

→ → Project All About You. I love the contrast of the dark oak island against the soft painted cabinetry beyond; it's that mixing of tones and finishes that stops a kitchen feeling flat. The brass tap and pot filler catch the light differently throughout the day. The small details are the ones that make a kitchen feel tailored rather than off the shelf.

"Spread the weight around the room so the eye moves evenly."

Kitchens work hard – some harder than others – but that doesn't mean they can't feel soft and characterful. A well-layered kitchen feels easy and inviting – somewhere you actually want to spend time, not just to cook and, let's be honest, clean. The layering here isn't about adding more; it's about softening what's already there so that the space feels grounded and welcoming. Start with materials. Kitchens are full of large, hard, reflective surfaces – joinery, worktops, tiles – so we need warmth, texture, and shape to create some movement. I like to use earthy accessories: wooden chopping boards stacked or leaned casually against a splashback, terracotta bowls, earthenware jugs, bunches of herbs, and antique finds like a pair of old weighing scales. And a few of your favourite cookbooks. These small, tactile pieces instantly take the edge off all that precision and make the space feel lived in. Natural materials age beautifully too – a little patina or wear only adds to the charm.

Hardware plays a big part in layering, too. Soft brass or aged bronze handles, knobs, and taps add warmth and contrast against painted cabinetry or stone. They catch the light differently throughout the day and bring a subtle sense of depth to the space. Mixing up the finishes here is where the magic happens, and is essential in creating subtle variations and adding even more depth and character. It's these quiet details that make a kitchen feel tailored rather than off-the-shelf.

Lighting deserves just as much attention. In the kitchen, good functional task lighting is key – you need bright, clear light for chopping, cooking, and cleaning without feeling like you're working in the shadows. But the moment guests arrive, you want the room to soften, to shift from "prep mode" to something warmer and more inviting. This is where layered lighting – and multiple zoned circuits – become one of my non-negotiables. Keep your overheads for the practical moments, then dial them down and let wall lights, pendants, or lamps take over. Nothing transforms a kitchen faster than lowering the lights; it turns a workspace into a place people want to linger – just long enough to do the dishes.

Rugs and runners can work wonders too. A vintage runner in front of a range or sink instantly adds colour, comfort, and character underfoot. Just make sure it feels robust enough to live there – expect it to have spillages and collect dirt, so nothing too precious, and ensure it can be cleaned.

And finally, let your kitchen breathe. Open shelving can be beautiful, but only when it's edited – not every mug, gadget, or "just in case" spice jar needs to star in the line-up. Kitchens might look like showpieces in photographs, but in real life they're working rooms with a social life. They're meant to look gorgeous and survive the chaos of actual humans. A few marks on the worktop or a dented pan? That's not a disaster – that's character, the culinary equivalent of laughter lines. Sometimes you have to let things go and allow the room to look like it's lived in, not curated by a gallerist.

A layered kitchen should feel easy, imperfect, and full of quiet confidence – that's the true heart of the home.

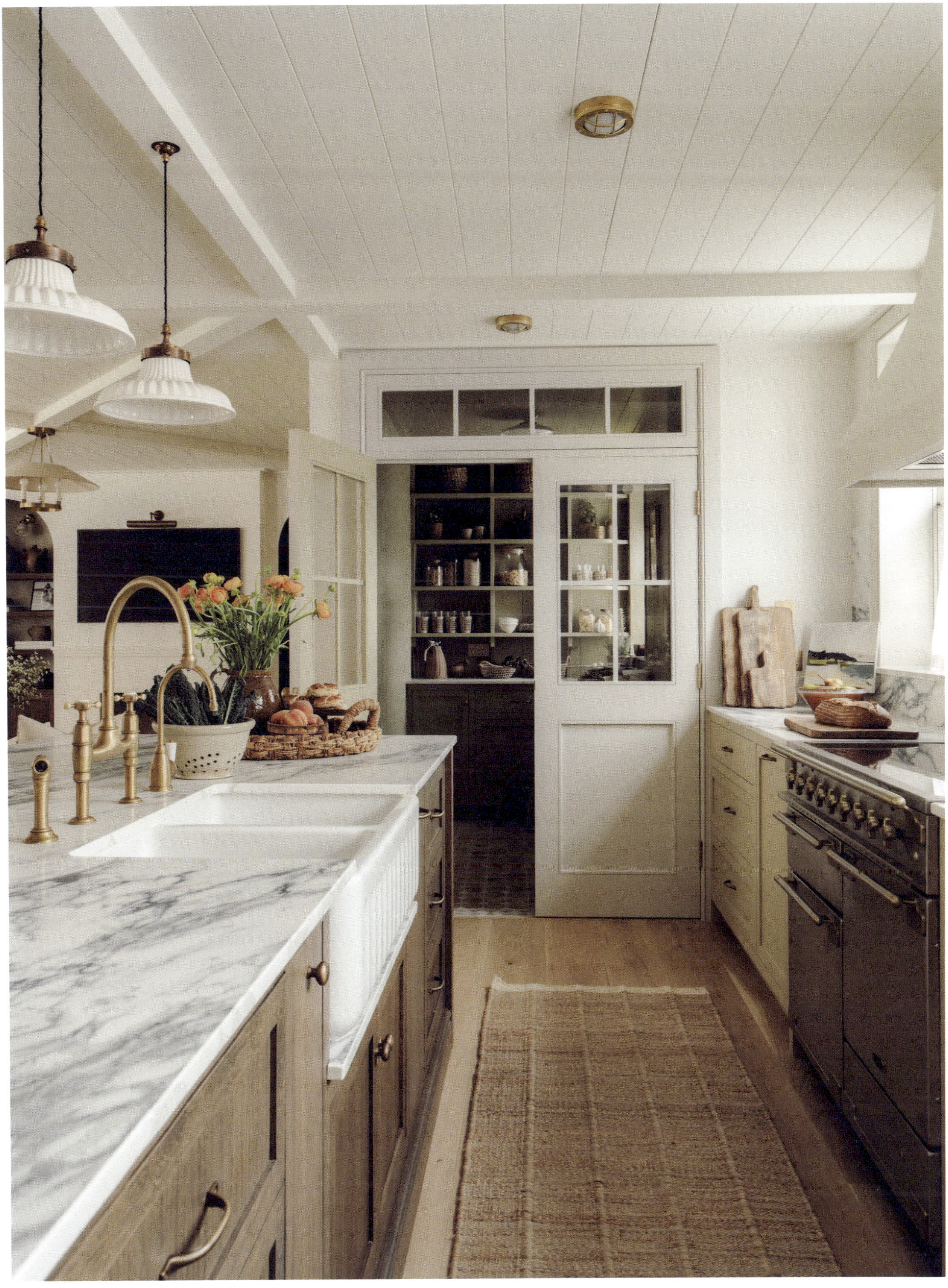

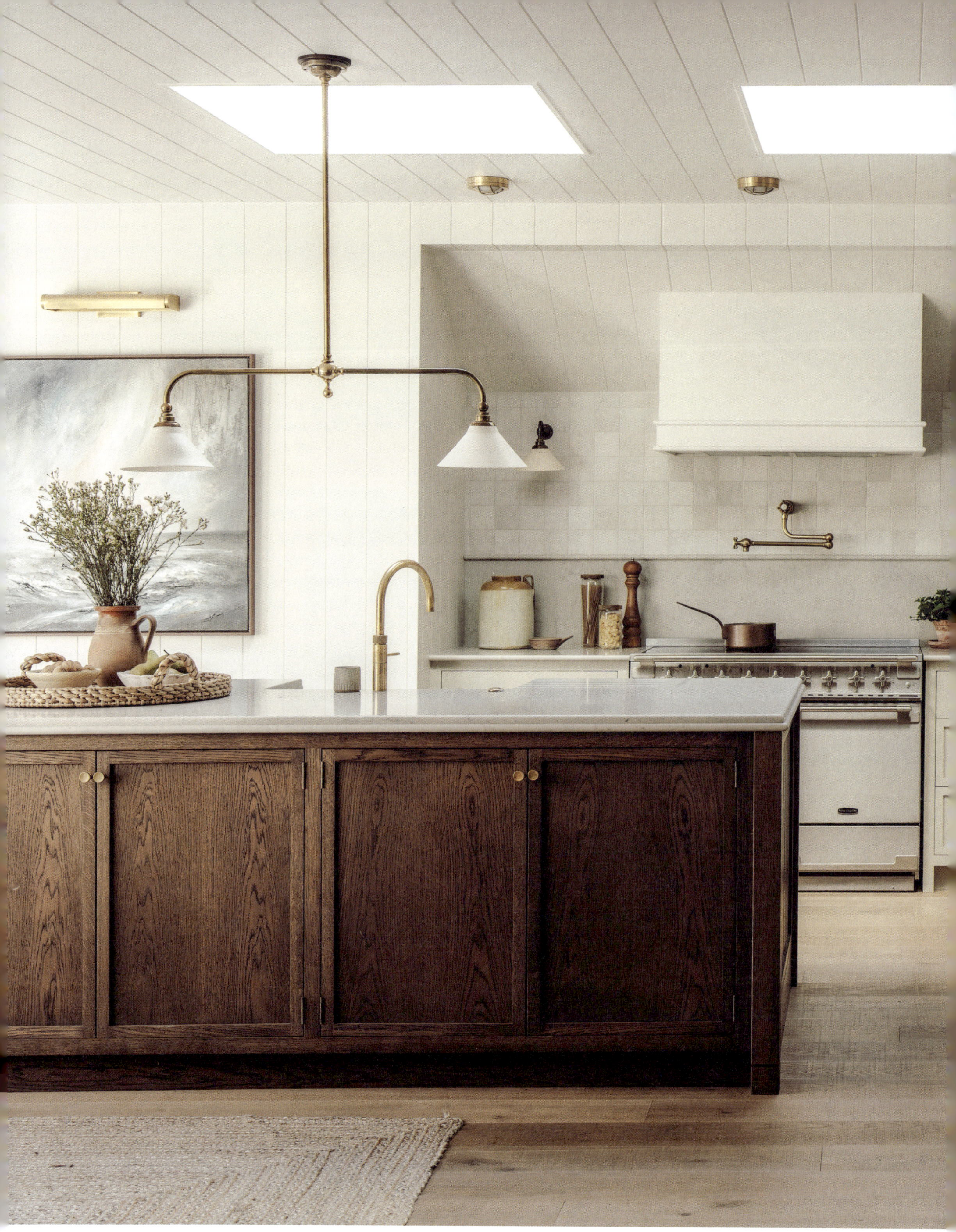

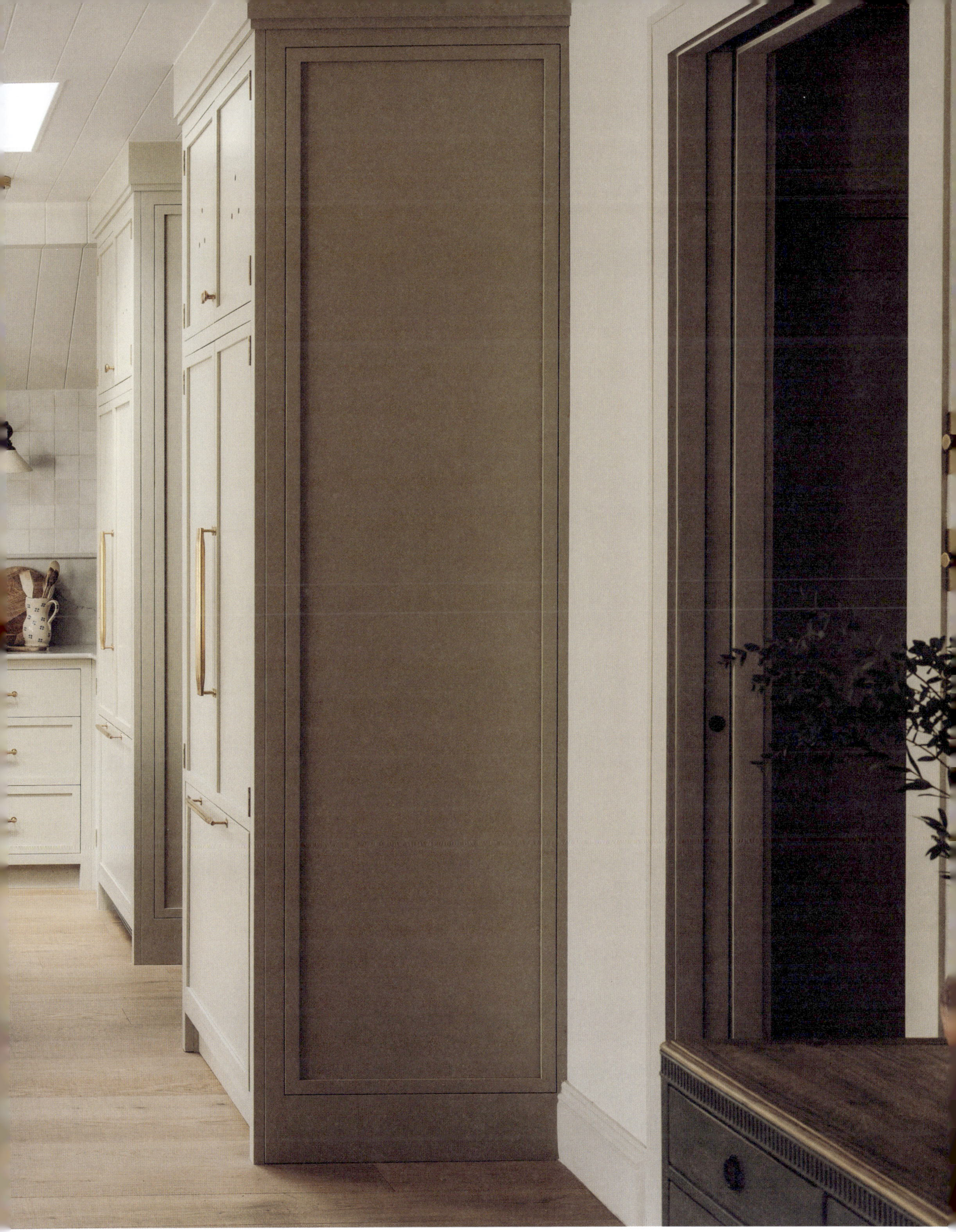

Layer with Intention

DESIGN NOTES

Layering might look effortless, but it's rarely accidental. Behind every perfectly "casual" throw or artfully un-styled corner is a bit of quiet know-how. These prompts will help you layer with intention.

1. START WITH A STRONG BASE

Before you even think about cushions or candles, make sure the bones are right. Your furniture, rug, wall colour, and joinery set the tone for everything that sits on top.
Try this: Clear one room of decorative extras. Just look at the fundamentals. Do they feel calm, balanced, and proportionate? If not, adjust the base before layering anything back in.

---

2. MIX YOUR MATERIALS

Texture is what brings a room to life. Rough needs smooth, matte needs gloss, linen needs velvet, timber needs metal. Too much of one thing and a space feels flat; contrast creates depth.
Try this: Gather a handful of materials from around your home – ceramic, glass, linen, timber, metal – and place them together. Notice which combinations feel rich, which feel dull, and which surprise you. Use those insights in your next arrangement.

---

3. COLLECT SLOWLY

Layering isn't a one-day job. The most soulful rooms evolve over time, filling with pieces found, gifted, inherited, or stumbled upon. That slow mix gives a home movement and personality.
Do this: Choose one surface and refresh it using only items with a story – something inherited, something picked up on a trip, something lovingly imperfect. See how the energy shifts.

---

4. LET IT BREATHE

Not every inch needs filling. Layers only work when they have space around them. Balance visually "busy" areas with quieter ones so the room doesn't slip into clutter.
Try this: Remove everything from a coffee table or console. Then put back only what genuinely adds something – a book stack, a bowl, a candle. Always start with the larger objects. Stop before it feels crowded.

---

5. REPEAT SOMETHING

A few repeated tones, textures, or shapes make layers feel intentional rather than random.
Practise: Choose one element – a colour, a metal, a texture – and echo it twice more in the room. Notice how repetition gently pulls everything together.

---

6. DON'T CHASE PERFECTION

The best-layered spaces are never perfect. They're a little crooked, a little lived in, and much more interesting because of it.
Try this: When you think you're done, step back and remove one item. If the room still feels balanced, you've layered just enough. If it feels too neat, loosen something – a loose throw, a wonky basket, burnt down candles, mismatched cushions. Let life show.

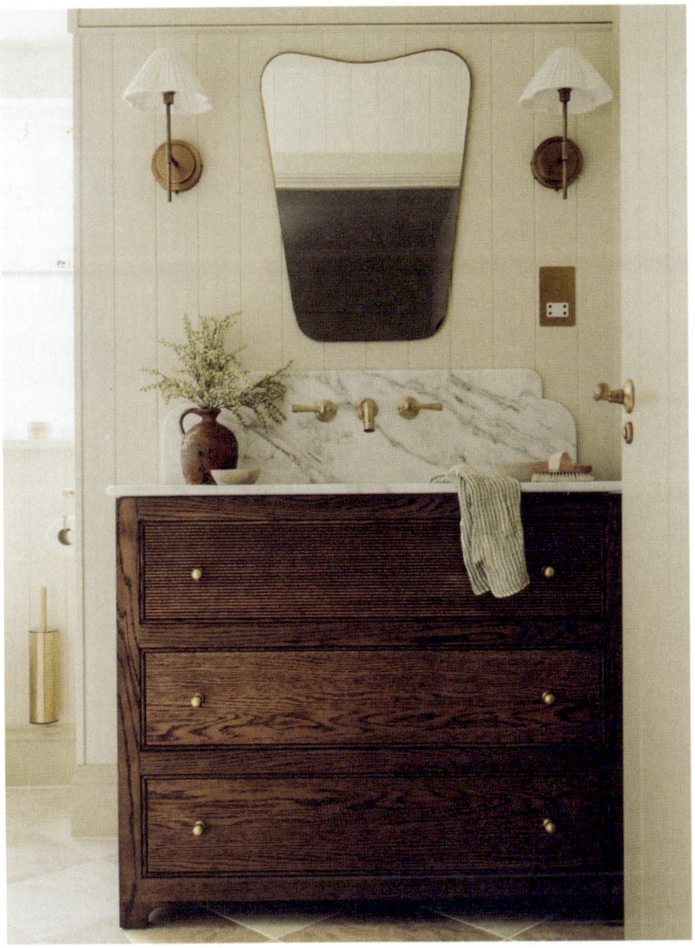

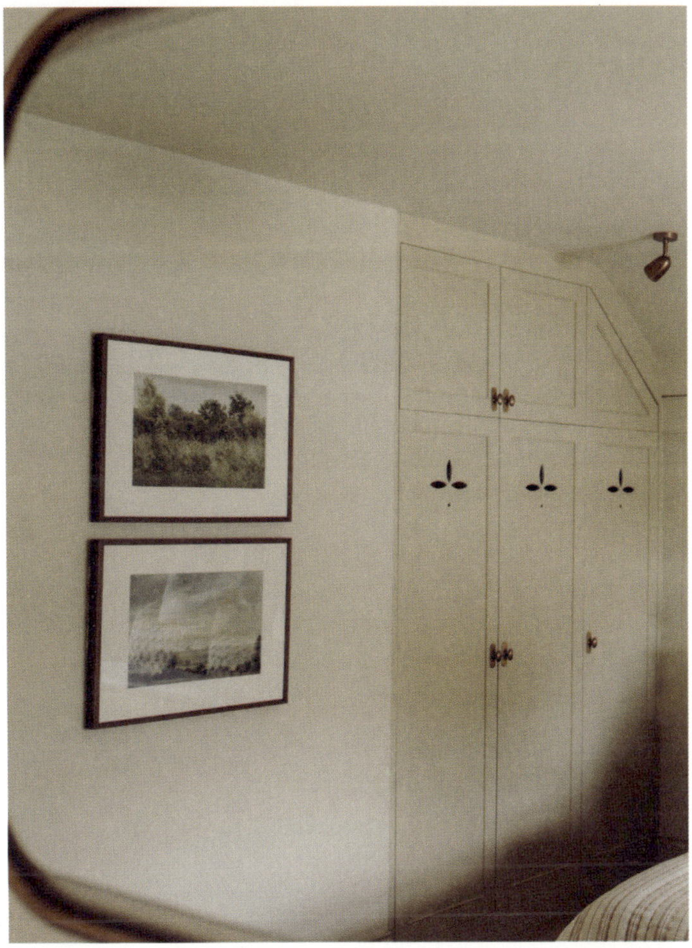

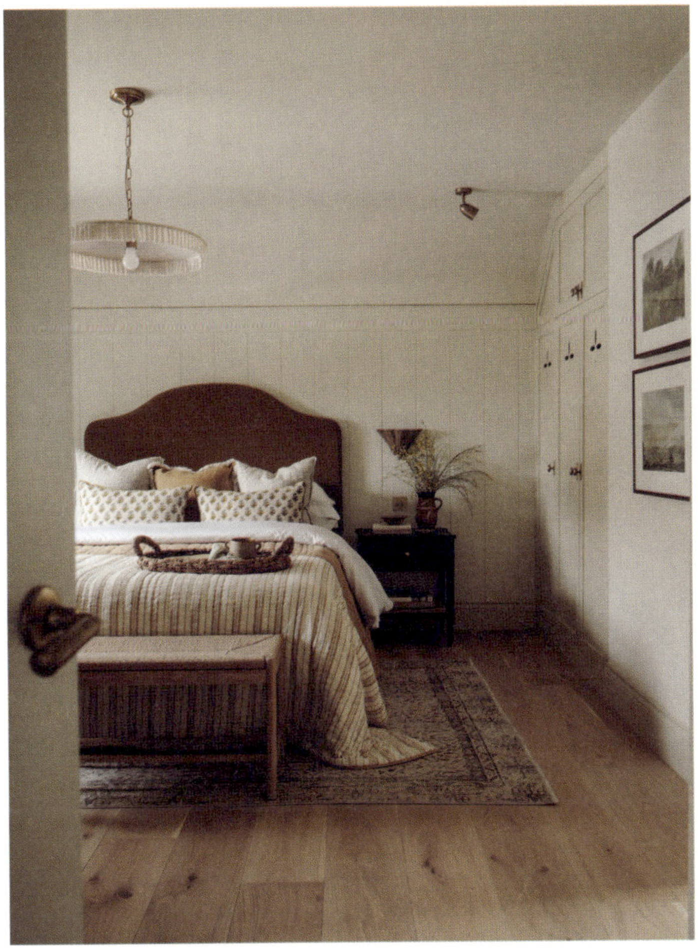

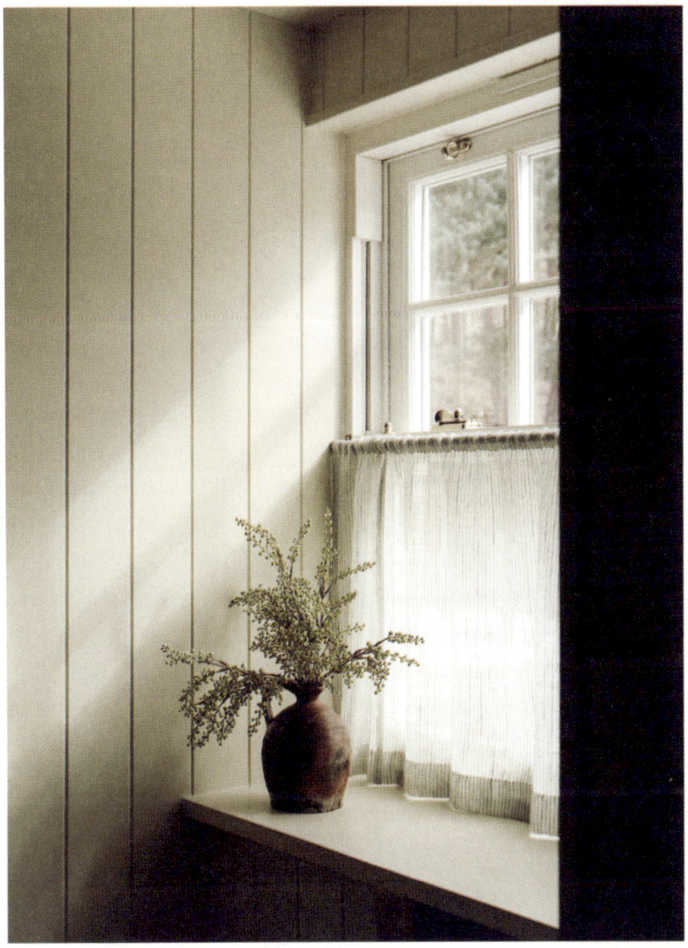

"*One is always drawn to what one loves.*"

RALPH WALDO EMERSON

Curate

FIND THE RIGHT PIECES AND MATERIALS

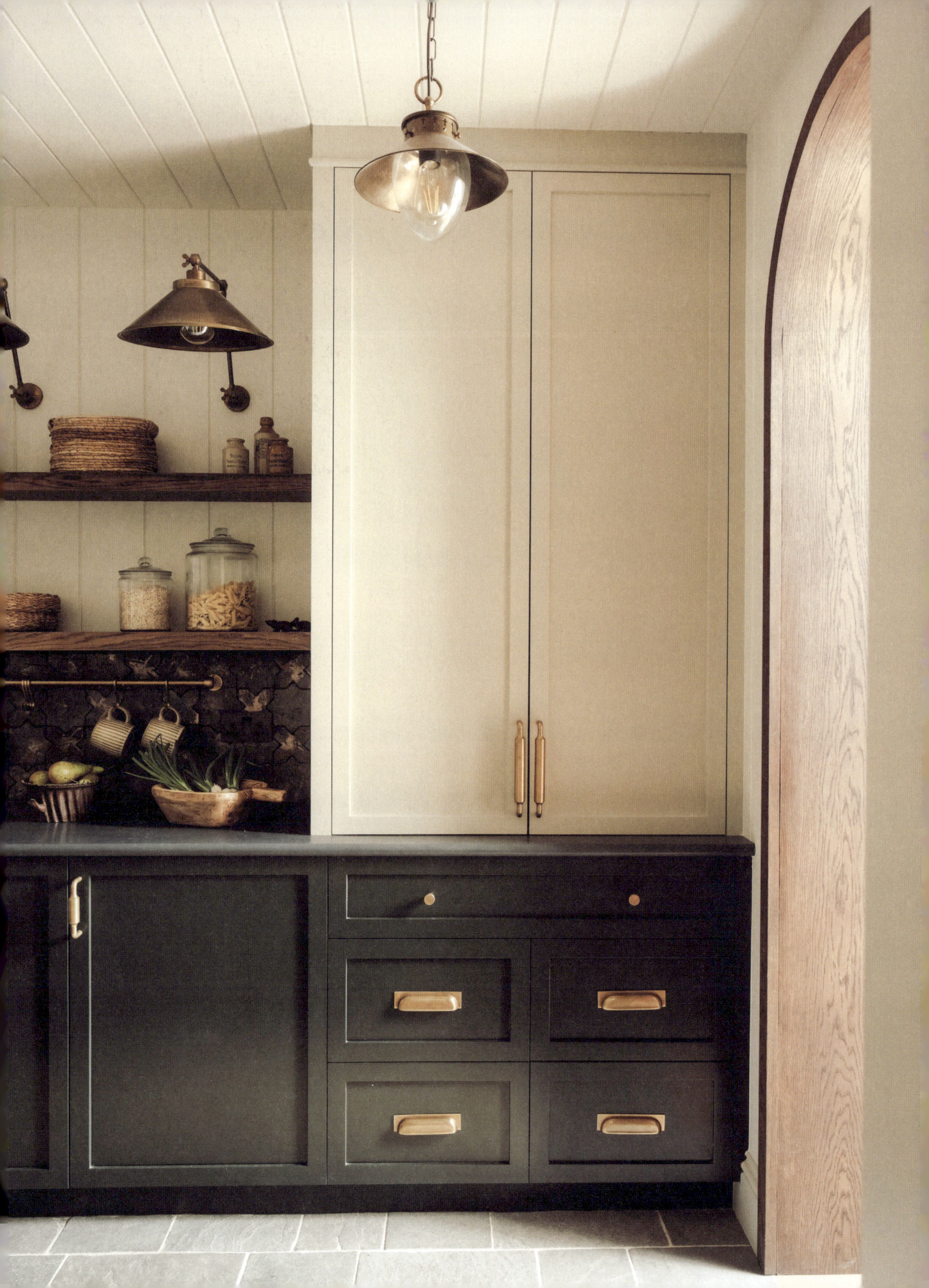

CURATING WITH *INTENTION*

Every home tells a story, but it only becomes your story when you start choosing pieces with intention. Curating a home is about forming a relationship with what you bring in. That chair you found in a vintage shop, the ceramic bowl your friend made, the linen that softens with every wash – these pieces become part of the rhythm of your home, and part of the rhythm of your life.

Curating is about choosing. And choosing well requires patience, curiosity, and sometimes, restraint. This is the part most people skip in favour of quick solutions. We're used to instant everything: instant delivery, instant style, instant "room makeovers". But a well-curated home resists the urge to rush. It asks you to slow down, to look, to touch, to question, and to wait for the right thing rather than settling for the almost-right thing.

Timelessness comes from this slowing down. When you choose materials because you love them, not because they're fashionable, they last. When you pick finishes for how they feel, not for how they look in a product photo, they age beautifully. When you choose furniture because it suits your life, not someone else's aesthetic, it stays.

A truly timeless home isn't one that avoids change; it's one that embraces it. Materials that weather, fabrics that soften, timber that warms, metal that patinates – these are the foundations of a home that feels lived with, not just lived in. We can't talk about timelessness without talking about sustainability. They are, in many ways, the same thing. Buying well means buying less. Choosing quality means choosing longevity. And sourcing pre-loved pieces – antiques, vintage, restored items – is one of the most sustainable choices you can make.

I often tell clients that antiques are the original eco-friendly purchase. They've already lived one (or several) lives. They've proven their durability. They've earned their character. And buying antique isn't just environmentally responsible, it's emotionally enriching. You inherit a little history with every

← One of my favourite rooms at Project Green Park. Even though a pantry is a functional space filled with the items a household needs, we'll still tuck in a few antiques around the edges to add interest and depth. We chose dark cabinetry with a dark quartz top, the brass hardware left to patina rather than stay precious.

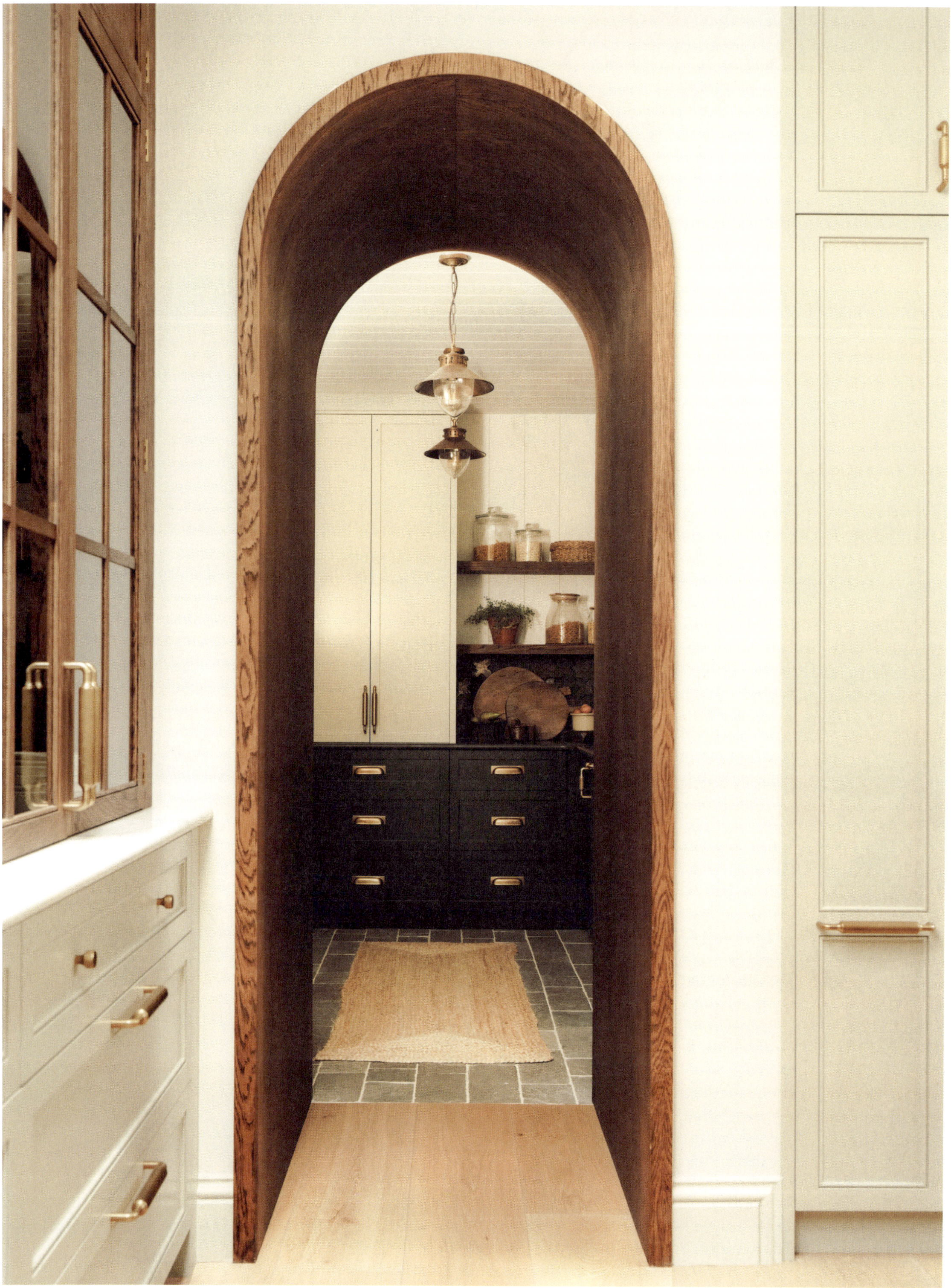

← The view through to the pantry from the kitchen. We designed a book-matched timber-lined door opening to add architectural interest and a bit of wow a factor. We pulled a slightly darker timber through onto the shelves and added oversized bronze wall lamps for impact.

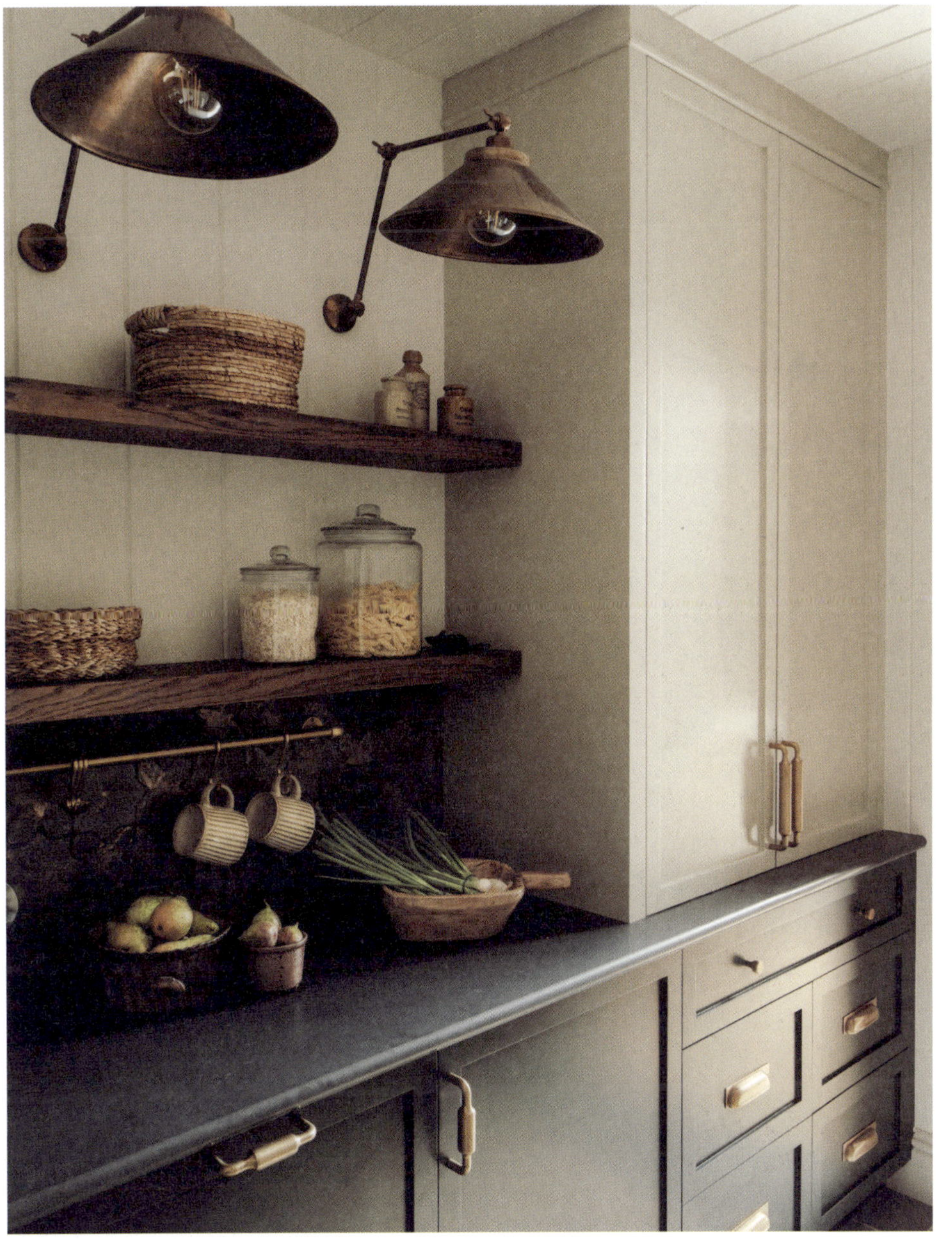

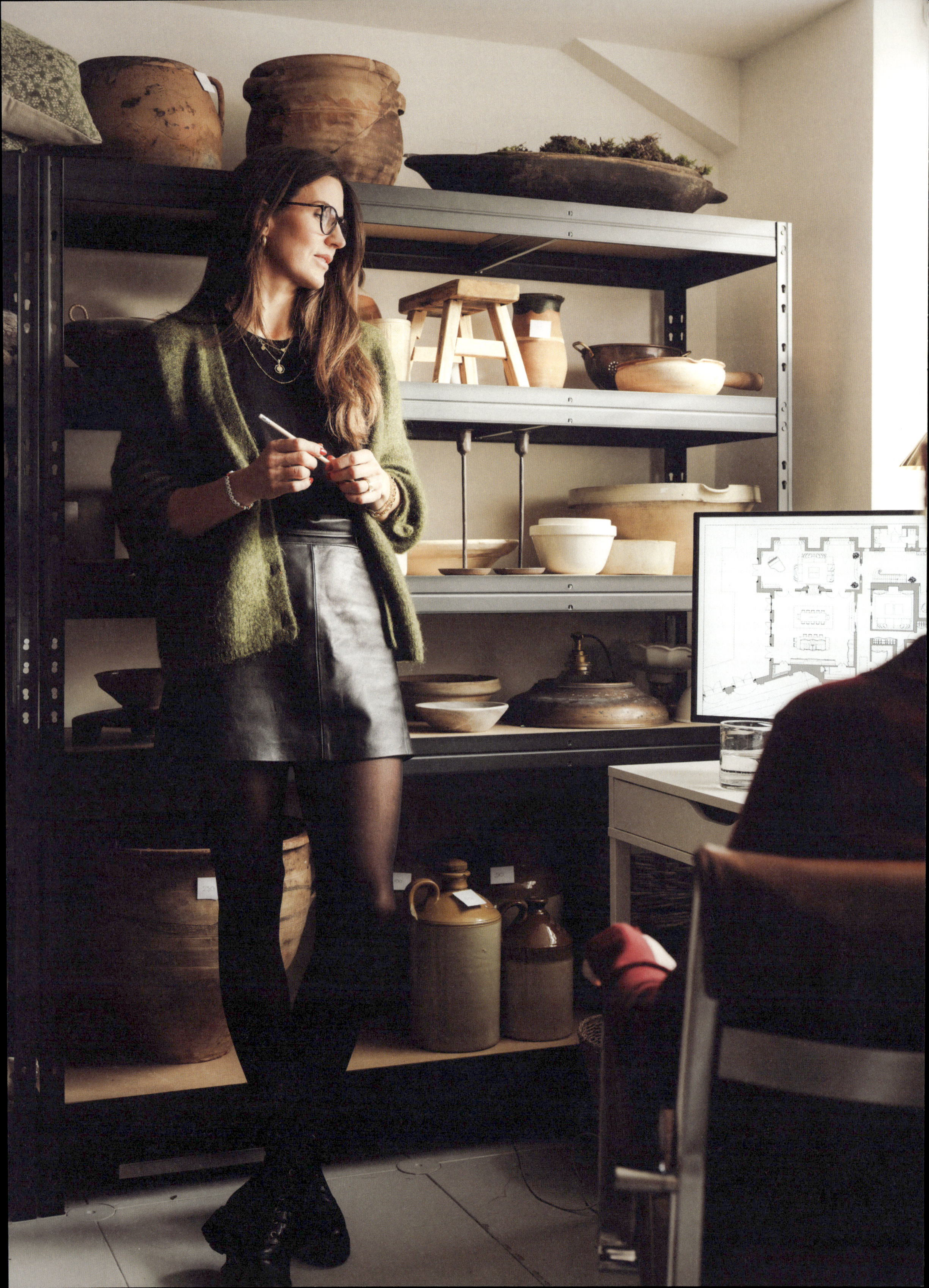

scratch and quirk. You also gain something else: a sense of origin. "Where did this come from?" "Who made it?" These questions deepen your connection to a piece – they remind you that your home is not just filled with objects, but with stories worth keeping.

Even when you're buying new, think sustainably: choose solid materials, natural fibres, well-made joinery. Ask yourself whether this piece has a future in your home. Will you still love it in ten years' time? Could it move with you? Could it be repaired or reupholstered? Could you hand it down to your children? Curating is choosing pieces that can withstand both time and life.

People often ask me how I find things – not just the beautiful ones, but the right ones. The answer isn't glamorous: I look at everything. I give it a good feel. I turn things over. I pull out drawers. I tap tabletops, smell timber, and examine hinges. I ask questions. I browse relentlessly. I follow my curiosity down rabbit holes. I allow myself to fall a little in love with the oddballs and the not-quite-perfects.

Good sourcing is part-instinct, part-trained eye and part-willingness to take a chance. You won't always find what you're looking for – sometimes you'll stumble across something you didn't even know you needed. And sometimes you'll fall hopelessly in love with a piece, hesitate for a moment, and then someone else snaps it up. Your heart will break, and yes, it may forever be "the one that got away". But strangely, that's part of the thrill – the missed treasures make the found ones feel that bit sweeter.

And the hunt is half the pleasure. Sourcing teaches you patience, curiosity, and the art of waiting for the right thing. It invites surprises. It encourages exploration. And it's far more rewarding than hitting "Add to Basket" at 11 p.m.

A curated home is built piece by piece, moment by moment. It grows with you. It evolves as you do. And if you allow yourself to enjoy the search – not just the end result – the home you create will feel layered, grounded, and unmistakeably yours.

← In the studio that is part-instinct, part-trained eye, always a hive of activity. Plans on screen, sourced pieces coming and going on the shelves, and the patient work of finding the right thing happening in between. Every project is a team effort, and the studio is where we all come together to make it happen - collaboration at the heart of everything we do.

The Art of Sourcing

If I have a true design weakness, it's sourcing. I can lose hours in a market or online in a late-night scrolling spiral. I'll fall head over heels for a chair with one good leg, or drive across the country to see a cabinet I "just need to check in person". Some people collect shoes, I collect stories disguised as furniture. My love affair with sourcing started early. As a child, I was the one turning over rocks, rummaging in dusty boxes, absolutely convinced there was always treasure somewhere to be found. That instinct never really left – I've simply become better at spotting the treasure.

→ Doing what I love best. On this day I was hunting for finds at the Ardingly Antiques Fair. You never quite know what's going to catch your eye until it does – the joy of the find is in that surprise; that small jolt of recognition when something just feels right.

Selecting furniture, art, and accessories with intention is where a home truly begins to reveal its character. Anyone can fill a room, but curating one requires a little more heart – and imagination. It's not about finding the "perfect" piece; it's about choosing things that make you smile, settle your shoulders, or pull you in for a closer look. A home with soul doesn't come from matching sets or pristine catalogues; it comes from a thoughtful mix of old and new, treasured and found, bold and quiet.

I always tell clients to buy the pieces that mean something to them. The rest follows. A vintage chair with a history will sit quite happily beside a contemporary sofa. A modern lamp looks even better when paired with an antique side table. Homes with depth are the ones that aren't afraid of contrast – where the clean lines of something new play against the warmth of something old. And honestly, isn't it a lovely thought to wonder who once rested their cup and saucer on that little nineteenth-century walnut table? What they might have been wearing 200 years ago? Curating is as much about imagination as it is about design – you're not just choosing furniture, you're adding your own history, stitching together stories.

Art often intimidates people, but it shouldn't. You don't need a gallery wall of masterpieces to have meaningful art in your home. Some of my favourite pieces cost less than the frame they're in. I have been known to frame £2 postcards, charity-shop prints, torn-out book pages, even old tea towels that held a memory. The value isn't in the price; it's in the joy. And sometimes a humble piece, treated with the same care as fine art, becomes more special than anything expensive.

Selecting intentionally also means understanding that not everything has to be instantly perfect. Let pieces evolve as your home does. Let an object surprise you. And let there be room

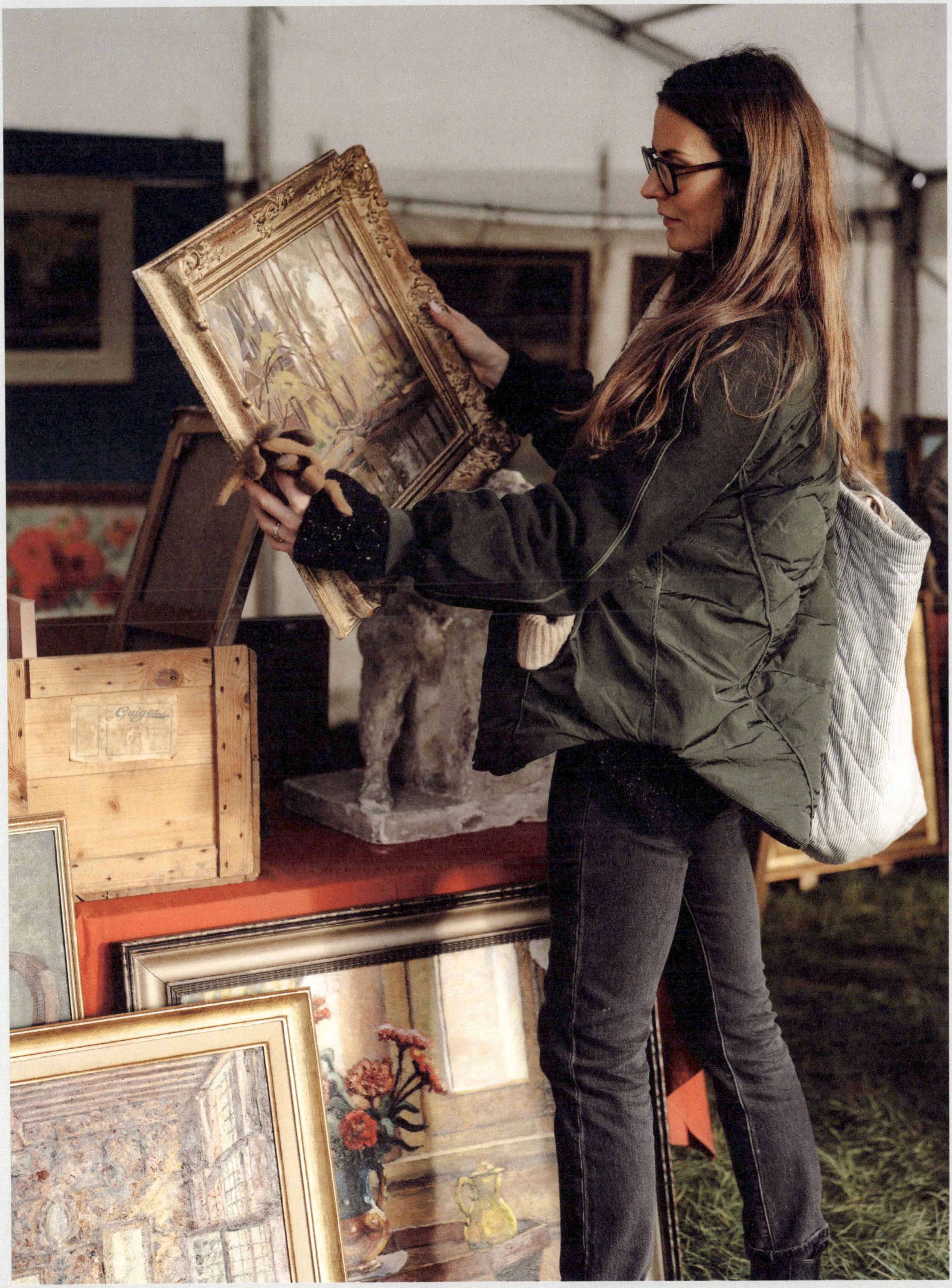

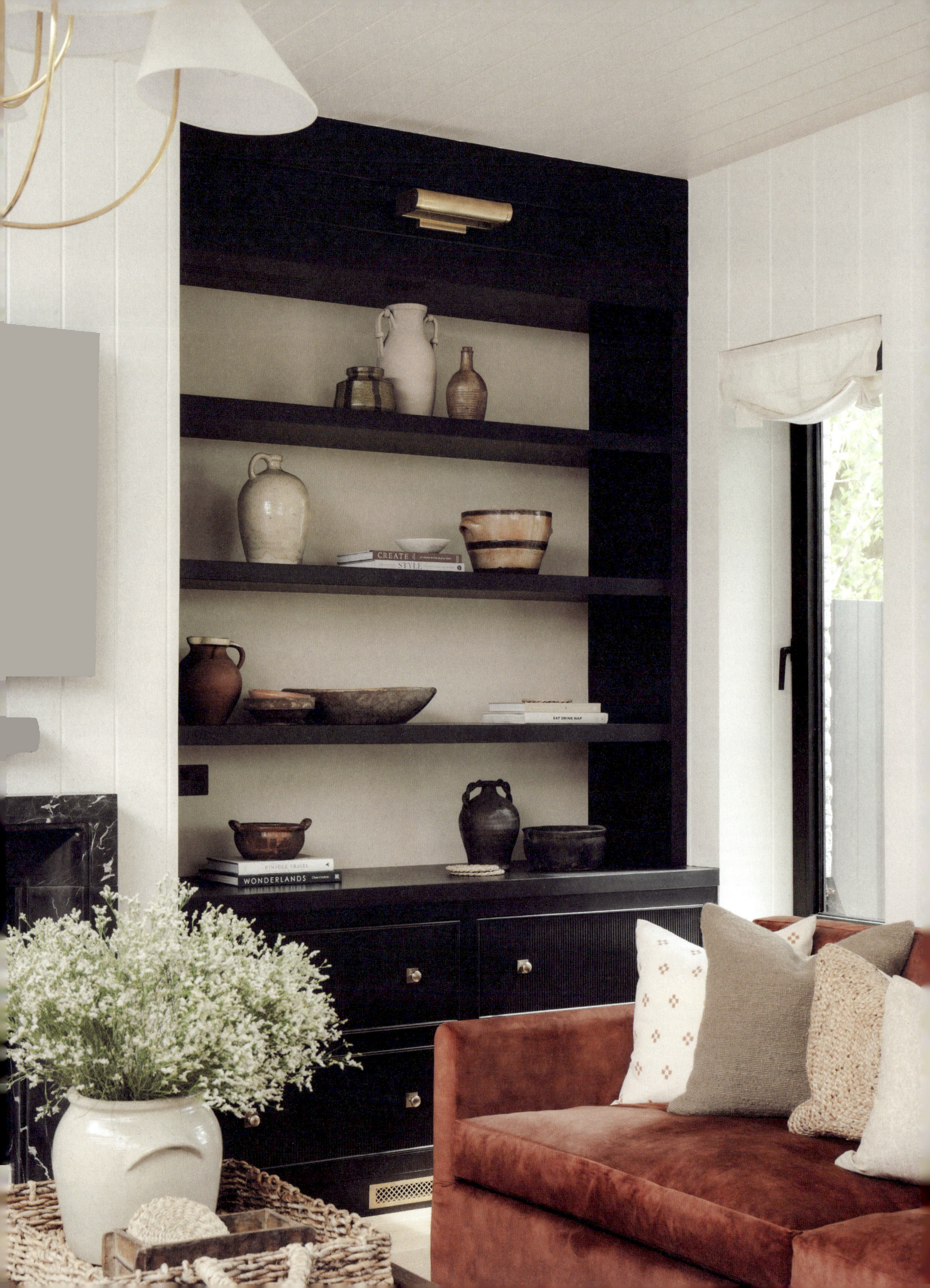
CREATE
STYLE
EAT DRINK NAP
WONDERLANDS

for discovery – the item you didn't expect to love, the accidental find, the thing you almost walked past but somehow couldn't leave behind.

Accessories, too, should have purpose. Not in a functional sense, but in the atmosphere they create. A stack of books that genuinely interests you, a family heirloom, or a ceramic bowl you picked up on holiday. These objects quietly narrate your life. They create warmth, texture, and a sense of place.

When you select with intention, you're not decorating; you're shaping the daily experience of your home. These pieces become the things you reach for, lean on, move around, and live alongside. They quietly enrich the background of your life, not because they match, but because they matter.

"Anyone can fill a room, but curating one requires a little more heart – and imagination."

← Designing from scratch doesn't mean starting without soul. Even with new furnishings, like in this living room, we dress with old and new — vintage pieces, Indian block print fabrics — to give the space its depth and character, and stop it from feeling flat. Every item is sourced with real intention. Nothing here is decoration for decoration's sake; each piece earns its place.

→ On final install days, we arrive with a collection of finds sourced over time - laid out on the floor, then carefully placed where they're needed. I'd rather have too much than too little, so we can have a play around until the spaces feel authentically styled.

→ → The flow here was created by using natural earthy colours and textures on the furnishings to carry you softly through the spaces. The gentle repetition of tones and textures helps the rooms feel like part of the same story, guiding you with ease from one to the next. By keeping the palette rooted in nature, the inside and outside feel seamlessly connected, blurring the boundaries between home and landscape..

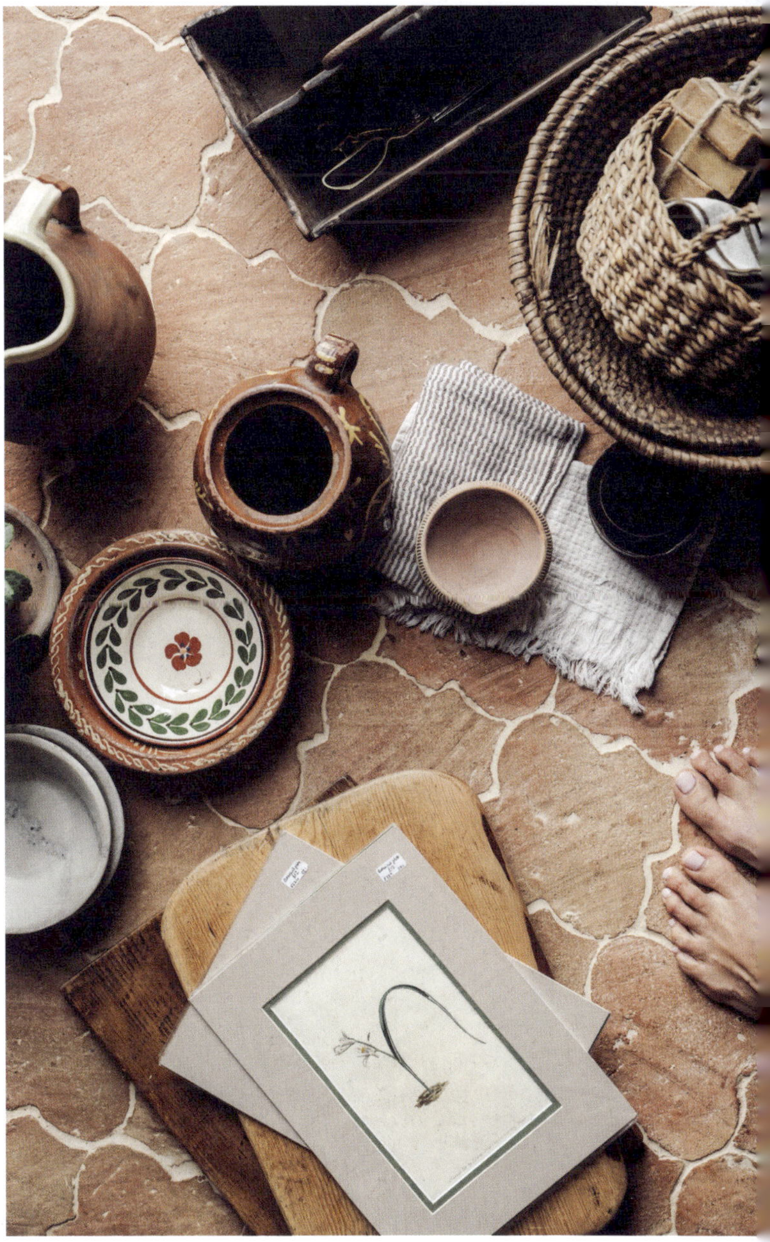

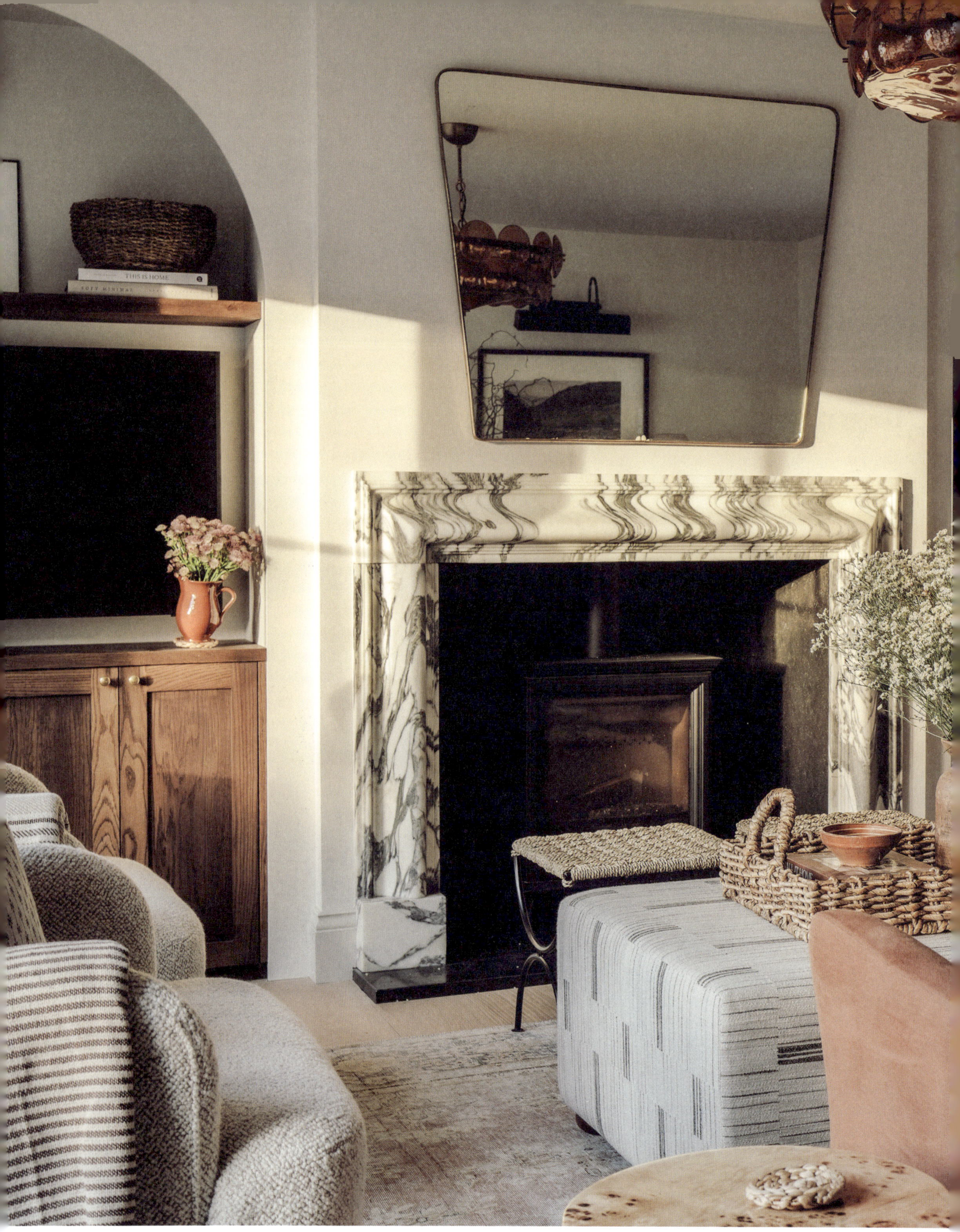
THIS IS HOME

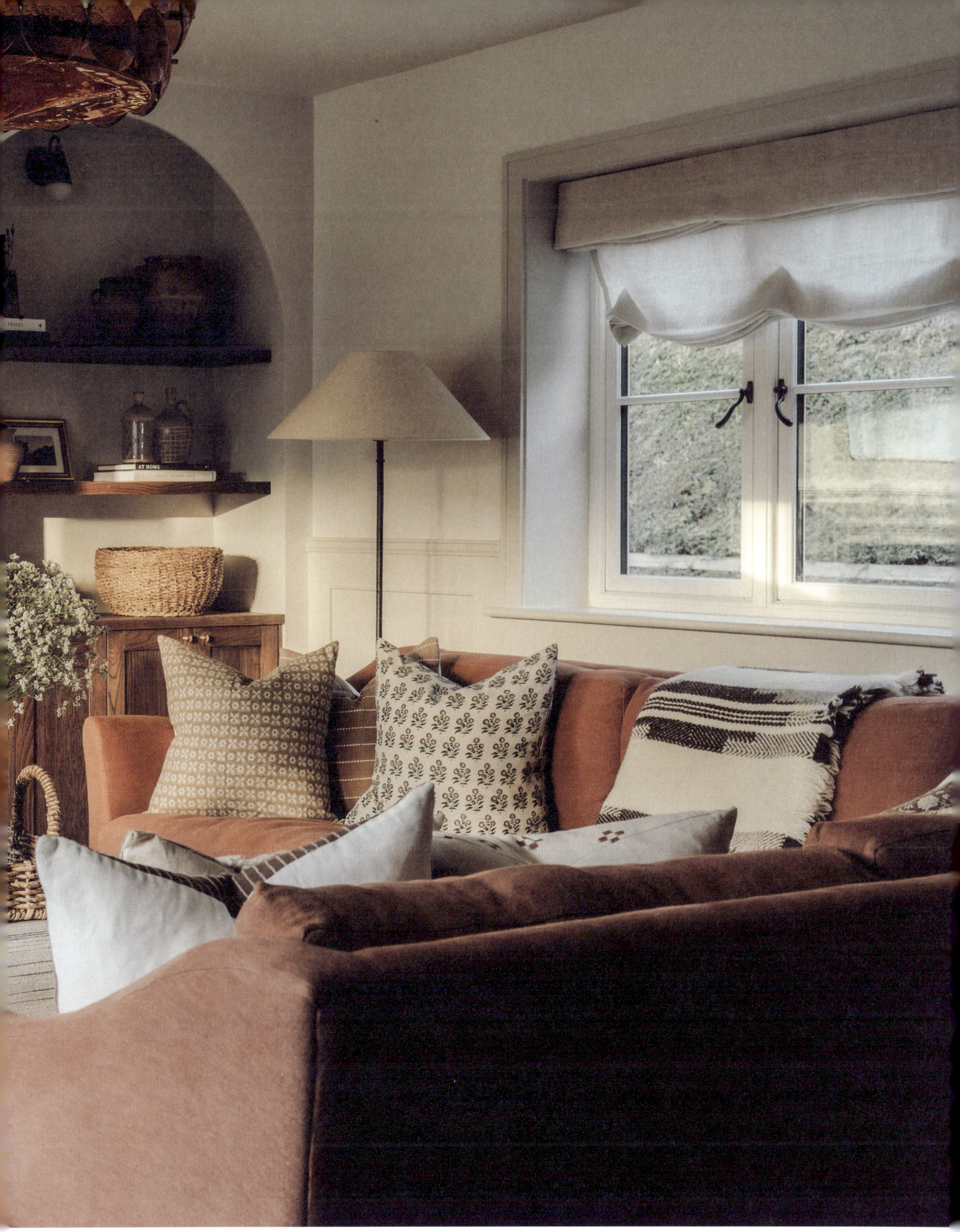

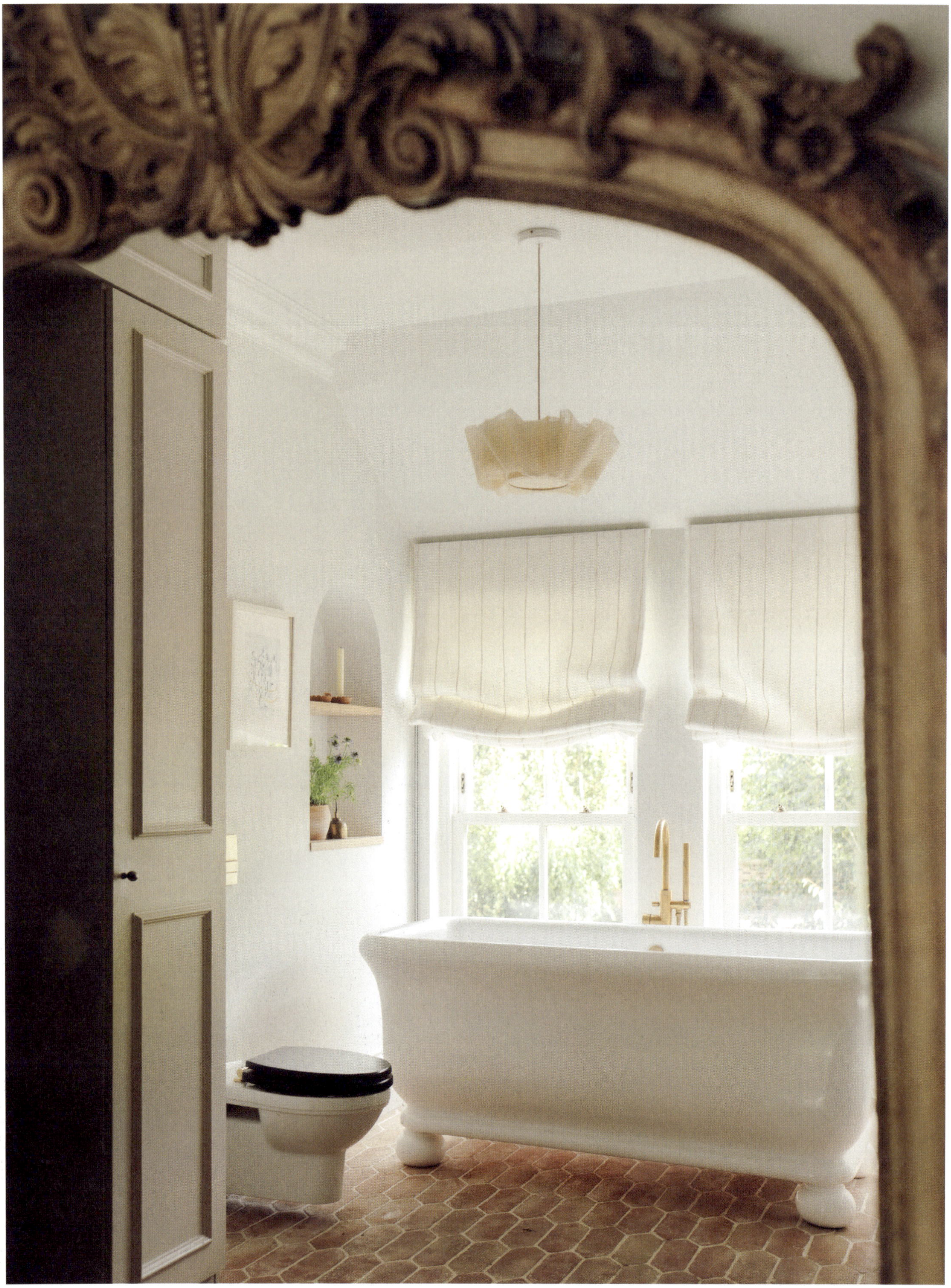

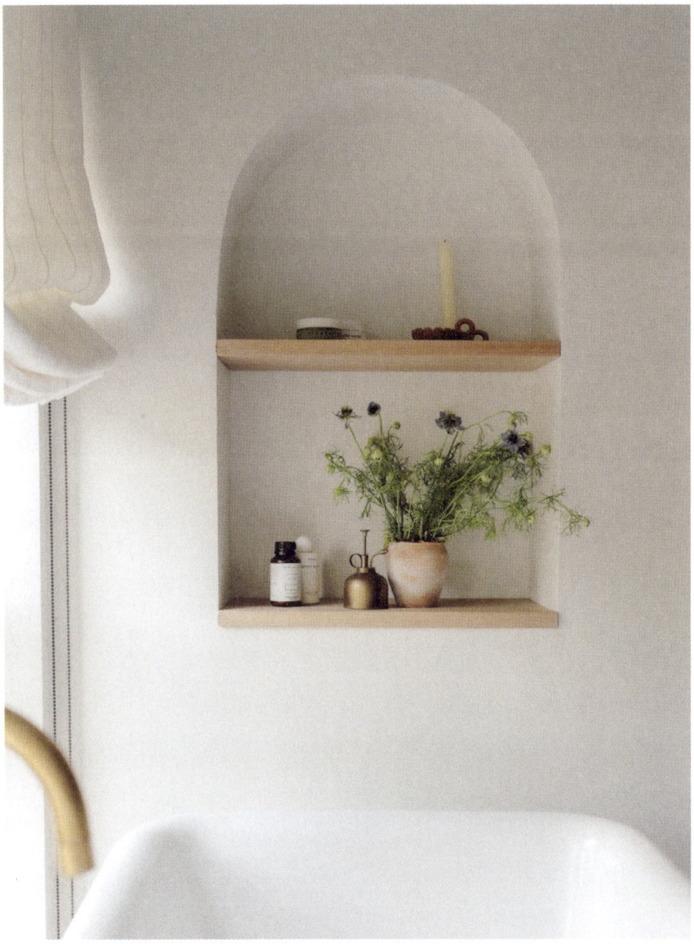

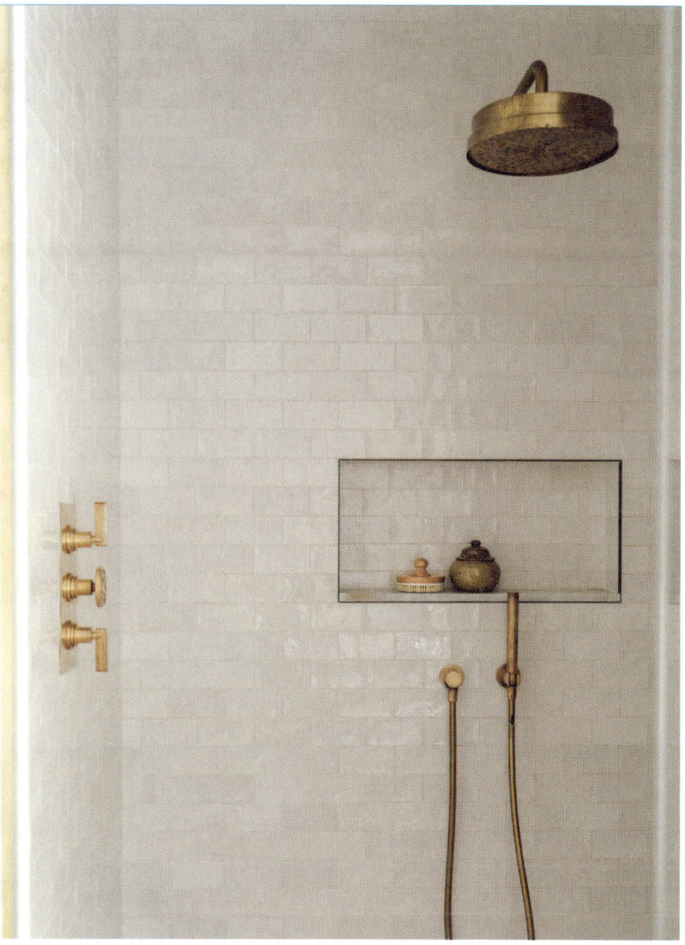

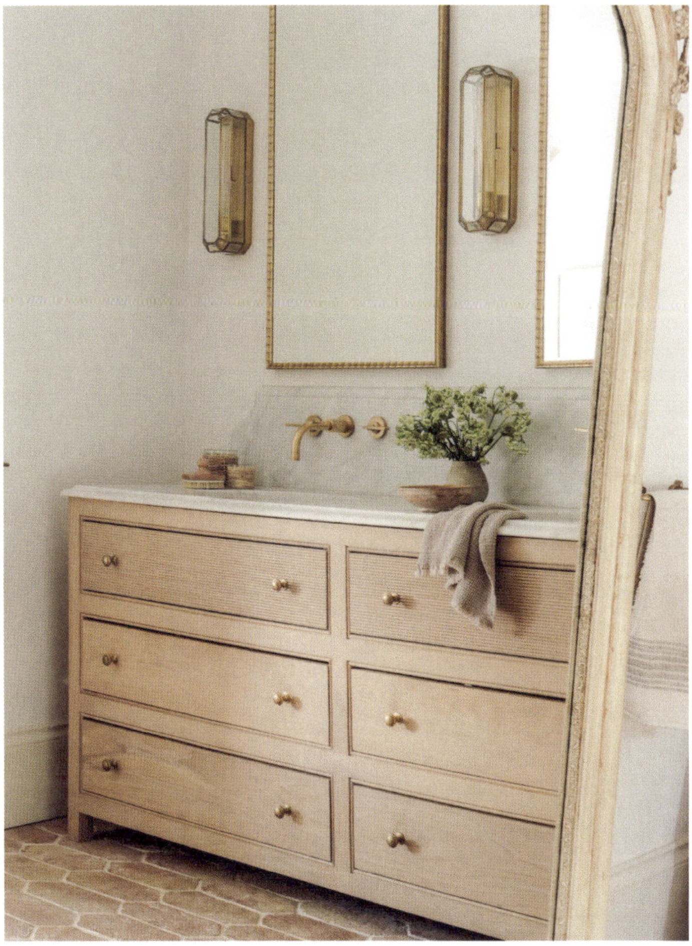

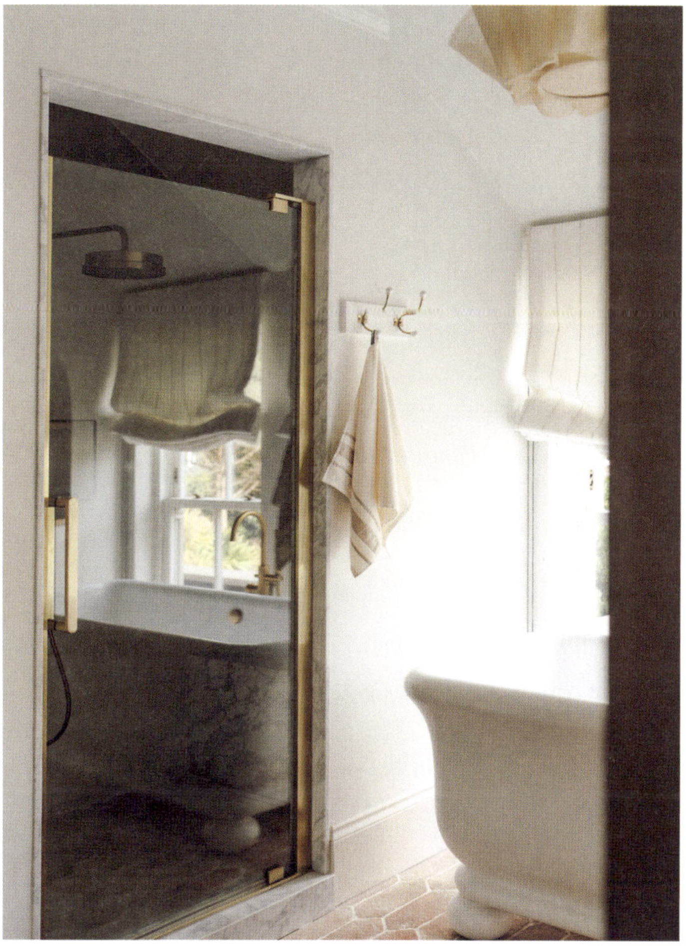

Choosing Quality Over Quantity

There comes a moment in every home where you realise that more things won't make it feel better, but better things will. Quality isn't about price or prestige; it's about longevity, comfort, and the quiet confidence of pieces that hold up, year after year, without demanding applause. Choosing quality over quantity is one of the most transformative shifts you can make when curating a home. It asks you to think long term, to be patient, and to invest in pieces that earn their keep and stand the test of time.

Quality pieces behave differently. A beautifully made sofa doesn't just sit in a room; it supports you, softens with age, and never develops that mysterious tilt that cheaper ones always seem to inherit (where the seat cushion becomes so flat it looks like its melting over the front). A well-crafted dining table becomes a witness to years of meals, homework, celebrations, and the occasional craft disaster – and somehow looks better for it. Even something as simple as a solid timber side table can outlive every trend that comes and goes around it.

A drum I'm always beating! Investing in quality also means buying less, and that's the beauty of it. "Buy cheap, buy twice" has never felt more true than when you're replacing a set of dining chairs for the third time. A single great armchair is infinitely more valuable than three mediocre ones. One wonderful lamp can pull an entire room together. Fewer, better pieces reduce visual noise and make everything you already own feel more intentional. Quality has this extraordinary way of making a space feel calmer, clearer, even grown-up, without losing any of its warmth or personality.

And yes, quality sometimes costs more upfront. But it pays you back in durability, comfort, and the joy of owning something that actually lasts. There is nothing more irritating than replacing the same item three times because it was never quite right to begin with. The cost of "nearly-right" adds up quickly. The cost of "just-right" lasts decades.

Choosing quality also connects you to the maker, the material, and the craft. When you invest in something well made – a hand-thrown ceramic bowl, a perfectly weighted door handle or cupboard knob, a beautifully upholstered chair – you're supporting skill and craftmanship, not mass production. And that alone adds a layer of meaning to your home. I also like to think of it as warm, fuzzy, guilt-free living!

Ultimately, quality over quantity isn't about creating a perfect home; it's about creating one that endures. One that feels steady, thoughtful, and built with intention – a home that grows with you, and doesn't fall apart along the way.

→ The principal bathroom at our All the Arches project – to this day, one of my favourite rooms, and where we first combined the use of terracotta. The vanity is our Goldbourne design from our range with Parker Howley: beautifully crafted, made here in the UK. This is what choosing quality over quantity looks like in practice – a piece built to be lived with, not replaced.

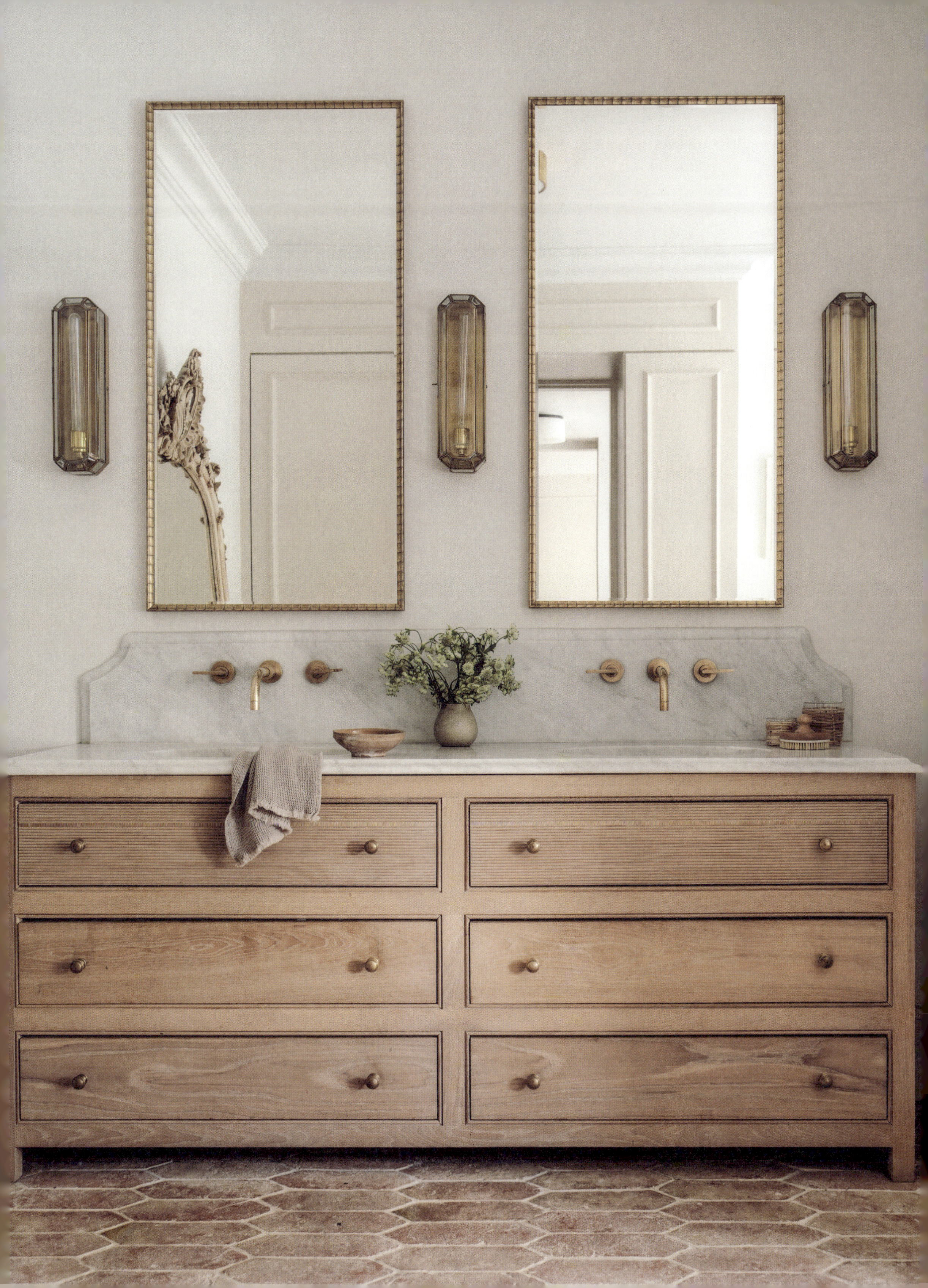

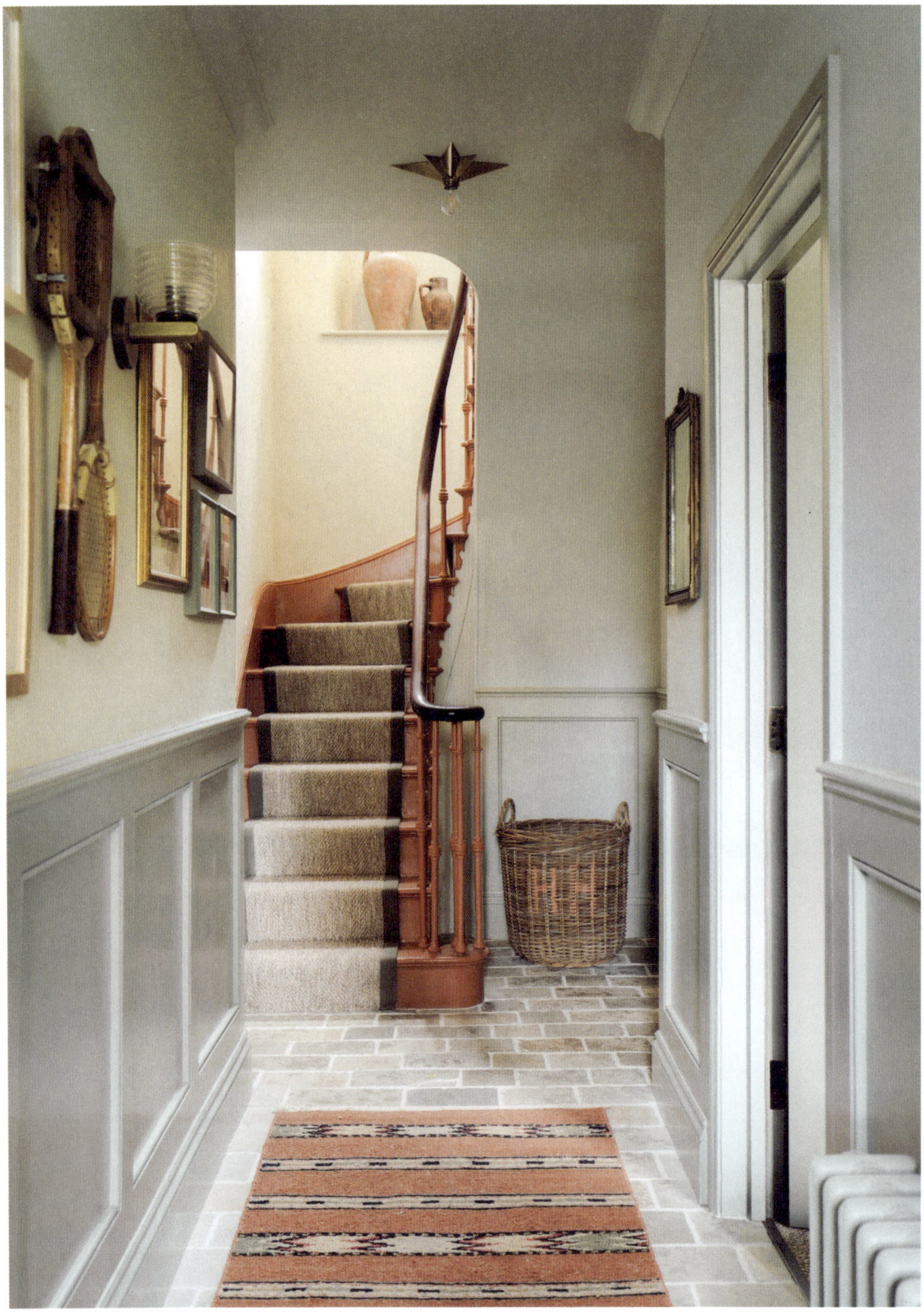

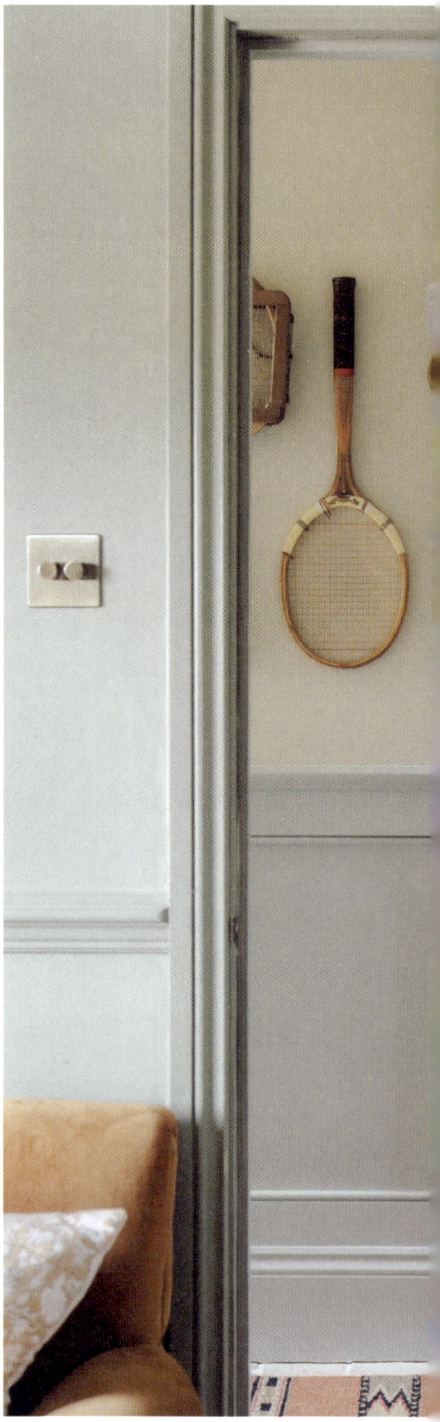

↑ This beautiful house in the centre of Stow-on-the-Wold had been stripped of its original features. We worked with joiners to reinstate them – the oak bench and timber panelling replicated to match what once would have been there. Made to feel timeless but also made to last.

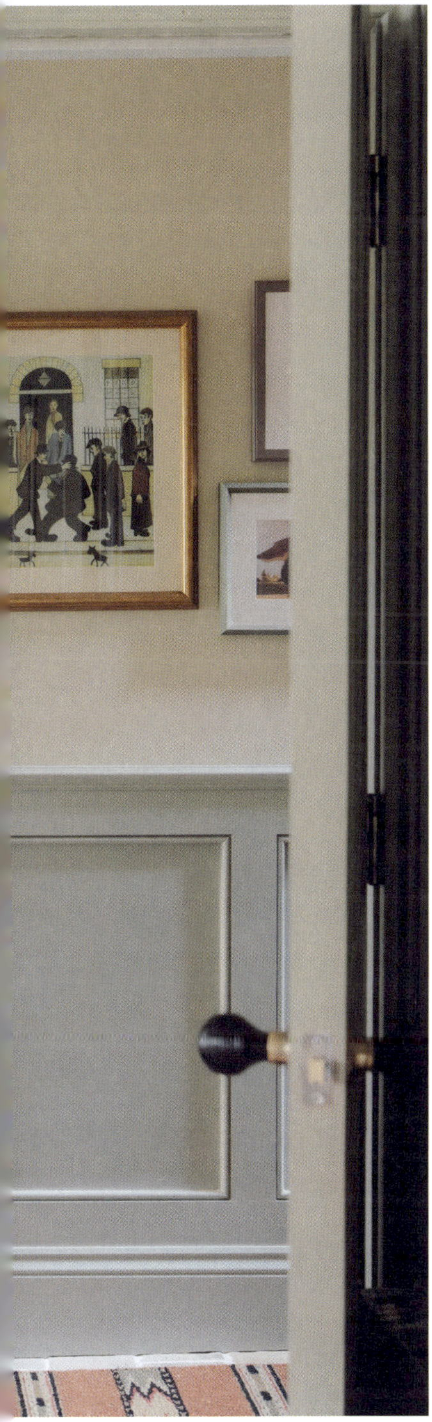

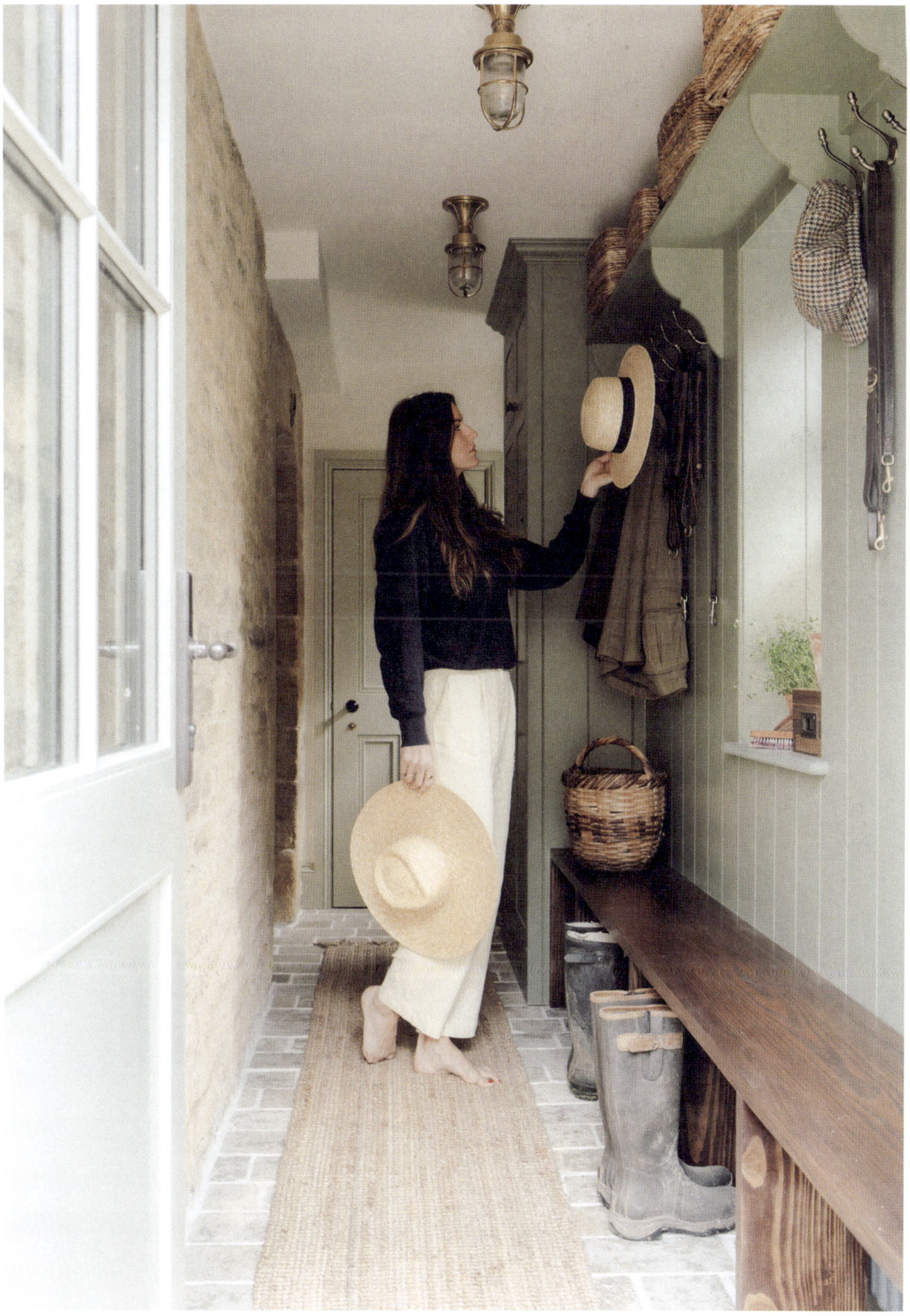

Mixing Styles

I grew up learning to mix styles long before I ever realised it was "a thing". When my parents moved to Wimbledon in my teens, London essentially became my back garden. I spent my time zig-zagging across the city hunting for treasure. Saturdays meant Spitalfields or Camden Market, back when Camden still had glorious punk rockers stomping around in platform boots and safety pins, and Spitalfields sold more dusty wonders than artisanal granola. I'd weave through those stalls with £10 in my pocket, convinced I was about to uncover something extraordinary.

→ This living room shows how to mix styles considerately – different eras that still gently talk to each other. The archway and panelling are classically English, so I brought in a sculptural pedestal coffee table to push against that, an antiqued brass chandelier for tradition, and a faded Persian rug to tie it together. Nothing clashing, just everything having its own place.

London is a masterclass in mixing eras without overthinking it. Turn one corner and you're in a narrow Marylebone backstreet where Georgian townhouses sit calmly beside modern glass-fronted boutiques. Turn another and you're swept into the Liberty store where Tudor beams, Arts & Crafts florals and contemporary fashion coexist as if that combination has always been entirely reasonable. The whole city is a collage of centuries, all stacked, layered, and bumping shoulders. That sense of joyful juxtaposition sank into me early; it taught me that old and new don't just coexist, they enrich each other.

So when people ask how to mix styles at home – Swedish and Gustavian antiques with a mid-century chair, an Impressionist painting above a modern console, a Persian rug beneath a Belgium sofa – I never pretend to be an authority. I just know what I love, and I know that trying things is the only way you learn. Mixing well is about experimenting, playing, shifting something a little to the left, and seeing how it feels. There's no formula because taste isn't mechanical; it's more emotional.

Most people get anxious about combining periods or styles because they think their home has to "make sense" to someone else. But truly, mixing styles is a lot like getting dressed. Some days you're in jeans and a blazer; some days you're in a vintage jacket with trainers; some days you're jewellery-heavy and dramatic. It works because you wear it with confidence, and because you have a few reliable staples you trust.

Interiors are exactly the same. A handful of grounding pieces – a great sofa, a beautiful rug, a table or two that have lived a life – allow you to be as playful or unexpected as you like around them. When you mix eras well, it doesn't feel chaotic, it feels alive. It feels like your home has a personality – a real, evolving character shaped by all the places you've been and all the things you love.

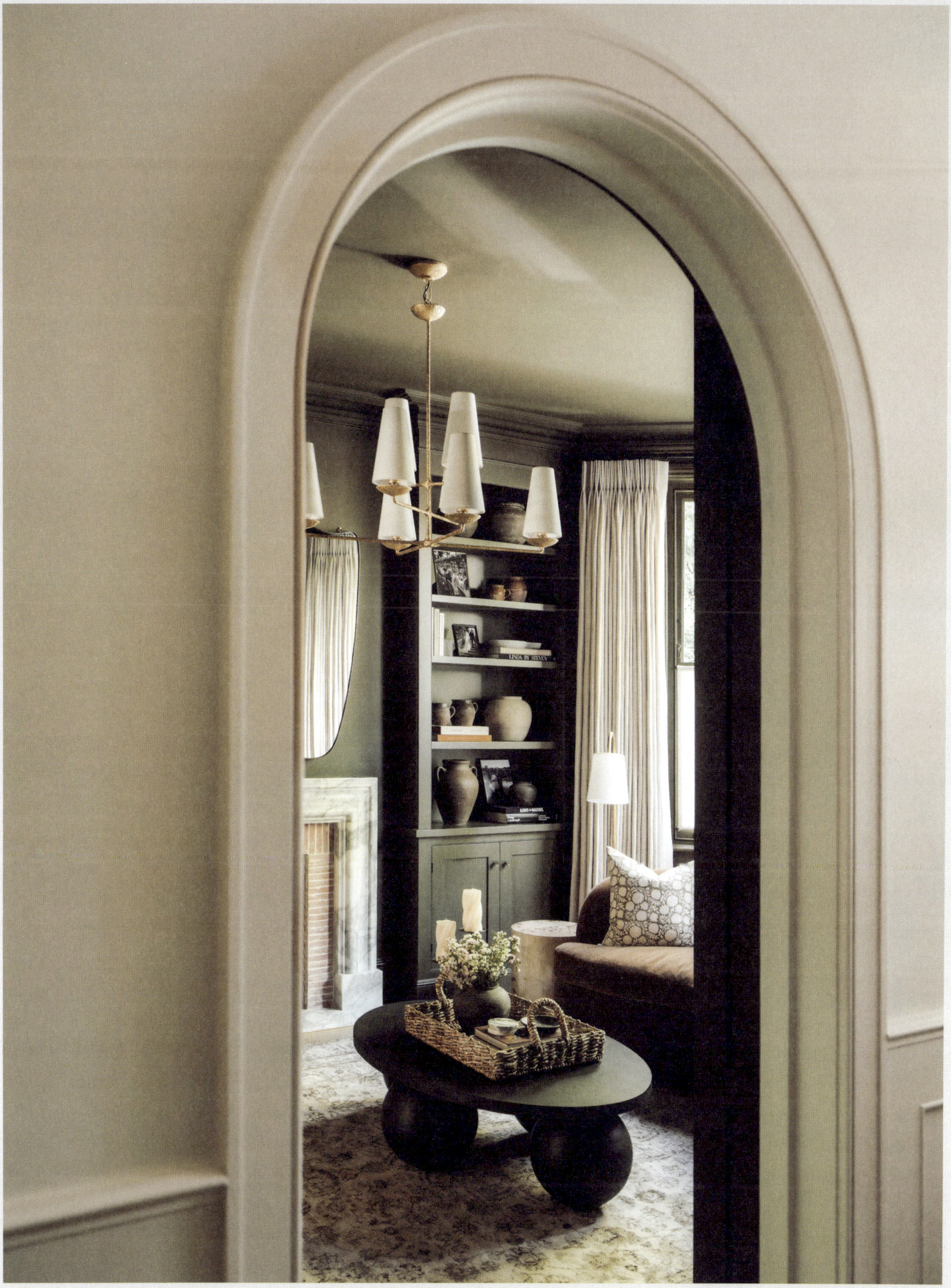

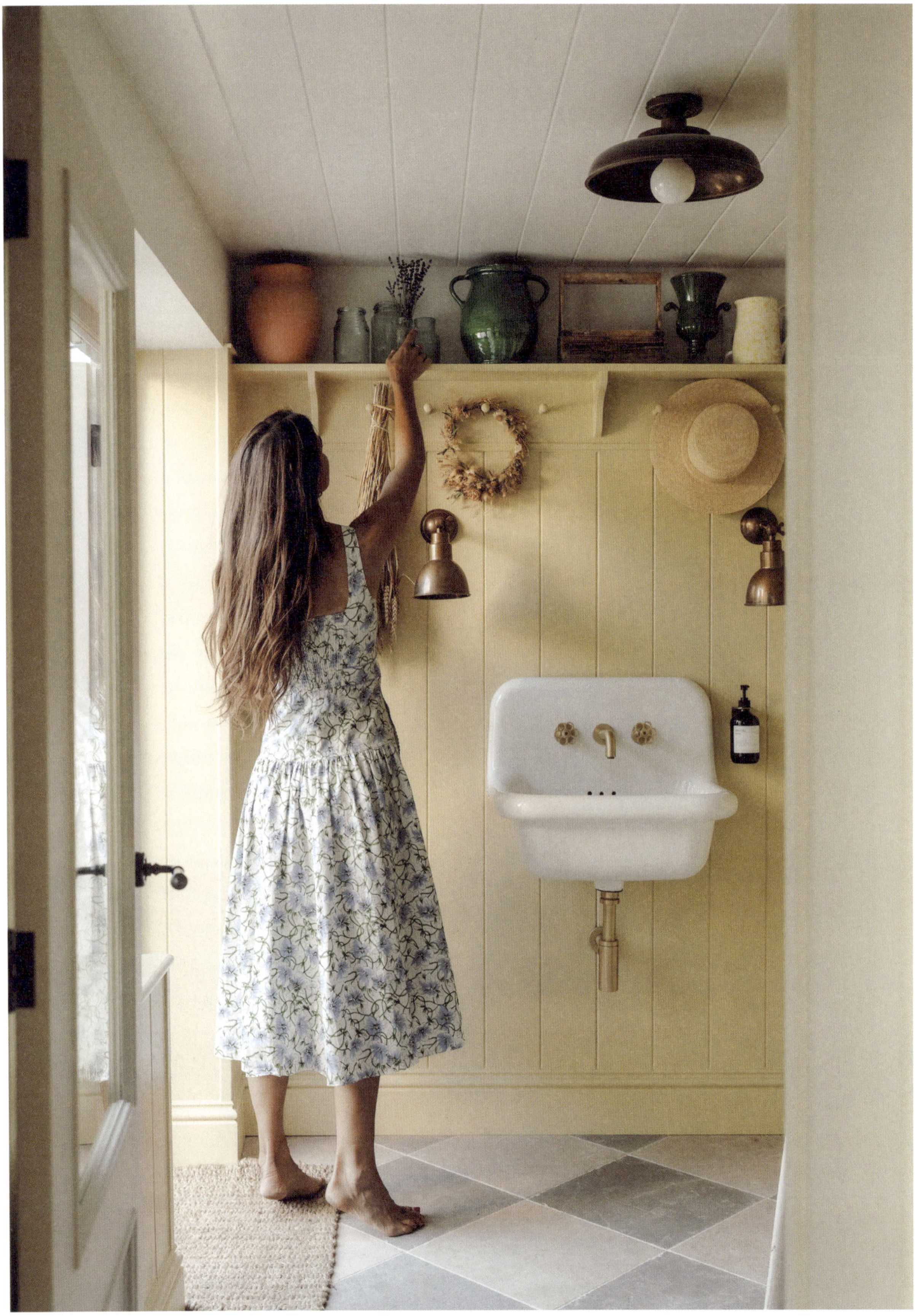

→ The kitchen at the home of my good friend Pollyanna Wilkinson. Her brief was colour, but earthy vibes and timeless. Mixing styles can be subtle – it doesn't need to shout. Here it's the warmth of olive cabinetry against limestone floors, brass details against soft stone worktops, an old enamel sink alongside considered new joinery.

↑ In the boot room, checkerboard floor tiles set the scene for a styled collection of her own pots and vases.

→ → The view from her kitchen into the open-plan living space. The connection to the garden mattered most to her, so we used biophilic-inspired colours throughout her home.

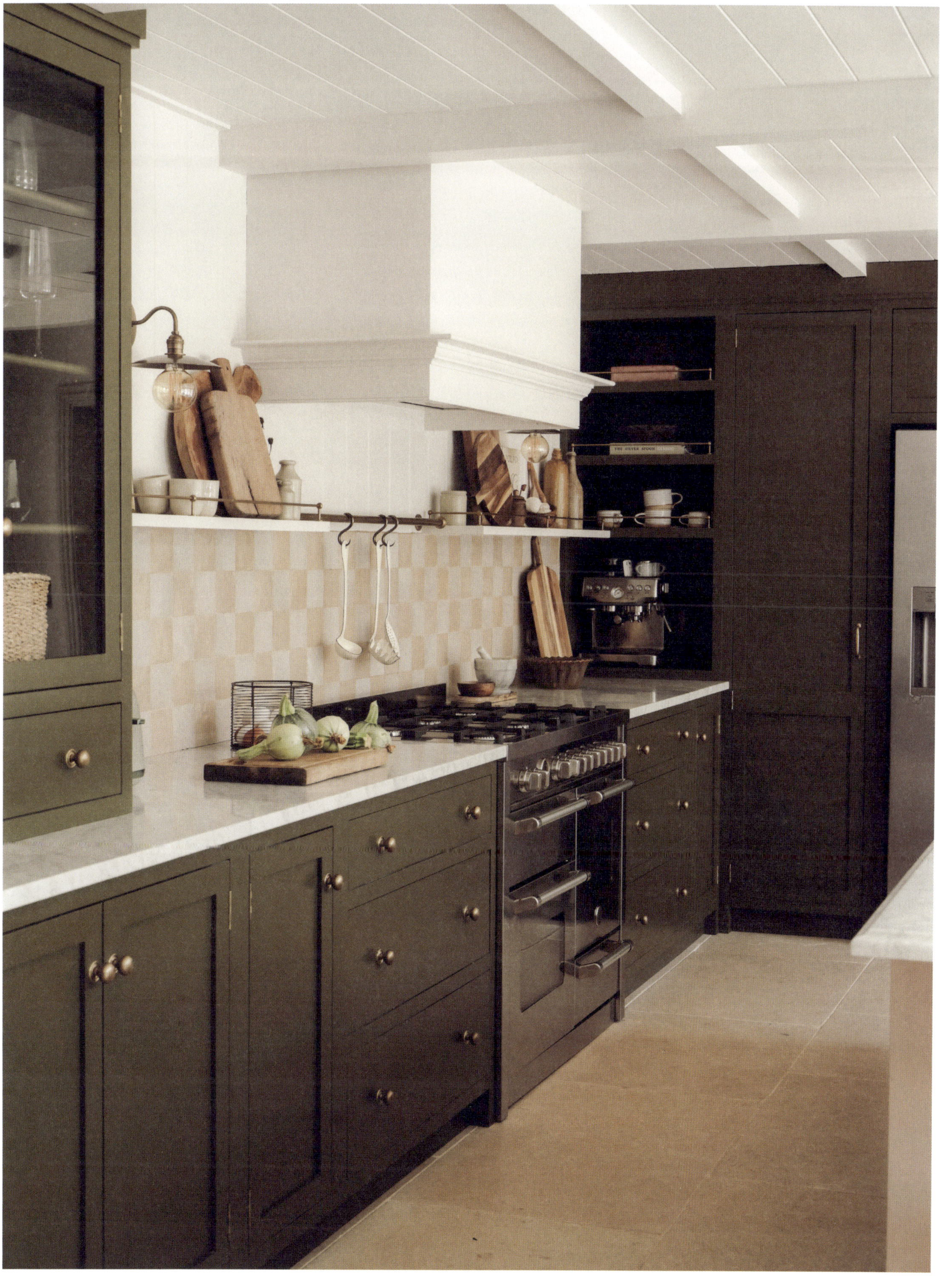

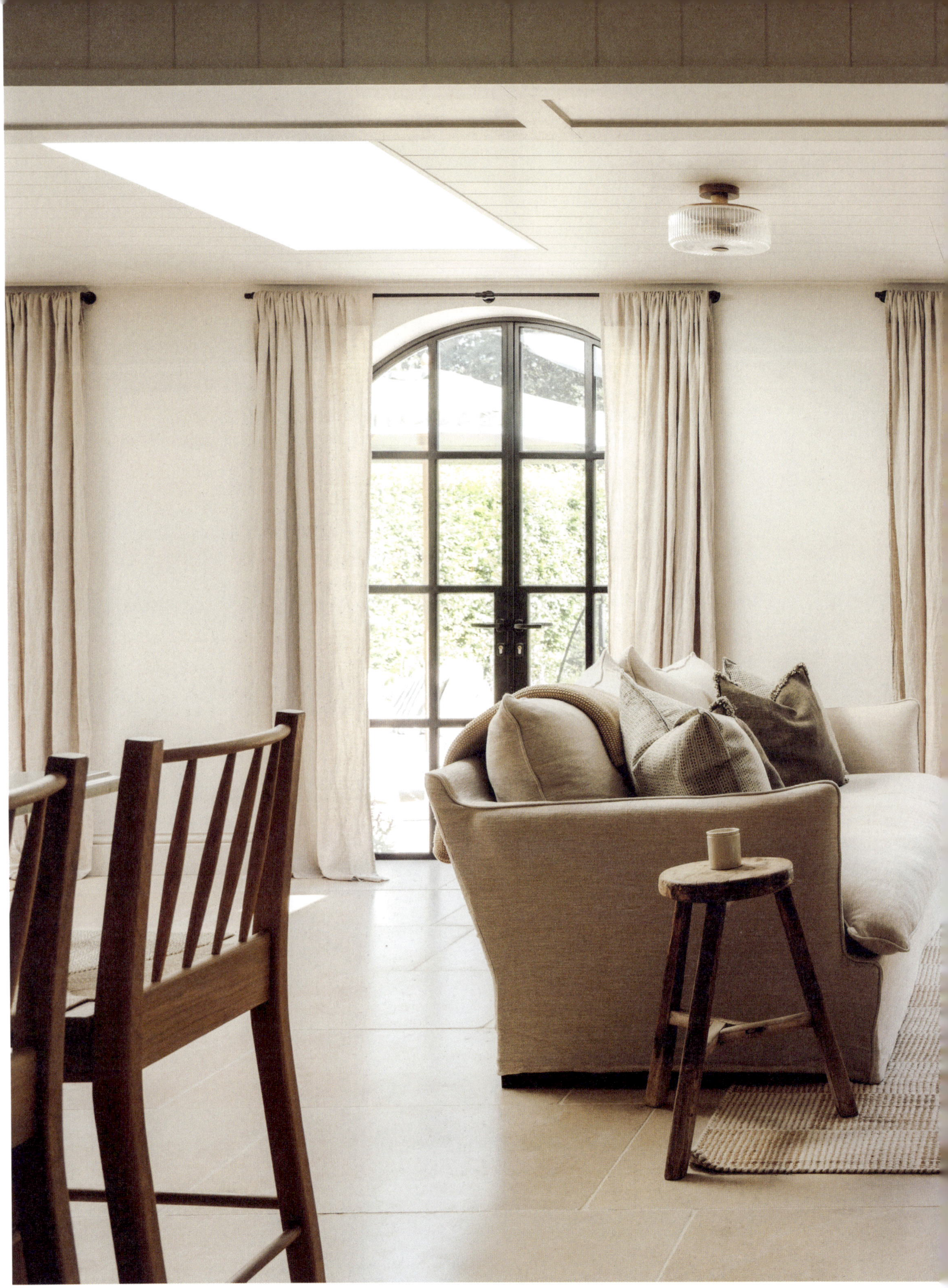

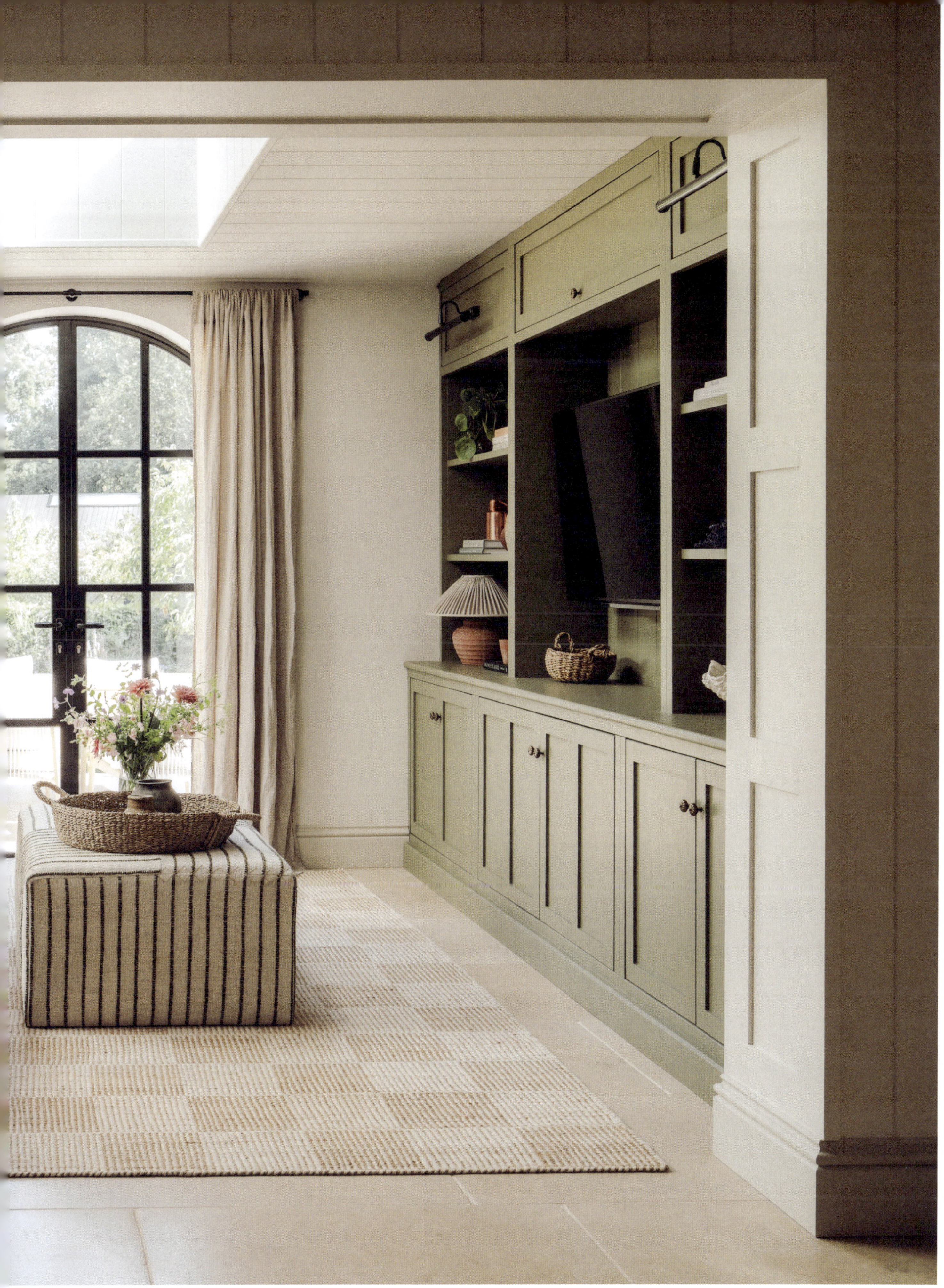

Edit with Confidence

Curation isn't about having more; it's about choosing better. A curated space feels intentional and personal without feeling cluttered. These prompts will help you edit with confidence and display with real purpose.

1. EDIT BEFORE YOU ADD

The instinct is always to bring more in. The braver move is to take things out. A well-curated space is allowed to breathe.
Try this: Walk through one room and remove anything that doesn't earn its place – anything you wouldn't consciously choose again today. Notice how much lighter the room feels without it.

---

2. LET THINGS HAVE MEANING

The most curated spaces aren't filled with expensive things – they're filled with considered ones. An object with a story will always outperform a beautiful object with none.
Do this: Look around the room and ask of each piece – do I love it, does it mean something, or is it just filling space? Keep the first two. Question the third.

---

3. DISPLAY IN ODD NUMBERS

Groups of three, five or seven feel dynamic and natural to the eye. Even numbers can feel formal or static.
Try this: Take a shelf or surface and rearrange your objects into groupings of three. Vary the height within each group. Notice how the composition immediately feels more alive.

---

4. CREATE VISUAL REST

Not everything deserves equal attention. A curated room has a hierarchy – a few hero pieces, some supporting players, and plenty of quiet space in between.
Try this: Identify the one object in a room you'd rescue in a fire. Give it more space around it. Let it be seen properly.

---

5. VARY THE HEIGHTS

Flat arrangements feel static. When objects sit at different levels – a tall vase beside a low stack of books beside a small sculpture – the eye moves and the display feels considered.
Do this: Introduce at least three distinct heights to your next arrangement. Use books, boxes or small plinths if needed.

---

6. BRING THE OUTSIDE IN

A stem, a branch, a handful of dried grasses – organic elements are one of the simplest and most effective curatorial tools there is. They add life, imperfection, and seasonality.
Try this: Replace one decorative object on a surface with something foraged or grown. See how it shifts the energy of everything around it.

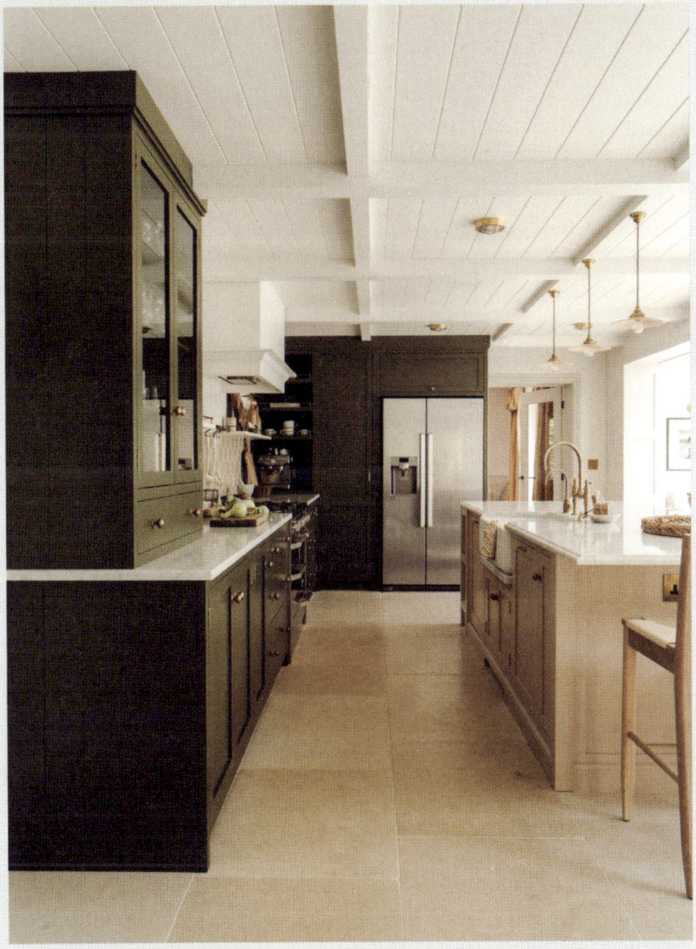

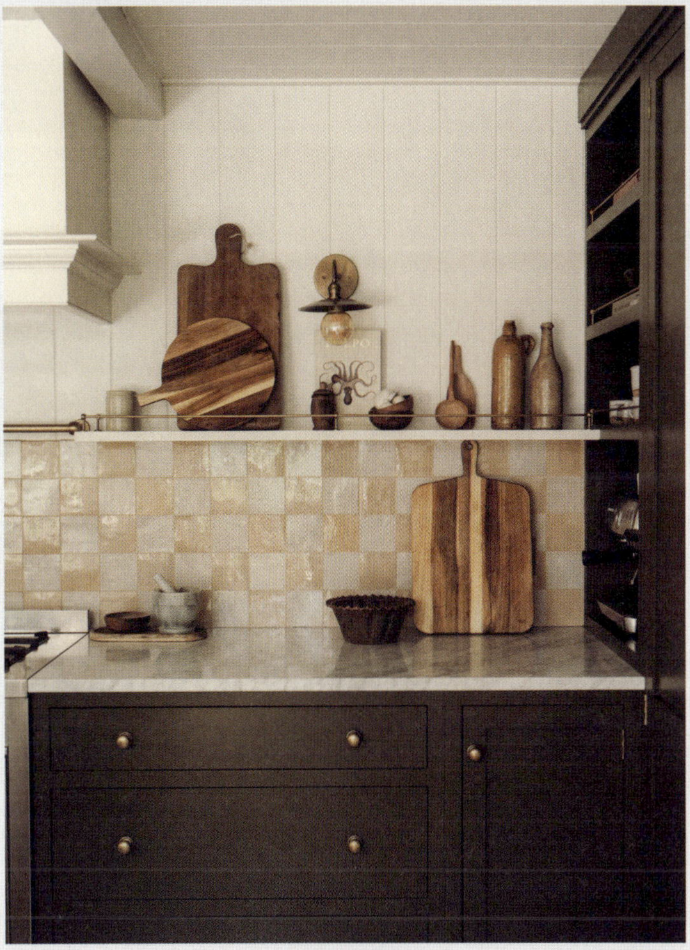

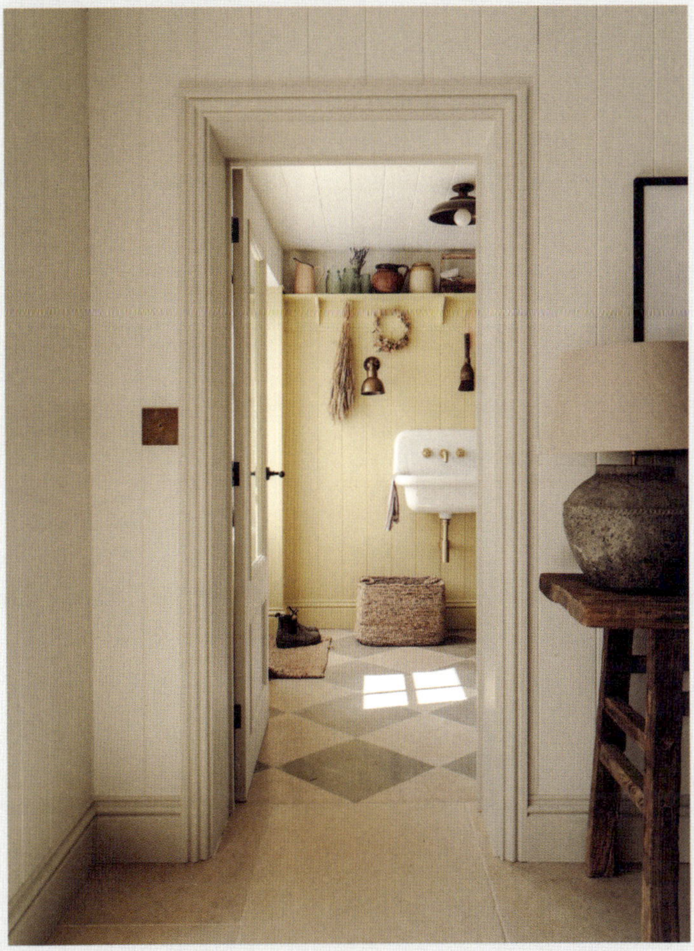

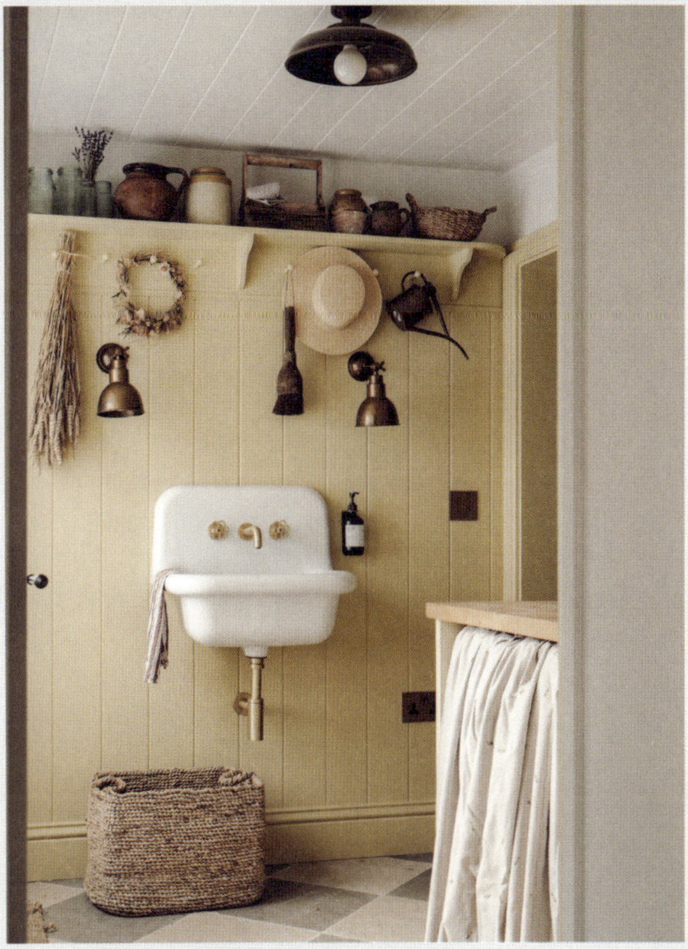

“The only way to make sense out of change is to plunge into it, move with it, and join the dance.”

ALAN WATTS

Evolve

ADAPT YOUR HOME AS LIFE FLOWS

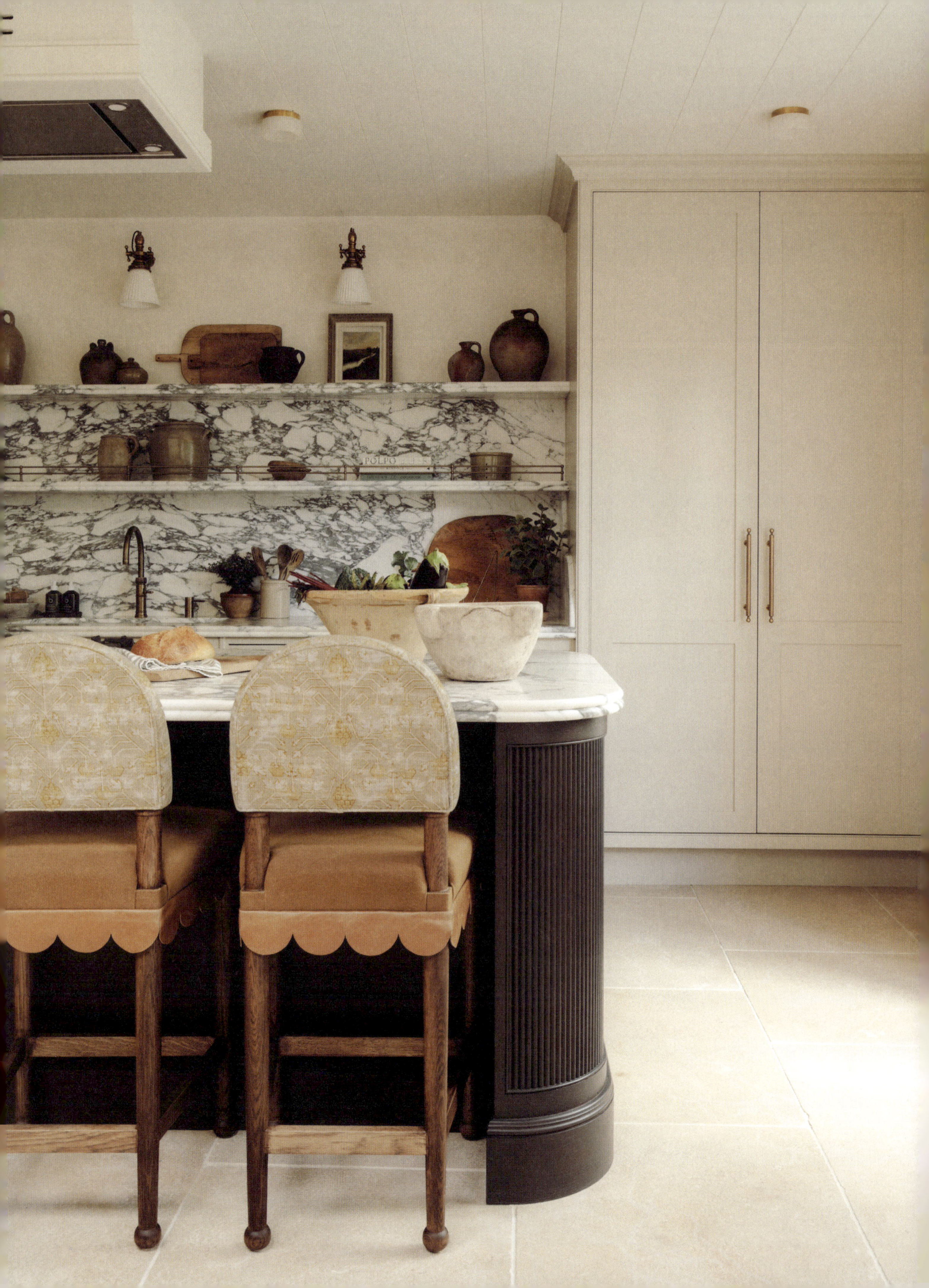
POLPO

THE EVOLVING *HOME*

I've always believed a home should behave a bit like a living organism, quietly expanding, contracting, adapting, and occasionally moulting, depending on what life is doing with you at the time. The trouble is, most of us try to freeze our homes at one ideal moment. We design for the life we think we'll have, rather than the life we're actually living... or the life we'll be living two years from now when a surprise puppy – or indeed baby, a new job, or a teenager's unexpected drum kit – lands in the middle of it all.

Growing up, our family home was constantly shifting shape. My mother would announce, mid-Tuesday, "I think the dining room is actually a library," and by Wednesday the table would be in the hallway and we'd be eating at a card table because she was "still getting the feel of things". It drove me mad at the time, but it taught me something foundational: spaces work best when you let them evolve with you.

And yet, in my work as a designer, I see a kind of nervousness around change. Clients will whisper, almost guiltily, "Is it terrible that I'm thinking of repainting the living room?" as though I'm about to hand them a detention slip. But here's the truth: paint is the least permanent commitment you will ever make. If you're going to be impulsive anywhere in life, let it be with colour, not haircuts or relationships.

But before we get into the fun of change, here's my grounding principle: design with lifestyle in mind. Not the polished, imaginary lifestyle where you meditate daily and your kitchen island is always spotless and adorned with a perfectly symmetrical fruit bowl. I mean the real one featuring your actual rhythms. Do you work from home now? Are you caring for ageing parents? Are there toddlers who believe every horizontal surface was created for climbing? These things matter far more than whether your sofa perfectly matches your rug.

A future-proof home isn't one where you've predicted every life scenario; it's one where the bones are smart. Quality flooring, decent wiring, lighting that can be dimmed and layered, well planned out joinery and storage that doesn't require Olympic-level contortion to access – these are the "backbone

← The clients originally wanted timber floors, but with the room being south-facing, we advised on limestone instead to avoid sun damage down the line. A London townhouse, but first and foremost a family home – built to be lived in, not just looked at.

→ → The kitchen at our Notting Hill project. The honed marble was a real splurge, but it's the veining that gives this kitchen so much of its depth and character – worth every conversation it took to get there.

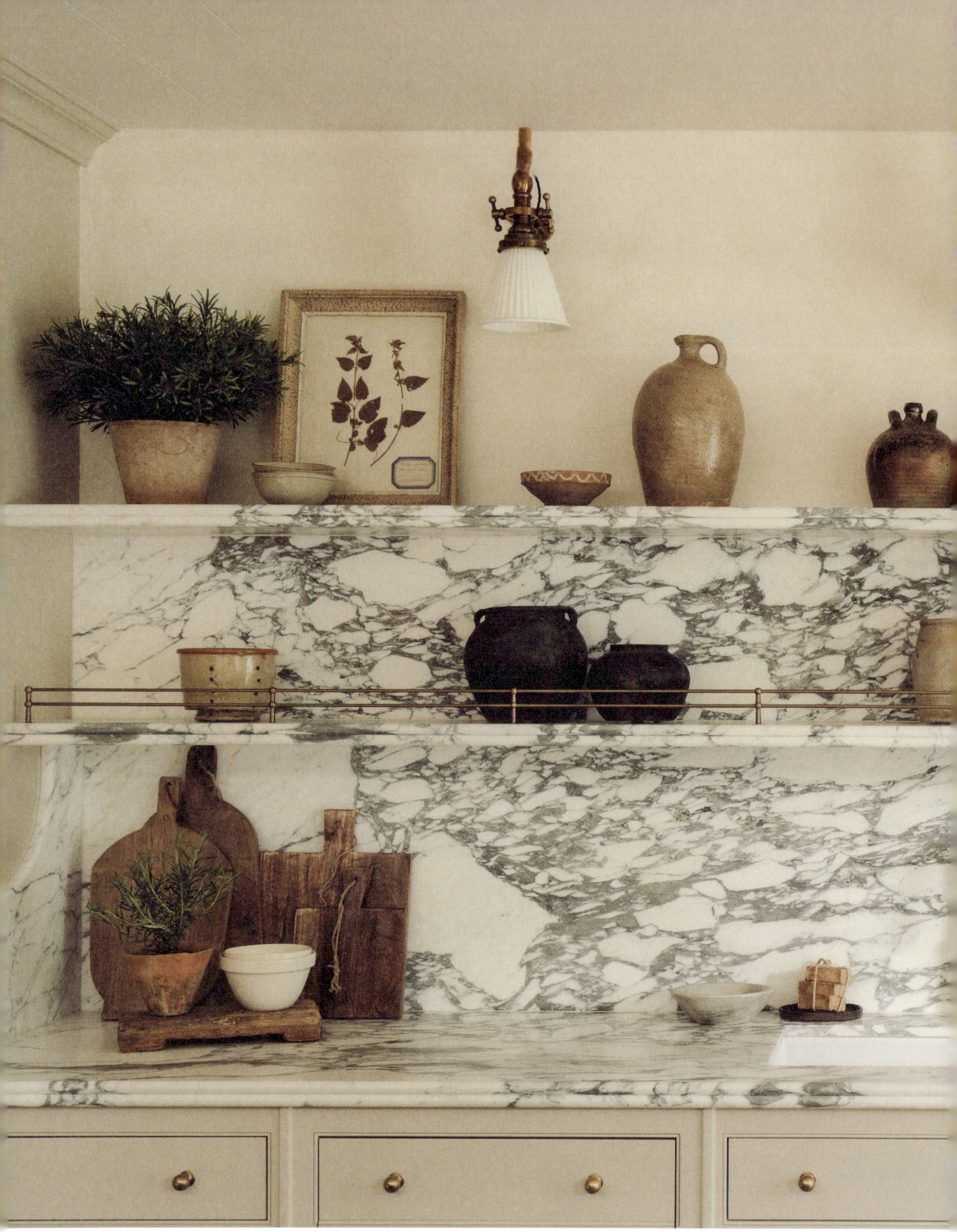

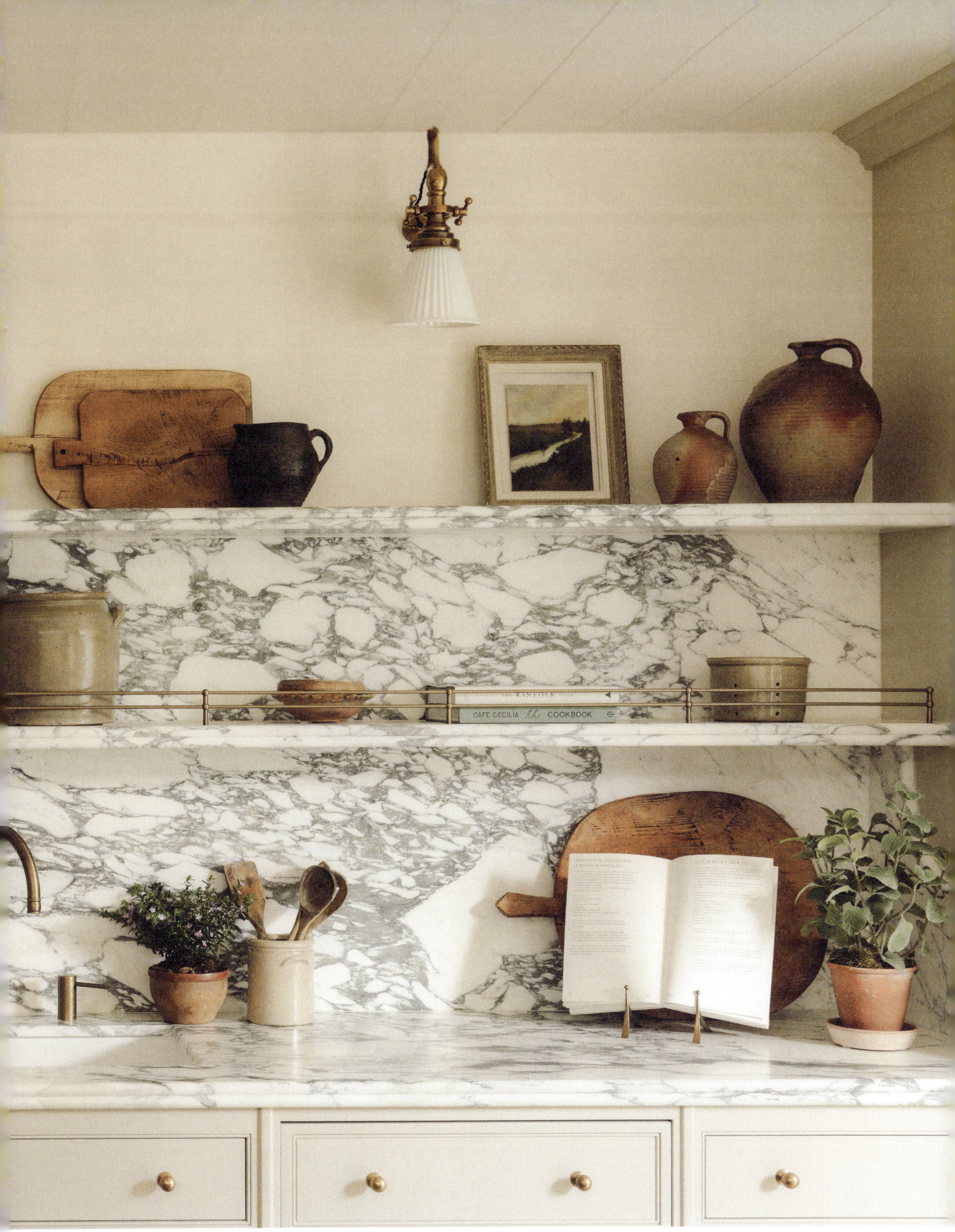
KINFOLK
CAFE CECILIA
COOKBOOK

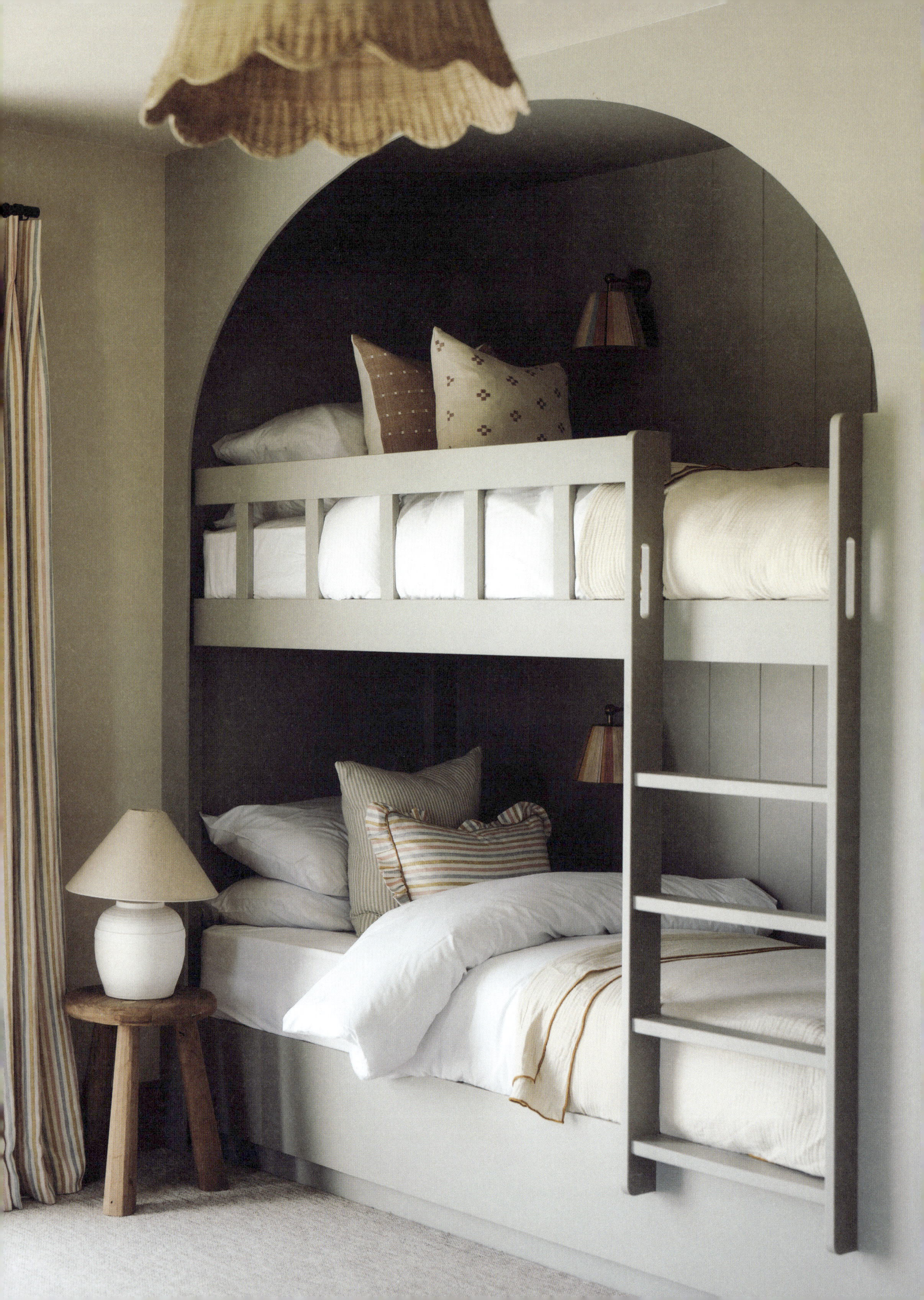

investments" that pay you back over and over because they don't need replacing every time you shift direction.

Once those bones are in place, create a neutral backdrop that stays steady even as everything else moves. Think of it like a beautifully cut town coat that is timeless, unassuming, and able to pair with every different pair of shoes depending on the mood or the season. Walls, floors, built-in cabinets – keep them calm and adaptable so you can be as expressive as you want everywhere else.

Because here's what no one tells you: most of the evolution in a home happens not through renovations, but through small, layered choices. The painting you bought on holiday in Cornwall. The little brown patterened velvet slipper chair you inherited that you swore was hideous until one day around perimenopause you suddenly "got it". The artwork your child made that somehow has more soul than the print you spent £300 on. The stories accumulate, and your home starts to feel richer – not because everything is new, but because everything feels lived.

Of course, we must talk about the emotional impulse to change things. Nothing sends people into a paint-sampling frenzy quite like returning from holiday or ending a relationship. I've had clients who, newly returned from a few weeks in Ibiza, are convinced their Edwardian terrace should now be whitewashed top to bottom "for freshness". And look, maybe it should. Or maybe you're just trying to extend the holiday feeling. That's human. But before you go redecorating in a fit of post-breakup or holiday catharsis, pause. Ask yourself: "Is this a true desire for evolution, or am I trying to reset my life through my walls?" Both are valid, but the former lasts longer.

And then I harp back to sustainability. Evolution doesn't mean ripping everything out and starting again (in fact, that's the opposite). The most sustainable home is one that changes slowly, intentionally, and with respect for what's already there. Repainting, repurposing, reupholstering – these are all small interventions that reduce waste and give old pieces new meaning. Evolution is gentler than renovation. And much cheaper.

Ultimately, an evolving home is an honest home. It reflects the season you're in, without pretending you're somewhere else. When your family grows, the house expands to meet it. When life quiets, the house exhales. When your tastes shift, the house shifts too – not dramatically, but gracefully, like someone adjusting their posture. The biggest takeaway? A home isn't a finished product; it's a relationship. And like any relationship worth keeping, it benefits from attention, communication, and the occasional refresh.

"The most sustainable home is one that changes slowly, intentionally, and with respect for what's already there."

← The kids' bunk room at Project Ziggy Rocks. A calm, adaptable backdrop in a soft sage paint- built to flex as the kids grow, with plenty of room left for the stories and layers that make a space feel lived in.

Flexible Design

Flexible design is one of those concepts that sounds terribly architectural and intimidating, but in reality, it's as simple as: "Can this room do more than one thing without driving me mad?" Our lives are not static, so our rooms shouldn't be either.

Modular furniture is a good starting point. I'm not talking about the enormous sectional sofas that require a forklift to move, but well-made pieces with lightweight components that can shift as your needs do. A modular sofa that can become two lounging chairs when you host friends; ottomans that double as coffee tables or extra seating; a dining bench that quietly moonlights as homework storage – these pieces work overtime.

Multipurpose rooms are the real unsung heroes of evolving homes. A guest room that's also a study. A dining room that transforms into a playroom with the help of a cupboard that hides toys with military precision. A landing with a built-in desk that becomes homework HQ. Most homes are full of underused corners that could be doing far more with just a bit of thought.

Adaptable storage is equally powerful. Adjustable shelving, hidden drawers, modular wardrobes – these aren't just organisational upgrades, they're lifelines. When your hobbies change (or your children's do), you want storage that shifts with you. I've seen clients spend thousands extending houses when all they really needed was smarter storage and a willingness to rearrange a little.

Flexible design isn't about perfection; it's about permission. Permission for your home to reflect who you are today, without locking you into yesterday's decisions.

→ The bunk room at Project Sandbanks. Tucked into the eaves, a built-in bed nook and window seat both with hidden storage beneath, proof that flexible design isn't about extending the house; it's about making the corners you already have work harder.

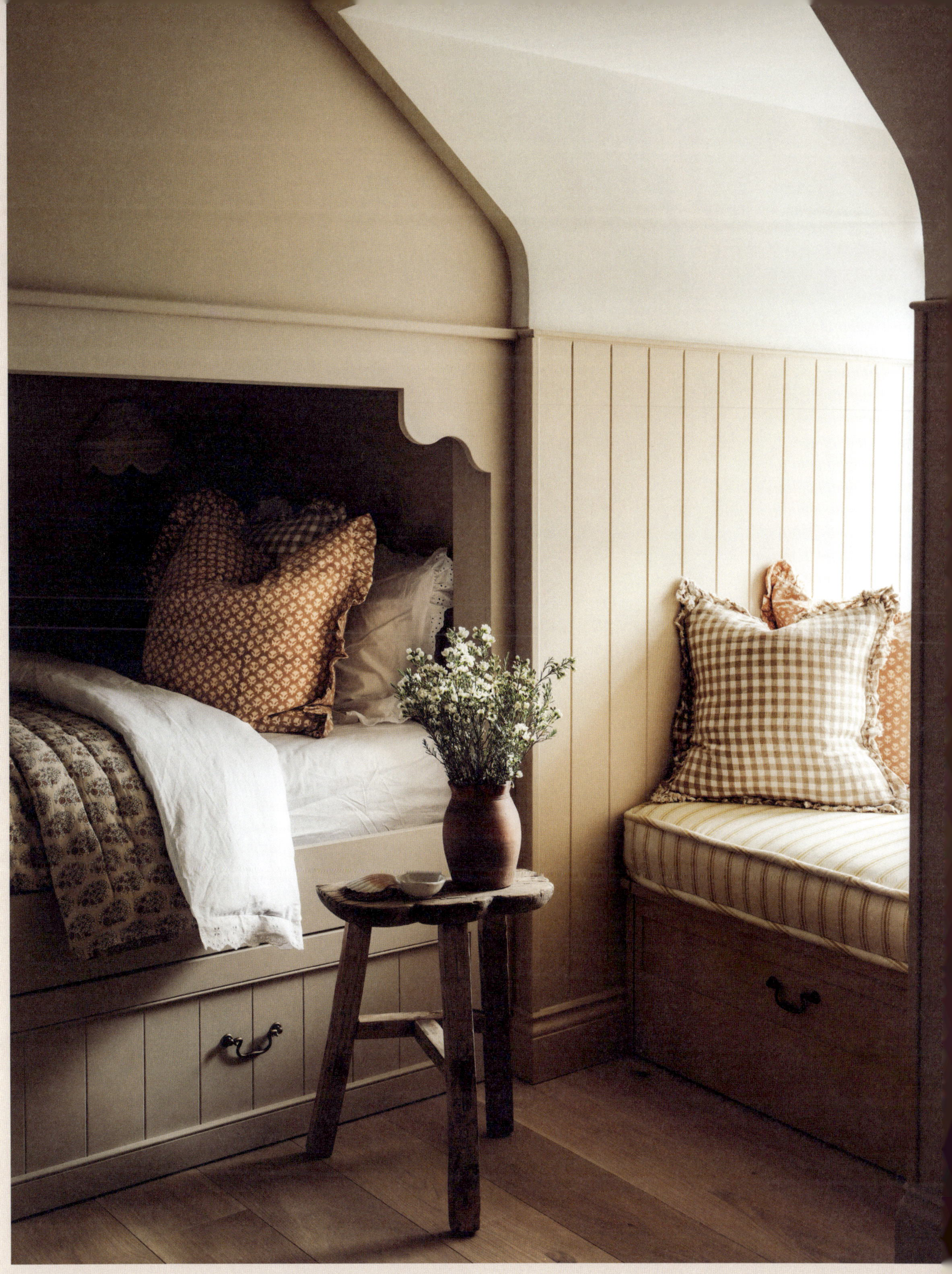

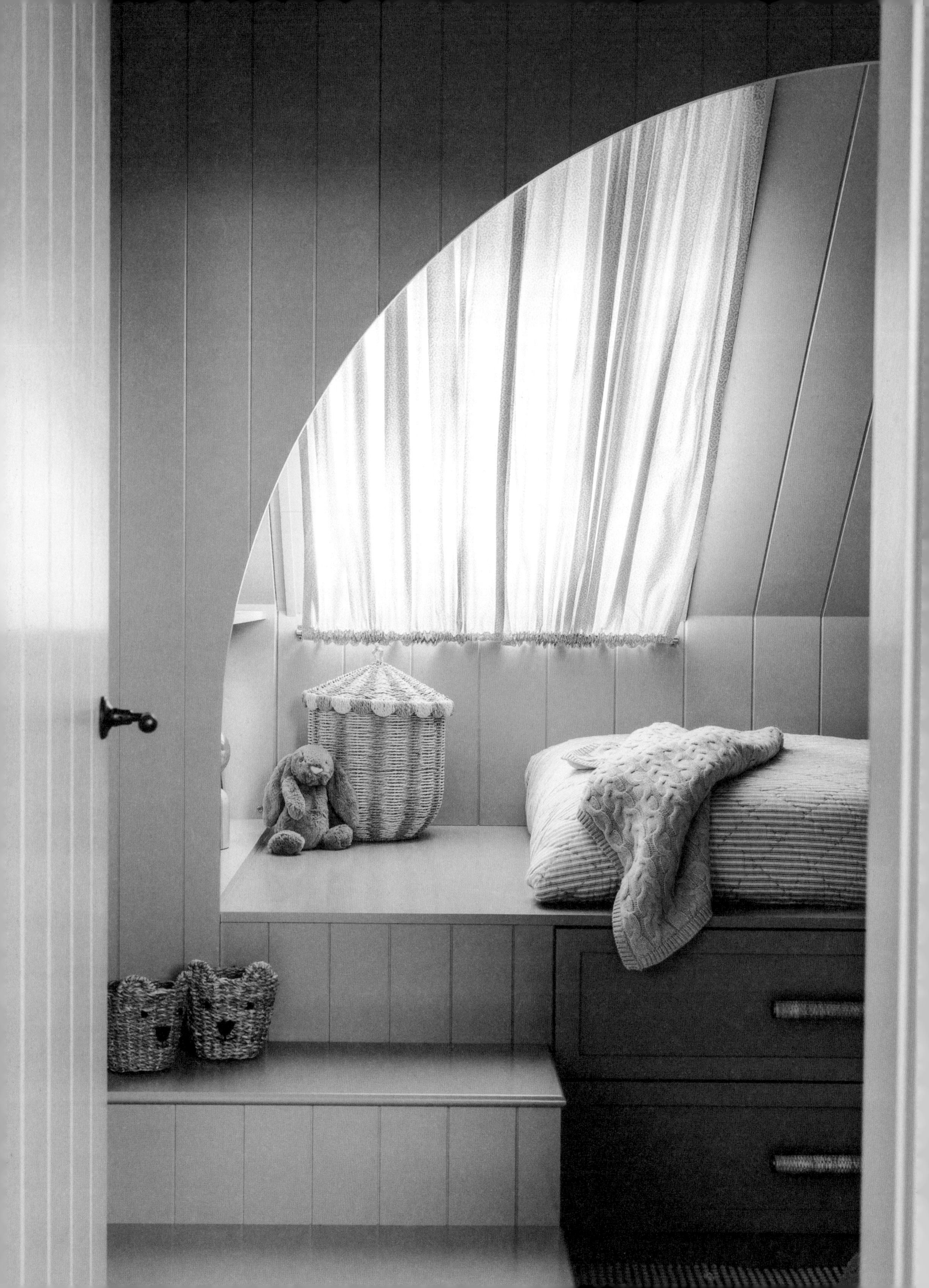

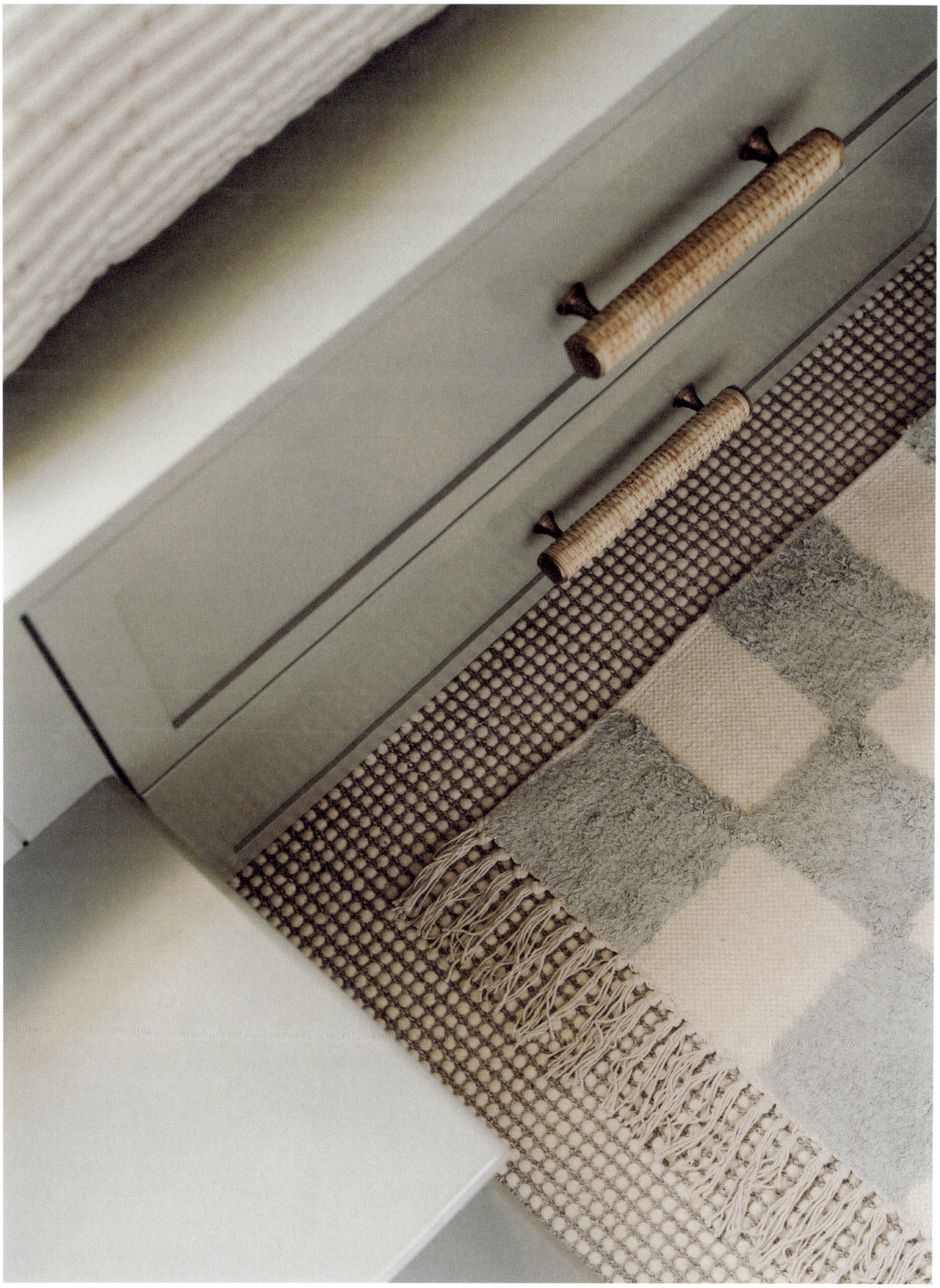

← Project Sandbanks. A tiny box room in the eaves, designed as the nursery for our clients' new baby boy. We maximised every inch of storage while creating something fun and a little magical, a space built to carry him through his primary years, not just his nursery days.

↑ The details: a built out step for climbing into bed, soft sisal wool carpet underfoot, and bamboo handles bringing in a little earthy texture.

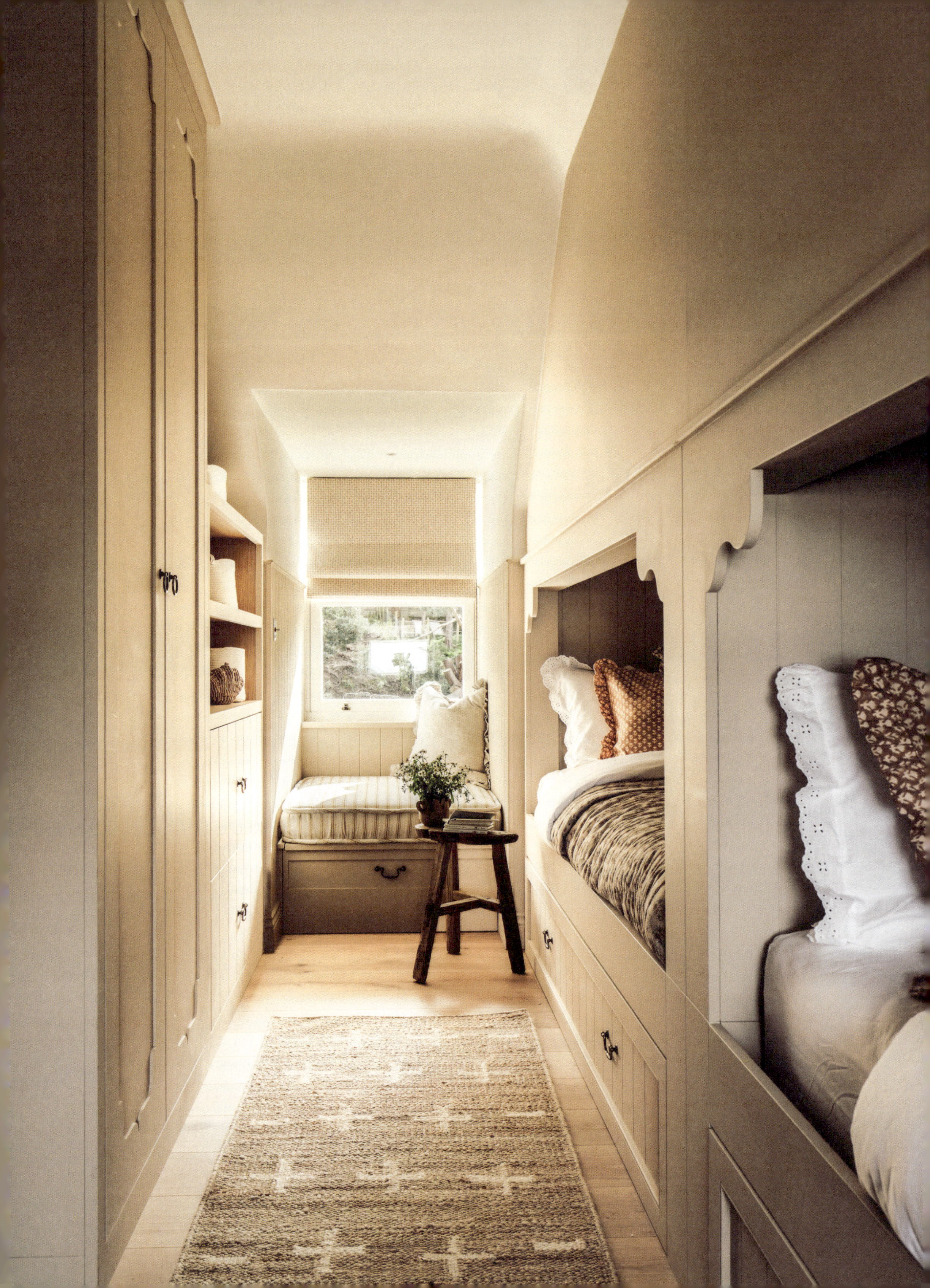

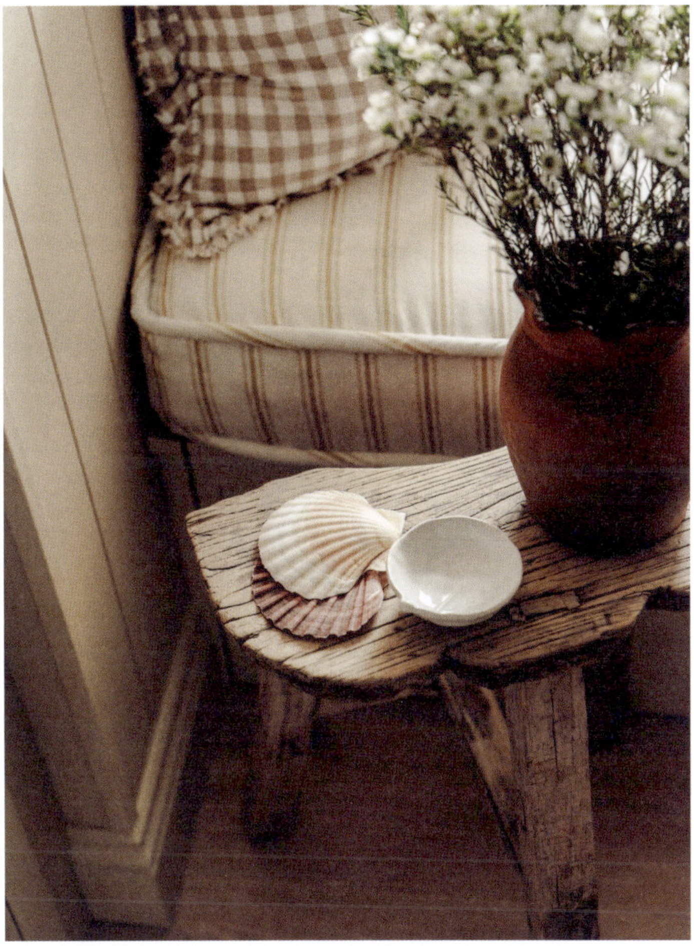

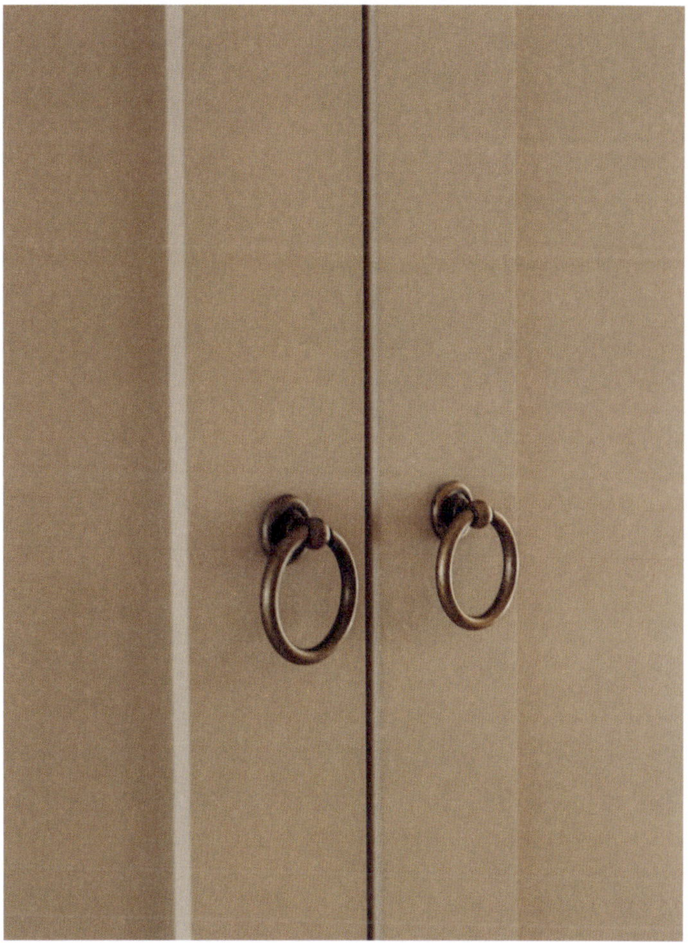

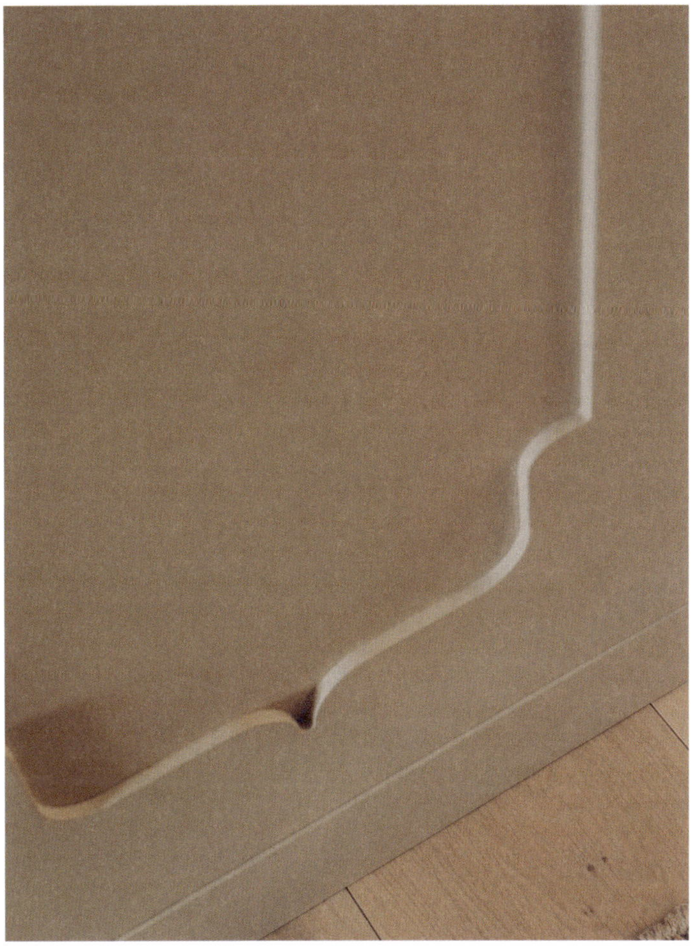

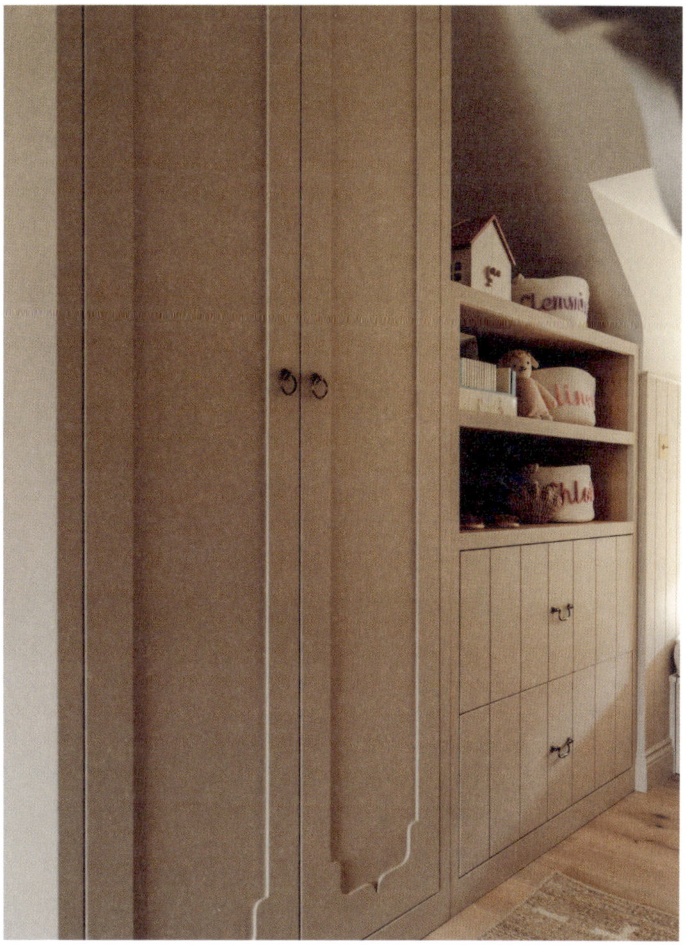

Refreshing Your Space

> *"Even the act of painting can be therapeutic, and is a visual declaration that something in your life is shifting."*

Refreshing your home doesn't have to mean a dramatic "after" moment worthy of reality TV. Most real transformation happens in the small things – the gentle tweaks and swaps that recalibrate the energy of a room without blowing the budget, or your sanity.

Reupholstering, for instance, is magic. One fabric change can turn a tired family heirloom chair into a knockout hero piece. The same goes for cushions, curtains, and throws – soft furnishings can completely shift a room's temperature, from warm and cocooning in winter to breezy and open in summer.

And paint. Oh, paint. If homes had a reset button, this would be it. A new colour isn't just aesthetic; it changes the way you feel in a room. Even the act of painting can be therapeutic, and is a visual declaration that something in your life is shifting. Lighting upgrades are another refresh with outsized impact. Swap a shade, change a bulb temperature, introduce a floor lamp, or reposition a pendant and suddenly your room has a pulse again.

Then there are the tiny, joyful updates – a new basket tray, moving art around, framing that print you've had rolled in a tube for two years. Accessories are the easiest way to indulge in trends without sacrificing longevity. And the beauty is you can change them again next season with zero guilt.

Refreshing is not about erasing the past; it's about creating space for the next layer of your life to settle in comfortably.

→ If there's one room built for taking risks, it's the downstairs loo. Small enough that a bold wallpaper or punchy paint colour won't overwhelm, big enough to shift the whole house's mood the moment you walk in. This one leans into a botanical print and sage panelling for something rich and characterful.

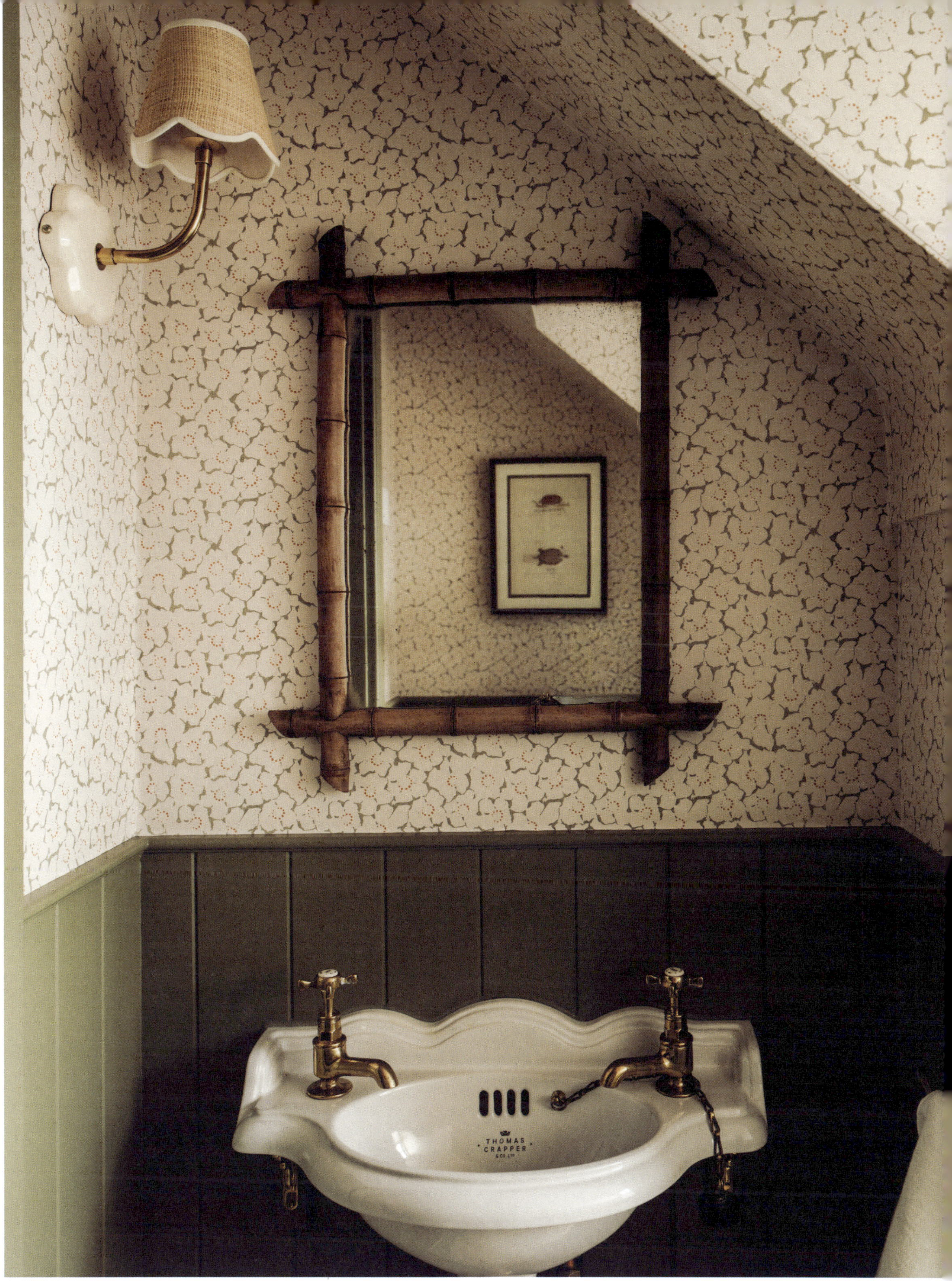
THOMAS
CRAPPER

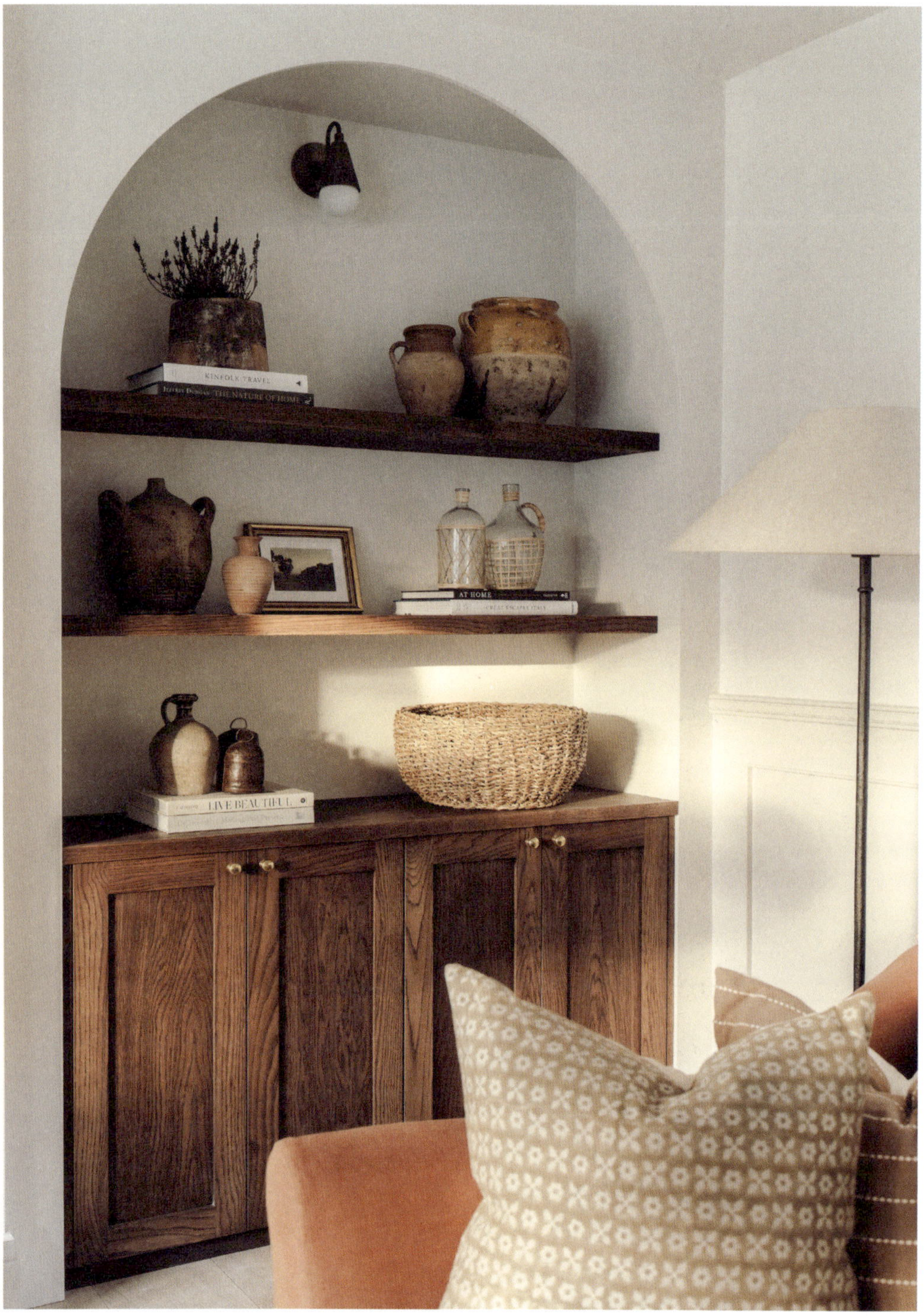

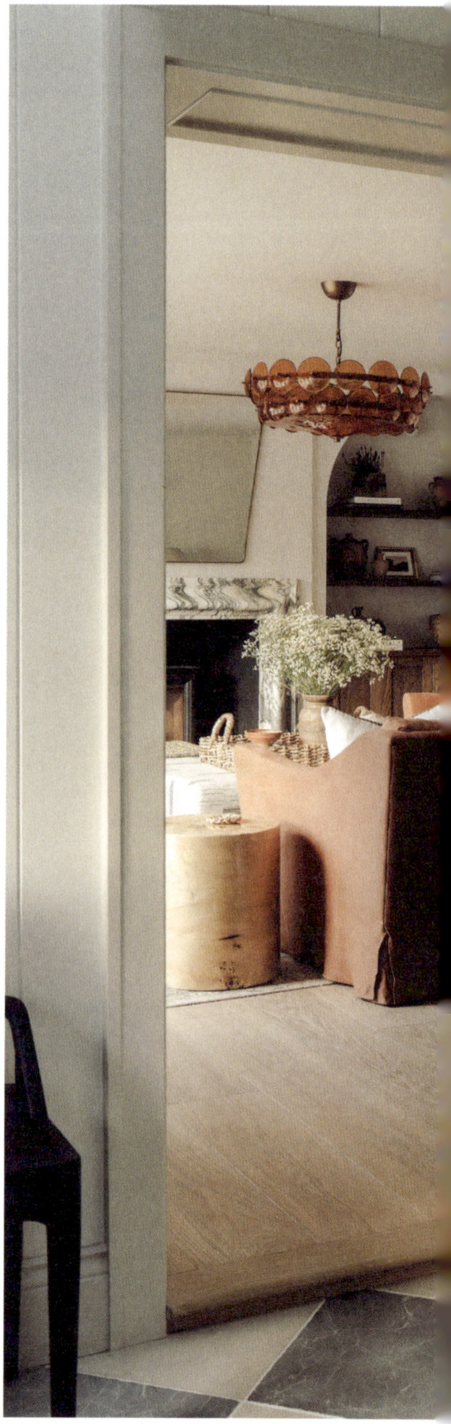

↑ Rust velvet, dried stems, warm timber – this room feels deeply autumnal. Yet a few small swaps could shift its whole mood: seasonal flowers, a lighter throw, even a different scent in the air. Proof that refreshing a space doesn't need a renovation - just a willingness to let it evolve.

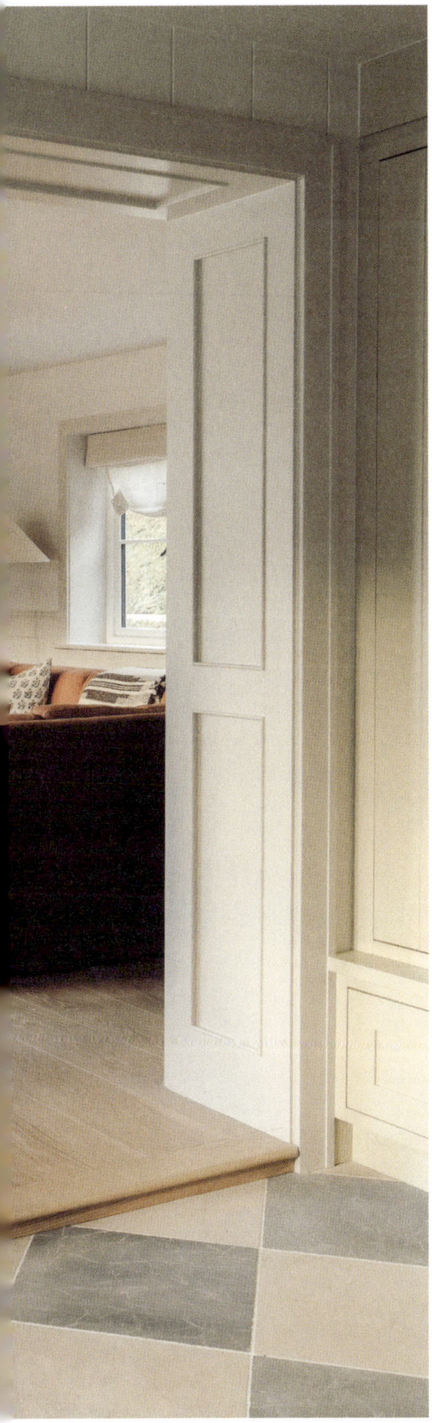

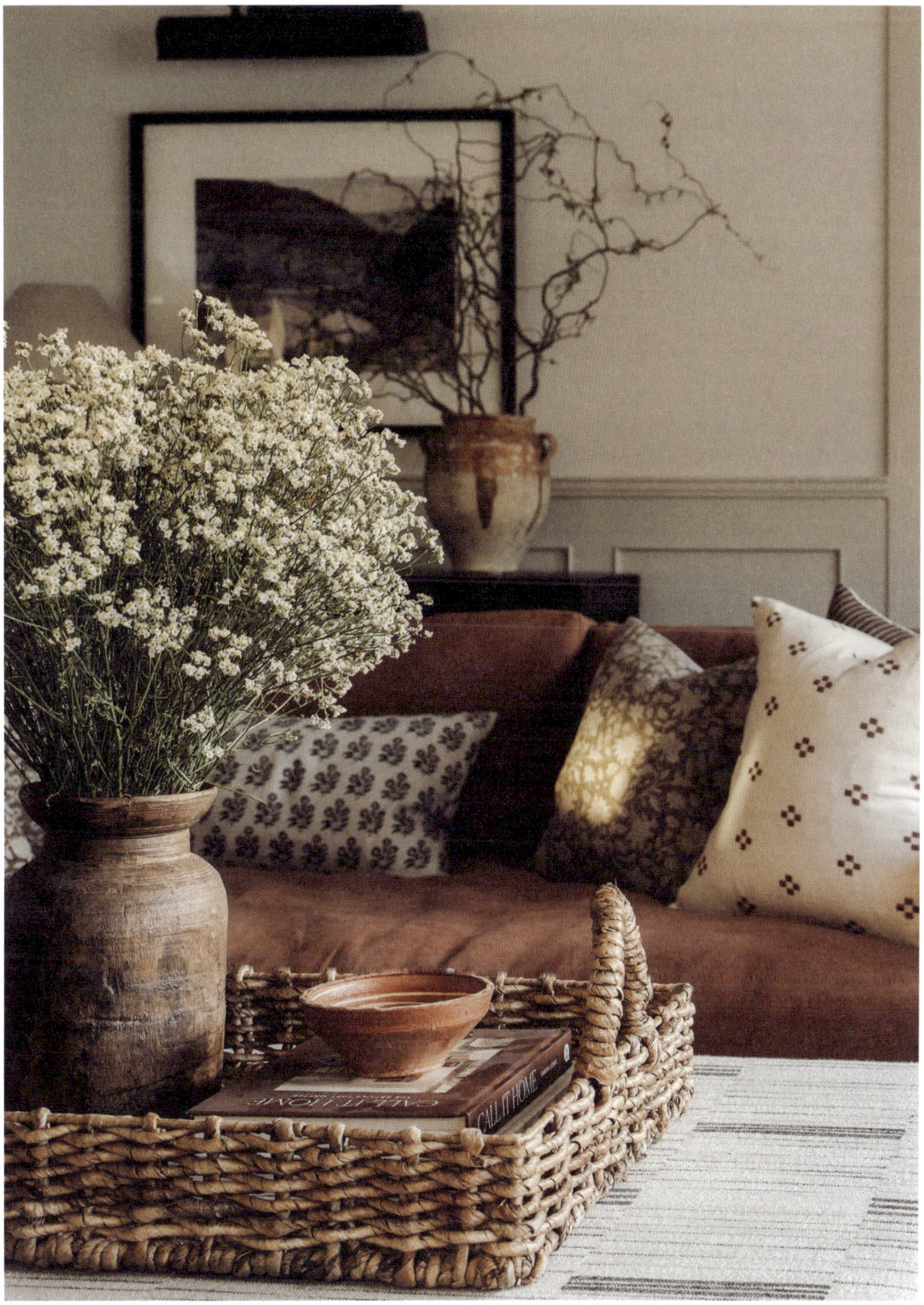
CALL IT HOME

Below are some soft, practical prompts to help you loosen perfectionism's grip and let your home feel easy, honest, and fully lived in.

1. LEAD WITH COMFORT, ALWAYS

If a space looks beautiful but doesn't feel good, it isn't truly working.

Try this: Sit in every seat in your living room. Which seat do you actually want to sit in? Which one feels stiff or "for guests only"? Let your body – not your décor instincts – make the call.

---

2. LET SIGNS OF LIFE STAY VISIBLE

A book on the armchair, a jumper thrown over the banister, a candle half-burned – these are signs of use, not failure.

Practise: Choose one everyday item you're always tidying away. Leave it out for twenty-four hours and observe how it feels to simply let it be part of the landscape of life.

---

3. MAKE FUNCTION YOUR GUIDING STAR

A room that supports your daily rhythms is worth far more than one that looks "done".

Do this: Stand in the doorway and ask: "What do I actually use this room for?" If the layout doesn't support that, shift one piece of furniture to better align with the reality of your life.

---

4. ADOPT A *WABI-SABI* GAZE

Look for beauty in the imperfect – the frayed edge, the scratch, the slightly wonky pottery bowl.

Try this: Walk through your home and identify one "flaw" you've been meaning to fix. Instead of correcting it, see if you can reframe it as patina, story, or character.

---

5. CREATE POCKETS OF REST

Relaxation doesn't happen by accident, it needs homes within your home.

Practise: Pick one corner and make it softer. Add a lamp, a throw, or something tactile. This becomes your exhale space.

---

6. GIVE YOURSELF PERMISSION TO USE THE GOOD THINGS

The "special" candle, the luxurious throw, the nice glassware – use them on an ordinary day.

Try this: Choose one item you "save for later". Use it tonight. Notice how your home rises to meet you.

---

7. EMBRACE THE CREATIVE MESS

A lived-in home is a creative home – papers on the table, paints on the counter, a project mid-flow.

Practise: Allow yourself one zone where creativity is can be imperfect. No tidying. No guilt.

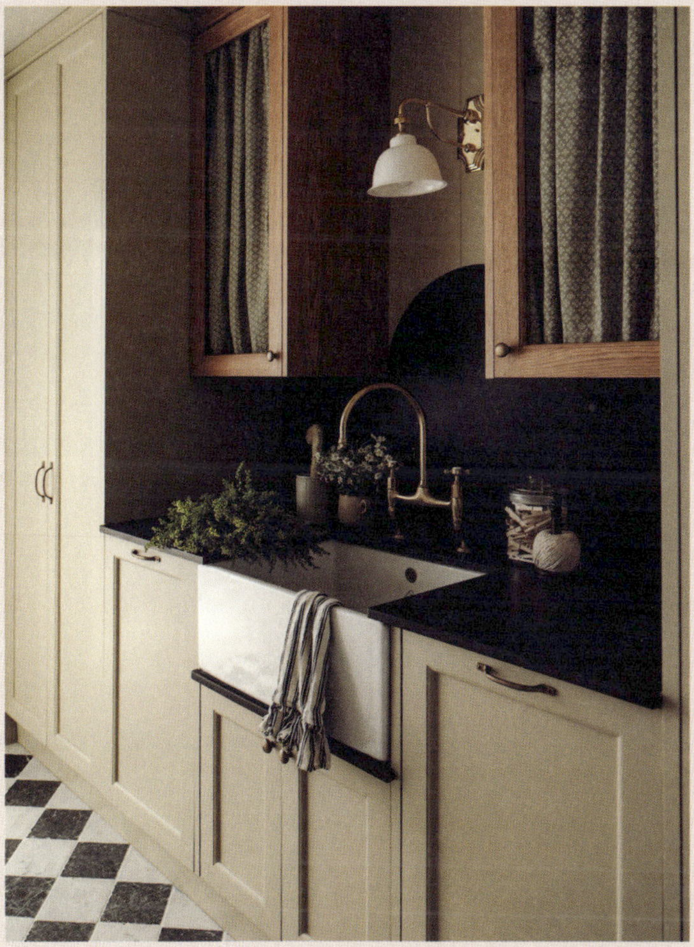
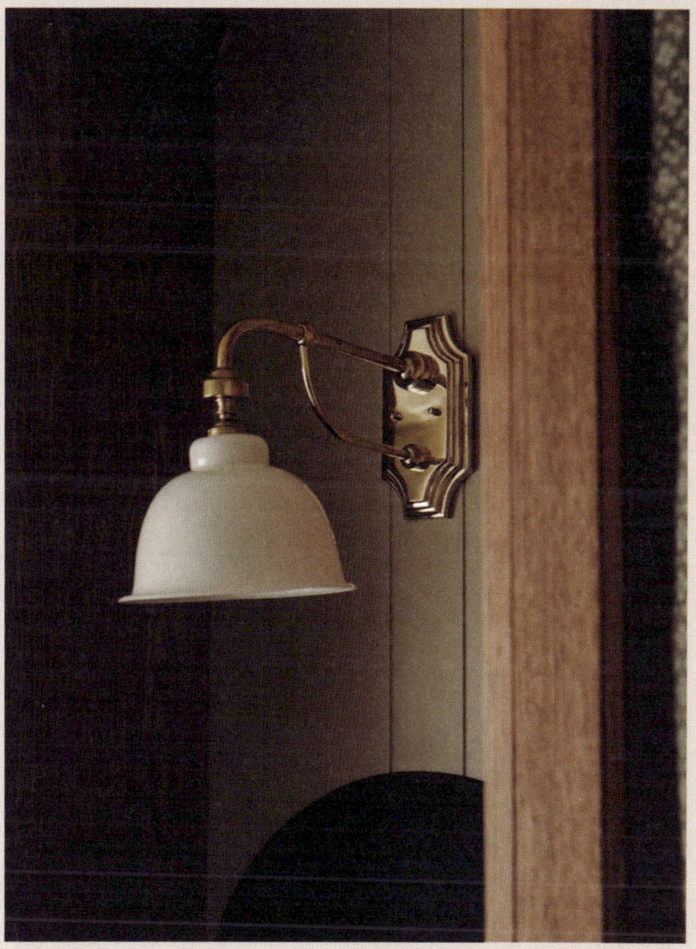
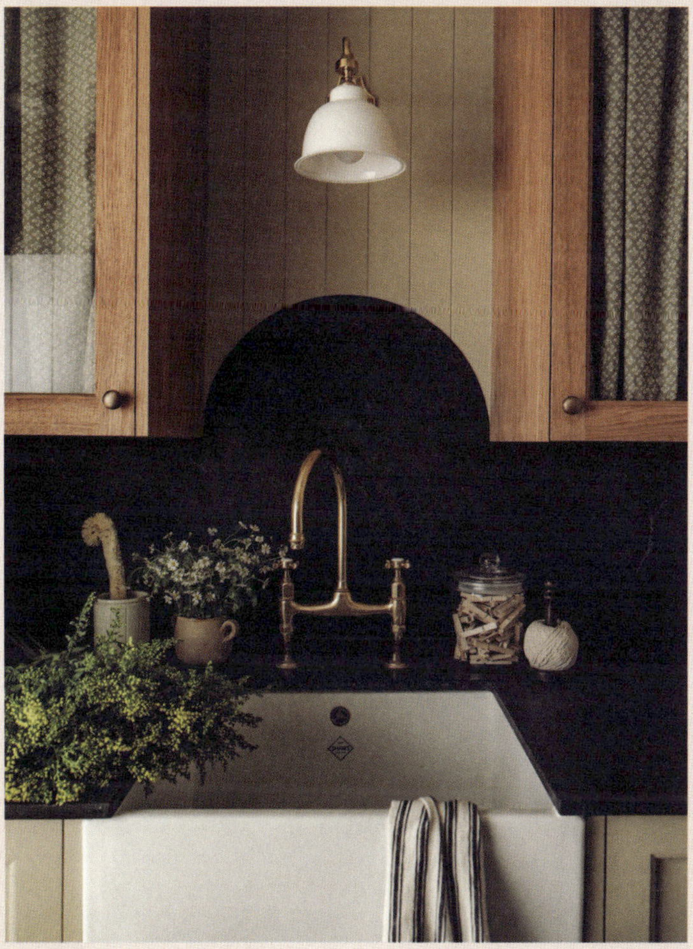
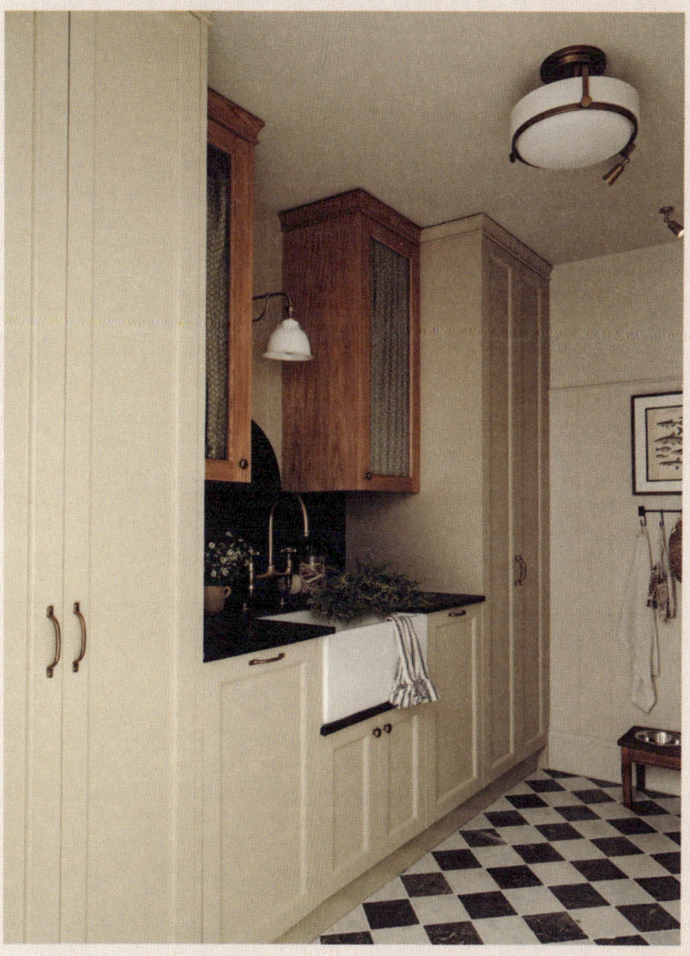

“Have nothing in your house that you do not know to be useful or believe to be beautiful.”

WILLIAM MORRIS

Live

ENJOY YOUR HOME

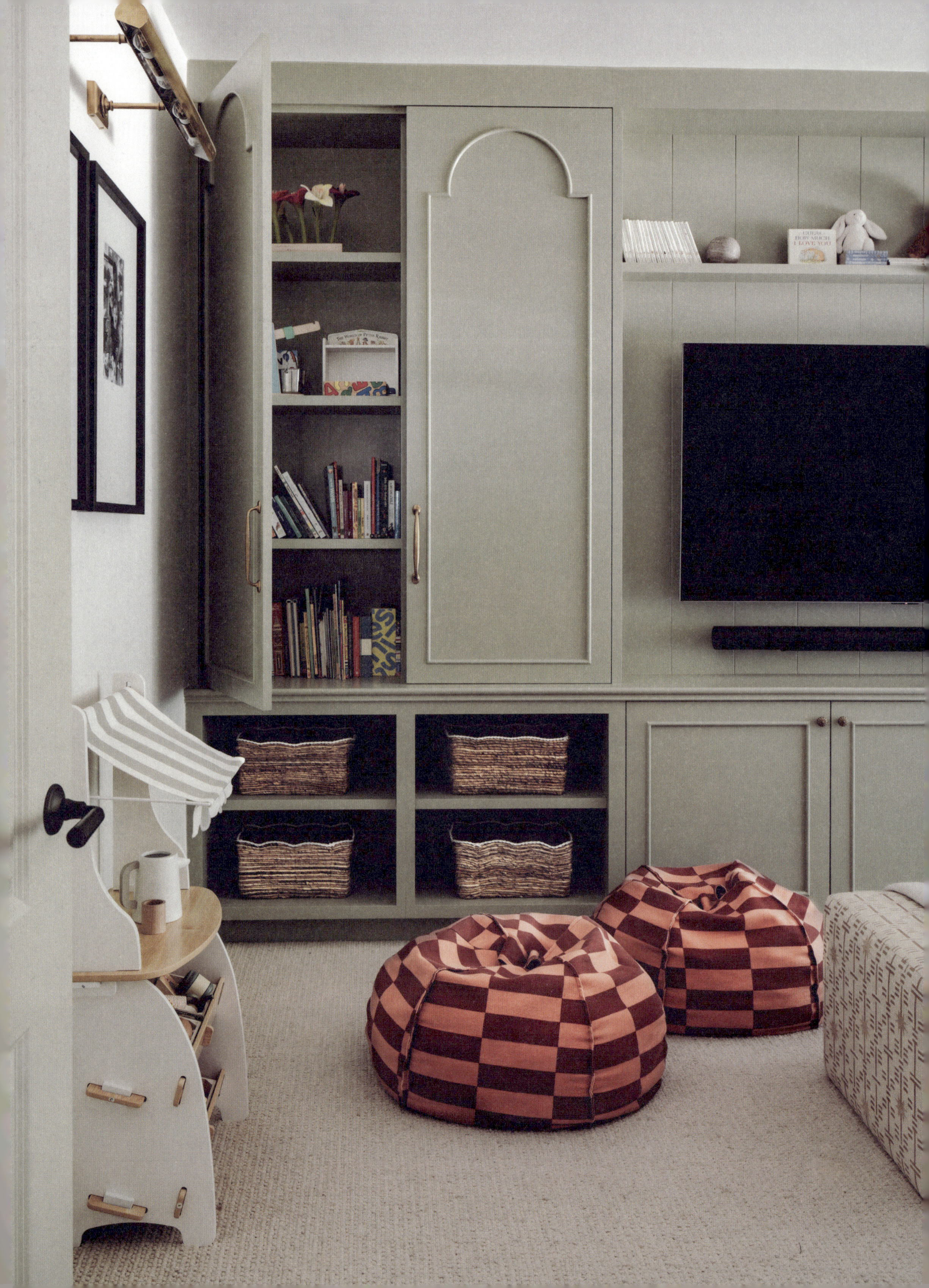
The World of Peter Rabbit

BEYOND THE PERFECT *PICTURE*

I learned early on that there is a difference between a house that looks perfect and a home that feels lived in. For years, clients have proudly shown me inspiration images – immaculate rooms with perfectly plumped cushions, curated coffee tables, and colour palettes timed to seasonal trends. They tell me, almost apologetically, "Mine will never look like this." And my response is always the same: "Good."

If you've ever tried to live inside a picture-perfect room, you'll know how exhausting it is. You find yourself plumping cushions before sitting down, then upon getting up again, hiding anything that doesn't "go", and scolding the dog for daring to shed. You start living for the image instead of living in the space.

Real homes thrive on the beautifully human things – movement, mess, history, laughter, accidents – and those treasured objects that only matter because they matter to you. I never expect my clients' homes to remain exactly as they were on the day we handed them over, nor should they.

To truly live in your interior, you have to embrace a subtle but radical mindset shift, choosing authenticity over perfection. You give yourself permission to let your home evolve with you rather than policing it into some static ideal. I'm a designer, and yet the most important design advice I can give is this: If something is comfortable or genuinely useful, it belongs. Even if it doesn't quite match. Even if it wouldn't make the cover of a magazine. Your sofa should ask you to sink in, not sit up straight for fear of leaving a mark. Your bedside table should hold what you reach for half-asleep – a book, water, a tangled charger. And if your dining chairs don't match but your table is always full, consider that your quiet design triumph.

The Japanese philosophy of *wabi-sabi*, an aesthetic and attitude that seeks the beauty in imperfection, totally changed the way I view interiors. It taught me to recognise the soulful in the slightly worn, the poetry in imperfection, the quiet beauty in things that are asymmetrical, softened, and lived with. Wear isn't a failure; it's evidence of life.

← Project Green Park, playroom – a space that lives by the chapter's own philosophy: "if it's comfortable or genuinely useful, it belongs". Mismatched checkerboard bean bags, open baskets for easy access, a wall of storage built for actual play rather than display. This is what a room looks like when it's designed to be used, not styled for a photograph (ok maybe just a little) – *wabi-sabi* in miniature, where the mess is the evidence that it's loved.

→ → Yes, the TV is front and centre. That's by design. So much energy gets spent hiding screens behind panels and barn doors, but in a family space built for actual use, sometimes the most honest choice is to let it be seen. As the chapter puts it: if something is genuinely useful, it belongs – even if it wouldn't make the cover of a magazine.

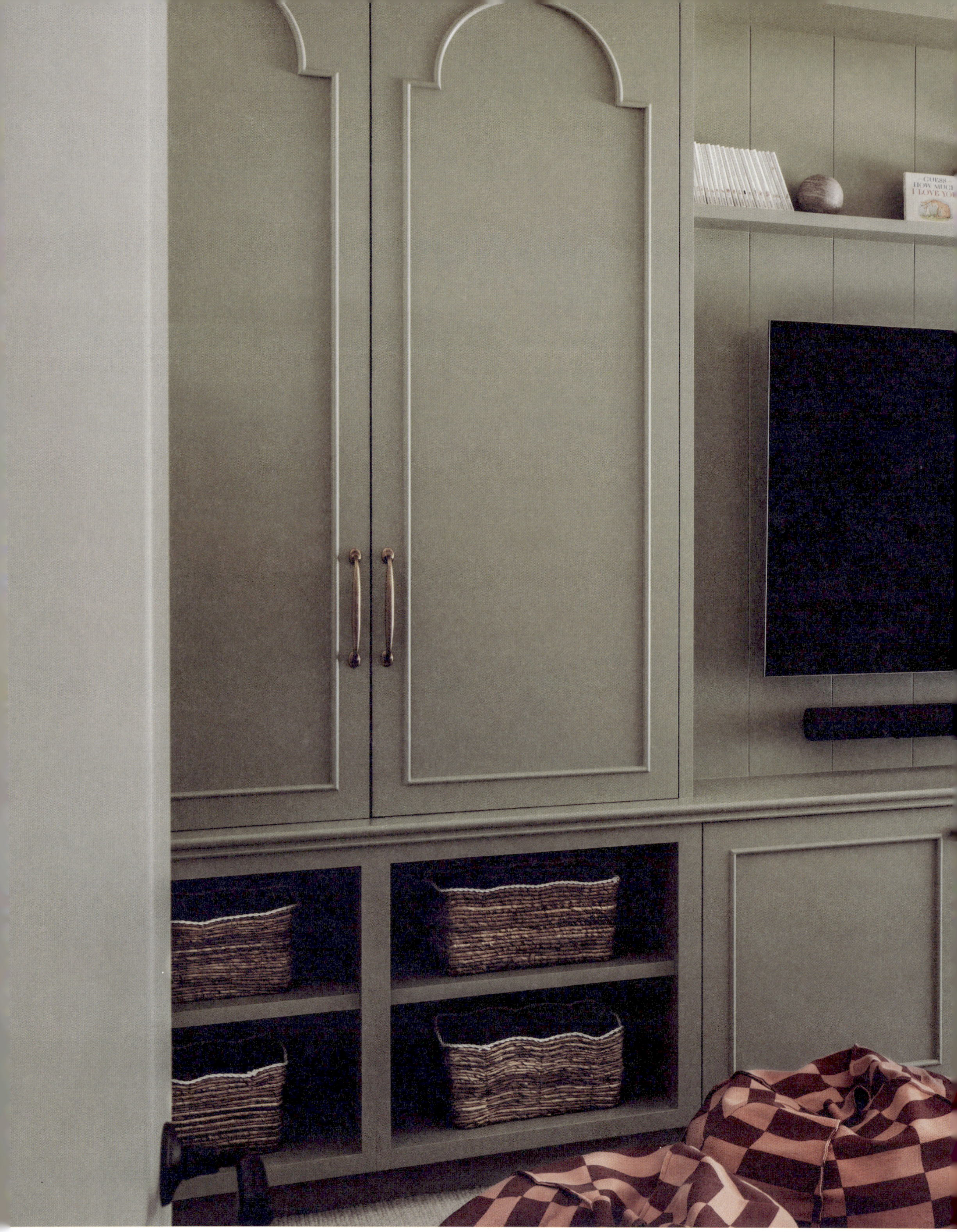
GUESS

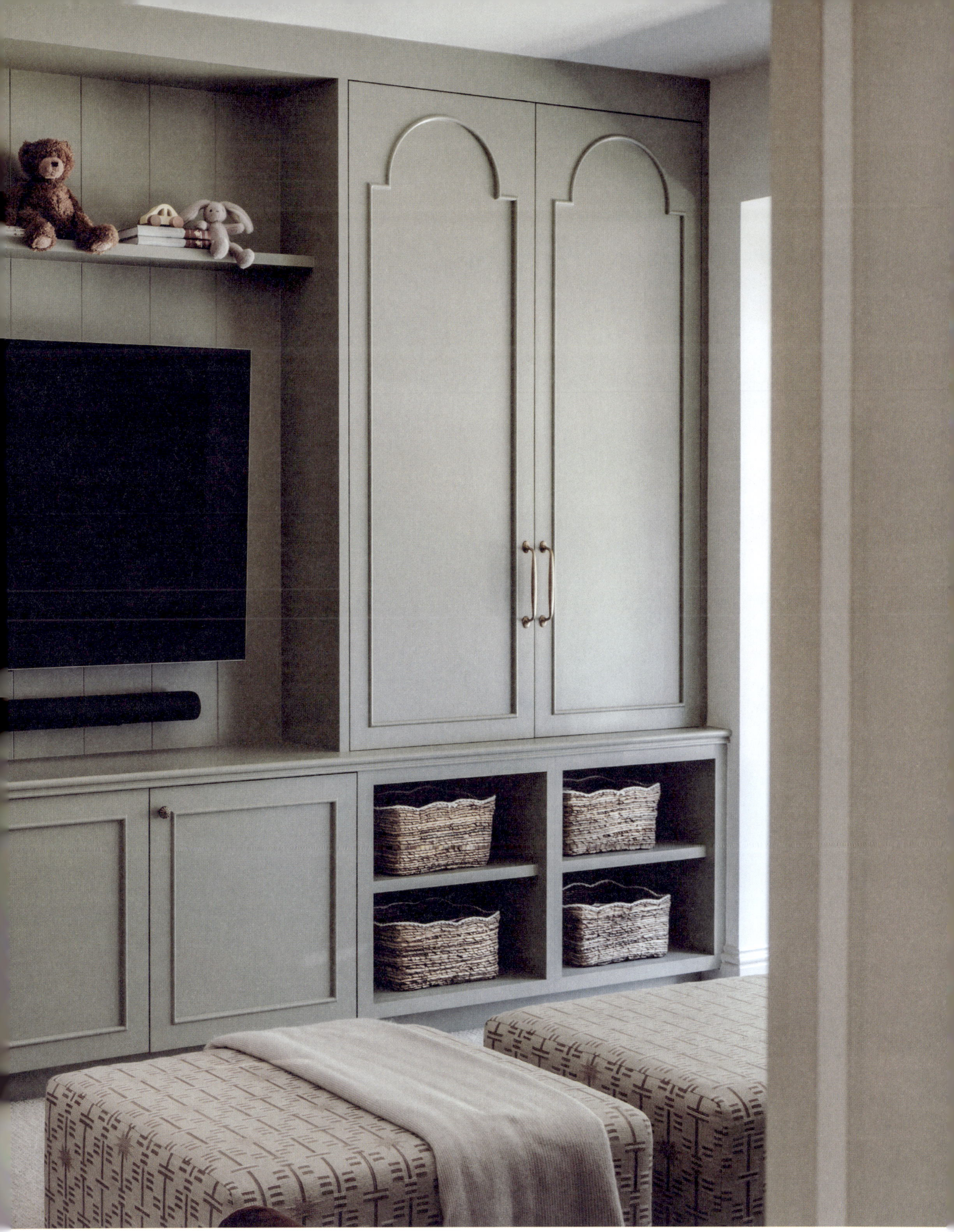

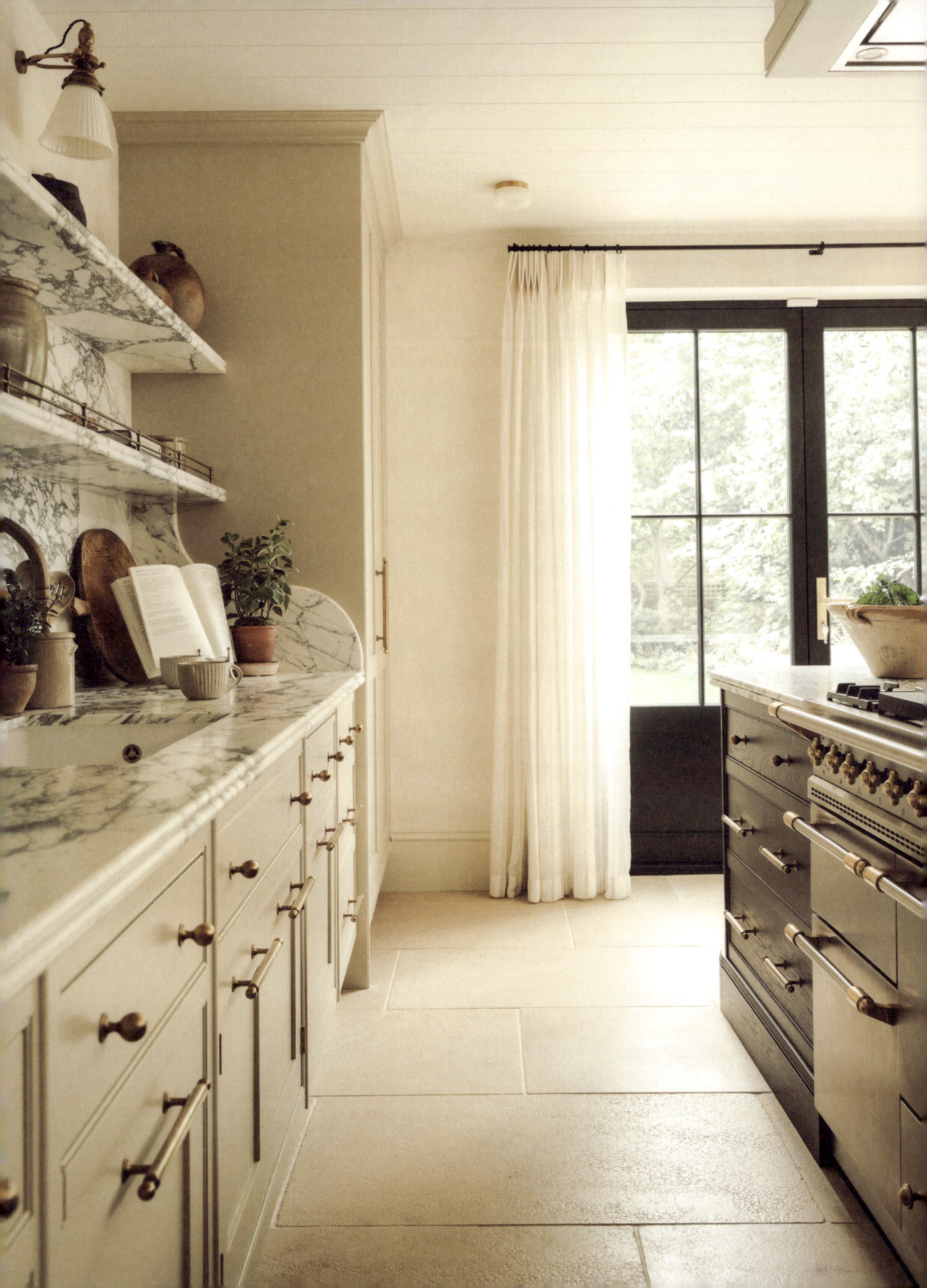

A few years ago, during my daughter Ziggy's night feed, my husband accidentally knocked a much-loved Vaughan table lamp off the bedside table. Certain it was finished, he carefully scraped the shattered pieces into a plastic bag. When he told me the next morning, I rescued it from the wheely bin outside immediately – all eighteen fractured pieces – utterly unwilling to let it go.

That moment led me to discover *kintsugi*, the centuries-old Japanese practice of repairing broken objects with lacquer mixed with powdered gold. Rather than hiding the damage, the cracks are traced, honoured, and illuminated. Breakage becomes part of the object's story, not something to erase. *Kin* means gold. *Tsugi* means joinery. Golden repair.

The philosophy is quietly profound: something can be broken, mended, and become even more beautiful because of what it has survived. Not despite its history, but because of it. That idea lodged itself deeply in me, and not just in how I think about objects. Perfection is sterile. Imperfection is alive.

Living authentically means embracing signs of life. A little everyday clutter is simply a sign that life is happening. And life, last time I checked, isn't a tidy business. Function always trumps aesthetics. Arrange your furniture so that conversations flow easily, create spaces that invite relaxation rather than admiration, let your living room be a room where people actually want to live. If the "correct" layout doesn't work for the way you move, rest, or gather, simply change it. Design should always bend to your life, not the other way around.

And, perhaps most importantly, allow things to evolve. You are not the same person you were ten years ago, or even two. So why expect your home to stay frozen in time? Repaint the room, move the furniture, replace the cushions, donate things you've outgrown, add things that reflect the person you're becoming. Your home is a living, breathing organism, so let it grow! When you let go of the pursuit of perfection, you create space for something far more meaningful: real comfort, genuine warmth, and a home that reflects your beautifully complicated, sometimes messy, ever-changing humanity. There really is no place like it.

"Real homes thrive on the beautifully human things – movement, mess, history, laughter, accidents."

← The kitchen is the hardest-working room in the house, and it shows here in the best way – marble open shelving within easy reach, a freestanding range built for serious cooking, doors that open straight onto the garden. It's beautiful, but beauty was never the starting point. As the chapter puts it: function always trumps aesthetics. Design should always bend to your life, not the other way around.

Relaxation, Creativity & Connection

When you allow your home to be lived in – not curated, not staged, just lived in – you create the conditions for something magical: ease. Ah, yes. The kind that allows you permission to curl up on the sofa without adjusting the cushions first. The kind that lets kids spread out Lego or puzzles or paints without you worrying that they're disrupting the "look". The kind that encourages your guests to talk longer, linger deeper, breathe slower.

"Relaxation happens when a space feels forgiving rather than precious."

A real home makes room for rest. Relaxation happens when a space feels forgiving rather than precious. It could be a reading corner with a lamp you love, or an extra deep sectional sofa that tolerates sprawling limbs. Lighting that softens in the evening so the day can melt away. These small gestures are what allow your nervous system to settle.

A real home also nurtures creativity. When everything doesn't have to be perfect, you give yourself permission to experiment – rearrange a shelf, move a chair, try a new colour, pick up a hobby without worrying about the mess it'll make. Creativity isn't neat; it's exploratory. Your home should encourage that exploration.

And, beautifully, a lived-in home deepens connection. People connect more easily in spaces where they feel they won't "ruin" anything. A slightly rumpled sofa with mismatching cushions invites closeness. A kitchen that looks used and lived-in invites conversation. A dining table with a scratch or your kids' scribbles invites a relaxed meal rather than a formal performance. When people feel at ease, I find they tend to relax more easily and open up – first to the space, then to each other. Living well at home isn't about polishing; it's about softening. It's about homes that feel loved, and in turn, love us back.

→ Project All About You - home to three kids, a dog, and a cat, this is a kitchen built for noise and life, not stillness. With a household this busy, the room had to be forgiving rather than precious: warm timber, soft brass, and a layout that doesn't flinch at muddy paws or mid-cooking chaos. As the chapter says, a kitchen that looks used and lived-in invites conversation - and in a family this size, that's exactly the point.

→ → An anteroom between bedrooms, turned into the loveliest kind of storage - a marble topped antique chest catching the morning light. Proof that even the in-between spaces deserve the same care as the rooms either side of them.

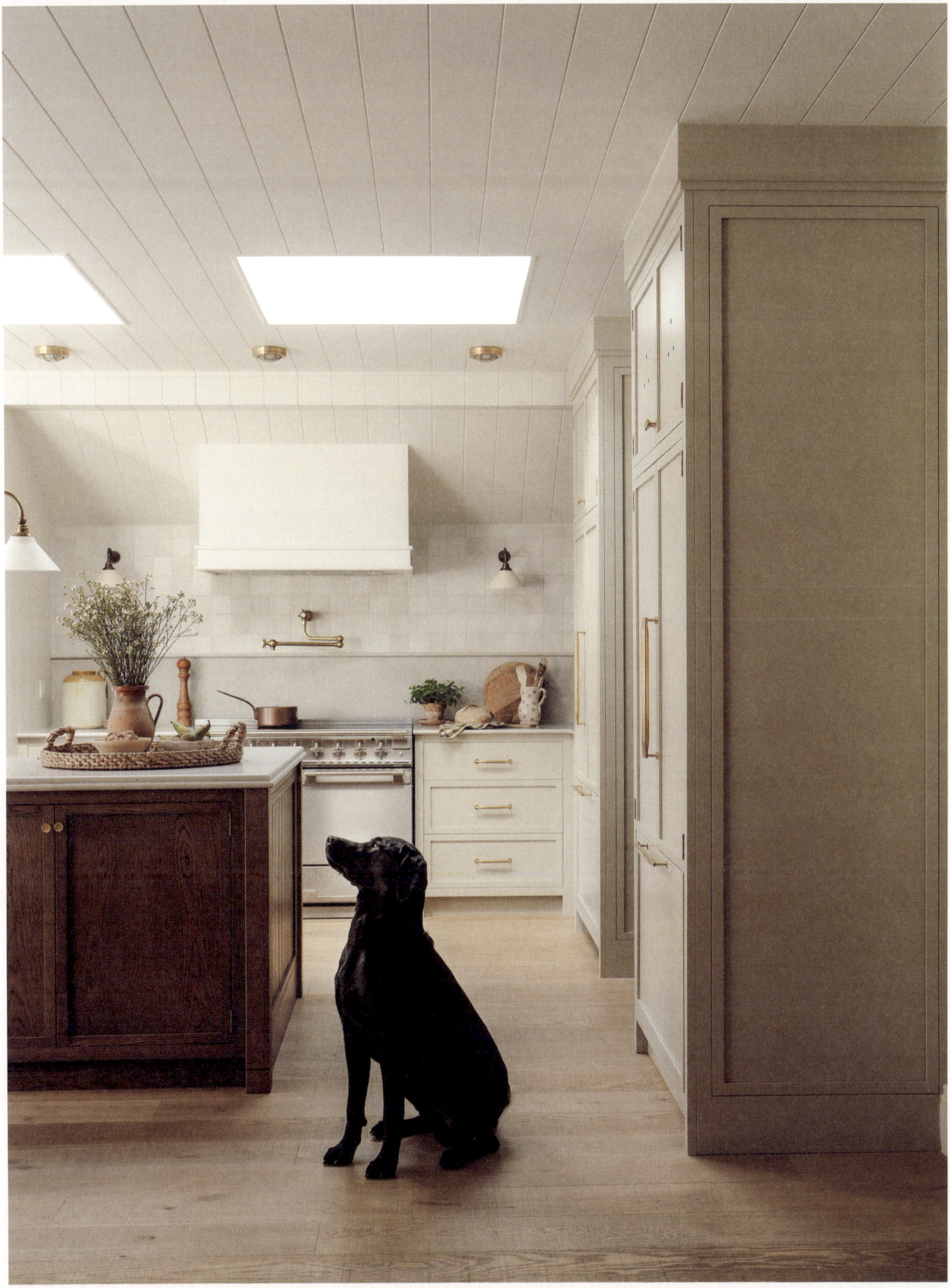

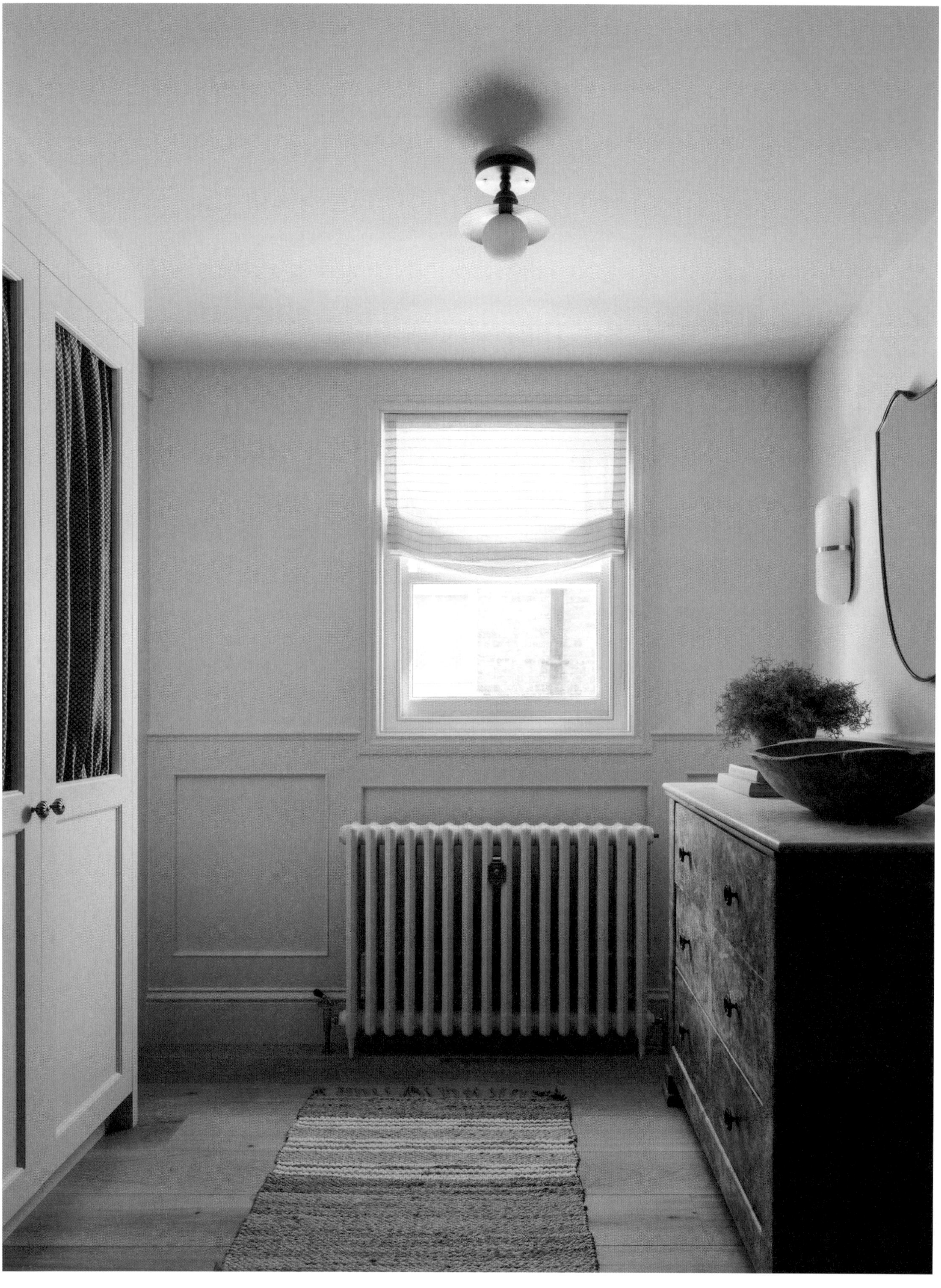

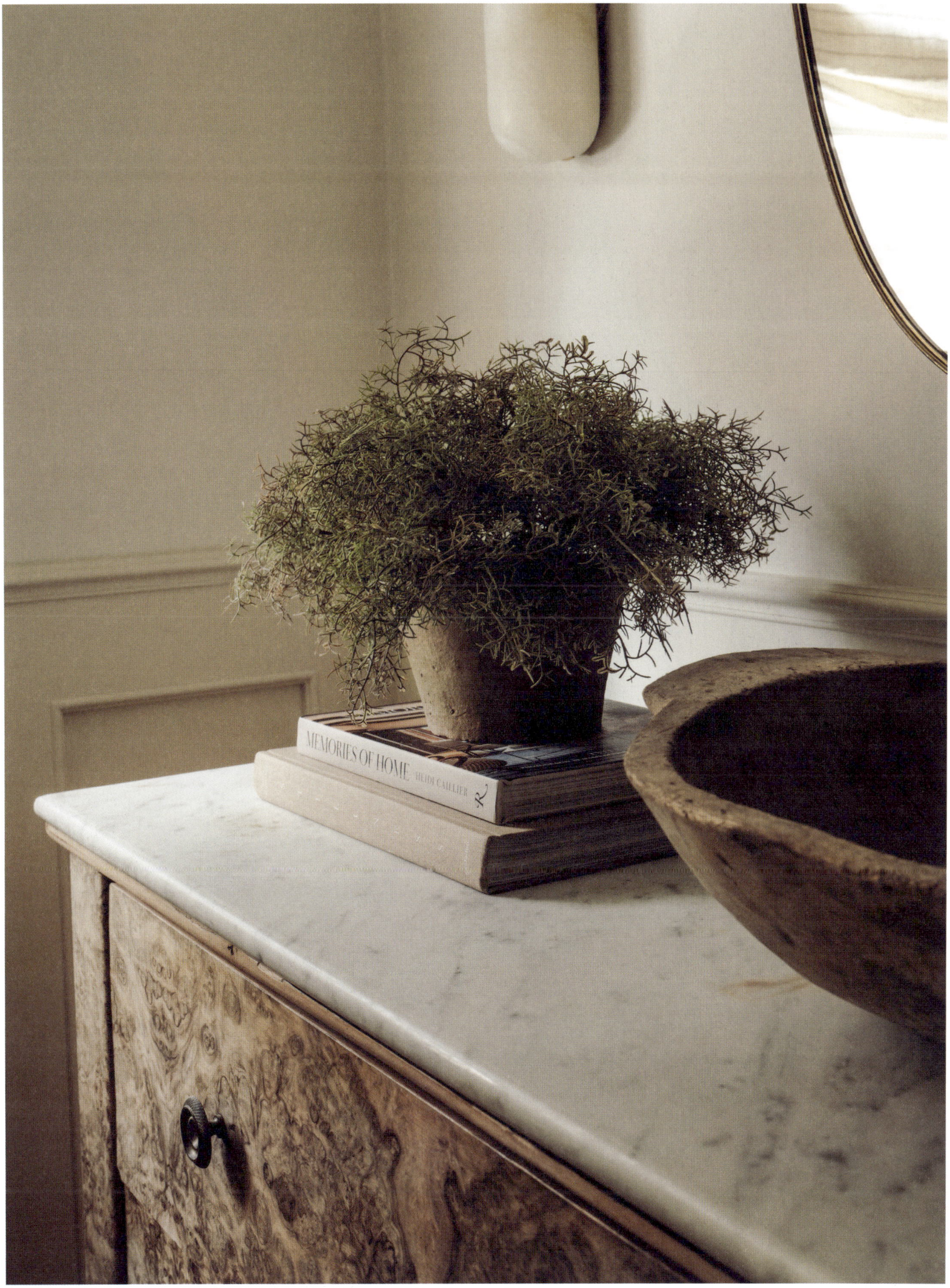
MEMORIES OF HOME
HEIDI CAILLIER

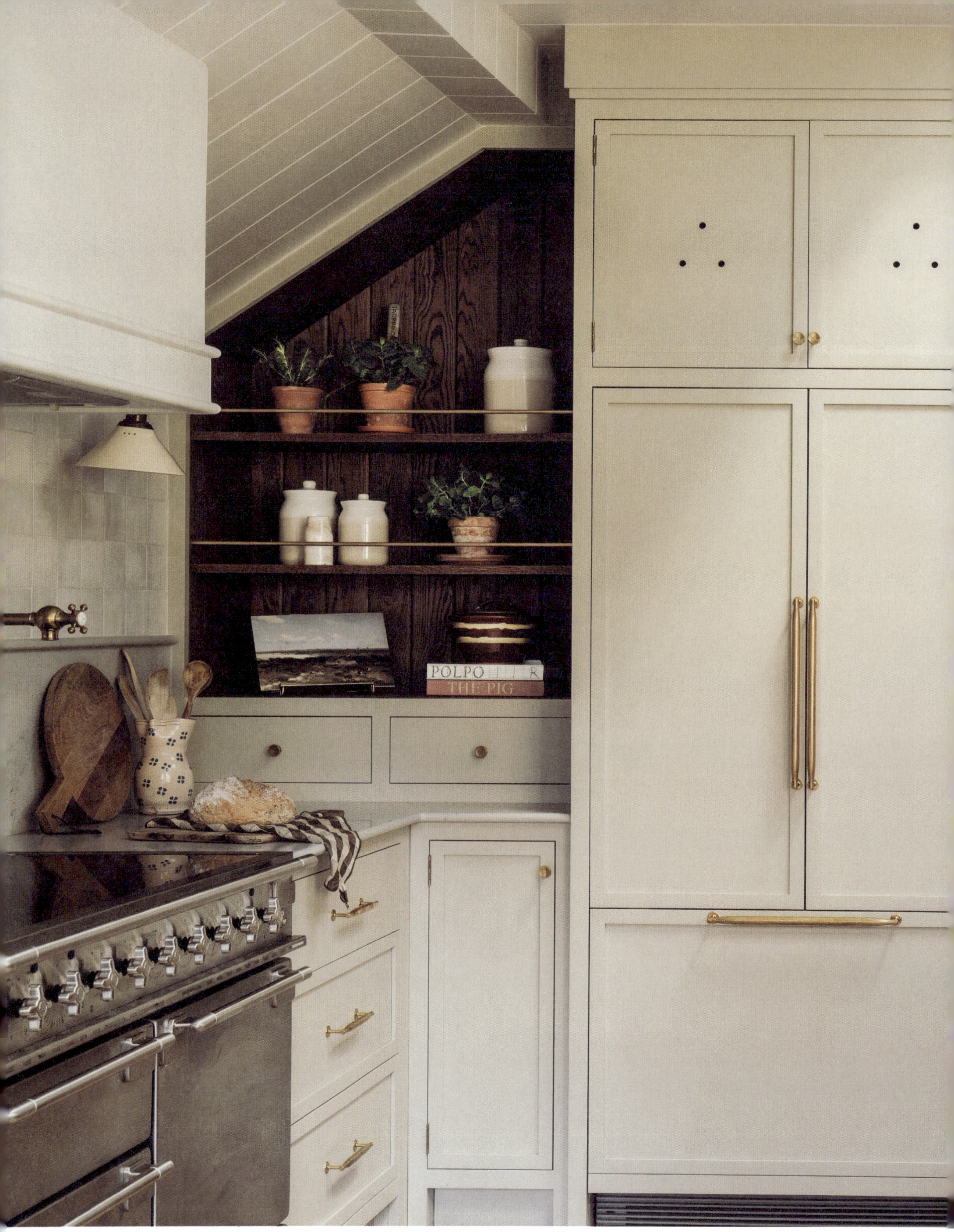
POLPO
THE PIG

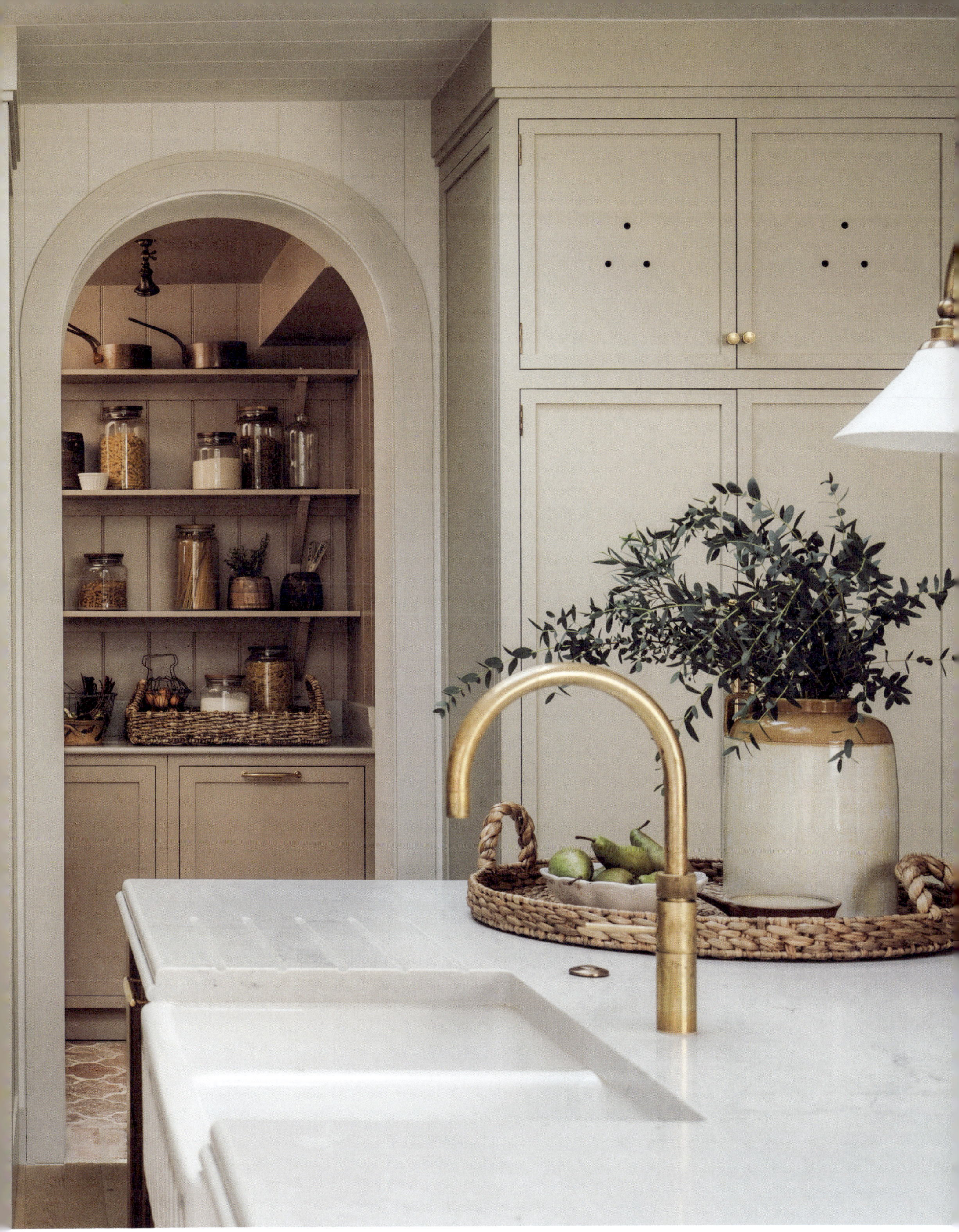

Daily Rituals

> *"Sacred spaces give shape to habits, and habits give shape to our days."*

I've come to learn that if perfection is the enemy of living, then ritual is its quiet counterbalance. Not routine in a rigid sense, but the small, repeated acts that slowly deepen our relationship with a space. The moments that remind us, often without words: "This is my home – and I belong here."

Homes that feel the most grounded aren't necessarily the most beautiful; they're the ones that have little pockets of meaning built into them. I often think of them as sacred spaces – not in a religious sense, but in the sense that they're protected, intentional, and deeply personal.

For some people, a sacred space might be a coffee nook – a well-placed machine, a shelf of favourite mugs, the comforting hum – that certainly signals the start of my day. For others, it's something quieter – a small spot for crystals and meditation, a particular spot where the light falls just right in the morning, a place to breathe and reset. It might be a chair you curl up in with a book, or a sofa claimed for evenings of Netflix, feet tucked under a blanket with a cat curled on your lap. These spaces don't need labels or rules, they just need permission to exist.

In a fast-paced, noisy world, these small ritual-led spaces act like emotional glue. They help steady us. Sacred spaces give shape to habits, and habits give shape to our days. They offer predictability without boredom, comfort without stagnation. When life feels uncertain, it's often these quiet rituals – the same corner of the sofa, the same mug, even the same side of the bed – that remind us we're held by something familiar and there is no comfort quite like it.

From a design point of view, this is where interiors stop being about how things look and start being about how they work emotionally. When you pay attention to rituals – morning meditation, a particular way of working, a regular evening wind-down – you can design a home that flows with you rather than against you. Furniture stops blocking movement; lighting starts supporting mood; spaces begin to anticipate your needs instead of frustrating them.

And this is why good design is never one-size-fits-all. What feels sacred to one person might feel meaningless to another. Effective design for wellbeing comes from intention and from understanding what matters to you, and embedding that meaning into the choices you make.

When rituals are considered, interior design moves beyond arranging furniture and finishes. It becomes a quiet practice of care – creating spaces that nurture the body, steady the mind, and gently support the soul – and that is the sweet spot when a house truly starts to feel like a home.

→ Project Notting Hill Townhouse - this snug had one job above all: comfort. The sofa was built extra deep for the client's gaming setup, the kind you sink right into. But as a central living space just off the kitchen, it still needed to hold its own - hence the layered gallery wall, sculptural lighting, and rich textures that mean it looks as good as it feels. As the chapter puts it: sacred spaces give shape to habits, and habits give shape to our days.

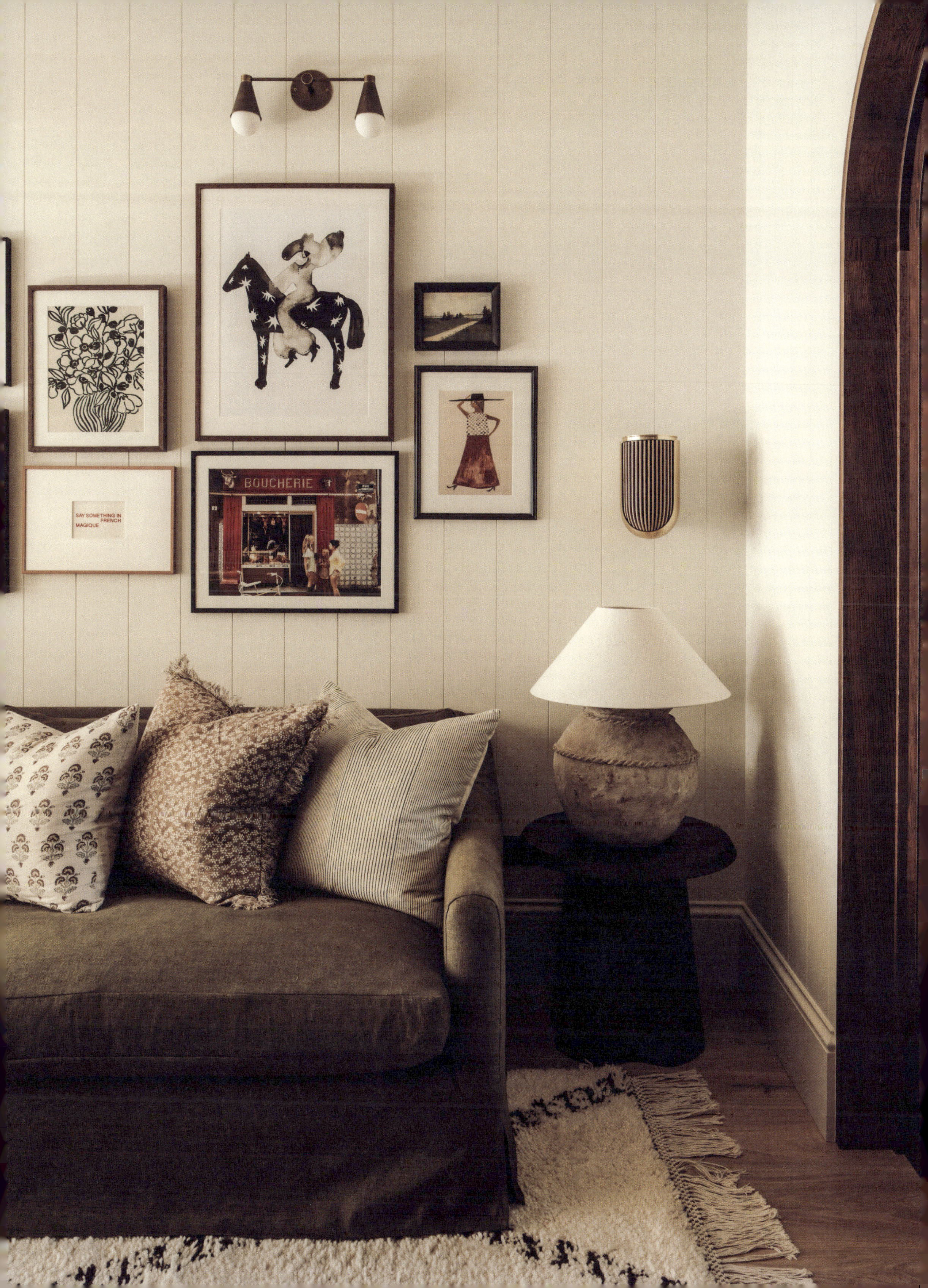
SAY SOMETHING IN
FRENCH
MAGIQUE
BOUCHERIE

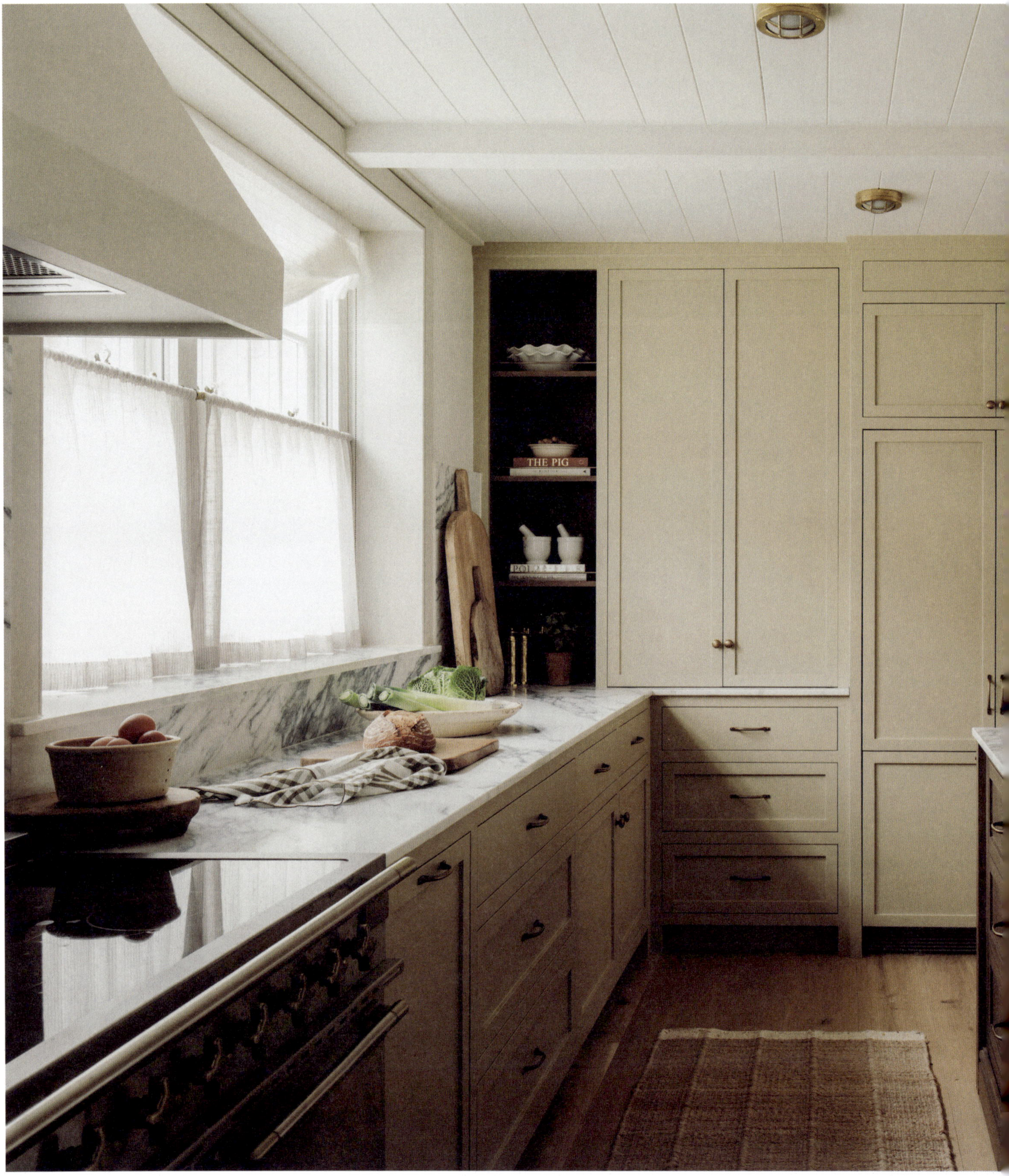

↑ Project Sandbanks – two spaces, two different jobs. The kitchen is kept bright and light; the kind of room that invites everyday living rather than just cooking. Through the glazed panelled door, the pantry shifts mood entirely: a soft green chosen to let the jars, glassware, and provisions take centre stage. As the chapter says, good design is never one-size-fits-all – it comes from understanding what each space needs to support, and shaping it accordingly.

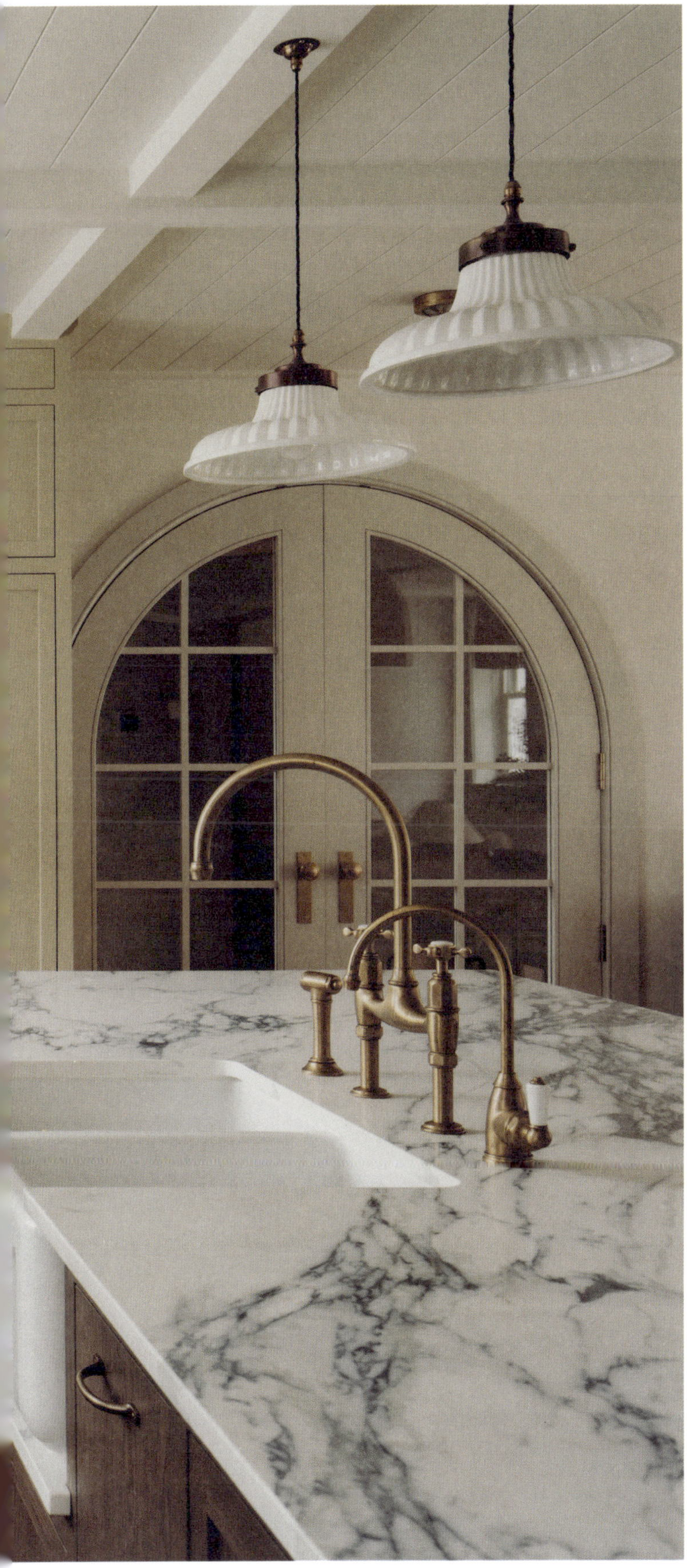
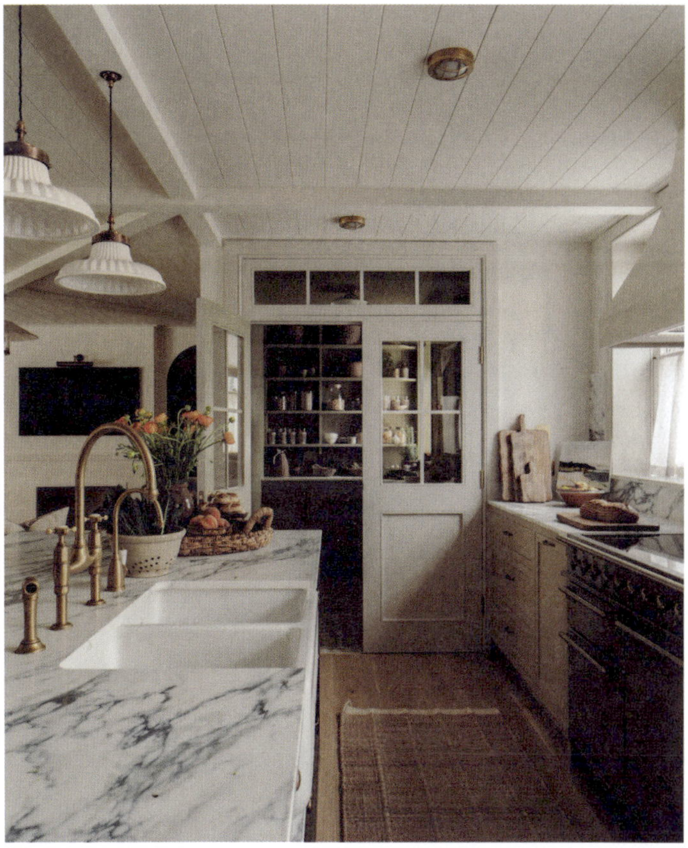
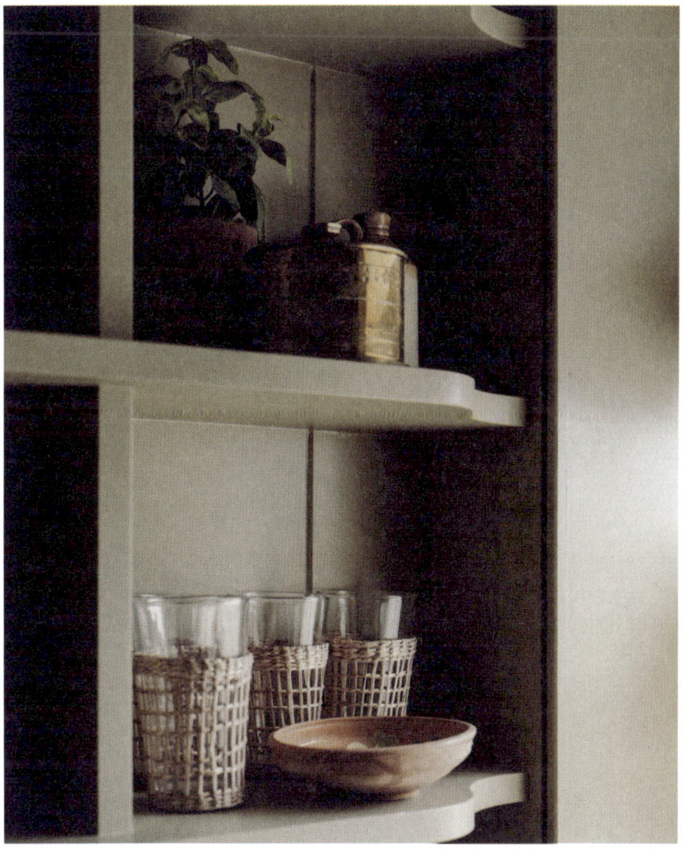

Make Space for Authenticity

DESIGN NOTES

Living isn't about getting everything right; it's about letting things breathe. These suggestions are here to help you loosen your grip on perfection and make space for ease, authenticity, and everyday humanity.

1. CHOOSE COMFORT FIRST

If a space looks good but doesn't feel good, it isn't doing its job.

Try this: Sit in every seat in the room. Which one truly feels comfortable? Which feels stiff or "for show"? Let your body, not your eyes, be the judge.

---

2. LOOK FOR THE BEAUTIFULLY USEFUL

The things you use every day deserve care and attention.

Practise: Identify three items you reach for daily. Do they deserve a better place? Could they be made more accessible, or more joyful to use?

---

3. DO A *WABI-SABI* WALK

Imperfection is not something to fix; it's something to notice.

Try this: Walk from room to room and find one imperfection that tells a story – a mark, a chip, a worn edge. Let it stay. Appreciate it. Let it soften the space.

---

4. CREATE ONE LIVED-IN CORNER

Homes need places that invite you to land.

Practise: Choose one corner and claim it with a chair, a lamp, and a blanket. Style it for use, not aesthetics. Make it unmistakably yours.

---

5. AUDIT YOUR INSTAGRAM INFLUENCE

Comparison quietly erodes contentment.

Do this: Unfollow any accounts that consistently make you feel "less than" about your home. Notice how quickly your own space begins to feel enough again.

---

6. BLESS THE EVERYDAY CLUTTER

A lived-in home carries evidence of life.

Practise: Choose one recurring mess – shoes, toys, post – and create a simple, forgiving system for it. Aim for ease, not perfection.

---

7. LET ONE ROOM EVOLVE

Homes grow when we allow them to change.

Try this: Move a piece of furniture, swap a rug, or adjust the lighting in one room. Let it breathe into its next chapter.

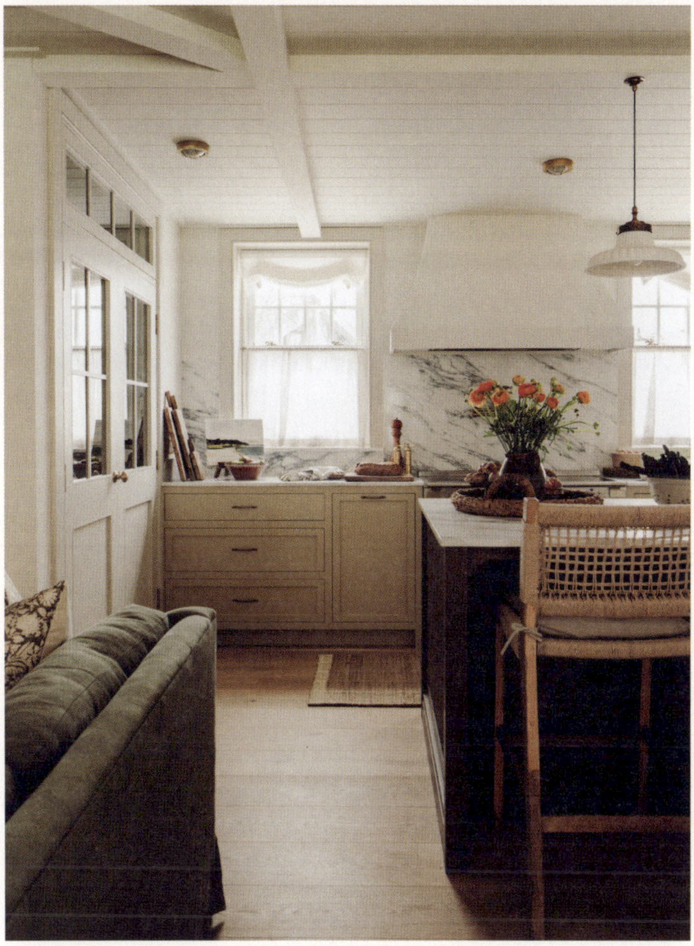

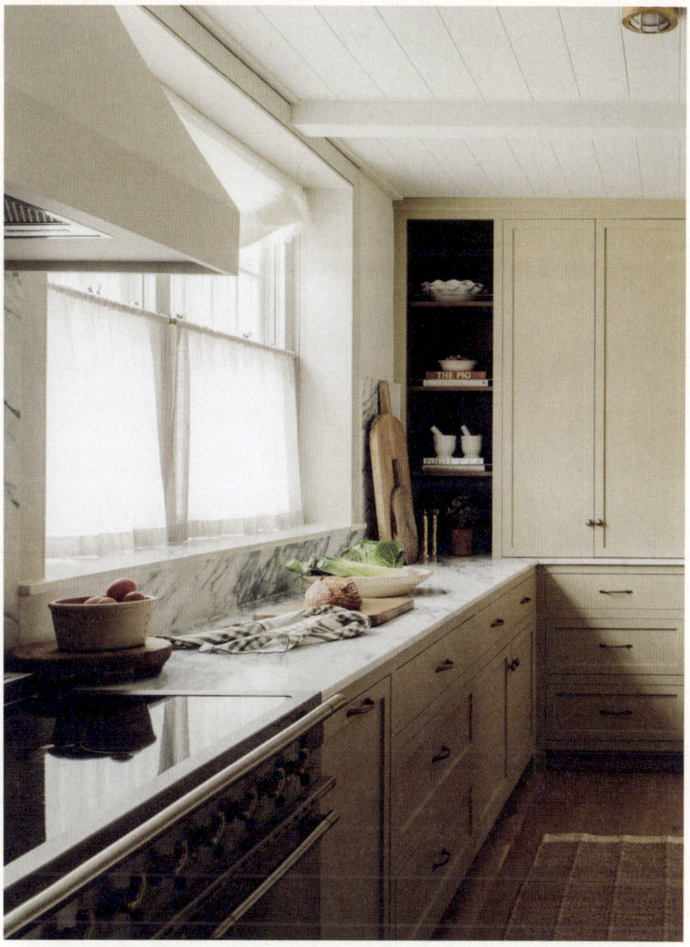
THE PIG

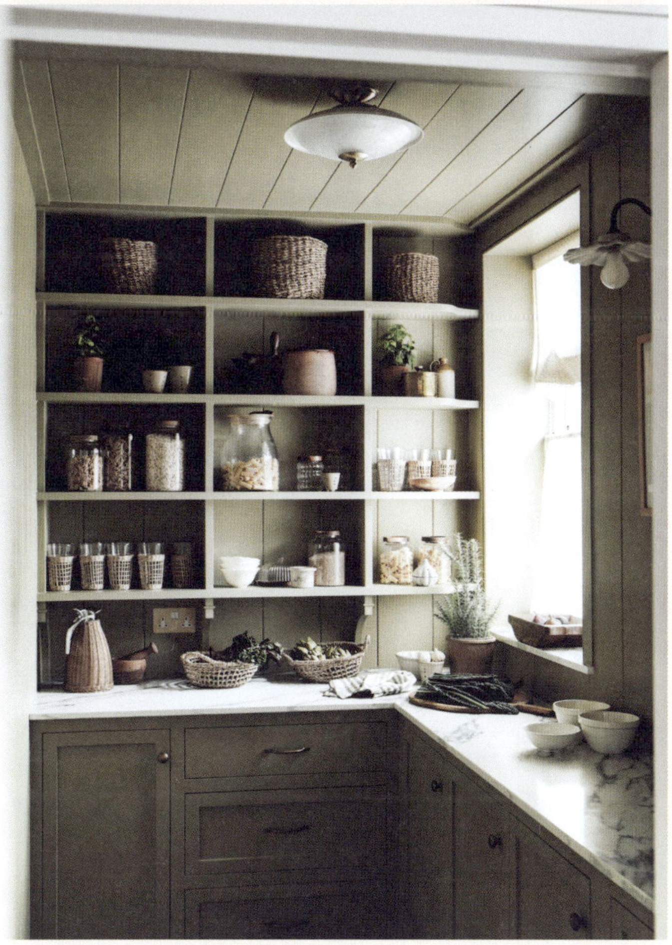

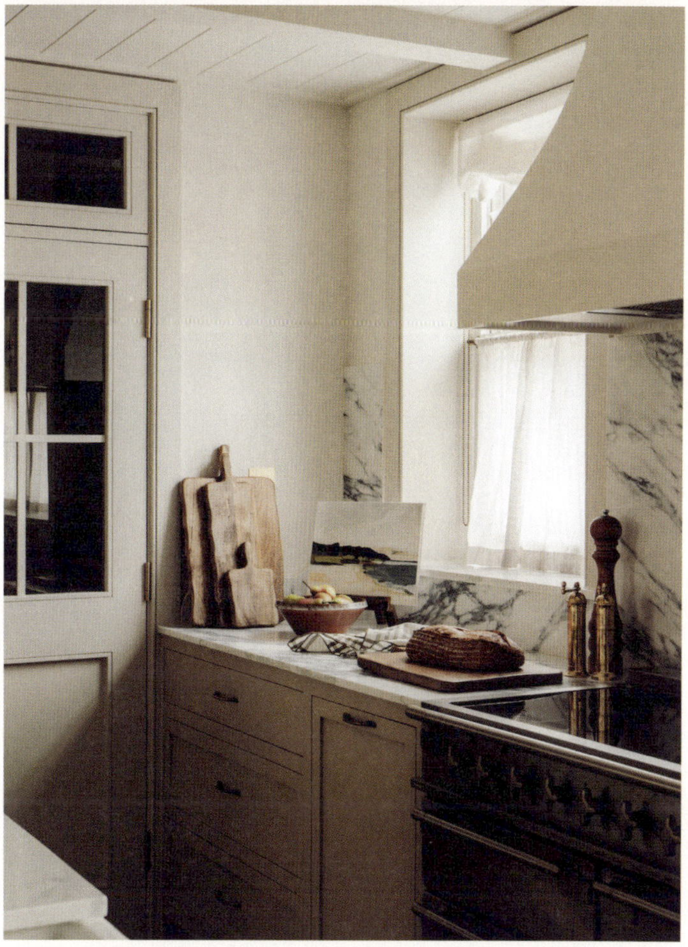

“Good design is making something intelligible and memorable. Great design is making something memorable and meaningful.”

DIETER RAMS

Gather

SHARE YOUR HOME

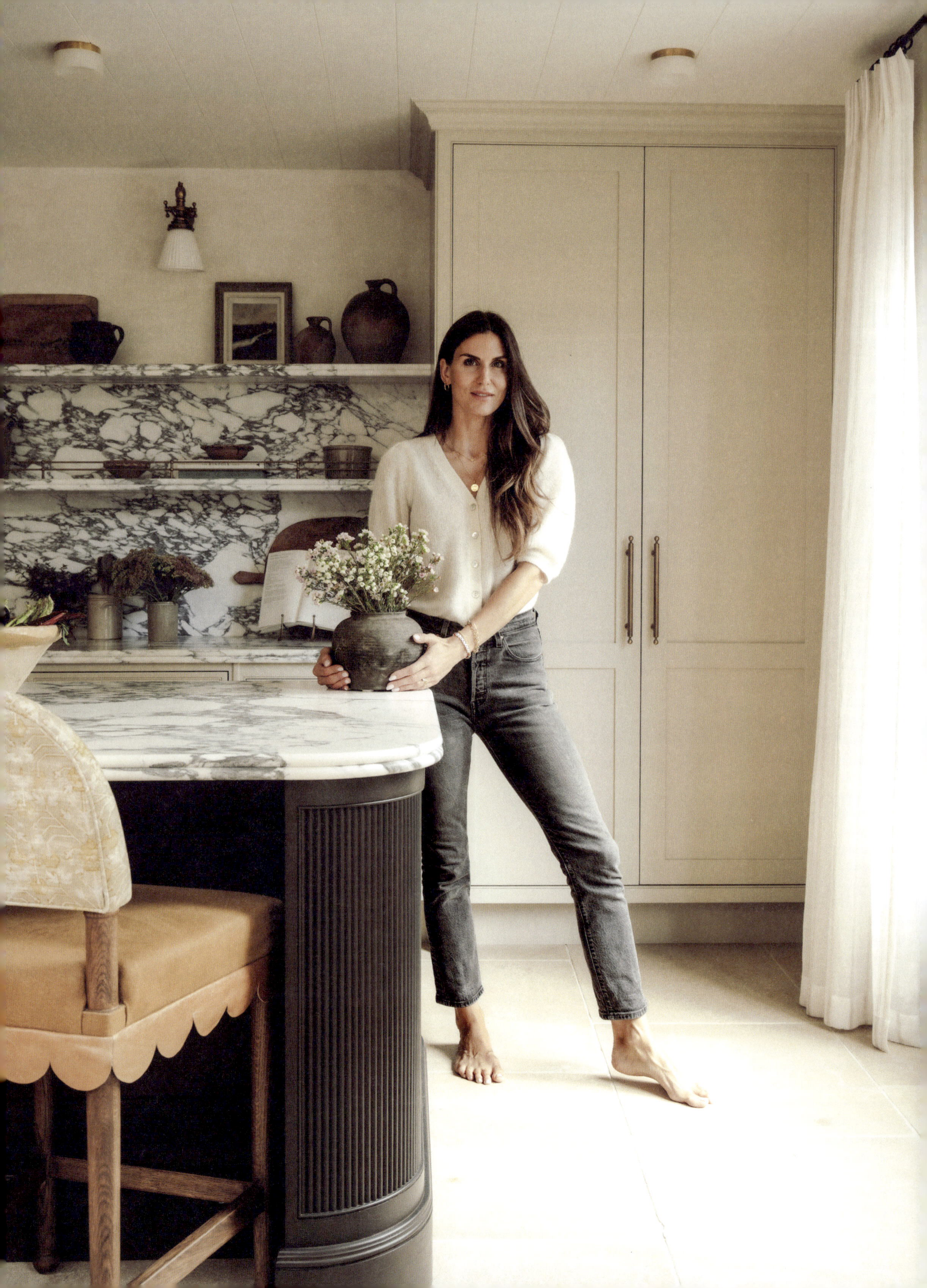

SHARING YOUR *HOME*

A home earns its meaning through use. Not just through daily routines, but shared ones. Meals stretched longer than planned, conversations that move from room to room, quiet mornings with extra mugs on the counter, bums perched on bar stools. However carefully designed, a house only becomes a home when it happily holds the people we love most.

Sharing your home isn't about scale or occasion. It doesn't require open-plan living or a table that seats twelve. It's simply the act of making space both physically and emotionally for the people you care about. Family, friends, neighbours, old faces, and new ones. The joy comes not from how your home looks during these moments, but how it behaves.

Homes that are shared feel different. They soften over time. Furniture shifts, layouts evolve, and rooms take on layered roles. A dining table becomes a desk, then a homework station, then somewhere guests linger long after the plates are cleared. This adaptability is a strength, not a compromise.

There's also a generosity in allowing others to experience your home as it truly is. Not staged, not paused, and not apologised for. When we stop treating our spaces as something to protect, and instead as something to offer, the pressure eases. Hosting becomes less about performance and more about presence.

Importantly, sharing doesn't mean surrendering your own comfort. The most successful homes are clear about how they work. Where people sit, where coats go, and where conversations happen. This clarity allows guests to relax, because nothing feels uncertain or precious. A home that's easy to share supports connection without demanding effort. It allows people to arrive as they are, stay as long as they like, and leave feeling restored rather than managed.

In the end, the memories that matter most rarely involve how a room looked. They're shaped by how it felt to be together inside it. And I believe that is the quiet measure of a good home.

← Me at our Notting Hill townhouse project, leaning on what might be the most used spot in the whole house – the island. It's where bums perch on stools, conversations move from room to room, and people linger long after the kettle's gone cold. As the chapter says, a house only becomes a home when it happily holds the people we love most – and for me, that always starts right here.

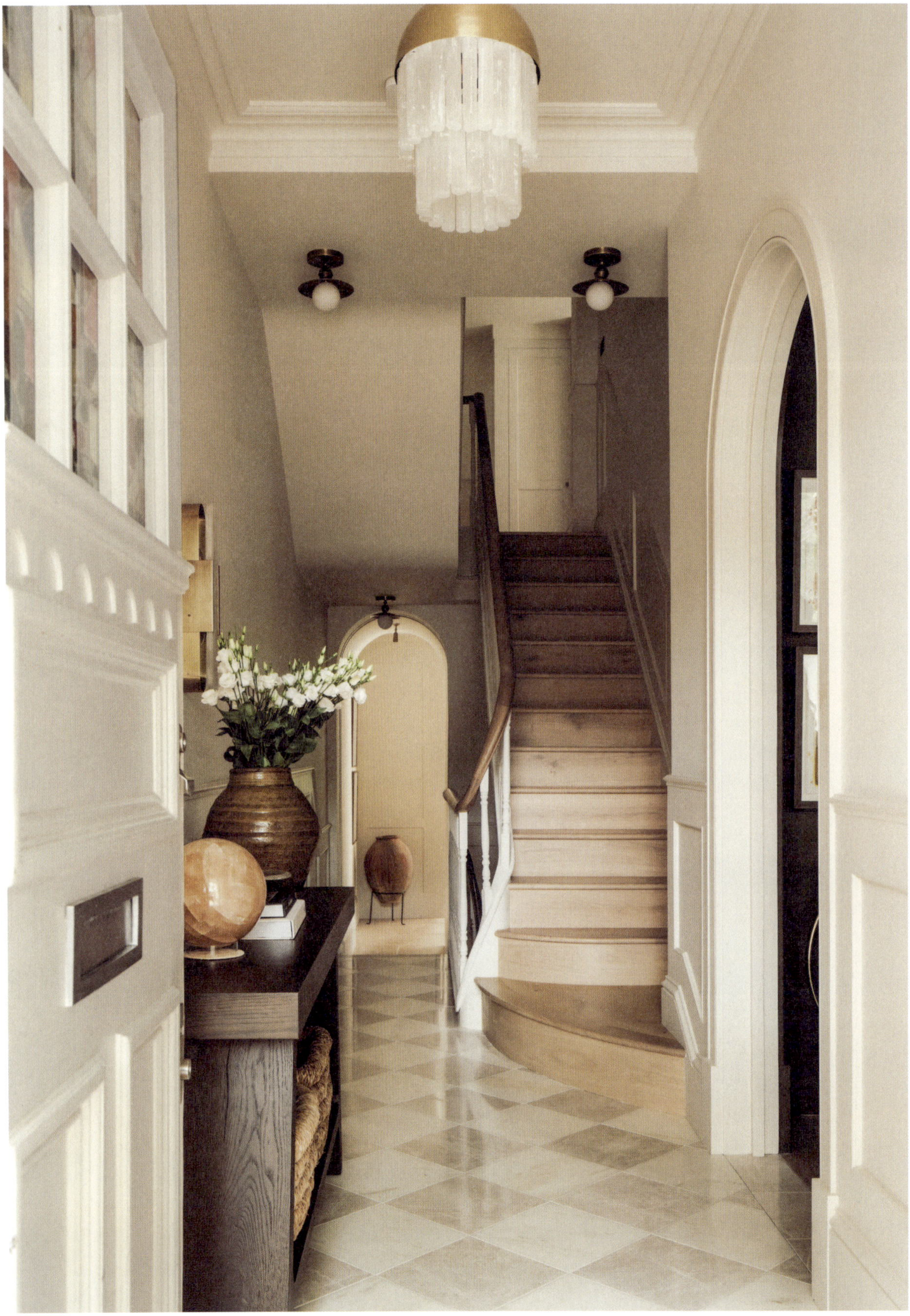

↑ → From a welcoming entrance hallway through to the open-plan kitchen and dining beyond, natural tones and an easy flow carry you between rooms. This solid elm farmhouse table is designed to feel just as comfortable with two as it does with ten – a space made for year-round entertaining.

→ → Open-plan living at its best – this space moves effortlessly from kitchen island to dining table to sofa. Woven pendant lights and arched doorways tie the rooms together, while the deep olive sofa, piled high with cushions, becomes the natural gathering point. It's social living in its truest form.

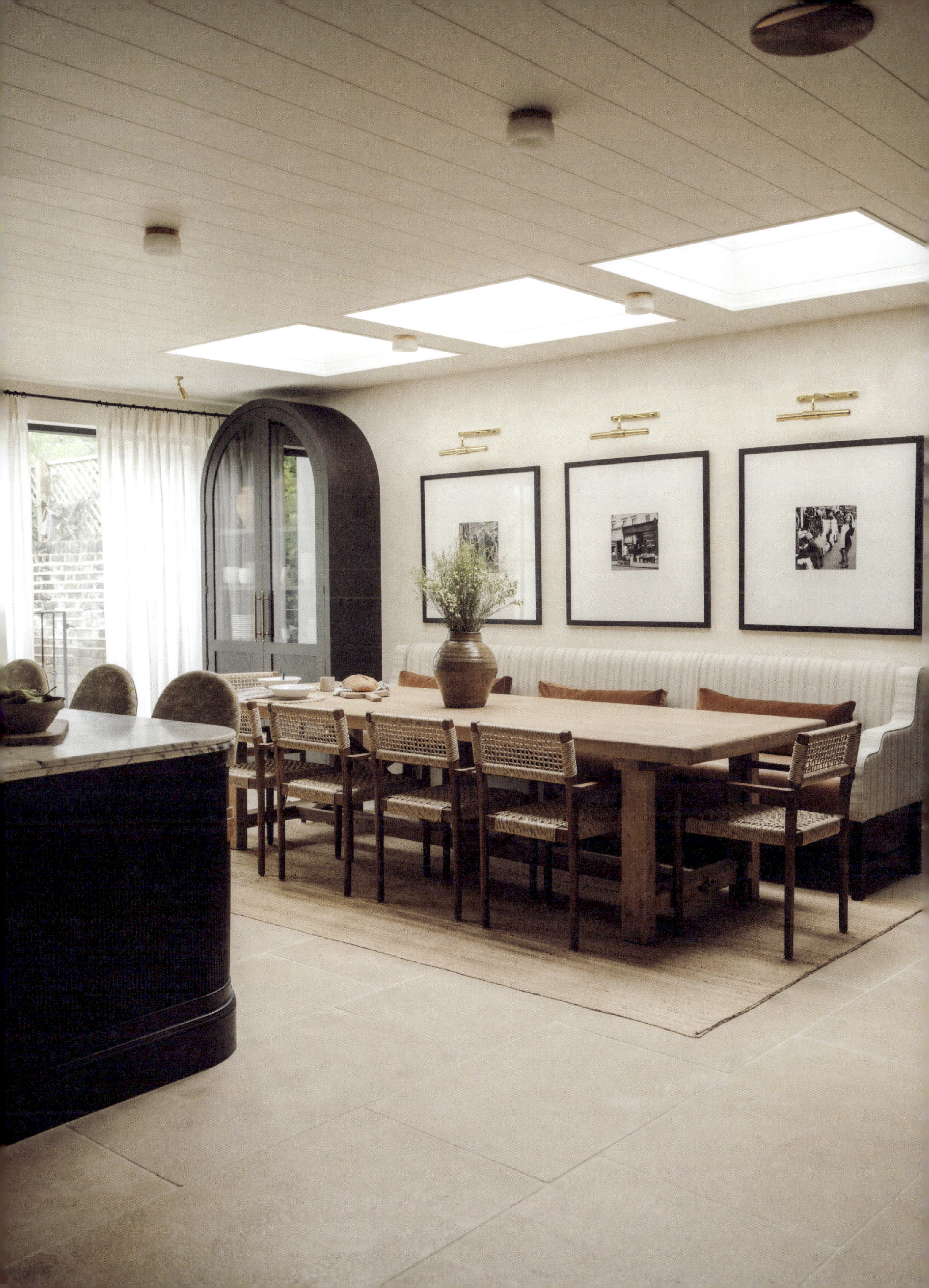

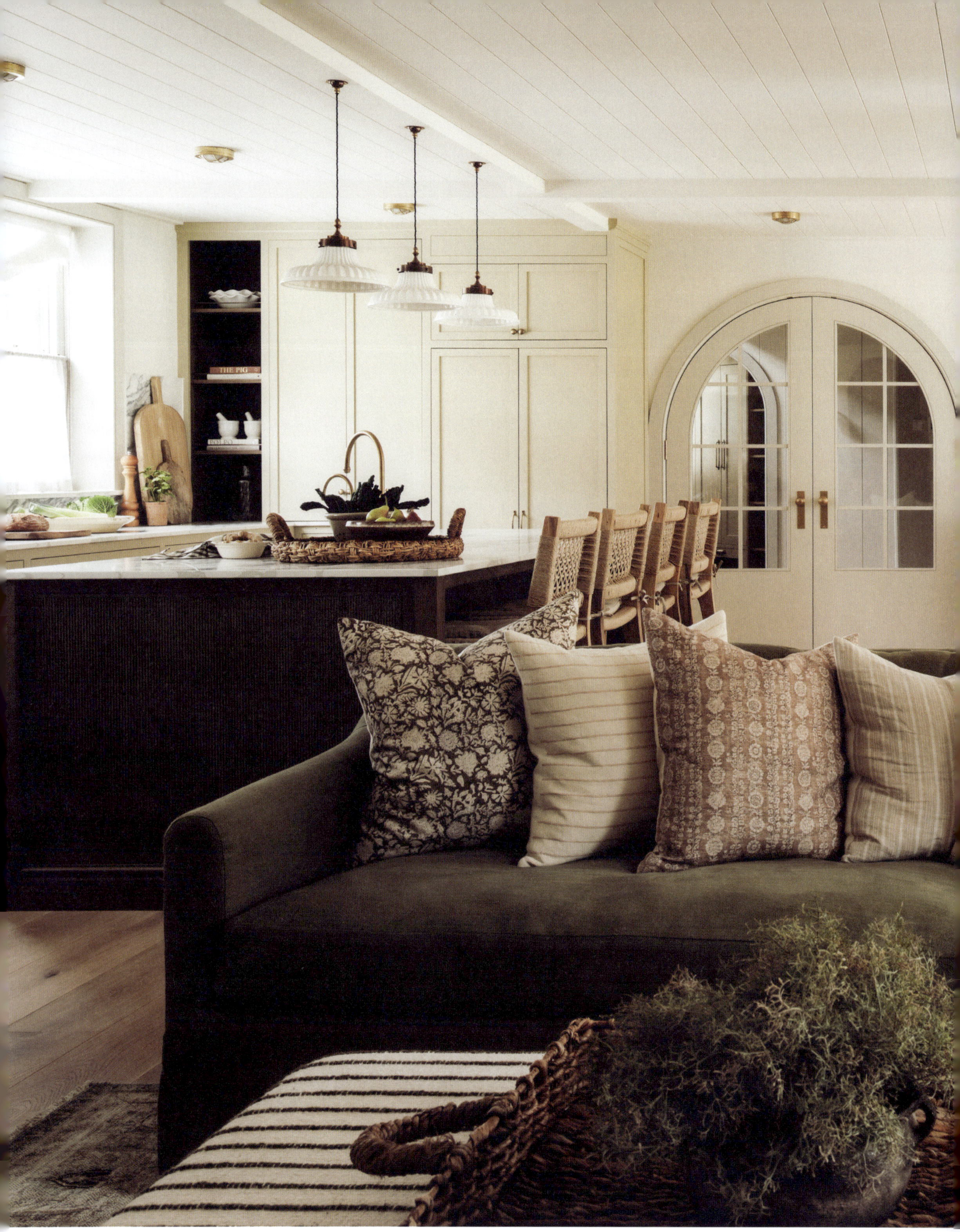
THE PIG

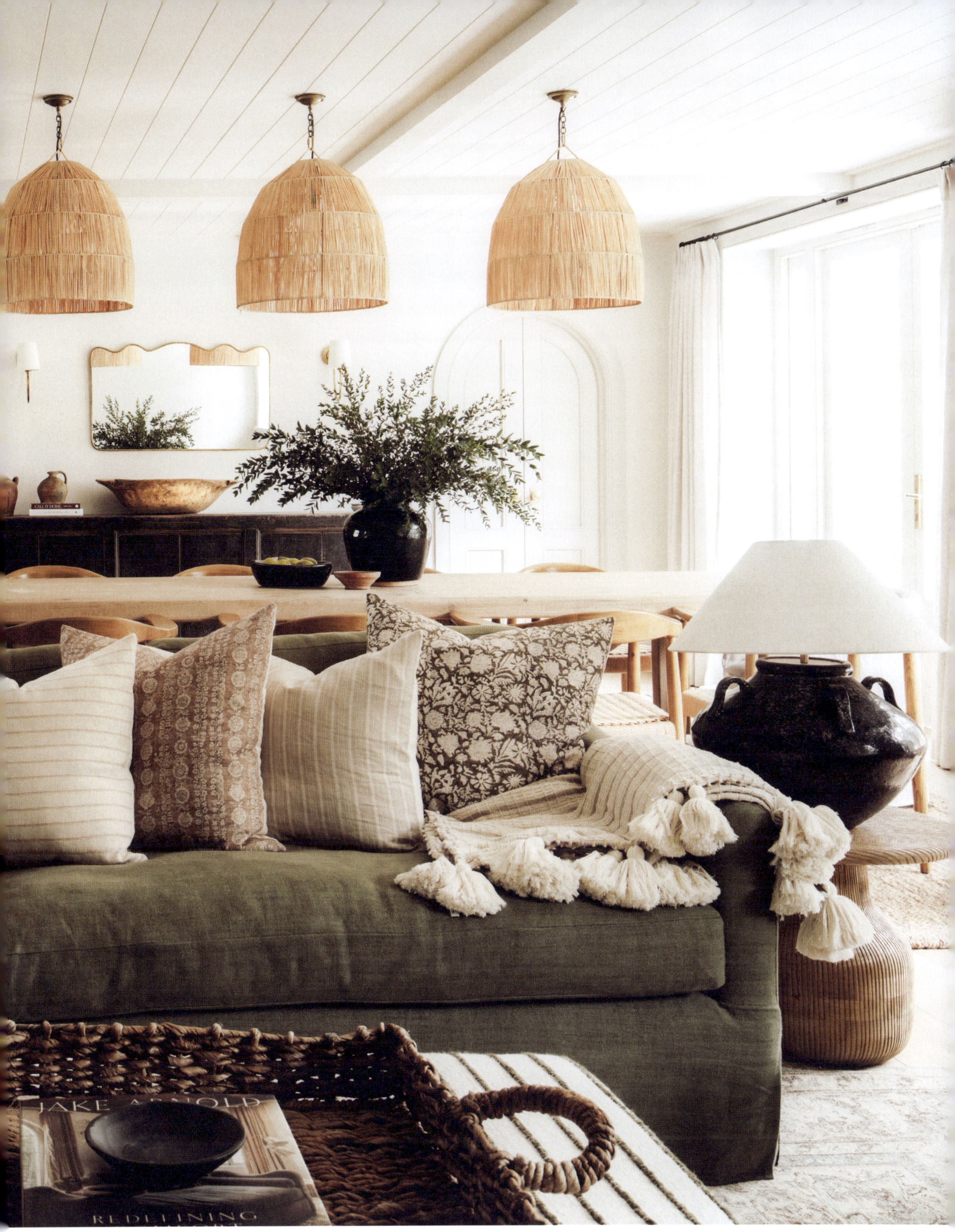

Hosting & Gathering

Homes that host well are, in fact, rarely overdesigned. They don't announce themselves as entertaining spaces. Instead, they work quietly in the background, supporting gathering without interrupting it.

Designing for hosting starts with understanding how people move through your home. Where do they arrive? Where do they naturally gravitate towards? Where does conversation start to drift or stall? These moments matter more than furniture or decorative finishes. Sometimes I find that the more relaxed the home, the more relaxed people feel as soon as they enter.

Clear entry points make a difference, too. Good lighting, somewhere to place a bag or coat, a sense of orientation. Guests relax quickly when they know where they are and what's expected of them – even if that expectation is simply "make yourself at home".

Living rooms are much happier when they're arranged for people, not screens. Turn the seating inwards, add a generous rug and a footstool, and suddenly the room feels like it's leaning in for a chat rather than waiting for the opening credits. People stay longer, sink in more, and actually talk to one another instead of hovering at the edges. Even if the TV is the main event most nights, it doesn't need to run the show when friends come over. A living room shouldn't feel permanently set up for a film marathon, with the furniture poised like it's saying, "Shhh... it's about to start." A few small layout tweaks can completely change the mood, and make the space feel far more relaxed, sociable, and alive.

In shared spaces like kitchens and dining rooms, surface space still matters, but it doesn't need to be bare. A bit of everyday "stuff" can in fact make a room feel warmer and more inviting. What people really need is clarity. Somewhere obvious to place a glass, rest a plate, or drop a bag without feeling like they're disrupting anything precious. When surfaces feel intentional rather than overloaded, guests relax. It's less about clearing everything away, and more about quietly showing people where

→ Seating turned inwards, a generous rug, a low stool within reach – this corner is arranged for people, not screens. The kind of room that leans in for a chat rather than waiting for the opening credits.

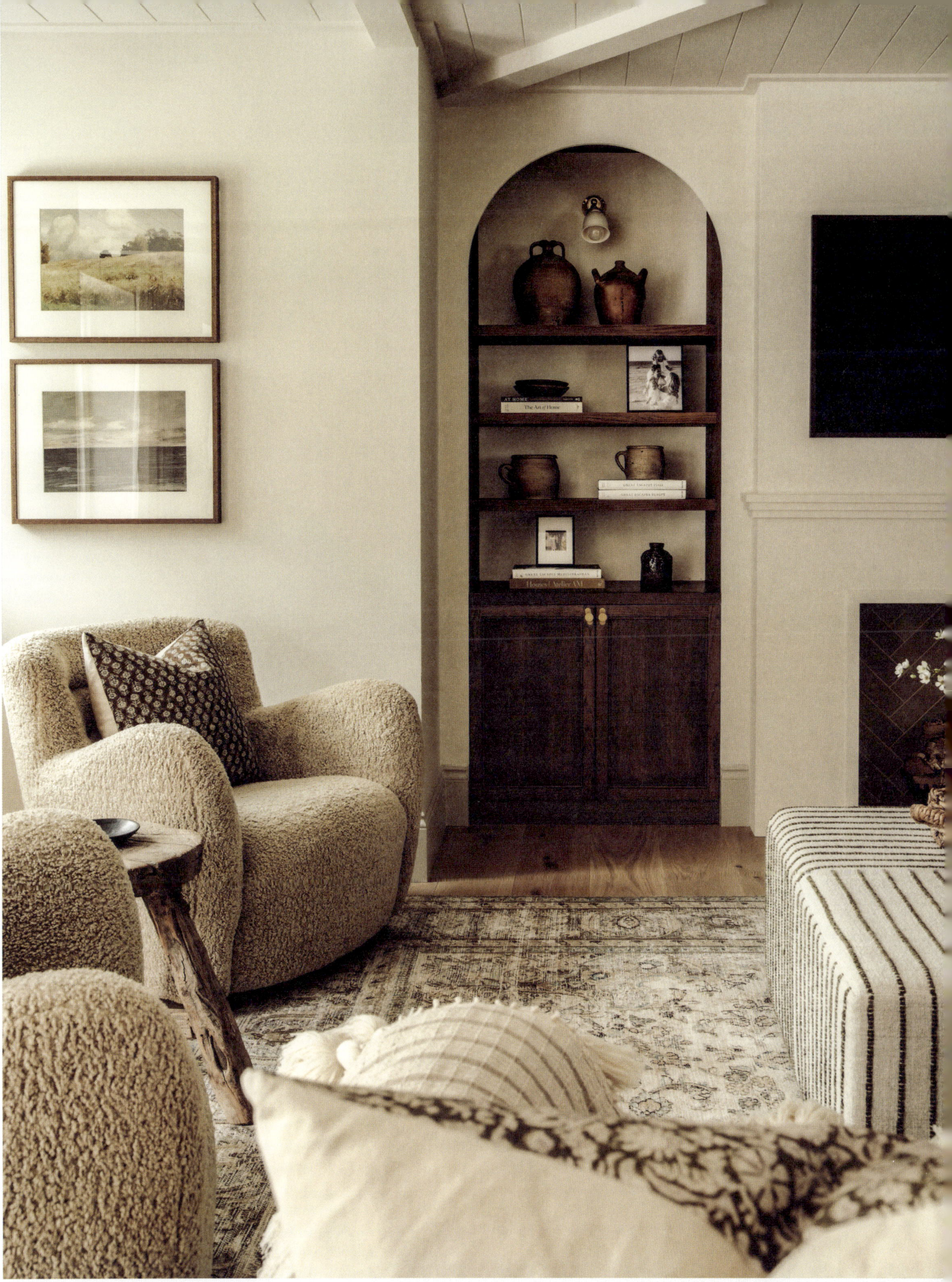

they're welcome to land. Flexibility matters, too. Open-plan living can be brilliant for gatherings, allowing people to flow easily between kitchen, dining, and living areas. But the homes that host best always offer moments of retreat as well. That's why, when I design open-plan spaces, I'm careful to zone them thoughtfully. A snug side room, a defined dining area, or a quieter corner for one-to-one chats gives people permission to drift, perch, or step back without leaving altogether. These subtle separations keep gatherings relaxed and fluid, rather than intense or overwhelming.

"There's also a generosity in allowing others to experience your home as it truly is."

Seating should always favour comfort over symmetry. A mix of chairs, benches, and banquettes allows people to choose how they sit and for how long. Banquette seating in particular offers an easy way to increase capacity without sacrificing comfort, especially in family homes.

Ultimately, spaces that encourage gathering don't try to control the experience. They simply support it. When the layout works, hosting stops feeling like something you manage and starts feeling like something you're part of.

→ Project Green Park – two ends of the same gathering space. The dining area opens fully to the garden through floor-to-ceiling glass, with a long table and a mix of chairs that lets people choose how they sit and how long they linger. Beyond it, the kitchen island does double duty as the social hub – woven stools lined up for quick chats, drinks, or homework, while the room flows easily into the living area beyond. Open plan, but never undefined: each zone has its own purpose, so gathering stays relaxed rather than overwhelming.

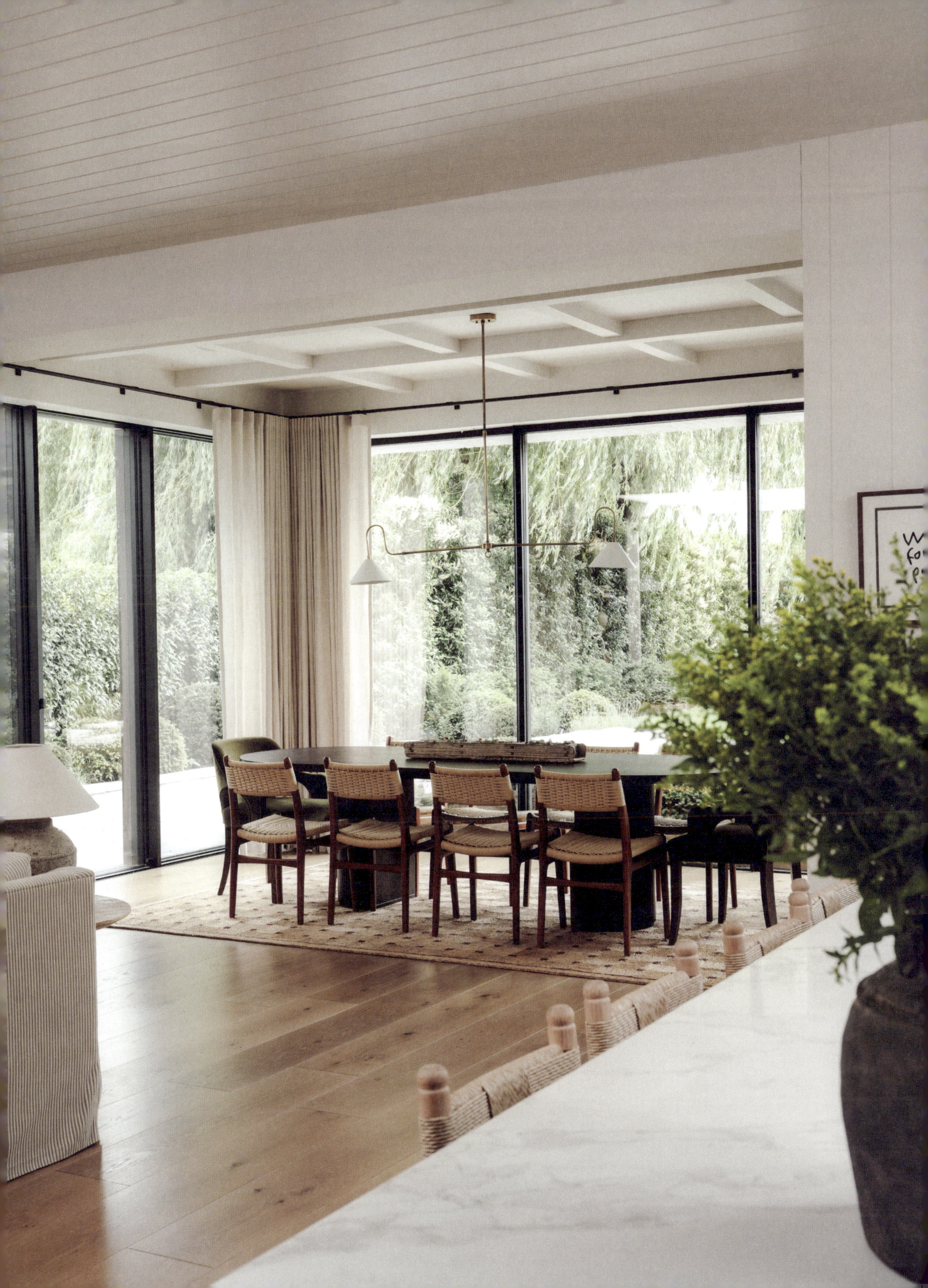

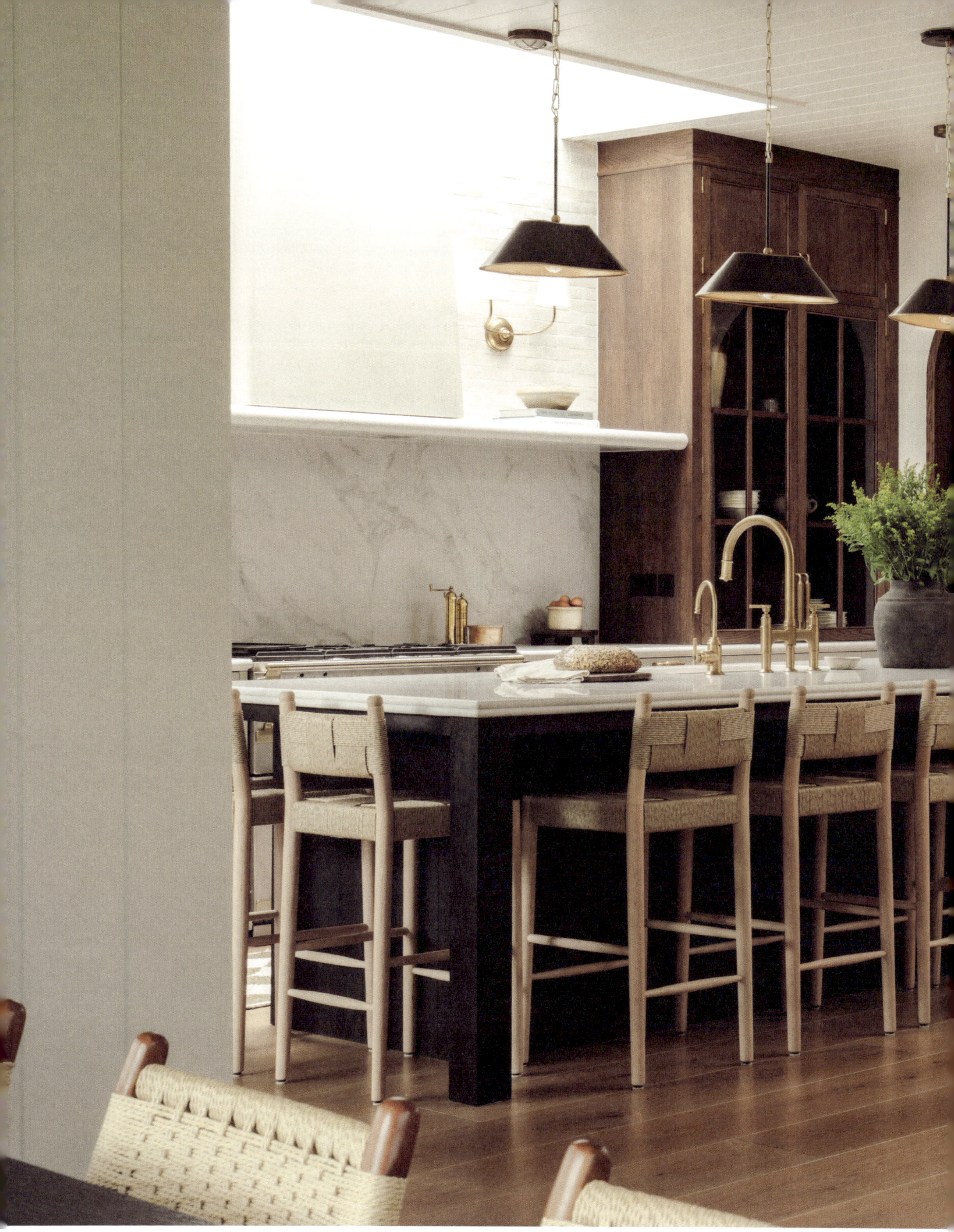

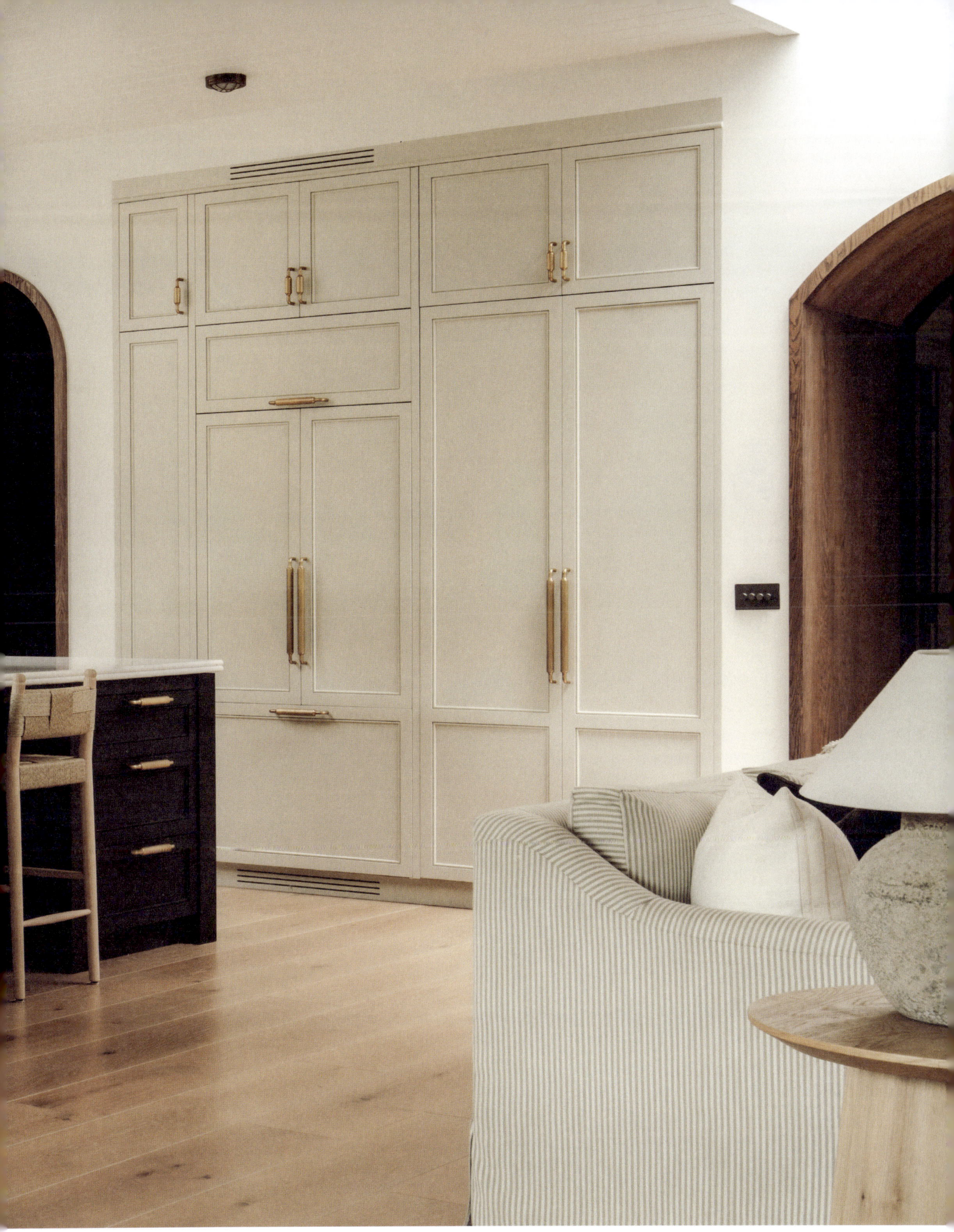

The Art of Hospitality

→ Guest bathroom built on consideration – warm brass details, soft lighting, and a towel always within reach. Small touches, but as the chapter notes, they're often what guests remember most.

→ → Here, layout does a lot of the hosting. A mix of seating – bouclé armchairs, a striped sofa, a rust velvet corner – gives people the choice of how and where to sit, with the fireplace and styled shelving anchoring the room rather than the TV demanding centre stage.

Hospitality isn't a style; it's an attitude, expressed through space. The most welcoming homes don't rely on grand gestures or perfectly set tables. They rely on consideration through small, thoughtful decisions that make people feel comfortable without drawing attention to themselves.

A guest room is a good place to start. It doesn't need to mirror a full-time bedroom, but it does need to feel intentional. A proper place to sleep, soft lighting, somewhere to put the overnight bag, a surface cleared just for them, and maybe a few hooks to hang their bits. These cues tell a guest they're expected and welcomed, not accommodated as an afterthought. Where space is limited, flexibility becomes key. A guest room that also functions as a home office is often the most practical answer, as long as both roles are properly considered. Storage, desks, and shelving can work hard day to day, while thoughtful sleeping solutions, such as a well-designed foldaway bed, allow the room to shift easily when guests arrive.

Bathrooms matter just as much. An ensuite is lovely, but when that's not an option, privacy takes centre stage. Guests should be able to find a bathroom easily and without feeling like they're sneaking through your life or sprinting down a hallway in a towel. The less awkward the journey, the more relaxed everyone feels. It's a small detail, but it makes a surprisingly big difference to how comfortable guests really are.

Beyond layout, atmosphere does a lot of the hosting for you. As the day turns to evening, lighting should soften and slow things down. Overhead lights are rarely kind; lamps create gentle pockets of warmth that invite people to settle in and stay a while. Dimmers help, of course, but so do candles. A few flickering flames instantly bring a sense of *hygge* (a Scandinavian term for a state of warm calm), making a space feel cosier, calmer, and more human. It's an easy way to shift the mood without saying a word.

The dining table is often where hospitality gets overthought. Perfect place settings and rigid arrangements can create pressure rather than pleasure. A table set with care doesn't need to be formal, it just needs to feel considered. Comfortable chairs, enough space for plates and glasses, and lighting that flatters faces rather than objects go a long way. And honestly, mismatched glasses, a slightly wobbly chair leg, or a serving plate you once superglued back together can in fact help guests relax. Those small imperfections add character and make a table feel lived-in rather than staged.

Effortless hospitality isn't invisible because it lacks effort; it's invisible because the effort has been placed where it matters. In foresight rather than performance. In comfort rather than control. A home that practises this kind of hospitality doesn't impress. It reassures. And that's what people remember long after they've gone.

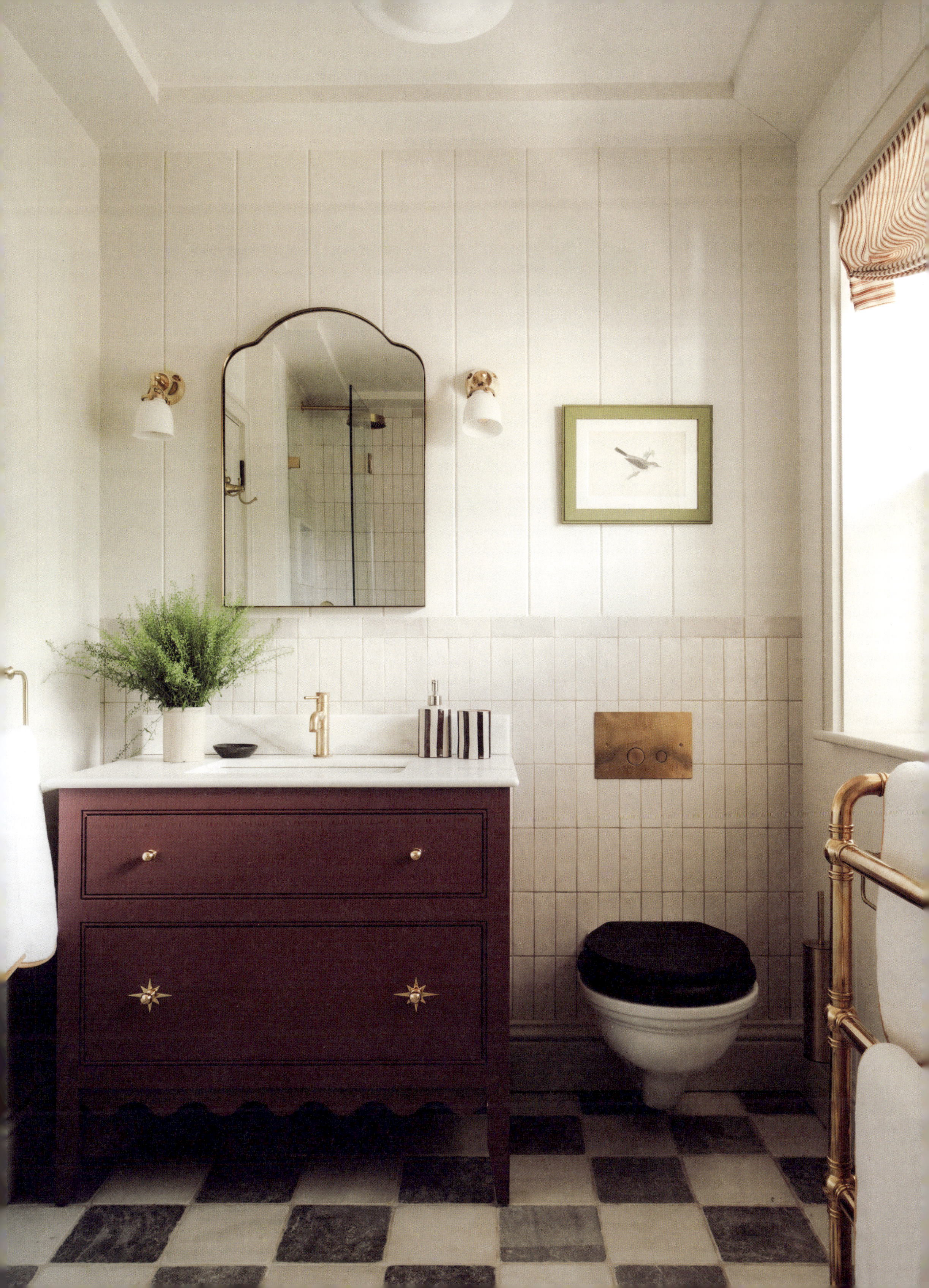

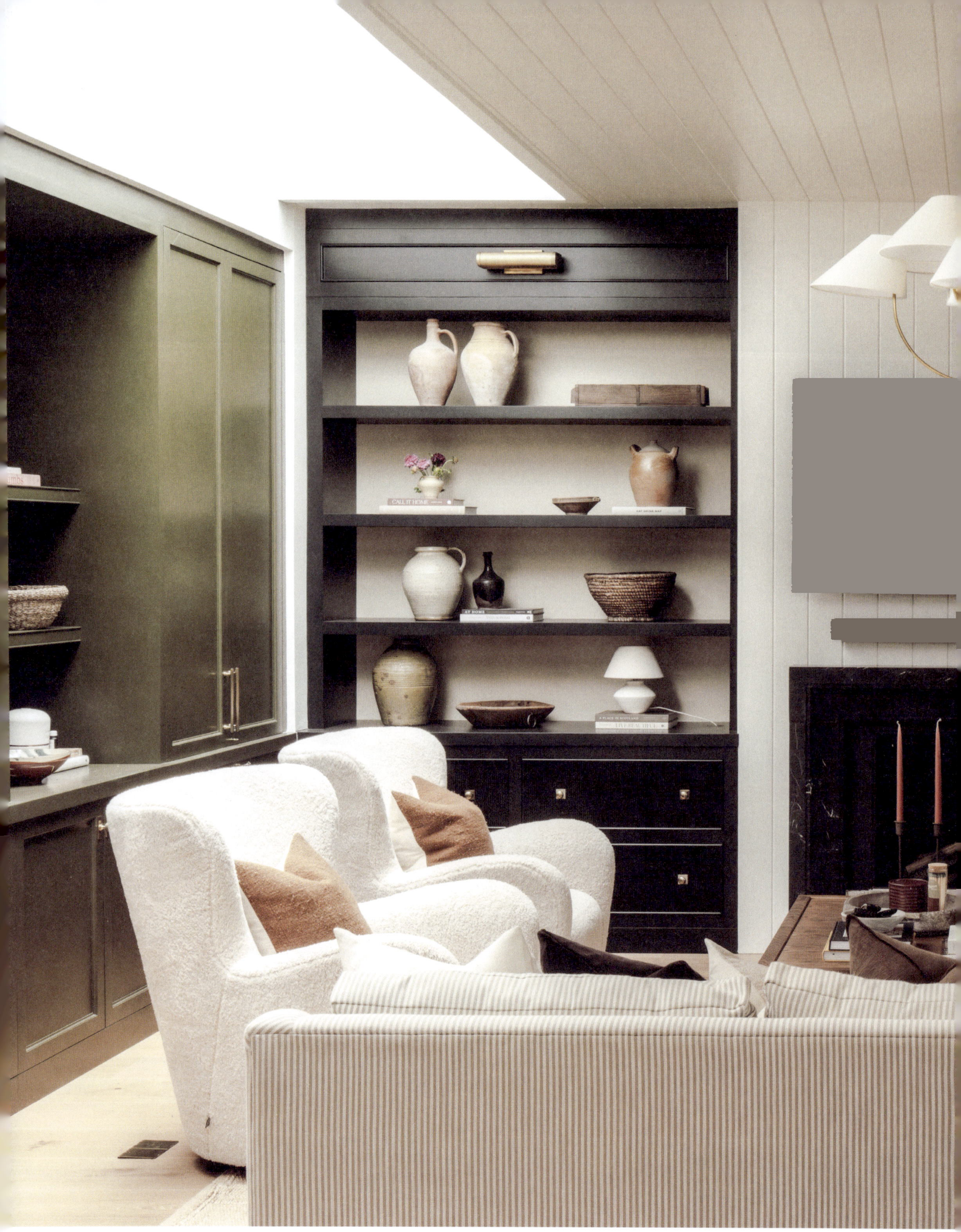

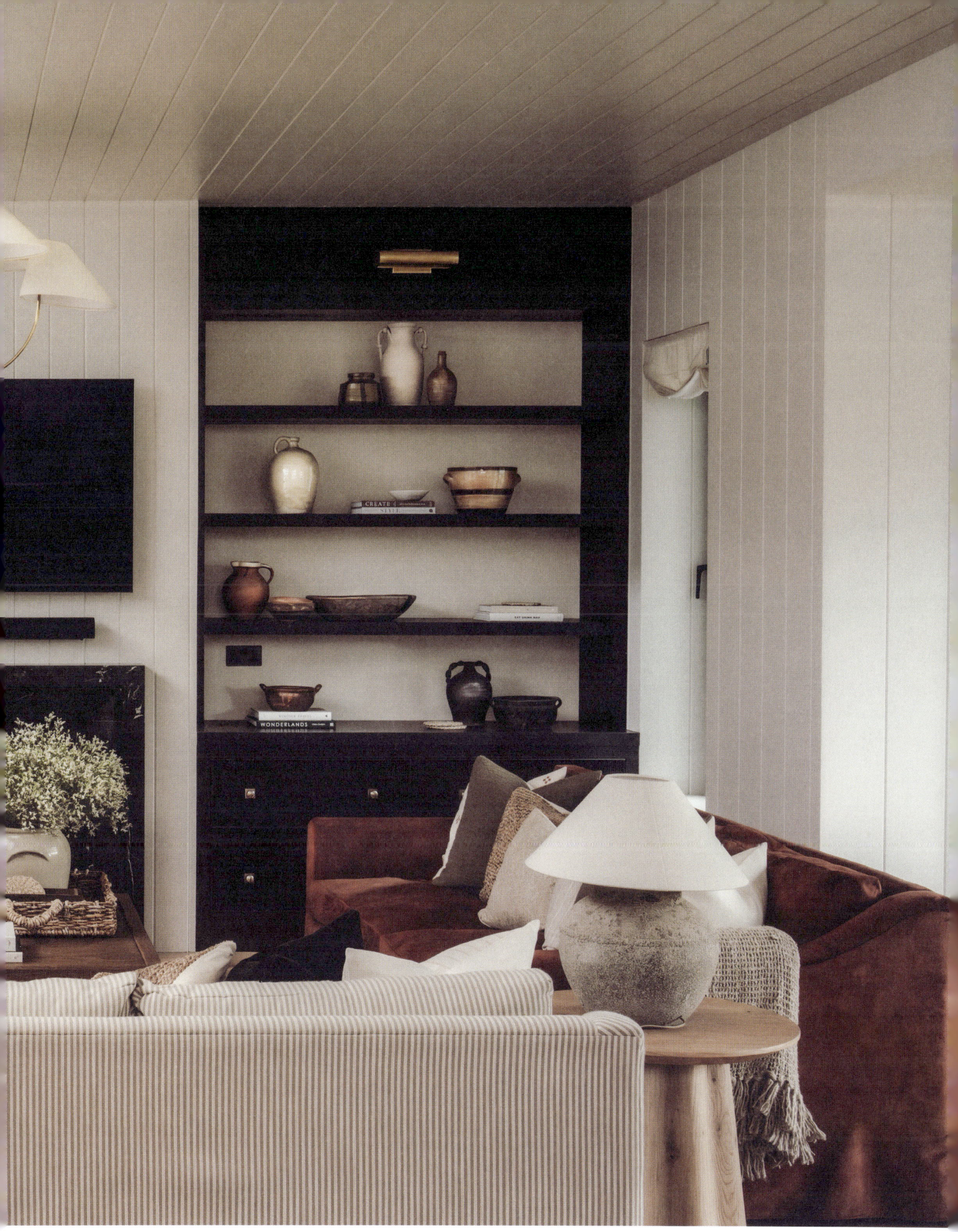
CREATE
WONDERLANDS

Design a Home to be Shared

DESIGN NOTES

These prompts are here to help you notice where small adjustments could make hosting feel easier, calmer, and more natural. Think of them as practical nudges; ways to design a home that's generous without being performative.

1. CLEAR THE LANDING SPOTS

Guests relax faster when they know where things go.

Try this: Walk through your home as if you were arriving for the first time. Is there an obvious place to put a coat, a bag, or a glass? Clear a surface in a shared space so guests don't have to ask.

2. TURN SEATING TOWARDS PEOPLE, NOT OBJECTS

Conversation needs orientation.

Practise: In your living space, turn chairs inwards and away from screens. Anchor the room with a rug if needed. Notice how it feels when you invite people to face one another.

3. MAKE ROOM AT THE TABLE

Generosity is often about space, not style.

Try this: Clear your dining table completely, then set it again with only what's needed. Check chair comfort and spacing. Ask yourself if you'd happily sit there for a long meal.

4. DESIGN FOR STAYING, NOT PERCHING

If people are comfortable, they linger.

Practise: Identify where guests tend to hover or stand. Add a chair, a bench, or a banquette. Prioritise comfort over symmetry – uneven seating is better than unused seating.

5. RECONSIDER THE GUEST ROOM

Hosting works best when the space works all year.

Do this: Look at your guest room (or spare area). Could it double as an office, reading room, or storage space? Focus on comfort, privacy, and intention rather than completeness.

6. WALK THE NIGHT-TIME ROUTE

Hospitality continues after dark.

Try this: In the evening, walk the route a guest would take to the bathroom. Is it well lit? Private? Easy to navigate? Adjust lighting or layout to remove hesitation.

7. SET THE TONE, THEN STEP BACK

Atmosphere does more than decoration ever will.

Try this: Choose one quiet, sensory detail before guests arrive – a candle lit in the evening or a simple bunch of flowers on the table. Keep scent subtle and familiar. Then stop adjusting. The room doesn't need managing once people are in it.

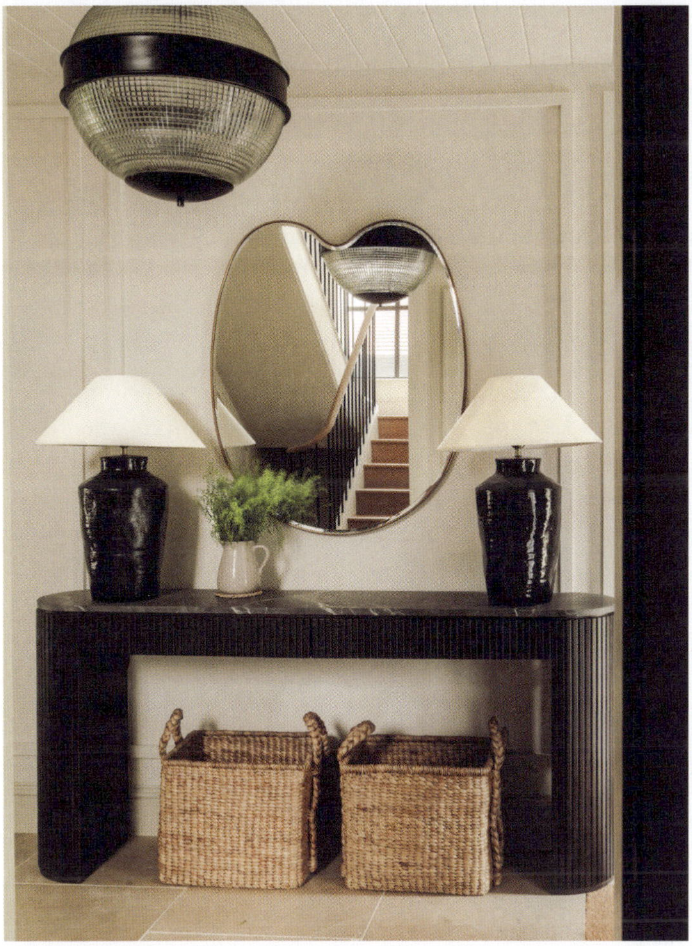
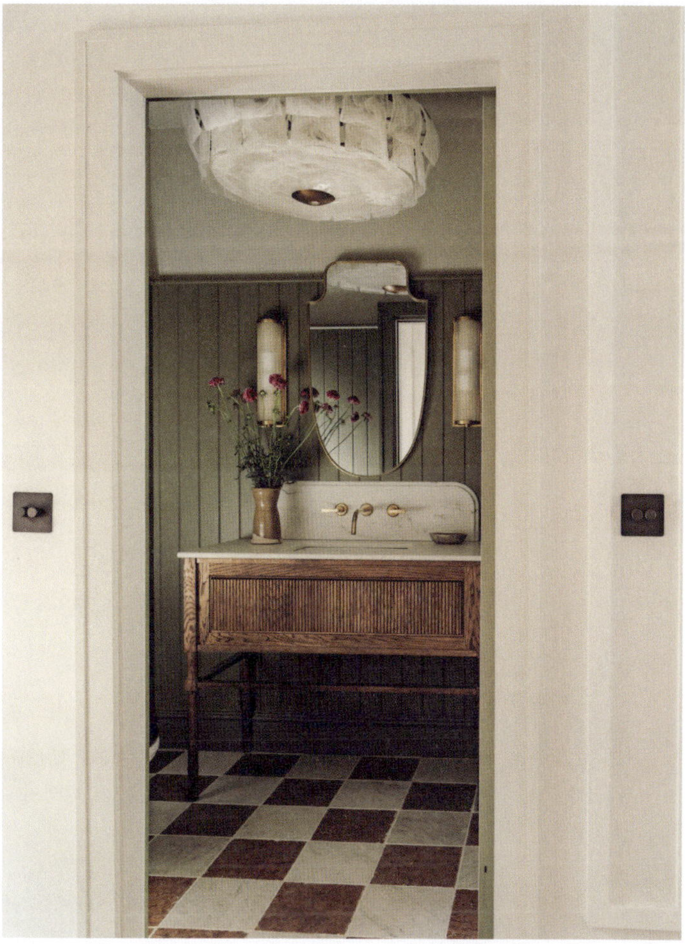
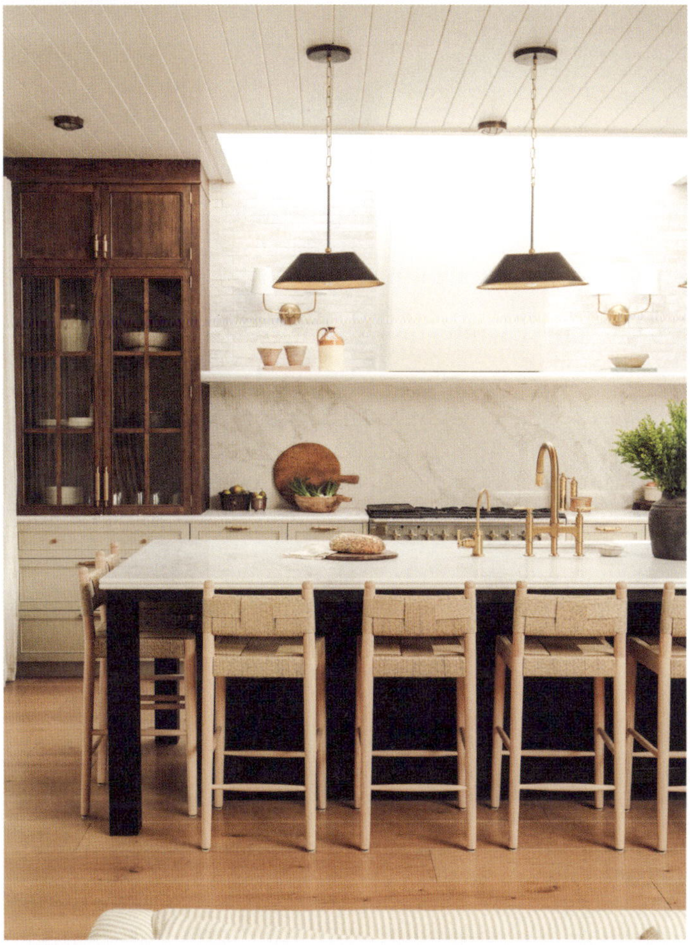
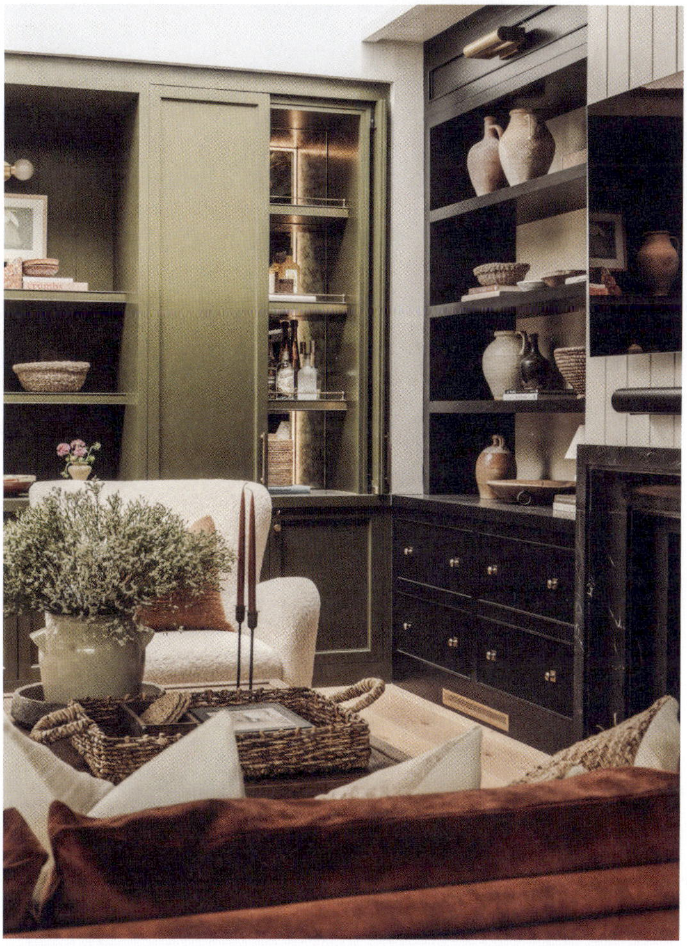

Directory

PAINT BRANDS

Annie Sloan – Creator of Chalk Paint. Beloved by upcyclers and furniture restorers. *anniesloan.com*

Benjamin Moore – US heritage brand, widely stocked in UK. *benjaminmoorepaint.co.uk*

COAT paints – Stylish paints made with natural ingredients. Palette includes a range of shades developed with House Nine. *coatpaints.com*

Edward Bulmer Natural – Plant-based pigments. Zero VOC. Stunning earthy tones. *edwardbulmer.co.uk*

Farrow & Ball – Iconic British heritage paints. Rich pigments, matt, and estate emulsions. *farrow-ball.com*

Little Greene – Historically inspired palette with exceptional depth of colour. *littlegreene.com*

Lick Paint – Modern curated palette. Peel-and-stick testers. Direct delivery. *lick.com*

Mylands – Professional-grade London paint house. Excellent chalk and gloss. *mylands.com*

Paint & Paper Library – Sophisticated, nuanced colours. Architects' favourite. *paintandpaperlibrary.com*

Zoffany – Luxury interiors palette, coordinates with fabrics and wallpapers. *zoffany.com*

WALLPAPER SUPPLIERS

de Gournay – Hand-painted scenic wallpapers on silk or paper. Bespoke & iconic. *degournay.com*

Designers Guild – Bold colour, floral, and geometric patterns. Can be found in their own stores and stockists. *designersguild.com*

GP & J Baker – Heritage floral and classic archive wallpapers. Coordinates with their fabrics. *gpjbaker.com*

Lewis & Wood – Bold oversized botanicals, animal prints, and rich wovens. Coordinates with their fabrics. *lewisandwood.co.uk*

Nobilis – Parisian house founded 1928. Blends traditional French elegance with contemporary design across fabric, wallpaper, furniture, and rugs. Collections are designed to coordinate beautifully with one another. *nobilis.fr*

Osborne & Little – British house founded 1968, beloved for sophisticated prints and patterns. Strong wallpaper ranges alongside fabric. Sister brand to Designers Guild's more maximalist aesthetic. *osborneandlittle.com*

Peony & Sage – Vintage and French-inspired prints. *peonyandsage.com*

Phillip Jeffries – American specialist in natural, textured and grass cloth wallcoverings. The go-to for woven wall materials — seagrass, jute, sisal, bamboo — as well as more decorative options. *phillipjeffries.com*

Sanderson – Morris & Co. archival range plus own their designs. *sanderson-uk.com*

FABRIC & TEXTILES

Chelsea Textiles – Hand-embroidered fabrics, crewelwork, and antique-inspired designs. *chelseatextiles.com*

Colefax & Fowler – Quintessentially English chintzes and linens. Trade and retail. *colefax.com*

GP & J Baker – Heritage archive prints. Flowers, botanicals, and Orientals. *gpjbaker.com*

Ian Mankin – Natural and striped tickings, linens, and cottons. Long-standing London fabric house. *ianmankin.co.uk*

Lewis & Wood – Cotswolds-based independent with a cult following. Bold oversized botanicals, animal prints, and rich wovens. Wildwood is their signature. Dedicated wallpaper studio at Chelsea Harbour showing full 3m drops. *lewisandwood.co.uk*

Molly Mahon – Block-printed fabrics and homewares. Distinctive blue and white. *mollymahon.com*

Morris & Co. – William Morris's original design house. Timeless hand-drawn patterns – Strawberry Thief, Willow Bough, Acanthus – rooted in the Arts and Crafts movement. Fabrics, wallpapers, and embroideries. *william-morris.co.uk*

Pierre Frey – Parisian family house founded in 1935. Sumptuous, printed linens, velvets, and wovens alongside exceptional wallpapers. Known for their archive depth and exuberant colour. *pierrefrey.com*

Sanderson – One of Britain's oldest fabric and wallpaper houses, founded 1860. Home to the William Morris archive as well as their own ranges. Quintessential English florals and nature-inspired prints. *sanderson-uk.com*

The Pure Edit – Relaxed prints with a focus on sustainable materials. Coordinates with their wallpapers. *thepureedit.com*

Zoffany Fabrics – Luxury velvets, weaves, and prints. Coordinates with their paint range. *zoffany.com*

ANTIQUES MARKETS & FAIRS

Alfies Antiques Market – Church St, Marylebone, London. Multi-dealer indoor emporium. Tues–Sat. *alfiesantiques.com*

Ardingly Antiques Fair – South of England Showground, West Sussex. Bi-monthly. *iacf.co.uk*

Bath Antiques Market – Guinea Lane, Bath. Wednesday mornings. 50+ dealers. Excellent ceramics and silver.

Bermondsey Antiques Market – Bermondsey Square, SE1. Friday mornings from dawn. Trade buyers and serious collectors.

Decorative Fair – Battersea Evolution, London. Bi-annual. High-quality decorative antiques. *decorativefair.com*

Kempton Park Antiques – Surrey. Fortnightly Tuesdays. 700+ dealers. Great for furniture and small items. *kemptonantiques.com*

Malvern Flea & Collectors – Three Counties Showground, Worcs. Monthly. *iacf.co.uk*

Newark Antiques Fair – Newark Showground, Notts. Six fairs per year and one of Europe's largest. *newarkantiquesfair.co.uk*

Portobello Road Market – Notting Hill, London. Every Saturday. Silver, prints, clothing, and curiosities.

Tetsworth Antiques – The Swan, Tetsworth, Oxon. Large permanent indoor market. Open daily. *theswan.co.uk*

SALVAGE YARDS

LASSCO – London and Oxfordshire. Britain's finest architectural antiques dealer. Flooring, ironmongery, fireplaces. *lassco.co.uk*

Retrouvius – Harlesden, London. Design-led salvage and reclamation. *retrouvius.com*

GENERAL DECORATIVE

Corston Architectural Detail – Considered fixtures and fittings which elevate any space. *corston.com*

House Nine Collection – Timeless, curated homewares designed by us. *housenine.co.uk/collections*

Konk – Bristol-based studio specialising in custom-made furniture. *konkfurniture.com*

Nkuku – Ethical firm specialising in handmade and responsibly sourced furniture and accessories. *nkuku.com*

Oka – Globally inspired British-designed furniture and accessories. *oka.com*

Olivia's – Unique, design-led homeware and accessories. *olivias.com*

Parker & Howley – Handcrafted bespoke furniture. *parkerhowleynco.co.uk*

Ruma – Considered artisan furniture and accessories. *ruma.co.uk*

Soho Home – Interiors collections from Soho House. *sohohome.com*

Soho Lighting Company – Hand-crafted lighting made in Cornwall. *soholighting.com*

Suffolk Latch Company – Traditional hand-forged ironmongery and hardware. *suffolklatchcompany.com*

Index

Index

About the Author

Jojo Barr has spent two decades shaping how people think about their homes. As Founder and Creative Director of House Nine Design, her London studio, established in 2014 after training at the prestigious KLC School of Design, she has built a reputation for interiors that are simultaneously beautiful, architecturally considered and deeply liveable. Her work spans high-end residential projects across the UK and internationally, alongside a virtual design service. In 2026, The Expert named Jojo the #1 International Designer on their annual Top 40 list for the second year running, reflecting growing global demand and recognition of her work. Alongside her design work, she shares her approach with a large online following (@houseninedesign), has her own homeware and interiors range, House Nine Collections, and co-hosts *The Ins & Outs* podcast with garden designer Pollyanna Wilkinson.

Acknowledgements

So much gratitude to everyone who made this book come to life, and somehow kept me sane while doing it.

Brad. My absolute rock. Thank you for being in my corner at every turn and never once letting me believe this wasn't possible, even on the days I was convinced otherwise. I love you.

To my mum and my sister Lou, thank you for your endless love, encouragement and belief in me, always. And to my dad, my greatest ever champion. I know you'll be cheering me on from somewhere.

To my friends, especially the local ones, thank you for helping with the kids, the ear to bend, the shoulder to cry on and the glass of wine when I was on the verge of losing it.

Every single project in this book is a team effort, and there is no version of this book that exists without the wildly talented humans at House Nine. Lizzie, you are my right arm, my right leg, and occasionally my sanity. Thank you for manning the fort every time I vanished to write, and for never letting anything drop, even when I gave you every reason to. Rosie, thank you for your creative magic and for the love and care you pour into every single project; it shows. James, thank you for keeping the balance in check, for paying my parking fines, and for nagging me about my expenses (it is, after all, your actual job, but I appreciate it nonetheless). Tara, my soul sister, you somehow always know exactly what I need before I do; slightly unsettling, mostly wonderful. Sasha, thank you for bringing the stories to life so beautifully. And Joey, my dear friend and photographer, thank you for making every shoot feel like a joy and not a chore. We could happily shoot on into the night if someone didn't eventually stop us.

To all of my clients, thank you for trusting me to get my hands all over your homes, and for so kindly letting me take over completely so we could capture these images. You opened your doors, put up with the endless snagging and zhushing of every cushion just so, and for that I am endlessly grateful.

To Quarto, for trusting in me and giving me the chance to write this book: Alice, Charlotte, Paileen, Vivianne, and Clemmie, thank you for your guidance, patience and for putting up with the avalanche of changes.

To Rhyanne, thank you for making the introduction to the wonderful Brionne at YMU, the dream literary agent, and always the best boost of confidence. And to Holly, my most brilliant agent, thank you for helping clear the way at every single step.

Quarto

First published in 2026 by Frances Lincoln,
an imprint of The Quarto Group.
One Triptych Place, London, SE1 9SH,
United Kingdom
T (0)20 7700 9000
www.Quarto.com

EEA Representation, WTS Tax d.o.o., Žanova ulica 3, 4000 Kranj, Slovenia
www.wts-tax.si

A catalogue record for this book is available from the British Library.

ISBN 978-1-80570-411-9
Ebook ISBN 978-1-80570-412-6

10 9 8 7 6 5 4 3 2 1

Design by CHD
Photography by Joey Kendal Brown

Editorial Director: Alice Graham
Art Director: Paileen Currie
Senior Designer: Isabel Eeles
Senior Editor: Charlotte Frost
Senior Production Controller: Rohana Yusof

Printed in Italy LT082026

FSC www.fsc.org MIX Paper | Supporting responsible forestry FSC® C016466